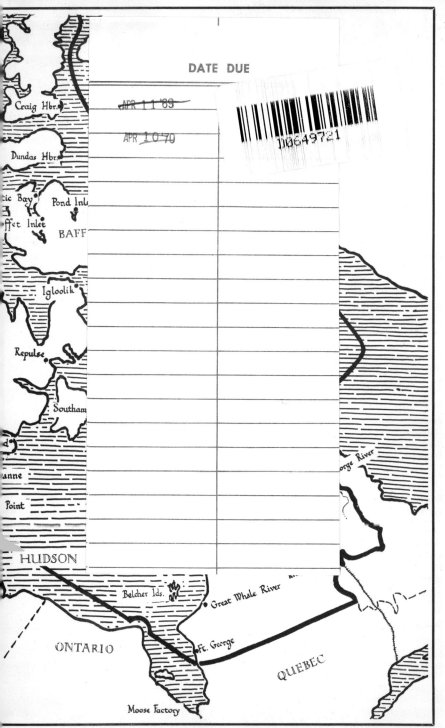

Craig Hbr.

Dundas Hbr.

tic Bay

Pond Inl

ffet Inlet

BAFF

Igloolik

Repulse

Southam

d

anne

Point

HUDSON

Belcher Ids.

Great Whale River

ONTARIO

Ft. George

QUEBEC

orge River

Moose Factory

torial area of two and three-quarters million square miles.

The author at fourteen
in his first Eton suit

Archibald Fleming
in the field

Bishop Fleming greets his friend King-o-wat-se-ak

The beautiful and remarkably functional Eskimo Kayak, "beyond comparison the best boat for a single oarsman ever invented"

This Eskimo's snow goggles are carved from willow twigs. The inside of the slits is charred to reduce reflection. Some goggles are carved from antler, and most have finer slits than those shown here. This Eskimo invention softens the terrific glare from Northern snows

A snow village in Baffin Land. Note the dark windows
made of skin membrane and the snow chimneys

An Eskimo baby rides piggyback

Donald B. Marsh

**This Eskimo holds a woman's knife, an
implement with a thousand household use**

Donald B. Mars

A polar bear pet

R.M.S. "Nascopie" in
the Polar pack

Courtesy of the Hudson's Bay Co.

S.S. "Pelican" at
Lake Harbour. From
an old glass plate

Courtesy of the Hudson's Bay C

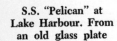

The famous "Distributor."
Note the paddle wheel

Boarding the "Nascopie"

Portrait of an Eskimo woman

This woman's face has been tattooed—
a custom of certain Eskimo

An Eskimo hunter

Eskimo woman sewing fur garments

Cutting blocks for an igloo

The very last job is chinking
the igloo. The chinks are
filled with soft snow to make
the ice home windproof

Donald B. Marsh

Eskimo child

At the top of the world

A young Eskimo

Bishop Fleming's historic first mission house at Lake Harbour

An engaging group of Eskimo children

The plane in which The Flying Bishop traveled in 1937

Bishop Fleming meets some old friends

This Eskimo child is obviously happy in the care of a pretty nurse at one of the hospitals founded by Bishop Fleming

St. Luke's Hospital, Pangnirtung, Baffin Land, the only hospital immediately north of the American continent

Archibald Cstr Axtec

☆   **Archibald the Arctic**   ☆

Archibald
the Arctic

by ARCHIBALD LANG FLEMING

The Flying Bishop

APPLETON-CENTURY-CROFTS, INC.
New York

☆ *To my spiritual children, the Eskimo* ☆

Contents

FOREWORD xi

1. The Awakening 1
2. To Baffin Land 36
3. Lake Harbour 56
4. Snow Village 78
5. Famine at Kinguckjuak 92
6. Journeys by Umiak and Kayak 109
7. Pagan Life 127
8. The Grant Episode 146

    Interlude I 167

9. Return to the Arctic 169
10. Of Myths and Angakoks 187
11. Where No White Man Had Gone . . . 203
12. Farewell to Baffin Land 224

    Interlude II 243

13. The Rescue of Matto 245

14. Archdeacon of the Arctic 265

15. Epidemic 281

    Interlude III 305

16. The Flying Bishop 309

17. Hospitals in the Far North 319

18. John Buchan Opens the Door 332

19. Decision at Eskimo Point 348

    Interlude IV 369

20. Reflections 373

    INDEX 395

Illustrations

(Preceding title page)

THE AUTHOR AT FOURTEEN

ARCHIBALD FLEMING IN THE FIELD

BISHOP FLEMING GREETS HIS FRIEND KING-O-WAT-SE-AK

THE BEAUTIFUL AND REMARKABLY FUNCTIONAL ESKIMO KAYAK

THIS ESKIMO'S SNOW GOGGLES ARE CARVED FROM WILLOW TWIGS

A SNOW VILLAGE IN BAFFIN LAND

AN ESKIMO BABY RIDES PIGGYBACK

THIS ESKIMO HOLDS A WOMAN'S KNIFE

A POLAR BEAR PET

R.M.S. "NASCOPIE" IN THE POLAR PACK

S.S. "PELICAN" AT LAKE HARBOUR

THE FAMOUS "DISTRIBUTOR"

BOARDING THE "NASCOPIE"

PORTRAIT OF AN ESKIMO WOMAN

THIS WOMAN'S FACE HAS BEEN TATTOOED

AN ESKIMO HUNTER

ESKIMO WOMAN SEWING FUR GARMENTS

CUTTING BLOCKS FOR AN IGLOO

THE VERY LAST JOB IS CHINKING THE IGLOO

A YOUNG ESKIMO

AT THE TOP OF THE WORLD

ESKIMO CHILD

BISHOP FLEMING'S HISTORIC FIRST MISSION HOUSE AT LAKE
HARBOUR

AN ENGAGING GROUP OF ESKIMO CHILDREN

THE PLANE IN WHICH THE FLYING BISHOP TRAVELED IN 1937

BISHOP FLEMING MEETS SOME OLD FRIENDS

ESKIMO CHILD IN THE CARE OF A NURSE AT ONE OF THE
HOSPITALS FOUNDED BY BISHOP FLEMING

ST. LUKE'S HOSPITAL, PANGNIRTUNG, BAFFIN LAND

Illustrations

(Facing this page)

THE AUTHOR AT FOURTEEN

ARCHIBALD FLEMING IN THE FIELD

BISHOP FLEMING GIVES IN HIS TONGUE KING-O-WAT-EE-AK

THE BEAUTIFUL AND REMARKABLE WESTGREENLANDER ESKIMO KAYAK

THIS ESKIMO'S SNOW GOGGLES ARE CARVED FROM WILLOW TWIGS

A SNOW VILLAGE IN BAFFIN LAND

AN ESKIMO LADY RIDES PIGGYBACK

THIS ESKIMO HOLDS A WOMAN'S KNIFE

A POLAR BEAR PET

R.M.S. "NASCOPIE" IN THE POLAR PACK

S.S. "PELICAN" AT LAKE HARBOUR

THE FAMOUS "PETER PAN"

BOARDING THE "NASCOPIE"

PORTRAIT OF AN ESKIMO WOMAN

THIS WOMAN'S FACE HAS BEEN TATTOOED

AN ESKIMO HUNTER

ESKIMO WOMAN SEWING THE GARMENTS

CUTTING BLOCKS FOR AN IGLOO

THE WORK LAST JOB IS CHINKING THE IGLOO

A YOUNG SEAL

AT THE TOP OF THE WORLD

ESKIMO CHILD

BISHOP FLEMING'S HISTORIC FIRST MISSION HOME AT LAKE HARBOUR

AN ENGAGING GROUP OF ESKIMO CHILDREN

THE PLANE IN WHICH THE FLYING BISHOP TRAVELLED IN 1927

BISHOP FLEMING MEETS SOME OLD FRIENDS

ESKIMO CHILD IN THE CARE OF A NURSE AT ONE OF THE HOSPITALS FOUNDED BY BISHOP FLEMING

ST. LUKE'S HOSPITAL, PANGNIRTUNG, BAFFIN LAND

Foreword

☆   ☆

As MY HUSBAND worked upon the pages of this book he and
I both realized that because of illness the sands of time were
running out. It was his earnest desire that should he not be
spared to see its publication I should undertake that task.
This it has been my privilege to do, and in this sad but
happy undertaking I have been greatly helped by others.

My especial thanks go to Miss Mildred Johnston, Secretary
of the Diocese of the Arctic, and to Miss Inez Bennett
formerly of the Diocese of the Arctic, for their labor of love
in typing the manuscript. I am also greatly indebted to the
present Bishop of the Arctic, the Right Reverend D. B.
Marsh, for his assistance. And I wish most particularly to
thank J. W. Anderson, Esq., Fur Trade Commissioner of
the Hudson's Bay Company, for his unfailing kindness in
responding to the many calls I made upon him.

Elizabeth Lukens Fleming

Huron Cliffs
Goderich, Ontario

☆ **Archibald the Arctic** ☆

1. The Awakening

IT IS STRANGE how, quite unbidden, scenes from the past come vividly to mind. Most often those that come to me are from my Arctic years—conversations or adventures with my beloved Eskimo, the sights and sounds of igloo life. Or suddenly, out of nowhere, come images of frozen wastes of ice and snow, of journeys across the immensities of trackless space. Yet often too I see again the setting of my early years, the joy and wonder of a childhood spent beside the River Clyde in Scotland. Very truly the Clyde is in my being with all its busy shipping and its gay regattas, its shrouded mists and its sunny radiances. My people were seafaring folk.

Of my immediate forebears I personally know little, perhaps because I was orphaned at an early age and was the youngest of nine children. My father was also the youngest of his family of six, and he, like many of the Flemings, followed the sea. When he left school he sailed first with his oldest brother, Captain George Fleming. On that return voyage the vessel, laden with sugar from the West Indies, sprang a leak and sank, but the crew took to the lifeboats and were all saved. With his big brother as tutor my father made rapid progress in the art of navigation and at about the age of twenty-three was given command of the fine three-masted 800-ton ship *Alepo*. In 1863 my uncle, Captain

George Fleming, was married to Barbara Lang, while my father, now master of the *Alepo,* married Janet Livingston who was Barbara Lang's favorite niece.

Seven years after my father had taken command of the *Alepo,* the owners decided to build a larger ship of iron. The *Rossdhu* was 1,340 tons, one-third larger than the then famous 921-ton sea clipper *Cutty Sark* which had been built of wood only five years previously. She was the answer of the Clyde to the American threat to British prestige on the high seas. She was a three-masted square-rigged ship with charming figurehead, white and black painted ports, grey hull and flesh-colored masts and spars.

In October, 1874, the *Rossdhu* left the Clyde bound for Calcutta and my father commanded her for twenty-one years until she was sold to the Turks. The *Phasis* replaced the *Rossdhu* but was wrecked on a coral reef in the China Sea by a typhoon. Captain Fleming was exonerated from all blame. For a short time after this my father commanded the *Anaurus* and then he retired from the sea. This period "was the high-water mark of the sailing ship."

In a British shipping journal of November 1949 a writer who signed himself R.W.V.B. states that he was an apprentice on the *Anaurus* and described my father as "a most distinguished gentleman with white hair and neatly trimmed beard, still very sprightly. . . . Captain Fleming was always at his best when we were running hard—and the *Anaurus* could travel."

I was born in Greenock, Scotland, at "4 h. 30 m. P.M." on September 8, 1883, and a month later was baptized by the Rev. Hugh MacMillan, D.D., minister of the Free West Church in that city and a man of more than ordinary ability.

Of my mother I remember, unfortunately, very little. She died on April first, 1890, after a period of illness. But from what I was told I can form some idea of what my mother looked like. She was of medium height and slight of build with very fair hair, very blue eyes, and transparent skin "as clear as alabaster."

I shall always remember with a deep sense of gratitude that because my parents were the kind of people they were I, even the last of their children, was endowed with a sound constitution as well as with sound ideals.

Because I lost my mother at such a tender age my first duty now is to record my indebtedness to my sister Barbara, who cared for me from the time that I was six and a half years old. I fear that I was at times a very dirty, naughty, highly strung youngster, at once her pride and despair. The wonder remains how she was able to manage so successfully to bring up our large family on scanty resources. The answer is surely to be found in the love and devotion that filled her heart. It must have been a difficult and vexing problem for her to wrestle daily with the whims and fancies of her brothers and sisters, some of whom were only a few years her junior, and having no authority behind her but the unfailing respect in which we held her.

While there were the usual differences of temperament that caused minor quarrels from time to time, ours was a happy household, probably because there were enough of us of different ages to create and maintain interest day by day. We must have been a noisy family, but we did have lots of fun. I have come to agree with Jane Austen in *Mansfield Park* that "Children of the same family, the same blood, with the same associations and habits, have some means of enjoyment in their power, which no subsequent connection can supply."

We lived a simple life, for very little pocket money was allowed. Unless my memory plays me a trick, which I don't think it does, I received two pennies (four cents) on Saturday—one to spend and one for Sabbath school.

I do remember deriving great pleasure from one extravagance—an iron hoop about three and a half feet in diameter. In these early days girls played with wooden hoops which they kept rolling by striking with a wooden stick. Boys, on the other hand, had thin iron hoops with which they gained greater speed, and instead of striking the hoop with a stick as did the girls the boys used what was known as a cleek, a straight iron rod of the same thickness as the hoop but with a hook at the end. The hoop was controlled by pressure from the cleek. After considerable persuasion I obtained enough money to purchase a hoop and cleek and walked over a mile to the nearest blacksmith where I spent the best part of a Saturday morning watching the smith shoe a horse and then make a hoop for me. How pleased I was because the smith had put an extra twist in the handle of the cleek which made it look superior to the ones owned by some of my playmates!

Most vivid among my minor memories is a great dancing bear that came one day to our door. The bear was led by a huge man with bushy black whiskers, round Astrakhan cap, and high boots. Barbara gave the man some food and told us that he came from Russia, which in our minds was very far away. Each spring, too, an Italian appeared upon the Esplanade. I can still remember his sleek black hair, swarthy complexion, and the peculiar gold rings in his ears. He carried a small organ which had one leg and played music when he turned a handle. On top of the organ sat a monkey wearing a little cloth coat and a round red cap. As the Italian played the organ, the monkey moved its head in rhythm and held out a tin cup for contributions. I ran home in haste to get a penny for the monkey.

But I liked best the sailors from Spain or Portugal who went from door to door selling strings of onions tied to a pole and carried across their shoulders. They were the first people I saw who wore blue berets on their heads, and we thought they were the Spanish model of the Scottish tam-o'-shanter! It never occurred to us that the Scots might have copied the Spanish cap.

Unlike my next older brother John, who was a very good-looking boy with "a grand leg for the kilt," I had lanky legs and long feet, and in the summer I developed not a sun tan as I so greatly desired, but a goodly crop of freckles.

I was dressed in sailor suits with a white flannel dicky kept in place by a band of tape around my waist. It formed a wide V in the front of the sailor blouse or tunic. There were crossed anchors on the sleeve, and the wide square collar was edged with three rows of narrow white braid. On Sundays a long black silk scarf was knotted around the collar so that the loops hung down below the end of the vest in front and my nickel-plated bosun's whistle swung from a heavily pleated white cord. Long black stockings over the knees and a round blue sailor hat with the letters H.M.S. AJAX in gold on the black band completed the costume. Soon I graduated to my first knickerbocker Norfolk suit of good strong Scottish tweed with folded pleats down the back and sides, and a strip of doeskin cloth with four buttons below the knee, stockings to match with turned-down tops, and a cap bearing the school badge.

How well I remember the Sunday I received my first Eton suit—a short black jacket and vest, grey striped trousers and school tie. That day in church when the children's hymn began, "I'm a little pilgrim and a stranger here," I closed the hymnbook in disgust, thrust my hands into my pockets, and sulked. The sister standing next to me gave me a nudge but I took no notice. She nudged me again and whispered, "Sing, Archie," to which I replied, "No! I'm *not* a little pilgrim and I'm not a stranger here!" I was all of fourteen!

Our amusements at home were of the simplest kind. In the evenings I loved to watch Barbara's fingers moving quickly over the ivory keys of the piano while we all gathered around and sang such songs as "Up in the morning's no' for me," and "There was a lad was born in Kyle." Barbara not only played the piano but had a good contralto voice and was a member of the Choral Union Choir, and John sang tenor. At other times we played the usual parlor games, and Barbara on occasion let us play Up Jenkins, Battledore and Shuttlecock.

The furniture in our dining room was of plain solid mahogany and the chairs were covered with black horsehair. The parlor furniture was also mahogany but was covered with crimson plush, the backs being protected by elaborate threaded antimacassars. Later, my sister Isa, who was quite artistic and full of ideas, insisted on calling the parlor the Drawing Room. In the Greenock house the fireplace in the dining room was of black mottled marble, while the parlor fireplace and mantel shelf were covered with hand-sewn silk draperies of elaborate design which Isa had worked because they were the latest fashion.

Coal gas was used for lighting and the burner under the open glass globes gave a soft blue and yellow flame. In the drawing room and parlor a central chandelier hung from the ceiling with four lights and ornamental globes.

In our home Saturday was bath day and a time of very great activity. The girls took their baths in the afternoon and later put their hair in paper curlers, while the boys bathed before going to bed. There was no hot-water tank in the house so a huge iron pot and iron kettle were used to heat the water in the kitchen and then carried to the bathroom. To avoid all unnecessary work on "the Sabbath" the roast of meat was cooked on Saturday night and served cold on Sunday but with hot vegetables which had been carefully prepared on Saturday. All boots and shoes for use on "the Lord's Day" were polished and put under chairs in the bedrooms, while clean clothes and church collection money were laid out in readiness for the morning. Then too, all newspapers and novels were put out of sight and replaced by *Pilgrim's Progress,* Fox's *Book of Martyrs, The Sunday at Home,* church and missionary magazines.

In the hall at the front door beside the overladen wooden hat stand we all appeared dressed in our Sunday clothes with hair well brushed and combed. After Barbara was satisfied with our appearance we were given the sign and started off to church two by two. First, my sisters Jessie and Elizabeth, then John and George, while Barbara and Isa with the baby (me) brought up the rear. These were happy days.

My sister Barbara would never have sent her baby brother away from home to a public school but in any case that was beyond our narrow means, so I attended the Greenock Academy and later Dunoon Grammar School. The academy had a long and fine tradition; it charged fees for tuition and ranked with similar schools throughout Scotland. The headmaster was called the rector and wore a college gown and mortarboard as did the entire staff. At that time teachers believed that what boys needed was grammatical drill, declensions and conjugations in English, French, German, and Latin. I fear it could have been said of me what Samuel Johnson declared of Davy, "He finds out the Latin by the meaning rather than the meaning by the Latin."

Generally our teachers were capable, friendly, and patient. They not only instructed us in the rudiments but gave us a glimpse of the vastness of the world of thought and taught us that most valuable lesson, that we were only at the beginning of things and so ignorant that we had little conceit left in us. The only time I can remember trying to cram was for the "Leaving Certificates" which were considered necessary before entering a business or university career.

One Sunday evening in the winter of 1894 something happened which at the time appeared only of trifling importance but ultimately changed the whole course of my life. I was sitting by the blazing fire in the parlor of our house in Greenock reading a bluish-green-covered book entitled *The Young Missionary*. It told of the life and habits of some natives in Africa. As was customary in religious homes in Scotland at that time, novels and newspapers were not read on the Sabbath. Before I went to bed on Sunday evening a true story was generally read to me but on this particular occasion a change was made. My sister Isa had just returned from a visit to some friends in Dundee and instead of reading me a story she told how, while away, she had seen an Eskimo named Shoudlo from Cumberland Sound, Baffin Land. He had been brought south on board one of the whaling vessels and had black hair, copper-colored skin, and spoke a strange language. She then described how he lived by hunting the whales, polar bears, and seals, and traveled over the frozen sea with sledges drawn by dogs instead of horses. Finally, my sister said that there was only one missionary in that land of ice and snow from which this stranger came.

At once I was transported from the sweltering heat of African grass huts to the frozen realms of Arctic night with shimmering aurora borealis and houses built of snow! It was an exciting tale, even more so than any by Fenimore Cooper which I had read in the *Boy's Own Annual*, because this was a *true* story. That night in my prayers before getting into bed I asked God to bless the Eskimo and help me to be a missionary to them when I grew up. This vision soon faded but was never entirely lost.

Until we moved to Hunter's Quay, we spent our summer holidays in or near some hamlet on the Kintyre Coast of Argyle or on one of the many islands on the west coast of Scotland, where the outside walls of all the cottages seemed to be covered with climbing roses, honeysuckle and red fuchsia.

About half a mile from one such cottage, I remember going fishing with a young friend, gathering mussels, cockles, periwinkles and limpets, building a fire in a rocky shelter and boiling our catch in a can which was purloined from the house and which we kept hidden among the rocks when it was not in use. When the shellfish were cooked we sat down and ate them with relish, thinking that we had never tasted anything half so good at home. As I grew older I was fortunate in having many friends who invited me to visit them during the summer months and I had very happy times with them. Thanks to the use of a newly purchased Rudge-Whitworth bicycle, I was able to scour the countryside on one holiday and I gained a considerable knowledge of a wide and beautiful area in the heart of Scotland.

I was thirteen years old when my father retired and bought a house at Hunter's Quay, a small residential area two miles from the town of Dunoon which was the shipping district. Our house like the others was called a villa and stood in its own walled garden high up on the hillside overlooking the estuary of the Clyde, with fine views of the Holy Loch and Loch Long.

Our move to Hunter's Quay had some unexpected results as far as I was concerned. First, for some reason unknown to me the family rented a pew in the Presbyterian church at Sandbank two miles up the Holy Loch from our house. Each Sunday morning—wind, rain, snow, or sunshine—we walked the two miles there and two miles home again, but because of the distance it was out of the question for me to be enrolled in the Presbyterian Sabbath school. Instead, I attended the children's service in the beautiful little Episcopal church in the afternoon. This was the only place of worship in Hunter's Quay and was a daughter of St. Silas' church, Glasgow. It was unique in that technically it was not the Episcopal Church in Scotland but the Established Church of England in Scotland. The explanation of this strange arrangement seemed to be that the Episcopal Church in Scotland was considered very ritualistic while in St. Silas the ritual was simple and the teaching evangelical.

On first entering the church I was filled with surprised curiosity. It was so different and yet so attractive and it was not long before I came to like it. I shall never forget one of the first children's services I attended there. The incumbent was a tall Englishman who evidently loved children and knew how to teach them. After a very shortened form of evening prayer with one lesson and some familiar hymns he spoke to us of God as Our Father. He asked a boy to spell "Father" and then taking each letter in turn explained the meaning. God was a *F*aithful Father, an *A*lmighty Father, and so on. For me this was an entirely new experience and I loved it.

When I returned home that afternoon I was asked by Barbara to repeat the text, which we were always asked to do, presumably to give us a double incentive to attend to what was said. Greatly to her surprise and evident pleasure, I described in detail the whole service and what had been said about God as our F-A-T-H-E-R.

I am sure that this incident helped to break down in our house the naturally strong Scottish prejudice against the Episcopal Church and the idea of *read* prayers.

The following year a young friend of mine named Ernest Collie and I were appointed sidesmen in this Episcopal church and it was our duty to see that each child had a prayer and hymnbook and to take up the collection. Ernest wore the kilt and I my Eton suit and we both felt a tremendous responsibility resting upon us. Thus was the beginning of my gradual move towards the Episcopal form of worship.

When first we came to Hunter's Quay, it was considered advisable to transfer me from the academy to the Grammar School at Dunoon. At this time I was a tall, pale-faced, spindly boy with two great ambitions in life. I wanted to be big and strong like my father, and I wanted to build ships. Indeed, I spent most of my spare time making model boats of various kinds. It was the making of these rather than their possession that gave me pleasure, and as soon as each craft had been completed I gave it away to a playmate. Each day I saw ships, large and small and of almost every nationality, passing up and down the River Clyde and I dreamed dreams of the future and of the ships that I would build.

About a year before I passed my final school examinations I paid a visit to cousins in Glasgow. While there I met another cousin who was well known in shipbuilding circles. One day he asked me what I planned to do when I left school and on being told that I wanted to be a shipbuilder he kindly invited me to let him know when I was ready to start work since he might be able to get me into a first-class shipyard. Nine months later I received a letter from Mr. David McGee, manager of John Brown and Company's great shipbuilding yard at Clydebank, asking me to come for an interview. Needless to say, this caused great excitement in our household.

A week later when I arrived at the main entrance of the shipyard I was confronted with a notice which read NO ADMITTANCE EXCEPT ON BUSINESS. The great gates were closed but there was a small door leading to an office in the wall, where a fine-looking man in uniform accepted my credentials. As I was being piloted from the gatehouse to the main office building, I saw things that rejoiced my heart—vast arrays of tall derrick poles and great cantilever cranes swinging huge steel plates or bundles of long angle bars in mid-air, then landing them gently on top of a rusty-looking mountainous structure that was an Atlantic liner in the making; I heard the rat-tat-tat of dozens of riveters' hammers; saw a funny little stumpy locomotive with the name JOHN BROWN & Co. LTD. painted on its bulging sides, puffing and snorting as it shunted railway flatcars loaded with great steel girders. It was all very wonderful and I would fain have lingered if I could have found an excuse.

Opening a glass-paneled door, the boy ushered me into the entrance hall of the building where my eyes beheld still greater wonders. On my right was a large room filled with the most beautiful scale models of ships—ocean greyhounds, cross-channel steamers, torpedo boats, destroyers, cruisers, and great battleships. I knew that this was the place of my dreams.

I shall always be grateful for the way in which Mr. McGee received me and put me at ease. With all the innocent self-assurance of youth I told him that I had always wanted to be a shipbuilder and that I should like to visit the different departments in the yard so that I might be better able to design new ships. He drew me on to tell him all that was in my mind and then explained briefly how the work, involving some 8,000 men, was organized. "What you want is an apprentice manager's job and we don't go in for that kind of thing here," he said. My heart now missed a beat but, with a twinkle in his eyes, he added, "My boy David will be coming along next year so if you are willing I will arrange for you to spend twelve months in the shops and on the ships and see how you get on. If it works out well with you, I may let David try it." He then told me that I would take my place side by side with the workmen and receive no favors. I was young, enthusiastic, and impressionable so I came away from the great man with complete confidence in the future.

That first year not only enabled me to understand something of the practical side of shipbuilding but also the problems of the workingmen, which proved of inestimable value in days to come. During the winter months I attended evening classes in naval architecture and applied mechanics, thus gaining much valuable knowledge of the theoretical side of shipbuilding.

Just one year after I had started my rounds in the yard, I received a message to come at once to the manager's office. This was the first time that I had spoken to Mr. McGee since the original interview and I had lost some of my self-assurance and now thought of him with considerable awe. When I was shown into his office he was sitting at his desk but he arose immediately and once more put me at ease by shaking hands with me, which I considered an exceedingly gracious act. He surprised me by saying that he had had his eye on me, and asked if I was ready to begin work in the drawing office. Needless to say, I readily replied in the affirmative.

During my Clydebank days my week ends were most frequently spent with my sister Barbara, now married to a fine Scot named Magnus McCuaig, manager of the branch of the British Linen Bank in the busy industrial town of Alexandria, Dumbartonshire. In summer when the evenings were fine I cycled through the beautiful countryside away from the noise and smoke of the city. When winter came with its cold and damp weather, my time was given over almost entirely to study. I attended evening classes where I gained prizes in both elementary and advanced naval architecture; joined the Institution of Engineers and Shipbuilders in Scotland, Student Section, and eventually became a member of the council and finally vice-president. I also joined the Institution of Naval Architects in London, Student Section, and in 1905 attended the annual meetings, where I was thrilled to be introduced to many of the world's most outstanding naval architects and shipbuilders.

I found the two years' course in naval architecture and marine engineering at Glasgow University intensely interesting. The head of the department was the famous Sir John Harvard Biles. When, at the end of the course, it was announced that I had gained the drawing prize for naval design I was filled with confidence that sooner or later the dream of my life would come true and I would count for something in the shipbuilding world. Little did I imagine what God had in store for me in the not distant future.

Of my eight years in the shipyard, four were spent in the scientific department of the drawing office, including one year at the experimental tank where paraffin wax models twelve feet in length were tested in a 400-foot basin very like a tiled swimming pool. By means of an overhead electric-powered carriage, the models were dragged through the water at varying speeds to discover the resistance due to skin friction, wave making and eddy making. Experiments were also made to determine the best type of propellers and their position in relation to the hull of the vessel. The whole of the scientific work came under the immediate direction of the naval architect W. J. Luke, designer of many famous ships, including the Cunard Liners *Caronia, Carmania,* and *Lusitania.*

The intricate detailed drawings of the ships were worked out in the main drawing office while in the scientific department our task was to design the ships to meet the requirements laid down by the prospective owners.

A company might wish to purchase a ship that would carry a certain number of passengers of various classes with suitable sleeping, dining, and recreational facilities. But she would also be required to carry a given number of tons of general cargo and to provide air-conditioned space in separate holds for further quantities of fresh fruit, beef, or mutton. And to be a paying concern she would have to be able to make the voyage from her home port to another in some distant continent in a given number of days. It was our responsibility to find out all necessary particulars regarding the various harbors which the vessel would enter: docking facilities for loading and discharging cargo, the depth of water at low tide, the height of any bridges under which the ship would pass, and similar details.

After the length, breadth, depth, draft, and speed of the vessel had been determined, it was necessary to work out the space required for propelling machinery, including the number of boilers, the space required for the passengers, crew, cargo, fuel, fresh water, stores, lifeboats, and many other matters. When this had been done the shape of the underwater form of the vessel, the type and power of the machinery and propellers received special attention, and it was here that the experimental tank was invaluable.

At this stage the details of construction had to be gone into most carefully to ensure the maximum of strength with the minimum of weights. When the *Lusitania* was designed, it was decided that in order to reduce the weight of the hull, high-tensile steel should be used over a large portion of the main structure instead of the usual mild steel. High-tensile steel is similar to mild steel except that it contains a higher percentage of carbon and this makes it tougher and capable of withstanding the greater tension that develops when the ship is being pounded by heavy seas. I had to keep in touch with the makers of the huge plates by visiting the works and checking on the tests made of each separate plate. In these tests a small strip was cut from the plate and put into a machine with great jaws operated by hydraulic power. When the necessary adjustments had been made, a valve was opened and the jaws drew apart. It was amazing to see the strip of steel stretch like a piece of sugar candy and then, when the limit had been reached, to watch it snap with a cracking noise like a shot from a high-powered rifle. The machine automatically registered the pressure at breaking point as so many tons per square inch. This information, with the detailed plans showing the exact position of each plate on the hull of the ship, was duly recorded for the consideration of both the builders and the owners.

Launching calculations also had to be made and great care exercised to ensure that the huge vessel would stop when afloat and not run aground on the other side of the narrow channel. Unlike the Canadian practice, the ships on the Clyde are launched not broadside but stern first.

I was greatly interested in all the work, and thrilled when a ship on whose plans we had worked for many months was successfully launched, or when, after the official trials on the estuary of the Clyde or in the Irish Sea, it was proved that *our* ship would take her place in the world of commerce or in the Royal Navy and uphold the reputation of *our company* and of the *Clyde*.

While I was concentrating on this business of shipbuilding, other factors were entering into my life.

At the university I had heard a man fume against religion in general and Christianity in particular. Among other things he sneered at the idea that the Man of Nazareth was other than an ignorant peasant, a well-meaning idealist and a fanatic. Love, forgiveness, and that no man lives or dies unto himself, were all nonsense, for in this world it was every man for himself and the Devil take the hindmost. That the speaker was himself a fanatic could not be doubted but he spoke well and with considerable passion.

He made one interesting point about heredity and environment that set me to thinking. A new awareness of the cruel effects that these influences can have caused me much difficulty and uneasiness. Why were thousands of people hard pressed for the bare necessities of life, while others lived in luxury? Why were some men incapable of assuming responsibility while others had marked ability? Why were sickness and pain allowed to afflict mankind? Why was I left an orphan to fight a lonely battle and live in lodgings while my cousins and friends lived in happy homes and had parents who planned their future?

One week end when I was visiting my boyhood friend, Jack Lochhead, in Greenock, I went to church with him on Sunday and heard the closing sermon of a series on comparative religion. The minister summed up the main points of each of the great world religions and then set forth the claims of Christ as the supreme revelation of God.

I was impressed and encouraged but still the problem of heredity and environment persisted. Determinism and the new materialism were then being hailed as the great discoveries of modern science. I had yet to learn that the love of God at work in the lives of men was the true and effective antidote. Heredity and environment, as James Denny puts it, merely fix our trail but not our fate. Ancestry and circumstance may determine what our trials may be, but they do not determine the final issues of these trials.

That week I gave much thought to the enigma and one morning I spoke to one of the men in the office whom I knew to be a sincere Christian and asked what he had to say about it. His name was Daniel MacDougal, a Highlander some fifteen years my senior, short and stocky of build, with thick black hair and bushy eyebrows. When he looked at you his piercing black eyes seemed to nail you to the spot. When I had told him what troubled me, he remained silent for a time and then said, "Look here! If you and I start to argue about heredity and environment we won't get far and you will have the last word anyway. I'm not a preacher, I haven't studied theology, but I can tell you something—nineteen and a half years ago I was troubled as you are now and decided that I needed strength other than my own to live courageously, so I took Jesus Christ as my Master and determined to trust and follow Him. Since then I have failed Him for I have said and done many things that were not according to His will, but He has never failed me and has made life worth while. Why don't you leave the problems of heredity and environment for a while and take Christ as your Lord and Master? You'll never be sorry about making that decision. He will give you light."

For some moments after that Dan went on with his drawing while no word was spoken and all unconsciously I kept puncturing a new piece of soft pencil eraser with the point of a pencil. Suddenly I asked Dan if I could see him after lunch, and so it came about that on a fine sunny day he and I walked by the side of the Forth and Clyde Canal on the outskirts of Clydebank and there I renewed my baptismal vows (I had not yet been confirmed) and decided to follow the Master unconditionally and look to Him for strength day by day.

It was a difficult experience and many problems confronted me for which I did not find an immediate answer. But gradually peace reigned in my heart and as I gained a clearer view of life's values it was possible to adjust my thinking to each problem as it arose.

What began as an adventure, an experiment in faith, ended in experiences that have affected my whole life. Yet sometimes periods of exultant joy were followed by depressions for I had yet to learn to say with St. Francis of Assisi, "I need no more, I know Christ."

What had happened to me was what is commonly called conversion. As Amiel, that devout Roman Catholic, put it, "to be born again is to renounce the old life, sin and the natural man, and to take to oneself another principle of life. It is to exist for God with another self, another will, another love." Or, as Lord Tweedsmuir (John Buchan), when Governor-General of Canada, put it, "There is still for every man the choice of two paths, and conversion in its plain, evangelical sense, is still the greatest fact in any life."

A friend of mine, David Patterson, whom I admired greatly, took a keen interest in my spiritual welfare. His love for his Saviour shone forth from his face and in everything he did. The consuming desire of his life was to witness day by day to God's love that others might come to know the joyous reality of this fellowship. To David the practice of the Presence of Christ was a glorious reality because he had yielded himself to Christ "body, soul and spirit," which, as the apostle claimed, was his "reasonable service." When he and I went for a walk in the country we communed together about things spiritual, and it seemed to me then that we were like the disciples on the way to Emmaus and the Presence was with us though unseen.

One Saturday evening David took me to what was called the Carters' Mission. I cannot remember where it was except that it was deep in the slums of Glasgow. David had been asked to give the address but when we arrived we found that there was first to be an open-air meeting. This was an entirely new idea to me and I was curious to see what would happen because I could not believe that these people would be interested in a church service on Saturday night.

Shortly after we arrived a man who seemed to be the leader announced that we would go to certain places to "ring the bell" but before doing so we would ask for God's blessing. About a dozen men and an equal number of women all knelt on the floor while the leader prayed that "some sinner may come to repentance tonight." He then marshaled all the men, and we marched down the street until we came to a crossroad where we halted in front of three public houses. Here several of the men made brief statements telling what the Lord had done for them and appealing to all to put their trust in Him.

At the close of each testimony and to the accompaniment of a grinding concertina, hymns were sung. They were all unknown to me and I must have looked both stupid and unsympathetic. Each hymn had a chorus and as the tunes were all simple and catchy I was soon able to appear to do my part. One chorus shocked me for it was a parody on another hymn and ran, "Over there, over there, and there'll be no public houses over there."

One of the bartenders, dressed in a not too clean white apron, stood at his door laughing at us. How I hated the whole display. It seemed such a crude, narrow, and unworthy way of expressing the love of the Eternal God. I had much to learn and later came to doubt whether a more composed witness would have been effective under the conditions that then existed in these slum areas. The educated Scot and those who live near to nature frequently possess a rich ethical imagination, but this could not be expected of people who lived in such an environment where everything was almost of necessity either all black or all white. I was glad when we returned to the hall.

In those early days there were no motor vehicles but only horse-drawn carts and drays so that in the city of Glasgow there were thousands of men called carters employed to drive the horses. This mission was intended to reach these men and their families who were out of touch with any of the churches.

The meeting place was a former warehouse on the ground floor of a tenement. It was spotlessly clean but entirely void of any aesthetic atmosphere. On our return from the parade I was surprised to find the place well filled with an audience of both men and women but only a few children. When hymnbooks called *Sacred Songs and Solos* had been distributed, the chair was taken by a great big sandy-haired foreman carter who announced the number of the opening hymn. It was unlike any I had ever heard in either the Presbyterian or Episcopal churches, but the people sang with fervor. At the close of the singing the chairman said, "Let us pray," and when all heads were bowed in silence he addressed the Almighty reverently but in the most simple and homely fashion asking that God's blessing might be upon the meeting.

A "brother" in the audience was then called up to the platform and read a passage from the Bible. My friend David Patterson was next introduced by the chairman and asked to give his "message." To my surprise and pleasure he did so most effectively. His address was spoken in a quiet, natural voice and entirely free from shyness or affectation. His face became radiant as he spoke of the goodness of God in giving us His Son to be our Saviour from sin and our Strength to overcome in the hour of temptation. He ended by appealing to each and every one to bear witness to God's love. It was all so simple and sincere that the audience listened to him with breathless attention except for a whispered "Praise God," "Thank God," or the like. To me it was a wonderful and never-to-be-forgotten experience.

When David sat down the chairman rose and led in a prayer of thanksgiving for the message. Another and more reverent hymn than the previous ones was sung, after which I expected that the meeting would be over. Once more I was mistaken. The chairman now stated that "Brother" Patterson had brought with him a young friend and he was sure that the people would all like to "hear a word" from him. I was immediately covered with confusion. I rose from my seat at the back of the hall and, addressing the chair, replied that I was very sorry but I did not preach and felt that there had been some mistake. Immediately all eyes were turned on me and two men beside me urged me to go up to the platform and "just say a word." There was no escape, so I told the gathering that I had never spoken in a religious meeting in my life and had nothing prepared. I then quoted a verse that had been in my mind since the morning, "Labor not for the meat which perisheth but for that meat which endureth unto everlasting life," and said I did not know all that was involved in these words but I believed that if we put God first everything else would take its place, and ended, much to David Patterson's amusement, by nodding my head to the chairman and saying "Thank you." As I hastened to my seat the people spontaneously began to sing something that in part ran thus:

> "Saved and happy now,
> Saved and happy now,
> The Devil and his furniture are all turned out."

On the way home I asked David why he had allowed me to be embarrassed. But for once he was unsympathetic and replied that I had to begin sometime so the sooner the better.

Things went along quietly at the shipyard until I had completed the special course in naval architecture. Then James

Semple, head of the experimental tank, asked if I would join the staff there. Nothing could have been more to my liking because I had studied the problems dealt with there.

I had hardly settled down in this new and interesting work before I became aware that my friends in the office had planned a propaganda campaign to indoctrinate me so that I would become a socialist—in those days the term communist was unknown but Karl Marx was the prophet. They were even more determined to undermine my religious beliefs and turn me into an agnostic if not an out-and-out atheist. It was all done in a very friendly way but there was some pretty hard hitting. I was not skilled to meet the arguments that came thick and fast at me, and I had a difficult time.

These were days when science was supposed to have displaced theology and the reign of law had disposed of God. The millennium had dawned because education and science could answer all the questions and guarantee peace on earth. No one could foresee the supersession of Newton by Einstein in forty years' time. Men spoke glibly of the "assured facts of science" as unchanging and unchangeable and said "Hang theology, give us facts."

I now felt deeply the sense of my own insecurity and uncertainty regarding religion and life. I had been brought up in a Christian home and had accepted the Christian principles but now the tides of skepticism and materialism swept upon me daily and seemed about to wreck me. I spent many a bleak hour wrestling with these problems. Sometimes it seemed as if my whole religious outlook was in a state of disintegration and would suffer total eclipse. But somehow I was able to withstand their onslaughts, for I felt within me that there was something lacking in the agnostic philosophy which was being pressed upon me so relentlessly.

That the reign of law is operative as a vital principle I could not doubt but I wanted to get behind that universal law. Who made the laws of the universe? Only a mind can produce minds; hence, the idea of chance explaining the problems of life and creation seemed inadequate. In my perplexity I wandered for a time in the labyrinth of theological dogmas and the theories of interpretation.

Sooner or later a man must drink this bitter cup of intellectual doubt, for the eternal question forces itself upon the earnest seeker after truth—Where is now thy God? Is there no alternative to the depressing metaphysics of Hegel? Can we assume that, in spite of the evil, disease, suffering, cruelty, hate, the chaos and tragedy of life, order and meaning can be found? For months I walked in the dark valley of derision and doubt because no clear answer came.

Gradually in the time of my agony a shaft of light pierced the gloom. I saw that I was a literalist. The philosophy of dialectical materialism as found in Darwin, Hegel, and Huxley had hit hard at my childish conceptions of God but brought no satisfaction from the intellectual viewpoint. My heart was hungry and something within me gave the assurance that there was an answer to my problem other than disillusioned atheism.

There were moments of acute pain when I became despondent until I realized that my tormentors were in an even more difficult position than I, for the problems of unbelief are greater than those of belief, and they were without hope even in this world. I had yet to recognize the hand of God in this, as in all the vicissitudes of life.

As Beverley Nichols put it, "Even if religion is a drug it seems to be a rather more effective drug than the average atheist can purchase from the average apothecary." I learned that you cannot argue or explain spiritual things. When you try to be literal and explicit, you lose them just as you cannot analyze and dissect your feelings and still have them. With this intellectual emancipation a new stage was set.

I realized, too, that faith is a necessity to life. We exercise faith during all the twenty-four hours of the day when we eat food, drink water, sleep, travel by land or sea or air, when we pay our taxes or read our newspaper. Without faith man's life would cease. "Without faith no man can see God." God is no clever magician. Down through the ages He has revealed Himself to those who have sought Him. The orderliness of nature, its beauty and complexity resound with the affirmations of God. His name is Wisdom, Righteousness and Love. He is the Mind behind the universe—infinite and eternal—so that for us to fully understand Him will require eternity. Yet to the humble seeker He reveals Himself sufficiently to give assurance for both time and eternity. Without free will man would be a nonentity but because he has free will he is capable of evil as well as good; the innocent suffer from man's disobedience to the Divine Will. By the order in the universe, by the glorious possibilities for good in man, we understand something of the Creator. To ordinary men and women God has revealed Himself as supremely good, just and loving. We know that the Creator cannot be less than His creation and our task in life is to realize our at-one-ness with God. Then, as Jesus put it, "He that followeth me shall not walk in darkness but shall have the light of life." This, to me, became the key that unlocked the mystery of life. As we do the will of God, we know the truth and it is here that the Christian revelation enables men to rise to heroic heights and to become witnesses to the truth which is eternal and which makes men free.

This was a major spiritual crisis and involved internal conflicts and mental changes, the repercussions of which were not fully understood until many years later. What Spinoza called "the intellectual love of God" which finds God present in every man and in every place is not anthropomorphic but is a valuable step towards the Christian position. Of necessity it is inadequate since man is more than intellect, but I came to feel that metaphysics was merely an instrument towards the discovery of truth. It was not difficult to assume a critical attitude towards orthodox Christianity but the need of moral and spiritual uplift for ordinary individuals and the experiences of the saints through the ages demanded something more than fine philosophical phrases. From personal contacts with some of my friends in the office I knew that moral indifference to morality inevitably leads to immorality. It is not abstract reason that inspires men but the spectacle of the powerful results following an act of faith in Him Who said, "I am come that they might have life, and that they might have it more abundantly."

I was still at the beginning of the road. I had to learn that the Christian religion is not simply a theory or method that can be studied and analyzed but a life to be lived involving the union of the spirit of man with the Spirit of God. This sometimes manifests itself emotionally. I can still recall the internal conflicts and intellectual doubts preceding this all-important decision and then the thrill that overwhelmed me because of the sense of the reality of God as the Creator and lover of man's soul—my soul. Then it was that I walked with a new strength and had a sure and certain hope for the present and the future.

After a year at the experimental tank I was transferred to the main office of the scientific department and reveled in the work there. These were days of great expectation and promise. Because they had constant variety, they seemed to be more creative and allowed me to do the kind of work which would best prepare me for that dreamed-of day when I would become a builder of ships.

In the spring of 1906 I was spending a week end with some friends at West Kilbride, a small town some forty miles from Glasgow. There was another visitor in the house, a Miss Annie Sharp, who was a missionary-in-training under the China Inland Mission. At first I was afraid of her until I discovered that she was not what young people today call a "creep" but was full of common sense and good spirits as well as being a deeply spiritually-minded woman. Her stories of the work in China inspired me but when she asked me if I would not answer the call to help the needy millions in that land of mystery I replied, as I had done to others, that I did not feel called to be a missionary but to be a shipbuilder, adding as an afterthought that if ever I felt the missionary call it would be to the Eskimo of Baffin Land.

Months later I met Miss Sharp's brother-in-law, E. J. Y.

Simmons, and after dinner one evening he told me that a friend of his, Harold A. Boyd, had been ill and was traveling in Canada, hoping to restore his health. It appeared that Boyd, who was a Presbyterian, taught a class of "working boys" in a Sunday school in the east end of Glasgow and there was an urgent need for some man to take over the class for a few weeks until Boyd's return. Would I help out? My answer was definitely in the negative. I had never taught anybody in my life but had always been taught. Moreover, it was my practice to spend my week ends with my sister Barbara because I disliked the city on Sundays. My protestations were without avail. Here was a most urgent need—I was free—it was a genuine call. . . . So it came about that the autumn of that year found me attempting to teach a class of big lads in one of the worst slum districts in the city of Glasgow.

The work was sponsored by Hillhead Baptist Church but of the twelve teachers only four were Baptists. It is interesting to note in passing that one Baptist went to China, one Presbyterian married a minister of that communion, while of the three Episcopalians one went to India under the YWCA, one became a sister in the Community of the Epiphany, Truro, and later served in Japan, while I went to the Arctic.

On his return from overseas Boyd's doctor advised against his undertaking work of any kind on Sunday, so instead of helping for a few weeks I continued with my lads for two years. At Port Dundas I was to learn something of the dire squalor and degradation to which human beings can descend in a great industrial city. I was shocked and disheartened, but concerned first about what could be done to help.

The first claim upon my attention were the boys I was called upon to teach Sunday by Sunday. Most of them worked in a local iron foundry, and it did not take me long to realize that their problem was very complicated. Poverty was not by any means the sole cause of the evils with which I was confronted as I visited the sordid tenement homes of my pupils.

As I came to know these people it was not difficult to

understand that to raise the moral and spiritual standards was even more important than improving their material standards but I saw that one affected the other in the most intimate way. It also became clear that a fine idealism based on a purely "mental" God could not solve the problem either. What was needed was an awakening of the souls of men to their need of the God and Father of Jesus Christ. This alone would establish the dignity of man and reveal the wickedness of poverty which made Him a nonentity.

Any lingering idea that there was truth in the assertion of human self-sufficiency and independence was shattered by my new contacts. To give more money to men whose idea of a truly happy Saturday was to "blow yersel' oot" with whiskey while their children went hungry was not the real solution.

Saturday evenings were the worst. Drunken men brawled with one another or with their womenfolk on the streets, coarse laughter, dirty, ragged, yelling urchins playing in the gutters caused many a heartache.

Yet it was encouraging that despite their different religious views those who taught the children in the Sunday school had but one motive—to help the slum dwellers to a better way of life. The workers were untrained and several were ladies from the fashionable district of Kelvinside.

My particular class of older lads met at a convenient street corner at two o'clock on Saturday afternoon and boarded a tram. For a few pence we traveled into the open country where we then tramped our way for several miles past small streams and through quiet villages. On the way back we visited a cheap teashop and each had a cup of tea, costing one penny each, and a pork pie costing twopence.

There was always much chaff and good humor as we ate our humble fare and these outings built up a spirit of comradeship that was most valuable. As I write, it all seems so unsophisticated and void of the dramatic but the years that followed gave ample proof of the reality of the changes wrought in many of our lads by the Spirit of God.

In my group the boy on whom I felt I could count the

most was James. About a year after I met him he obtained work as a butcher's assistant with a substantial increase in pay. Unfortunately he became mildewed with the blight of respectability and gradually shunned his old friends. He now appeared in brand-new habiliments, a white hand-starched linen dicky with high collar and gaudy tie or boots that were not the kind men wore to work in during the week. The climax was reached when he appeared wearing a black bowler hat! His old friends felt stung. My own feelings were mixed. I liked James and understood his many fine qualities. I knew that in time he would adjust to his new state of prosperity and prove his worth but I was sorry that his blemishes created a nasty spirit of jealousy among some of his less fortunate friends. Later he moved from the district and became a loyal member of a Baptist church.

If James was the most hopeful of my lads, John was considered almost hopeless. His parents were both shiftless and chronic drunkards. If his mother could not get enough money to buy a glass of beer she drank methylated spirits. One Saturday afternoon when I arrived at their single basement room with some clean clothes for John to wear on Sunday I found him alone in the house. The place was without even the most necessary furniture. A few decrepit-looking pots stood on the broken cooking stove, some chunks of coal fell from a burlap bag, and two filthy blankets only half covered a pile of straw in a corner. Three empty wooden boxes took the place of chairs.

The pathetic sight filled me with sorrow. While we were talking the door opened and John's parents staggered in. Both were drunk. The woman was disheveled and the front of her dress was wet. She stood glaring at me for a moment and then suddenly flopped to the floor, making gurgling noises. The man swore at her and rolled her over on the straw pallet. He then turned and in strong language asked me who I was and what I was doing there. John explained and for a moment his father looked at me in silence, then suddenly, as if waking out of a dream, drew close to me and asked if

I had "any good in my mind" and would let him have the price of a "schooner" of beer.

Inexperienced as I was, I did not know what to do. I whispered to John to come away with me. We went down the street and round a corner to a cheap restaurant where a cup of hot tea and penny buns seemed to relieve the tension. John still carried the bundle of clothes I had brought him but that did not register in my mind at the time because the whole scene had been so disturbing. At Sunday school the next day John was dressed in his clean clothes and the improvement in his appearance was most marked.

A week later John was absent. None of the other lads in the class knew anything about him. On the next Tuesday evening I called at his home, to discover that his mother had pawned the new clothes during the previous week. This was the first of innumerable discouragements, and many times I returned to my lodgings so depressed by the stark misery that I found it difficult to sleep.

With the assistance of one of the mission workers, however, we were able to get John room and board with a respectable widow who lived in a different part of the city, where his parents could not bother him.

The plan was a complete success, and later I was also able to get John established as an apprentice boilermaker in the shipyard at Clydebank.

One morning in September, 1908, as I stood with friends on the deck of the ship that was to take me to Canada, I was greatly surprised to see a group of my Sunday school lads crowded close to the barrier on the dock. I immediately went ashore and thanked them for this unexpected kindness. Of them all John looked the most disconsolate, so I drew him apart from the others and immediately he broke down, telling me that I was his best friend. If I left him, he said, "I can-na keep it," meaning that he would be unable to live the Christian life among the men in the boiler shop. My reply was that I knew he had faith but that he thought that God could work only through me because I had been a channel of blessing to him. This, I said, was very wrong and dishonoring to God and that I felt in taking me away God was giving him the strength "to keep it." This seems to have been one of the turning points in John's life. His faith became stronger and he is now an elder in a local Presbyterian church. His only son served in the Royal Air Force during the Second World War and soon expects to graduate in medicine at Glasgow University.

Not long after I took up work at the mission I also became interested in a Bible reading fellowship known as the Scripture Union. Under this plan a brief portion of Scripture of from eight to twelve verses was appointed to be read each day throughout the year and my lads found it simple and helpful.

But to return to the Sunday school at Port Dundas. I must mention one occasion when a missionary on furlough from China was speaking to my class. After the session the speaker asked me if I planned to go to the mission field. Once again I explained my position only to be questioned further: "Have you any home responsibilities?" "No." "Are you planning to be married in the near future?" "No." "Well," said the missionary, "I have met numbers of young men who don't feel the 'call' because of the claims of relatives but you have none. May I ask you if you really feel 'called' to stay at home?" Then, when he was saying goodbye, there came a whisper in my ear, "Do pray about this. China needs you."

Shortly after this incident I was reading the paper one morning in the train between Charing Cross, Glasgow, and Clydebank. A friend who worked in the drawing office and who was soon to leave for China to work under the National Bible Society of Scotland threw a copy of a paper called *The Life of Faith* across the compartment to me with the remark, "There is something of special interest in that for you." I scanned the pages but could see nothing that attracted my attention until I came to "Letters to the Editor." There I read an appeal by the Rt. Rev. George Holmes, Bishop of Moosonee, Canada, in which he stated that he had gone up and down England all winter searching for a young man who would be willing to hazard his life for the Gospel among the Eskimo of Baffin Land. He had heard many sing:

> *"Take my life and let it be*
> *Consecrated, Lord, to Thee,"*

yet not one volunteer had come forward. The following morning, May twenty-four, 1906, the bishop was leaving Liverpool for Canada but if his appeal met the eye of one who was prepared to volunteer, that man was asked to communicate with the bishop's secretary, Mr. George J. Money, in London.

This struck me like a thunderbolt. I can still remember how I became faint and cold all over. The challenge had come and had to be faced. What was I to do? It was as upsetting as it was unexpected. I did not wish to change the even tenor of my life or to give up the dream that had been with me through the years. My whole training had been as a shipbuilder and not for missionary work.

After an unhappy week of indecision I wrote to the bishop's secretary, telling him my story and asking him for his advice. By return mail I received a kindly letter informing me that since an Arctic missionary, the Rev. E. W. T. Greenshield, was in England on furlough, my letter had been forwarded to him for his attention. Greenshield then wrote of the pressing need but also set forth some of the grave difficulties and dangers and privations that were commonly encountered in the Arctic. He suggested that I should communicate direct with the bishop, whose headquarters were at Chapleau, Ontario.

A full statement was sent to the bishop, but I raised two theological problems that were causing me difficulty and I felt that in all honesty they should be cleared before I committed myself to the work should the bishop finally wish to accept my offer of service. These were: What did "seeing now . . . this child is regenerate" mean in the baptismal service and in what sense were the words "eternal fire" in the Creed of Athanasius to be understood?

The bishop was a very busy man traveling over his vast diocese and the mails were slow in those days so that there were many delays. Finally he arranged with a friend in England to send me some books and papers dealing with the problems I had raised. Then one day in the spring of 1908 I received a letter from Bishop Holmes telling me that he and the veteran Eskimo missionary, the Rev. E. J. Peck, were in England, and asking if I would come to London for an interview.

This was not quite so easy as it sounded. London and Glasgow were a day's journey apart and the bishop was constantly on the move preaching and lecturing on behalf of the work in Canada. Moreover a young man in a junior position in a big firm does not readily ask for time off for personal affairs.

Then a strange thing happened. The British Admiralty had called for tenders to be submitted by the shipbuilders on the Admiralty List for the construction of some new vessels and I was sent by John Brown and Company to investigate the plans and specifications at the Admiralty Office in Whitehall, London. Was it only chance that both the bishop and Mr. Peck were in the city at that time?

On my return to Clydebank I did not find it easy to announce my resignation. I shall never forget the kindness of Mr. W. J. Luke who, following the death of Mr. David McGee, had been appointed manager of the great shipyard, or his urgent appeal that I should think it over. "Let some burly Highlander go to the Arctic," he urged. "Never have we given to a young man the training and opportunities that you have had. We gave them not out of charity but because we felt that you showed exceptional promise and in this we have not been disappointed. Stay with us and a great future lies ahead. Any man can be a missionary but not every man can be a shipbuilder." Mr. John Paterson who had succeeded Mr. Luke as naval architect echoed Mr. Luke's words.

I was much moved by this entirely unexpected consideration on the part of these men who held such important positions, and at their request I promised to say nothing about the matter in the office for one week. Then I was to tell them my decision. How difficult it all was! How torn I was as I looked ahead and wondered what was in store for me! But to me this challenge was an opportunity to endure in order to bring the Eskimo of Baffin Land the message of God's love. If it involved loneliness, hardship, cold, hunger, and misunderstanding, then that was the price to be paid. There could be no reserve of my committal to Him whom I called Master and Lord.

I had promised the bishop that I would leave for Canada in time to begin the study of theology at Wycliffe College, Toronto, by October first. And more important, I knew very well that although I had been wonderfully privileged in the training and experience given me in the shipyard and owed my two chiefs a great debt, yet I knew also that there were others eager and anxious to take my place, while not one of them would go to Baffin Land.

Inevitably the following months were upsetting. True, some of my friends approved of the step I was taking and to them I shall always be grateful. It is said of Albert fourth Earl Grey when he was at Trinity College, Cambridge, that by his sympathy, understanding, and faith "he lit many fires in cold rooms." So these good friends kept the fire of faith burning in my heart and I was given strength not to look back. It was David Patterson who reminded me that as it was with St. Paul so it would be with me: "My grace is sufficient for thee; for my strength is made perfect in weakness."

The majority of my friends shook their heads and seemed to think I had become mental. One friend in the office considered me a fool of classic type. He said so in plain, blunt, and uncomplimentary language. After I had received a farewell presentation from the office staff, this man refused to shake hands with me. At the time his lack of good will hurt me more than I can say. After a lapse of thirty-seven years I was greatly surprised to receive a most kind letter from my quondam friend and since then the old friendship has been renewed. He is now a warden of the church in his parish in Wales, where he has retired after a busy life as manager of a Clyde shipbuilding yard.

The voyage across the Atlantic on board the Allan Line steamer *Ionian* was restful and pleasant. We reached Quebec on the twenty-ninth of September and had time to make a hurried trip in an open horse-drawn carriage around the historic city. I was struck with the beauty of the mighty Saint Lawrence River and, like many another traveler, fascinated by the old French buildings and the winding, cobbled, and very steep streets.

I had promised Bishop Holmes that I would be at Wycliffe College, Toronto, by October first and on that morning I arrived. A number of students were chatting together in the rotunda of the building when I entered and immediately came forward and gave me a friendly welcome. They had heard of my coming. They took me to my room and did everything possible to meet my needs. Later I was shown into the principal's office and discovered that he was a genial Irishman and not the stern ecclesiastic I had imagined him to be. The Reverend Canon O'Meara was not considered to be a scholar but he was a great human being and from the first I was impressed by the way he put me at my ease, giving me a clear understanding of the studies I would take and the time of my bishop's visit to Toronto. Then with a smile he advised me to remove my mustache since first-year students were required to be clean-shaven! During that first interview and during the years that followed I found in Dr. O'Meara a warm friend.

In the drawing office in Clydebank I had felt that I was entering upon a career which had been my goal ever since I could remember. School, university and night school had had their day and I was now twenty-five years of age. Success and failure had been mine but I had been confident of the future. Yet here in this strange new country I was suddenly bereft of all my friends and acquaintances, registered as a first-year student in theology, having to begin all over again, to prepare for the vigorous life of a missionary in the faraway Arctic. I found it difficult to fit into the youthful viewpoint, particularly all the horseplay and nonsense, for I had given up everything to serve for Christ's sake in Baffin Land and I wanted to get on with the job. But it was a humbling experience and much later I came to realize that it had been a good thing for my pride to have been given a little rough treatment.

In addition to my studies in theology I was fortunate in gaining some knowledge and experience in elementary medicine. Canon O'Meara introduced me to Dr. W. H. B. Aitken, who took a genuine interest in me and worked out a plan which proved of great value to me later in Baffin Land. Through his kind offices I attended lectures on anatomy and medicine and worked at the outdoor clinic of St. Michael's Hospital. Here I first met Dr. Malcolm C. V. Cameron who became my medical advisor and from that time has given me without stint the riches of his friendship. Dr. Aitken also arranged for me to help at the Simcoe Street Free Dispensary and to observe maternity cases. All of this combined with my theological studies made a very heavy schedule but it seemed the only way of accomplishing my necessary preparation.

Before leaving this portion of my life I must record my grateful thanks not only to Principal O'Meara but to Canon H. J. Cody, Professor G. M. Wrong, and Professor W. T. Hallam, later Bishop of Saskatoon, for all the help they gave me as a stranger and a Scot. In later years it was Canon Cody who placed me deepest in his debt. Canon Cody was a very great man, richly gifted in many and diverse ways, not least in his human relationships. He never gave the impression of being encumbered by his vast knowledge, but wore the weight of learning and the burden of unequaled popularity and many honors like an easily fitting garment. During my entire Canadian life I had the privilege and benefit of consulting him about all the major decisions of my public and private life.

Early in November 1908 Bishop Holmes came to Toronto, bringing news that was both startling and upsetting. He wished me to go to Baffin Land the following July—that is, in July 1909—to spend two years there doing mission work and then to return to the college to finish my preparation for ordination.

I was torn between the desire to hasten working among the Eskimo and hesitancy in delaying the ordination which was my immediate objective and necessary for my ultimate goal. I knew that as an ordained man I would be far more effective and it disturbed me that I was being asked to go north but partly trained. My overwhelming enthusiasm was in no way diminished but my judgment balked. No independent young Scot accepts blindly the decrees of another and I had much wrestling with myself in prayer. Ultimately I said nothing. The Church to which I belonged was Episcopal and an embryonic missionary should not dispute the decisions of his bishop. Once this inner struggle was behind me, I began to make preparations to go north. Expectancy rose daily higher and higher as I realized that the great adventure in the Master's service had begun.

☆   # 2. To Baffin Land   ☆

ONE FINE CLEAR morning in the month of July 1909, I stood on a wharf in the landlocked harbor of St. John's, Newfoundland, watching the men load the cargo on board the *Lorna Doone*. She was a two-masted fore and aft sailing schooner of fifty-four tons, built in 1887 for fishing off the Grand Banks. In recent years she had not been able to compete with more high-powered fishing craft and was generally employed to carry freight from St. John's to small outposts on the Newfoundland coast.

We considered ourselves fortunate that the *Lorna Doone* had been chartered to take us on the long 1,200-mile voyage from St. John's to Baffin Land. It had been arranged that I should work during the first two years with Mr. J. W. Bilby who had already served as a missionary in the Arctic. This was only common sense, for I, an inexperienced young man, could not be sent to the Far North completely alone to establish a new mission and to evangelize singlehanded a pagan people. No matter how eager and willing, I knew neither the land nor its inhabitants, the language nor the living conditions.

On the voyage Bilby and I were also to be accompanied by the Rev. E. J. Peck, superintendent of the Church's Arctic work and himself a veteran Arctic missionary whom I had met in London on the occasion of my first interview with

Bishop Holmes. He was a short, stocky, bespectacled little man with an abundance of the most beautiful white hair and a heavy white beard. But I did not make the acquaintance of Bilby until we arrived in St. John's just prior to our sailing. Naturally I was somewhat curious about him. He was an Englishman of average height and well built, with heavy chin and nose, good brow, thick hair greying in the temples, and a black mustache. His nine years' experience at Blacklead Island Mission (the forerunner of the present Pangnirtung Mission) with Mr. Peck and Mr. Greenshield had given him an intimate knowledge of the Eskimo and their language.

For weeks we had been looking forward to this day when the cargo would actually be put on board the little ship, and now excitement seized us all. The entire contents of a mail-order catalogue seemed to be stacked alongside the *Lorna Doone*. It was essential to take with us every article that would be needed to build and furnish a four-room mission house and to provide us with food, utilities, medicines, clothing, and articles of barter. No vessel would be sent north with further supplies for *two* years. If anything were forgotten or overlooked we would have to do without.

All about us lay a jumble of lumber, window sashes and doors; barrels of coal oil, bags and crates of food supplies, utensils and household furniture. Between the slats of heavy crates I spied our kitchen stove and two small Quebec heaters, one for each bedroom. The coal had already been dumped into the hold. There were also such goods as cartridges and knives, cotton materials and blankets to be used for barter with the Eskimo. And then our personal baggage. I had put into mine a complete set of Ruskin, small and bound in leather, which, after all these years, is on my study shelves today.

During the process of loading, our spirits rose or failed according to the progress of the day. As we looked at the small size of the ship it sometimes seemed quite impossible that she could accommodate every bag and box and crate of that great pile. Yet what could we sacrifice? We discussed and debated,

debated and discussed, and the problem kept me awake at night. Yet in the end only the material for a small storehouse had to be left behind. The cargo did not all get into the hold, however, and the deck was finally loaded high above the bulwarks. On the day of our departure the *Lorna Doone* would not have been passed by an inspector from Lloyds!

Reference to our expedition had been made in St. John's newspapers so that there was always a group of citizens on the dock watching the loading. Man after man remarked, "Well! It will be all right if you don't run into rough weather."

The success of the loading was a tremendous relief to us all, and not least to me, because I had been sent down to St. John's earlier in the month before Peck and Bilby to attend to the outfitting of the expedition. Shortly after my arrival in the city an immaculately dressed young man came up to me in the lobby of the Crosby Hotel where I was staying and said, "Excuse me, but are you the man who is going to the Eskimo in Baffin Land?" Almost before I could answer he surprised me by saying in a pleasant, soft voice, "I go back to my home in Greenland." I was startled and for a moment speechless. Before I had recovered and while I was studying his face, noting his copper skin, brown eyes, black hair and high cheekbones, he smiled gravely and said, "I am Mene Wallace."

I now greeted him warmly if somewhat belatedly for he was the first Eskimo I had ever seen. I had, of course, heard of Mene Wallace because the Canadian press had carried dispatches about a group of Eskimo brought south by Commander Peary, and of how they had all died except one lad who would return to his homeland. In my mind I had associated this young man with New York and not with St. John's. My surprise and delight at encountering him were very real.

We soon became friends and because Mene had nothing to do but await the arrival of the ship that was to take him north he was glad to come with me on various errands when

I was purchasing our supplies. He was very lonely and talked with great freedom about his experiences in New York, although I could get surprisingly little from him about his life in Greenland. He was discontented and even bitter at having to leave the south. It was soon very evident that in civilization he had learned much that was good and useful but also much that was detrimental to his own best interest. According to Mene he had been adopted as a son by Dr. and Mrs. Wallace of the Museum of Natural History, New York. While admitting that they had treated him with every kindness and generosity, he had two complaints about them, both fantastic to a degree. First he claimed that they denied him his freedom! When analyzed this meant that they disapproved of his being constantly in the company of a music-hall actress named Vesta Tillie who was twice his age. Mene considered her to be his best friend. Then he claimed that Dr. Wallace was just waiting for him to die so that his skull might be put in the museum alongside that of his father! Later, I was told by those who knew the true story that Mene had become so spoiled and rebellious that Dr. Wallace felt only harm would come to him if he remained in the south. He regretted that the boy had been removed from his environment in the first place.

Arrangements had been made, therefore, for Mene to return to his home in Greenland and he had been sent to St. John's to await the arrival of his ship. My heart went out to him but I found him hard and void of any love for his own people. This may have been understandable after the adjustments he had been required to make, but it was distressing. He was completely lacking in religious faith of any kind, whether pagan or Christian.

Mene was on hand to wave us farewell on our great day. On Friday, July 30, 1909, at about 3:30 P.M. the start was made.

As the sails were run up and the *Lorna Doone* quietly passed down the beautiful harbor borne along by a fair wind, my heart was more tumultuous than the movement of the little ship as she slipped through the high rocky bluffs of the "narrows" and into the open sea. My life's work had begun.

The *Lorna Doone* was so small that there was no difficulty about getting to know each member of the crew. My first impression of the skipper Fradsham was that he belonged to the era of Elizabeth's buccaneers. He was in his middle thirties, thickset with crisp brown hair, deep-set quizzical blue eyes, and sensuous mouth. There was something about this man, whose skin the sun and wind had turned to deep red leather, that both attracted and repelled me. Before the voyage was over my first impressions were deepened.

The mate, who was somewhat older than the skipper, had a very quiet voice and referred to the other members of the crew as his "lambs." At first this struck me as silly but there was reason behind the expression. Such strength lay in his kindly nature that he was able to control those rough young giants of the sea without raising his voice and, unlike the skipper, he never resorted to swearing to get the work done. While some of the mate's religious beliefs were undoubtedly narrow, he was respected for having the courage of his convictions. Right at the start he made it clear that only works of necessity and mercy were permitted on the Lord's Day. Anything more was a desecration. This included shaving so henceforth Bilby and I performed that task on Saturday night. Mr. Peck's Victorian whiskers relieved him of difficulty in this connection.

The cook was the hardest-working man on the ship and from the first I liked him. As the days went by we became great friends and bit by bit as his natural reticence dissolved he spoke to me about himself. Behind his whimsical smile and unexpected thoughtfulness was passion held in check by the experiences of life and by personal allegiance to Christ. To know him was a privilege.

The other members of the crew were hardy, sober men but so shy that it took them almost half the voyage to become friendly. Accommodation on board the *Lorna Doone* was somewhat limited. Our quarters were the skipper's cabin, which measured roughly nine feet six inches long and nine feet wide with one bunk on either side. These were occupied by Fradsham and Peck. A couch intended for the mission house was placed along the forward bulkhead to provide a bunk for Bilby, while three trunks, a suitcase, and a handbag with a mattress laid on top formed my sleeping place. It had to be disposed of before breakfast each morning so that we could get at our possessions in the trunks and made up again each evening, and in rough weather it disintegrated so rapidly that on more than one occasion I landed on the cabin floor with one or more of the trunks on top of me.

For two days the schooner sailed smoothly and speedily forward, propelled by a light offshore wind, but the second night she was suddenly struck by a wicked squall, the forerunner of a heavy thunderstorm. Peck and Bilby were writing up their diaries while I was reading. The sudden impact of the wind caused the ship to heel over so sharply that we, with the stove, boxes, and books were hurled to leeward in one confused mass. The seas flooded the deck and cabin and unfortunately swept overboard two chairs and some valuable lumber.

When we stumbled on deck the wind literally screamed in the rigging. It had whipped up a very rough sea, and angry waves roared on our port side, causing the boat to twist and turn violently. It was tremendously exciting although we were thoroughly shaken up and carried the bruises with us for some days. It is these sudden squalls that make the Newfoundland-Labrador coast so dangerous for sailing craft and account for the large number of schooners wrecked each year.

The following day we arrived at St. Anthony, the headquarters of the Grenfell Mission. Having learned in Toronto much about the work being done among the deep-sea fishermen I looked forward with eagerness to this visit. This was the first mission station I had ever actually seen with my own eyes. A Dr. Wakefield was in charge and he, with the members of his staff, gave us a warm welcome. In the evening Dr. Peck preached in the church to a goodly congregation. We spent the whole of the following day there and to me it was a tonic and an inspiration.

From then on we made frequent stops at tiny settlements and islands along the bleak Labrador coast, ostensibly to fill our two water casks, or to buy cod or salmon with which to replenish our poorly stocked larder. To our surprise we found that at each settlement we met relatives of first one member and then another of the crew so we soon concluded that there was a double motive involved! Thus Battle Harbour, Cape Harrison, Cape Harrigan, Cut-throat Harbour, Blow-me-down Mountain, and Cape Mugford became something more to me than mere names on the map.

The fisherfolk always received us most kindly, inviting us into their dwellings and offering us the best they had, which was generally a mug of "real strong" tea and a piece of bannock with a little treacle on it. The more I saw of the "Liveyeres," as they are called (the name is derived from the expression "live here"), the more I admired the calm courage of these men who risked their lives in their cranky little dories to gather in the silver harvest of the sea.

On Tuesday, August 10, we were sailing along quietly before a light breeze in what the sailors referred to as "sociable" weather and enjoying the sunshine. We worked our way through narrow passages called "tickles" between small islands. At times we were so close to the shore that we could see not only the fish-drying stages and the dwellings perched high on the rocks, but the ragged children playing at the water's edge. The nets spread out to dry in the sun fluttered gently in the wind.

Our idyllic peace was suddenly broken by a series of shocks as the ship bumped on the rocky sea bottom. The bow of the *Lorna Doone* was fast on the rocks but the stern was afloat so Fradsham ordered everything possible moved from the bow to the stern in order to lighten the fore part of the ship. Then there was much hauling at a rope attached to a small kedge anchor astern and with the help of the men from a nearby schooner the vessel was swung off the rocks and we were afloat once more. This was the third time we had scraped bottom.

When the weather was fine I loved to stand out on the bowsprit and watch the soft lapping ripples at the bow. Then, too, I had long talks with members of the crew who told me of their experiences when engaged in the annual spring seal hunt. Each year hundreds of men from St. John's and the "outports" of Newfoundland set out for the ice fields where the families of harp seals are to be found. Each year tens of thousands of these mammals are slaughtered.

It is a great gamble because the men are paid according to the number of seals obtained by their particular ship, but generally it is considered profitable and, besides the money, they have the excitement and good fellowship involved. All the members of our crew had been to the sealing, or "the swilling" as they called it. Among the many songs they sang this one has remained in my memory—

> 'Way down on Pigeon Pond Inlet
> When Daddy comes home from the swillin',
> (Maggoty fish hung up in the air,
> Fried in maggoty butter!)
> Cakes and tea for breakfast,
> Pork and duff for dinner.
> Cakes and tea for supper,
> When Daddy comes home from the swillin'.

One of the highlights of the voyage was our visit to Hopedale, about halfway up the Labrador coast, where the Moravian Brethren have an important mission station. Years before I had read with intense interest the story of their work first in Greenland and then in Labrador. The first to preach the Christian faith to the Eskimo of the North American continent was the "Society of the Unitas Fratrium," better known as "The Moravian Brethren"—a small German Protestant communion whose missionaries reached Labrador (Nfld.) in 1752. According to the British Admiralty Records quoted in Hunt's *Life of Sir Hugh Palliser*, Governor of Newfoundland, the Eskimo at that time were considered to be "the most savage people in the world." In spite of this, or perhaps because of it, the Moravians felt drawn towards them and on May 18, 1752, a little sailing vessel called the *Hope* left London, England, bearing the first missionaries. On the 27th of July the tiny craft reached Davis Strait Inlet on the Labrador coast. Heavy fog veiled the land and for five days the ship remained becalmed.

Some Eskimo saw the ship from the shore and approached it in their kayaks. John Christian Erhardt, one of the missionaries aboard who spoke the language, went out to meet them in the ship's boat. The natives appeared to be friendly and on Erhardt's invitation came aboard. Eventually a suitable site was found for the mission, and the material for the buildings and supplies for twelve months were put ashore. By the last day of August all the provisions had been landed and the main portion of the buildings completed. Five days later some Eskimo told Erhardt that a large number of their countrymen were to be found farther up the coast. The missionary accepted the invitation to visit this settlement and set sail in one of the ship's boats on the morning of September 13. He was accompanied by six members of the crew, and the schooner *Hope* was left at anchor with only the mate aboard. The seven men who set sail vanished into the unknown. One can but conjecture their fate.

The Moravian Brethren finally established a permanent settlement at Nain in 1771 and from that time onward they had the whole responsibility of the missionary work among the Eskimo of Labrador.

Because of my familiarity with their history I felt that I was visiting friends at Hopedale and as events proved I was not mistaken. After more than forty years I still communicate with Mr. and Mrs. Lenz who were then missionaries-in-charge. There was warmth and pleasure in their welcome as we were shown over the substantial dwelling house. It was built of heavy timbers brought from far inland at the head of one of the fjords for which Labrador is famous. The church was disappointingly bare inside. Everything was made of wood, void of paint, and scrubbed clean with German thoroughness. Even the floor was well sanded. But the greatest surprise came when we were taken to the back of the buildings and discovered there a charming, well-laid-out garden.

Mr. Lenz asked if there was anything that he or his wife could do for me. My reply surprised and amused him for I said, "Yes! Could I please have a hot bath?" While Mrs. Lenz was boiling a great kettle of water on the kitchen stove, Lenz and I rowed out to the schooner to fetch some clean clothes. When the bath incident became known, it caused much merriment and chaff on board the schooner. I could only remind the jesters that it was now eleven days since we had left St. John's and that on the *Lorna Doone* no bath or toilet accommodation was provided. This reply did not make the slightest impression for to them the situation was ridiculous. Fradsham could not get over the incident and teased me unmercifully for days to come.

It was here that I met the Labrador Eskimo for the first time and I longed for the day when I could speak with them in their own tongue. Mr. and Mrs. Lenz and Peck and Bilby all urged me to begin then and there with a few simple words of greeting.

After we left Hopedale the air became heavily moisture-laden so that the men wore their oilskins and sou'westers. Soon it increased in density and swept past us like white vapor, obscuring everything. The man at the wheel found it difficult even to see the man on the lookout at the bow. How Fradsham managed to grope his way along I do not know.

Our next stop was at a tiny Eskimo settlement a short distance southwest of Cape Mugford which is known to the white men by the menacing name of Cut Throat Harbour. We were forced to take shelter here because of a strong north wind against which our little schooner could make no progress. It was at such times as this or when we were becalmed, or in the ice fields, that we longed to have auxiliary power. A number of fishing schooners had also sought the shelter accorded by this safe anchorage, and the following day being Sunday, services were conducted first for the Eskimo and then for the fisherfolk. Then Bilby and I took the small rowboat and visited each of the schooners to invite the crews to attend an open-air service on shore at 7 P.M. That night we joined some eighty fishermen and six "schooner girls" (cooks on board the schooners—they were either wife or daughter of one of the crew) while Peck conducted the service with some assistance from Bilby and me. There on the sloping hillside gathered a strangely assorted group of the Eskimo and white men and women. The Newfoundlanders, like the Welsh, love to sing and it was an inspiration to hear their voices ring out so clearly and sweetly the words of some of the old hymns.

We spent about an hour after the service chatting with our new-found friends, who were surprised at our expedition. It seemed incomprehensible to them that we could seriously contemplate living alone in Baffin Land with only the Eskimo as companions.

Just as we were pushing off in the ship's boat to return to the *Lorna Doone,* our oars were suddenly silenced. The voices of the Eskimo in their own language had lifted in a farewell song as they stood on a rocky point where we had to pass. That scene remains riveted in my memory. It was a still evening, the sea being perfectly calm and almost motionless, while the waves lapped gently on the beach, the rugged Labrador mountains stood out in darkest purple against the now faintly lighted western sky. There on the rocks at the water's edge in dim outline we saw some twenty Eskimo singing their mournful song of parting. My thoughts went back to the middle of the eighteenth century when the ancestors of these very Eskimo were a wild pagan people who only a few miles away in August, 1752, undoubtedly murdered John Christian Erhardt who came to tell them the story of Redeeming Love about which they were now singing. Our boat lay silent in the water as the strains of the song came floating out to us and our hearts were full of thanksgiving for this demonstration of the power of the Gospel of Love. The recollection of this scene was to be a strength to my faith when things were difficult in the early days in Baffin Land.

At six o'clock the next morning we weighed anchor but made little headway so the skipper ordered the two long oars or sweeps to be used. We all took turns and found the rowing very hard and disappointing work. We seemed to make small progress and our hands became red and blistered.

At noon the skipper remarked that the barometer was falling and at about three o'clock a hurricane swept down upon us from the wild cliffs at Cape Mugford. Soon the sea literally roared while the thunder cracked and great sheets of lightning flashed across the dark and lowering sky. The storm broke upon us with great suddenness, causing the masts and spars to groan with the pressure from the bulging sails. The crew worked desperately to shorten sail while the biting northwest wind threw the spray high over the bulwarks, slopping the decks and flooding the galley. To add to our miseries, the flurries of sleet froze and congealed on the rigging and the cargo-littered deck. Fradsham said that we had been driven many miles off our course into the Atlantic.

The violence of the storm ceased as quickly as it had burst upon us, but then to add to our discomfort, we lay becalmed except for a heavy swell. Thick fog settled down upon us. After weary hours of suspense a break came in the sky, the sun fitfully dispersing the vapor. At first the light and dark shadows seemed to magnify the height of the waves and to make the sullen sea look even worse than before. But finally the air cleared and a light breeze from the south sprang up. The order was given for all sails to be set. It brought new life to every man on board to see the canvas bellying against the clear blue sky.

At the end of three days landfall was made and we rejoiced to see the rugged coast of Labrador once more. Our joy was short-lived, however, for the next day we ran into fields of scattered ice. The fact that the *Lorna Doone* was old and was not strengthened in any way to withstand the pressure from the ice fields caused us some anxiety. We began to wonder when, if ever, we would reach Baffin Land. Fradsham the skipper was a man of courage and resourcefulness but knew nothing about navigation and told me quite emphatically that he did not believe in "them new-fangled instruments." When I foolishly asked him how then could we hope to reach Baffin Land, he looked at me with a mocking smile and said, "That's all right, we don't need any of them fancy things to tell us how to get north." He worked entirely on dead reckoning and like all the schooner men was never happy out of sight of land.

New experiences kept crowding in upon me. In Scotland and at Wycliffe I had often tried to visualize myself in the Arctic but it had been beyond the powers of my imagination to anticipate the thrill of seeing polar bear, whales, seal, and walrus during this voyage. The walrus particularly amused me, looking like a certain type of dour Scot with down-drawn mouth. One evening while we were working our way through scattered ice we came upon a large herd of these amazing creatures. The ship was sailing so quietly that they did not leave the ice until we were almost upon them. Suddenly the leader raised his head and sniffed, scenting danger. It was no ordinary panic that overtook them; at his signal, like so many churchwardens making an orderly exit from a meeting, they dived neatly beneath the waters.

Aided by a freshening breeze, we successfully rounded the Button Islands named after the English explorer, Captain Thomas Button, who discovered them in 1612. We then ran into raging seas as we entered the Hudson Strait. This turbulence is caused by the interplay of the forces of the wind, the Polar current sweeping down the Baffin Land coast and other currents coming out of Hudson Bay and Ungava Bay. By noon we had to work our way through scattered ice fields, and drenching rain added to our discomfort.

As the sun rose the next day the wind veered to the northwest, the weather cleared and the ice dispersed so we headed across the Hudson Strait. We ran into still greater ice. The extraordinary magnificence of the icebergs that we passed that morning has never left my memory.

At about noon land was sighted. Emotion welled up strong within me although I saw only a low, grey monotonous coastline with the rain coming down in torrents. Because of the rain it was impossible to stay on deck and the wretched little cabin smelled of bilge water. Everything was dreary beyond words yet surely, I thought, tomorrow would end the voyage. However, the skipper wisely decided to seek a safe and quiet anchorage for the night. After the trials of the past week we were all in need of sleep and rest. So we crept along the uncharted coast until we dropped anchor between two small islands.

At daybreak we pressed on again, sailing westward, and continuing in sight of the coast until we drew near some islands believed to be the Saddlebacks although no one was quite sure. Suddenly the wind blew up and the conditions of the previous day repeated themselves. The rain thrashed down upon us with such deluging force that the skipper began to search for an anchorage without delay. The mainsail was quickly lowered and we moved in cautiously towards the land, not knowing what rocks and shoals might lie ahead. We edged along until we were well surrounded by islands which afforded some protection and then a small boat was lowered and sent to measure the depth of the water. After considerable delay the men returned to report that the harbor we had sought was shallow and full of shoals. The ship's course was then altered and we tried our luck among some other islands lying to the west. The decks were slippery and dangerous and we were all soaked to the skin and stiff with cold. It was with the greatest relief that at about eight o'clock we finally cast anchor. We called the place Doone Harbour, which it is called to this day.

Excitement was not yet over, however. Suddenly thick smoke was seen rising from the galley. Somehow or other the planking near the cookstove had ignited down underneath the floor boards. There is nothing more horrible at any time than fire at sea, not to mention fire in that remotest desolation. The boards were ripped off and salt water thrown on the blaze which seemed to gain headway despite our best efforts. But after long toil and suspense, the fire was extinguished and in utter exhaustion we rolled into our bunks, deeply thankful that we had been spared this most sickening of disasters.

During the next three days everyone showed the effect of the strain of the voyage and the uncertainty of the future. Once it was realized that we were close to our destination restraint seemed to take leave of us. Among the crew tempers that had merely flickered now burst forth, small aggravations assumed immense proportions and constant grumbling took the place of agreeable conversation. As for Peck, Bilby, and myself, we felt caught in the pages of some Ibsen drama where a condition of frustration and despair is wrought by the recurrence and repetition of a depressing note. For during those three days a thick, wet fog enveloped us in its shroud. We lay blinded and idle.

As suddenly as it had settled the fog cleared and to our astonishment and delight we made out a beacon of stone and wood at the top of a small rocky islet. The sight of this beacon caused more argument than anything that had happened during the voyage. We did not think that it could be a guide to our ultimate destination, Ashe Inlet, for if our calculations were correct, that lay twenty miles to the west. When speculation was at its height the skipper shouted that he spied a small black object moving on the water.

"Walrus," scoffed the sailors, "seal, polar bears, whales." By now the excitement was so intense that the skipper himself ran up the rigging of the foremast, telescope in hand. "Canoes," he cried. "Canoes—two of them."

Nearer and nearer drew those tiny kayaks. In each sat a young Eskimo paddling for all he was worth. The first to arrive was a fine-looking man named Noo-voo-le-a. He soon told us that he had met "teachers" once before at Blacklead Island when he had been a very sick boy. He had been kept alive because of the food and care he had received from the missionaries.

From Noo-voo-le-a we also learned that Ashe Inlet had long since been abandoned but that Robert Kinnes and Company of Dundee, the managing owners of the whaler *Active,* had a mica mining depot at Lake Harbour which lay only fifteen miles up the fjord from where we were now becalmed. It seemed obvious, therefore, that we should go to Lake Harbour. Noo-voo-le-a volunteered to pilot the schooner since Fradsham did not know the channel of the fjord. As if in answer to prayer a light breeze sprang up filling our idle sails and by six o'clock we dropped anchor just off the little shack which was the miners' headquarters during the summer months. The final rattle of the anchor chain, the salty smell of the sea at low tide, the sight of an ever-increasing crowd of Eskimo gathering on the shore, the feeling of adventures past and adventures yet to come all combined to wipe out the agony of our voyage. A new chapter in my life was about to begin and I breathed a prayer of thanksgiving for all of God's mercies and for the brave men of Newfoundland who had brought us safely to our destination.

Lake Harbour is well named. It is practically landlocked and very like a Scottish lake surrounded by rugged hills void of vegetation except moss, lichen, heather, and a few small flowers which lack fragrance or scent.

As soon as possible Peck, Bilby, and I rowed ashore and were greeted at the water's edge by a large company of Eskimo. I shall never forget our first welcome to Baffin Land. The people thronged around us exclaiming, "How wonderful!" "How loving!" "It is good!" "The teachers have come!" "We are happy!" "Yes! Truly we are happy!"

After we had shaken hands with each and every one, including the shy little babies peeking out of their mothers' hoods, Peck made a speech. He said first how glad he was to see them and then that he had brought two younger teachers who would stay with them and help them to know and serve the Great Spirit Whom we call God. His address was punctu-

ated by loud exclamations of joy and satisfaction from the
Eskimo. At the end one woman, evidently a person of impor-
tance, thanked Peck, calling him "The Speaker" and saying,
"We wanted teachers and now they have come."

Peck was greatly impressed by the warmth of this reception
and referred to the matter on several occasions. That the
Eskimo were friendly and loving could not be questioned and
this would mean everything to us as we entered upon the
work. But it was equally clear that these were indeed a primitive people. My heart sank because they looked so wild, dirty,
and unkempt. Some were dressed in garments made of sealskin while others wore a hodgepodge of ordinary clothing
received from the men on the whaler. All were sadly ragged
and disheveled. Could we ever hope to instruct them? That
night I could only pray, "Lord, I believe; help thou my
unbelief."

Driving wind and rain had come on again and by the time
we finally reached the miners' shack we were wet and cold.
We were given a kindly welcome by a man named Ross from
Inverness who told us that his companion, Brown, was with
a group of Eskimo at the mica mine some five hours' walk
inland.

Besides Ross we met a young man named Ritchie who
proved to be one of the crew of the Scottish trading vessel
Snowdrop which had been wrecked the previous autumn in
Frobisher Bay. His story was one of considerable hardship
but he spoke with great appreciation of the kindness he had
received from the Eskimo. He had traveled with two of them
through a cut at the southern end of the Grinnell Glacier and
spent the winter at the Saddleback Islands, about seventy-five
miles east of Lake Harbour. In June he accompanied them
to Lake Harbour to meet the whaler Active but had not been
able to secure passage. Peck agreed to take the shipwrecked
man south on the Lorna Doone, and Bilby and I were able
to supply him with some clothing.

While we were talking to Ross in his shack the wind had
increased in violence and when we went out we found that

because of the great waves we were unable to launch the boat. At Ross's invitation we spent the night in his cabin—dry but uncomfortable. When we returned to the schooner at five o'clock the next morning, we were asked by the skipper to explain why we were "absent without leave"!

Immediately after breakfast Peck, Bilby, and I returned to the shore, selected a site for the mission house and with the help of a number of Eskimo men and women cleared the ground of boulders. All day long loads of lumber and other freight were transferred to the shore by boat and then carried up to the site. The Eskimo proved themselves to be a happy and willing band of helpers, and I was astonished to see women with babies in their hoods carrying heavy loads up over the rocks from the shore and doing it all with much laughter.

Sunday August 29 was a glorious day of bright sunshine. In the early morning the water in the harbor glittered like steel, then as the sun rose the hills were "fired with the red glow of the rushing morn." Overhead the sky was cloudless and pale blue. But it was a disappointment to me that there was not a speck of ice or snow to be seen.

Peck arranged for a "time of teaching" that morning and for another in the afternoon, at both of which Bilby conducted the service and Peck preached. Nothing could have exceeded the attention given by the people to these services which were held in the open air under the shadow of a rocky cliff. One particularly enthusiastic woman, who seemed to have a large family connection, had been taught by a group of Christian Eskimo from Blacklead Island and from them she and some of her relatives had secured copies of our Eskimo Book of Common Prayer and had learned to sing several of the hymns. In speaking to Peck she said earnestly, "We want to know God truly, but are like those who do not know Him."

There were a few others like Noo-voo-le-a who had made a brief visit to Blacklead Island and had received some teaching but had not been there long enough to be prepared for baptism. The rest were pagans. The Eskimo services were conducted by Bilby but Peck preached the sermons. He was not eloquent and he had a thin, high-pitched voice but his earnestness and quiet simplicity combined with a wonderful mastery of the Eskimo tongue secured absorbed attention for him. When he was preaching his eyes lighted up, and his favorite theme was God the Holy Spirit the Paraclete—God's Advocate at work in the hearts of men. His evangelical passion was tremendous. Otherwise he would never have been able to accomplish the great work he did for the salvation of the Eskimo. This involved compiling an Eskimo grammar (twice published by the Canadian Government), the translation of the Scriptures, the Book of Common Prayer and many hymns. With the exception of myself, all who worked under him are dead, but the work he and they accomplished will endure.

On Monday and on each succeeding day we arose at five thirty in the morning, worked hard at the erection of the mission house, and returned to the ship utterly exhausted. The weather was fair but turned cold at night so that in the morning we had to force our boat through newly formed ice. The warmth of the sun combined with a light breeze generally broke up the ice by noon, but the Newfoundlanders became anxious lest the ship should be frozen in for the winter. As soon as the freight had all been landed, several tons of stones were gathered and taken in boats to the schooner so that she might have ballast for the return voyage.

By the end of the week the roof of the house had been completed. To our joy the first use to which our new dwelling was put was the holding of divine worship on Sunday, September 5. Thus was it dedicated to the service of God.

On Wednesday, September 8, and my birthday, Bilby and I were able to sleep in the house for the first time, albeit among piles of crates and boxes. I felt particularly happy that this should happen on my birthday although I kept this fact to myself.

The following morning the *Lorna Doone* weighed anchor

and with a fair wind and all sails set passed swiftly down the harbor and disappeared around Hawk's Head less than two miles away. For a moment a deep sense of loneliness swept over both Bilby and me. Yet we knew that we were not alone since He Who had called us to the work had promised to be with us to the end.

☆ 3. Lake Harbour ☆

THE ENSUING WEEKS were exceedingly busy. There was much to do before the house could be considered habitable for the winter. We also had to eat, and since the fastidious Bilby would not allow an Eskimo to touch his food this meant that we had to do all our own cooking. He decreed that we should take turns week and week about at this and the housework. For the first week he was cook and provided an excellent table. The next week he suffered my feeble attempts with Christian fortitude. It was a great burden to me for unfortunately I had no culinary skill whatever.

The climax was reached when early in my first week on duty an Eskimo brought in a newly killed Arctic hare. As the beastie lay on the kitchen dresser I admired its lovely soft white coat and its long ears and thought how nice it would be to have this change in our diet. Bilby thanked and paid the hunter and then disappeared to continue his work on the walls of the house. I examined the purchase, hung it up on a nail in the outside porch and gave all my attention to the preparation of our dinner. That evening I said, "By the way, Mr. Bilby, what is to be done with the hare?" "Why," he replied, "I hope you will let us have it for dinner, say on Thursday."

"But how can I cook it," I exclaimed, "since it has not even been skinned?" "That's the cook's job," was his terse answer.

My heart failed me. Never in my life had I skinned anything. Bilby finally relented to the extent of showing me how to do it and then had great fun watching my crude efforts. When the animal had been duly prepared for the pot he murmured, "You'll be an Arctic-trained man yet!"

He certainly put me through my paces in this and in other matters. I learned much and was kept very humble because I was constantly made aware of my ignorance of many things that made life possible in that land of my adoption.

During the first few weeks the Eskimo came to the house in droves to see how things were progressing. They always had a smile so that it was pleasant to have them around. After the services in the evenings the people brought the skins of caribou or seal to provide us with warm clothing for the winter. Like everything else, these were purchased on the barter system and I found the proceedings absorbing to watch. An Eskimo would bring in a number of skins, put them on the floor and grin from ear to ear. Bilby would then examine each skin with great care, pointing out the merits of this one or the defects of that. Then a woman would say that this was a good skin for an inner coat while that was so beautiful it must be used for an outer coat, and so on. Bilby would next ask the hunter what he wanted for the skins. Generally he got the reply, "I do not know!" Bilby next suggested various articles such as gunpowder (they loaded their own cartridges), tobacco or matches. When the decision had been made the merchandise had to be sorted out in the proper quantities. This was entrusted to me and I felt that I had been promoted from the position of cook to that of store clerk!

When one transaction was finished another began and since there was also a social aspect to this trading it was always late in the evening before we could go to bed. I remember one incident when a man asked much more than usual. Bilby hesitated because he considered the demands excessive. Suddenly a woman raised her voice and in a very positive fashion told the man that he ought to know better than to ask for so much. He knew how small the ship was that brought the teachers. How could they with such a little ship be expected to pay more than the captain of the great whaler? The others all exclaimed, "Yes! That's right!"

Between carpentering, cooking, language study, and Eskimo visitors our days were full. One morning late in September I was surprised to find young ice forming in the harbor. From the window of the house it looked as if a scum of oil were floating on the water, but when I went down to the shore I saw that innumerable rounds of thin ice had formed. They looked like a vast series of large lily pads each just touching the other. By noon this young ice was broken up by a breeze from the northwest, but it was not long before the same phenomenon repeated itself and as the next few days were without wind and quite cold the whole harbor was soon frozen over. With each succeeding week the ice became thicker and remained until the following July.

This ice puzzled me because it did not possess the brittleness which is characteristic of fresh-water ice. Instead it had a peculiar resiliency and bent under pressure before it broke. Later, when it had reached a thickness of two inches or so and we were able to walk on it, we saw this even more plainly. As we walked, the ice rose before us in a kind of wave as if it were made of rubber. It is claimed that the salt lodging between the pure ice crystals prevents them from interlocking tightly, thereby reducing the tensile strength and permitting a maximum amount of bending without fracture. Our footprints were recorded just as if we had been walking on new-fallen snow.

Bilby was very meticulous about checking our supplies and as he did this he became much worried about the quantity of coal landed from the *Lorna Doone*. He was convinced that there was a serious shortage. If this were true we were faced with a grave situation since there was little hope of obtaining more until our next supplies were sent from the south two years hence. In view of this predicament it seemed vital to ascertain the exact amount of coal on hand, and then to estimate the amount used per day in the kitchen stove. From this we could judge how much of the total supply would be required for the next twenty-four months for the very minimum use. We earnestly hoped that some would be available for the Quebec heaters in our two small bedrooms. The prospect of an Arctic winter in an unheated bedroom was without attraction.

At St. John's, Newfoundland, the coal had been simply dumped into the hold of the schooner. At Lake Harbour it was the last of the cargo to be discharged from the *Lorna Doone* and we were so busy trying to get the house built that we had paid no attention to it. As we discussed the matter I told him that, on the average, coal was taken at about forty cubic feet per long ton, but he was not satisfied with that. Instead, and with the greatest care, he weighed two samples of it on our small scales, then in this laborious fashion he measured the amount in the pile. The result of our calculations was most disappointing. Not only was it short in quantity but the quality was inferior. It was useless to complain or regret. We had to face the inconveniences involved, not grudgingly but willingly, for it was part of the price we had to pay as pioneer missionaries. After some discussion we worked out a system of rationing. A wooden box was placed in the outer porch and was filled each morning with coal for use that day in the kitchen stove. Then we agreed that the fire was to be banked with fine coal dust (of which alas! there was all too much) immediately after the evening meal and that all the drafts in the stove were to be closed until morning. Once a week we could each have a fire in our own room for bath night. Bilby chose Sunday and I Saturday.

The next decision was the most drastic. We agreed to leave the mission house in January and to live with the Eskimo in their snow villages until warm weather, longer than we had previously planned. By adhering to these uncomfortable and uncompromising measures we felt that we would be able to make the necessary saving in fuel.

On November ninth, it is noted in my diary that we were still busy carpentering all day. The house was far from complete—the wind and snow drifted in through the cracks. The outside temperature sank to 4.5 degrees below zero (36.5 degrees of frost) which was the coldest we had experienced so far. In my room the thermometer registered eleven degrees of frost and the ink in the bottle on my desk was frozen.

The following week was both a happy and an interesting one for me. When I went out to take the meteorological observations at nine o'clock in the evening I was greatly impressed by the beauty of the sky which was constantly illuminated by the pyrotechnics of the aurora borealis. At that time the weather was fine, and the nightly displays of this phenomenon were unusually resplendent. Overhead and to the south the sky was pulsing with lambent flame. At first there were a few shafts of light only. Gradually these became enlarged and spread out in ever-changing shapes. Sometimes waving banners flashed overhead, sometimes what I can best describe as masses of shimmering luminosity tinged with all the colors of the spectrum. It was as if a veil were flung across the darkness of the sky and yet through the veil I could see the stars. By and by the moon arose and bathed the world in silver.

Our next excitement was the arrival of the Dundee whaler *Active* which dropped anchor in the harbor on Friday, October first. The men had been very successful, having secured several large whales and many walrus. The stir in the settlement caused by the arrival of the ship was intense because it meant the closing of the mica mine for the season. The captain had to pay the Eskimo who had been working at the mica mine as well as some eighty Eskimo who had helped to man the whaleboats during the cruise. This was a slow business for, like all such Arctic transactions, it was done by barter. The ship did not finally depart until Monday morning. In the meanwhile there was perpetual hubbub in the colony of sealskin tents erected on the shore.

While the ship was in port we had many interesting visits from Captain Alexander Murray and the members of his crew. All expressed surprise at finding that we had established a mission and intended to winter in the land. One old sailor called us "shentlemen" and referred to the Eskimo as "Dir-r-r-ty peasts of Huskiemoes." He criticized the ration of rum given to the crew after they had returned to the ship in the whaleboats. Indeed he claimed that only a "puir weak cra-tur" could be satisfied with it since the cold in the North caused a man to be "ferry heavy on the dram." Poor old man!

He went on to tell me that there was too much of what he called "goings on" during the voyage and that every Eskimo woman, married or single, young or old, had a great ambition to be companion to a white man untrammeled by a contract of marriage since such contracts were unknown to them. He added that the Eskimo men seemed to raise no objections and this proved that they were "dir-r-r-ty peasts"! I did not like the man's attitude toward the people and concluded that he was exaggerating.

The following day the captain invited Bilby and me to midday dinner on board the ship. He apologized for the lack of fresh meat or vegetables but we found the fare a welcome change and enjoyed our visit. Since some of the Eskimo had still to be paid, the captain excused himself as soon as the meal was over. Bilby got into conversation with the chief engineer while I climbed to the poop deck. From here I was able to look down upon the crew as they hauled the bags of mica from the whaleboats into the ship's hold.

Eskimo men, women, and children were milling around the galley door eagerly watching the cook. It was with shocked surprise that I noticed some of the Eskimo women putting on lascivious airs and making shameless gestures to the members of the crew. The mate explained that because of the length of the voyage and the close confinement of the men they were given carte blanche to do as they pleased, when they pleased, if not on duty. Human nature being what it is, the inevitable happened. Only too plainly the old sailor's claim seemed to be confirmed.

Some years later, when the Hudson's Bay Company had

established their trading post at Lake Harbour, Mr. Ralph Parsons succeeded in persuading the authorities at the head office of the company in London to arrange that the men on their ships should have no "shore leave" while in the North but be given compensation when paid off at the end of the voyage. In this way a great change for good was brought about.

On Sunday, October third, a service in English was conducted on board the *Active*. We had a quantity of hymn sheets and distributed these to the ship's company. Bilby took charge of the service but gave me the task of leading the singing of the hymns, reading the New Testament lesson and giving a brief address. Several of the tough whaler men said they had not been inside a church for over ten years. The only service with which they were familiar was the Burial Service used by the captain when one of their number found his last resting place on some rock-bound shore. They pointed across the fjord to some wooden crosses, painted white. I doubted in my heart whether these hard men "frae Dundee" would join in the hymns as the Newfoundlanders had done on the *Lorna Doone*. But they did.

The following morning the *Active* weighed anchor and we stood on the cliff in front of the house waving farewell with a white tablecloth. The captain blew the whistle three times and soon the ship was lost to sight. This was our last link with the outer world until July of the following year. Again a feeling of loneliness swept over us.

Once the whaler had sailed we lost no time in finishing the house. On Wednesday, October sixth, the linoleum was laid in the kitchen and then in the sitting room. A few days later the bedroom floors were laid. Sunday, October tenth, was a great day for me because I was allowed to address the people at the afternoon service when Bilby kindly acted as interpreter. It was Peck's definite conviction that except under special circumstances a new missionary should speak only in the native tongue. Both Bilby and I appreciated the wisdom of the principle and adopted it for the future. Because of all the time taken up with carpentry and cooking I had found it impossible to do more than pick up a few words and expressions at random but now I began a programme of concentrated effort.

Here is our timetable as recorded in my diary on October 17. This was my week as cook.

6.45 A.M.   Got up, kindled fire in the kitchen stove, prepared breakfast, swept the floors of the kitchen and dining room, softened my sealskin boots, washed and shaved, laid the table in the dining room.

8.00 A.M.   Breakfast—coffee, porridge, condensed milk, toast, butter and marmalade.

8.20 A.M.   Washed dishes, cut up hare for stew, put harecot beans in pot to cook. [This was not the hare referred to previously!]

9.00 A.M.   Took meteorological observations.

9.10 A.M.   Made bed and put my bedroom in order and swept floor.

9.15 A.M.   Devotions.

10.00 A.M.   Language study (alone) memorizing portions of the intransitive verb.

11.20 A.M.   Fetched four pails of water (two trips) from the stream over the hill.

12.15 P.M.   Prepared table, etc., for dinner.

1.00 P.M.   Dinner. Hare stew, harecot beans, cornstarch pudding.

1.30 P.M.   Washed up dishes, pots and pans.

2.00 P.M.   Read in English—Ruskin's *Time and Tide*.

2.45 P.M.   Language study with Bilby and an Eskimo.

4.45 P,M.   Stopped language study to prepare supper.

5.30 P.M.   Supper. Flap-jacks with corn syrup, Pilot biscuit, tea, butter, jam.

6.05 P.M.   Washed dishes and put kitchen in order.

6.30 P.M.   Practice reading St. John, Chapter I in the syllabic characters so that I may be able to read a lesson on Sunday.

9.00 P.M.   Took meteorological observations.

9.30 P.M.   Retired to my own room after banking the kitchen fire.

10.00 P.M.   To bed.

The practice of studying the language with both Bilby and an Eskimo present was suggested by Peck and proved most helpful. Bilby gave me a lead and helped me with the grammar which, to my surprise, was most complete. I was then urged to learn from the lips of the Eskimo themselves the correct pronunciation, enunciation, and articulation of the words. In order to avoid individual peculiarities of sound, we had different Eskimo come as my teachers.

Each morning I studied Peck's *Grammar* which I had first begun to copy on the *Lorna Doone* because at that time it was not printed. By memorizing parts of the verb, some nouns, adverbs, and particles I was able to make up brief sentences. In the afternoon I visited the Eskimo in their tents and tried to put my knowledge into use. I also gathered new words (we had no dictionary) and experimented with those I had discovered on previous days. In this way, over a period of more than four years, I built up a vocabulary of some five thousand words.

One afternoon I called on an Eskimo family and sitting on an empty cartridge box near the little door sought to advance my attainments by asking questions. When I inquired of them the general word for "wood" I ran into difficulties. Finally, after several futile attempts, I touched the wood at the side of the door. At once their faces lighted up and I was given the word "a-vah-le-sanga." I knew that the termination "sanga" was the third person singular possessive, so I jotted down in my little black note book:

a-vah-le-sanga—his wood
a-vah-le-sak —wood

That same afternoon I gathered a number of other new words and noted them likewise in my little book. The following morning I spent an hour making up and memorizing suitable sentences in which my new-found treasures were incorporated. Later I sallied forth in the hope of demonstrating my knowledge and securing still further additions to my vocabulary. I felt confident of success. I first called on the people who had been so helpful to me on the previous day. Alas, while most of my new words were understood, I failed lamentably when I asked for a piece of wood. No matter how carefully I pronounced my words they shook their heads and each time said, "Nel-o-voong-a"—"I am ignorant." Clearly something had gone wrong. When I called on another family I met with the same unsatisfactory results. On my return to the mission house Bilby asked me how I had managed. On hearing my story, he laughed uproariously and said that I had been asking for a doorpost!

As I progressed in my studies I tried to acquire not only the structure of short sentences but the correct idiom, which is more difficult. This is one point of importance that few white men in the North seem to grasp. It is a simple matter to string together a lot of words but quite another to speak correctly. Only by close personal contact with the people can one gain a knowledge of the mode of speech and thought.

On Guy Fawkes Day, 1909, it is stated in my diary that I baked an apple tart which was considered a success. The entry also indicates my ignorance in the art of baking: at first the rolling pin stuck to the paste until I discovered that a little flour rubbed on the pin solved the problem!

So far so good, but the housework took up far too much time. Bilby acknowledged this but nevertheless was reluctant to ask an Eskimo boy to help us. The Eskimo had no idea of being anybody's servant and it was not our purpose to make him one. Nevertheless, we needed help if we were to provide help. After much discussion with Bilby, I persuaded him to allow an Eskimo boy to touch our food under certain conditions: He would help us because, being ignorant strangers in the country and without the help of women, we stood in need of his assistance. He would also be my companion and teach me the language. On this basis a boy might be willing to come.

As I watched the boys at play it seemed to me that one, named Yarley, was particularly bright. He was a dirty little barbarian, good-natured, ragged, rotund, and ridiculously amusing. I recommended him to Bilby as my choice. I also felt that he had the potential qualities of a forceful Christian leader. So Yarley joined us as our little "companion," relieving us of many of the chores and helping me immediately in the study of the language, in understanding the people and by accompanying me on tramps over the hills in search of game. Indeed he contributed greatly to the happiness of my days.

One morning shortly after Yarley had become a member of our household, he returned with water from the brook and with the news that he had seen a flock of ptarmigan on the hillside. I gave him my double-barreled shotgun and some cartridges with the warning to return before dark. In less than an hour he came back, his copper-brown face beaming with pleasure and good will as he laid two brace of ptarmigan on the kitchen table. I don't know who experienced the greater pride—Yarley or me—but when I congratulated him he grinned and said quite modestly that it was the gun. Then after a pause he told me it was a very good one and could he have it! I explained in my halting fashion that I only possessed that one shotgun but would lend it to him again.

Each day I came into very close physical contact with Yarley and in the heat of the kitchen I could not avoid realizing that he, to put it plainly, smelled. I spoke to Bilby about the matter but he doubted if we could do much. "After all," he admonished wisely, "consider the conditions under which the Eskimo live. But," he added, in his terse way, "it's up to you if you want to be a reformer."

I succeeded in getting Yarley to wash his face once a day, and his hands when he was cooking. How would he react to the idea of a hot bath? What would the other Eskimo say to him? The people had a right to be sensitive about their customs. As long as they were merely onlookers they were interested and amused at our strange ways, but it might be quite another matter for one of their number to adopt a practice different from their own.

I decided, however, to take the chance and introduce

Yarley to the Order of the Bath. One night after supper, when the kitchen was nice and warm, I put the copper boiler on the stove and filled it with water from the barrel in the corner. Then I placed a large galvanized washtub near the stove, with a plentiful supply of carbolic soap, towels, and a sponge (in those days the modern cotton face cloth was unknown). Yarley was tremendously interested and evidently thought he was going to see me have a bath.

It came as a shock to the lad when he was told that all was for him, not for me, and that he was going to take the first bath he ever had in his life. With some agitation he agreed and I stood by to see that the job was well done. The knowledge that after the washing was over he would possess new clothes, the towels, sponge, soap, etc., may have been a contributing factor to the success of the event! Who can tell? At any rate he came out clean and smiling as if he had been through a great adventure, and he did not take cold. But he watched me with suspicious looks for some days to come. It was also the subject of much comment among the Eskimo. Years afterwards when I visited the people on the Foxe Channel coast I found that they had heard all about it down to the most intimate detail.

I had not been long in Baffin Land before I began to sort out some of my impressions of the Eskimo. I felt that if I was to do effective work among these primitive people I must know them well, respecting their customs even while I tried to bring them God's word. One of my first discoveries was that they were true socialists in the matter of food. My first experience of it is still vivid in my mind.

Food had been very scarce but that afternoon one of the hunters arrived, bringing a fine fat seal with him on his sledge. As soon as the dogs had been unharnessed and the traces and other equipment stored safely in the porch of his igloo, a message was sent to each of the other snow huts calling the people to the feast. The women and girls entered first and took their places at the back of the igloo, while the men and boys gathered at the front. The man who had speared the seal now came forward and with great speed, indicating a fine knowledge of the mammal's anatomy, separated the skin, with the blubber attached, from the more edible portion of the carcass. The flippers were then removed and were given to the women who quickly and skillfully dissected them and passed portions to the children. The seal was now cut up into large pieces and each piece was handed round from one to the other until it was consumed. This was followed by a piece of blubber which was gorged with noise and avidity. One child was handed the nose and lips of the seal and in the eating of this delicacy used the strong whiskers as a sort of fork.

The seal was not cooked and since it had been swimming in the water only a short time before, the flesh was still warm. Indeed, owing to the coldness of the air in the igloo, clouds of vapor could be seen rising from the carcass. When the feast was ended the participants presented rather an unpleasant appearance; blood and grease covered their faces and hands. A small vessel containing some melted snow was passed round, and each person took a mouthful of water with which to clean up the mess. A ptarmigan skin, with the feathers on, was used as a towel. The feast was now over and the guests departed after expressing their thanks.

For the "civilized" man one of the greatest difficulties in the Arctic was and is "keeping in order" physically. In this connection Peck had been very definite that we should spend two hours each day in the open air no matter what the temperature. With the thermometer registering 50 degrees below zero our activities were bound to be strenuous and energetic! When the weather was fine I went for long walks over the hills and frozen lakes. Some of these excursions were taken after the day's work was over and the moon was shining with her cold beauty. The majesty of the wild scene and the invigorating air acted like a tonic and in my youthful exuberance I literally sang for joy! Often I would recite some of the prayers and the passages of Scripture that I had been memorizing or I would sing a hymn that I was preparing to teach the people. At other times I used to love to go out at night, after having taken the meteorological observations and, crouching in the shelter of a rock, watch the stars. With the help of a small astronomical atlas I was able to identify several of the clusters. The mystery and the majesty of it all did not fill me with a sense of loneliness. I was inspired, not by the thought of the terrifying vastness of the universe, but by the consciousness that behind all this amazing orderliness there was a Master Mind—the Creator. I would return to the house with a heart deeply stirred by a strange joy such as the Psalmist must have had when he wrote, "The heavens declare the glory of God; and the firmament sheweth his handywork."

On the twenty-fourth of November, when returning from my walk, I slipped and tobogganed down a hillside and landed in a snowbank. Fortunately no bones were broken but the hair on a certain part of my caribou-skin trousers had been rubbed off and the skin torn! When Bilby heard about my little accident and saw the garment in question, he became quite anxious. Indeed he predicted coldly that I would break my neck some day and then he would have a difficult time explaining the tragedy when the whaler arrived in the summer. What a strange man he was.

If a blizzard was blowing or the snow drifting heavily, I did not attempt to go out of sight of the house but got my exercise by running back and forth past the front door, much to Bilby's amusement.

At about this time we had excitement because of frequent visits from a wolf. When an Eskimo first reported that he had found wolf tracks in the snow, I went with the man in order to see for myself. On examination I was unable to differentiate them from those of a sledge dog. However, the wolf was plainly seen on several occasions. On Thursday morning, December 19, he came quite near the house but by the time we had secured our rifles he was almost out of range and none of us were successful in bringing him down. A few months later, when we were living at a snow village about thirty miles from the missing, the Eskimo killed three wolves within a few hours so we tasted our first wolf meat, which is tough and poor.

In the closing months of the year I devoted all possible time to the study of the language. Besides adding to my vocabulary and becoming familiar with the grammar, I read the Gospels and the Book of Acts in Eskimo, memorized parts of the prayer book and endeavored to find suitable tunes for the hymns so that people might learn them quickly. I also spent much time copying the hymns from Bilby's book and making reproductions on "Jellograph," which was a fore-runner of the modern mimeograph. In this way we were able to provide every family with at least one copy of each hymn.

We had to take all this extra trouble because two cases containing our new and enlarged Eskimo Service Book had unfortunately missed the *Lorna Doone* at St. John's. The lack of these books seemed to threaten the effectiveness of our work and caused us much heartbreak and additional labor. The service books contained not only the translation of the Book of Common Prayer but also 150 hymns which had been prepared at great labor by Peck and by the Rev. W. G. Walton and Mrs. Walton, the Anglican missionaries at Fort George on James Bay.

In the absence of the books Bilby and I resorted to the simple method of having the people, young and old alike, memorize the prayers and hymns as well as many portions of the Scriptures. We were surprised and delighted to find how quickly the Eskimo were able to do this until we remembered that, having no written language of their own, they were dependent upon oral tradition, which necessitated a retentive memory. What had at first seemed such an unnecessary handicap proved to be of inestimable value in the years that followed, both to the Eskimo and to the young missionary.

Our time was so taken up that before we knew it Christmas had arrived. The dawn of that first Christmas Day in Baffin Land was calm and still. We were disappointed that the sun did not show itself but the sky was completely overcast and low misty clouds could be seen hurrying westward. By eleven o'clock a strong north wind was driving the snow before it, causing a peculiar rustling noise as it swirled around the house.

It had been agreed that on this great day the house would be kept warm and that for the first time since the whaler had left us we would dress in civilized apparel. It gave me a strange feeling to enjoy the luxury of a white shirt, linen collar, fine socks, and leather shoes.

The day began with our Christmas service in English but as we were two only I fear our thoughts wandered to the South with its crowded churches, carols, and bells.

When worship was over Bilby said that, since he was cook, he wanted the kitchen to himself. I retired to my room for nearly two hours, spent first in private devotion, and then I had a glorious time reading Christmas letters and opening presents.

Perhaps I should explain that, at the suggestion of Peck, I had asked my friends to date all letters and parcels on the outside and I had promised that I would keep them unopened until that particular date twelve months hence. In this way I had the joy of receiving letters and parcels throughout the year, even when I was away from the mission house and living with the Eskimo.

Although relieved of all cooking responsibilities, I was allotted the task of "table maid" while Yarley proved a most willing and helpful dishwasher. Bilby, to my great satisfaction, left the arrangements and decorations of the table entirely to me.

It was our everyday practice to have our meals in the dining room, never in the kitchen. Three times a day the red tablecloth was removed and replaced by a white cloth. On this occasion we had a really fine linen cloth on the table, and linen napkins replaced our ordinary cotton ones. A pair of small brass candlesticks, some artificial flowers made by the blind in Glasgow, an embroidered centerpiece, a specially designed menu card bound with a little blue silk ribbon, fruit and candy, gave a festive appearance to the table which surprised and greatly pleased even Bilby.

Yarley was dressed in "white man's" clothes, including a large apron of bleached cotton made especially for the occasion by an Eskimo woman. I had trimmed the lad's hair and let him plaster it down with some of my hair tonic.

The food was cooked to perfection, well served and seasoned. Here is what the menu cards said:

> *Seal Soup*
> *Arctic Hare* (Jugged)
> *Arctic Ptarmigan* (Baked)
> *Caribou Steaks* (Fried)
> *Fresh Potatoes* (From St. John's, Nfld.)
> *Onion* (Canned—from England)
> *Plum Pudding* (Canned—from England)
> *Fruit* (Canned—from England)
> *Jelly* (from England)
> *Candies* (from Canada)
> *Coffee* (from St. John's, Nfld.)

We sat down to dinner at half past one o'clock and in an hour all was over! But what a happy time we had.

As soon as the house was once more set in order, we called the Eskimo to service and Bilby told them the story of Bethlehem. Never shall I forget the eager upturned faces and the look of joy and wonder written across the dusky features. From time to time, as was their happy way, the people indicated their pleasure, surprise, or approval by such expressions as E (Yes!), E-la-le (Certainly!) or Ka-pay (Wonderful!). As they listened, I prayed that the Saviour of the world might be born anew in the hearts of these dwellers in Arctic night.

After the service we invited our friends to a feast. Bilby had labored diligently to provide the kind of food likely to be enjoyed by our guests. Two large steaming puddings something like our Christmas pudding but not nearly so rich were served with molasses for sauce. These were followed by quantities of thick currant scones fried in marrow fat, and steaming coffee. Gradually the feasting ended and each Eskimo in turn expressed thanks. It was then my privilege to play selections on our little Victor gramophone with its funny metal trumpet. Music always stirred the Eskimo to glowing enthusiasm but they had a hard time understanding the gramophone and wanted to know where I kept the little man in the Talking Box.

Before we parted we gave each of our visitors a present as another reminder that on Christmas Day we commemorated God's Great Gift to all "the inhabitants of the world" and that this was a free gift that could not be obtained by barter.

Many of these Christmas presents had been generously supplied by the Women's Auxiliary of the Church of England in Canada. Bilby and I contributed various items from our common store or some personal possessions which we felt would be of special value to particular Eskimo. After the distribution of gifts we sang a Christmas hymn and closed with a prayer of thanksgiving, the Christmas Collect, and the Benediction.

When the people had departed after much handshaking and many expressions of thanks, Bilby, Yarley, and I had a busy time washing up dishes and cleaning the house. Finally all was in order once more so Yarley returned to his family while Bilby drank tea with me in my room and enjoyed Scotch cake and shortbread. We then went to bed, each to think his own thoughts of past days and of loved ones.

Owing to the excitement of Christmas Day, I forgot to wind the kitchen clock on which we were dependent for time since neither Bilby nor I kept our watches wound. In the extremely cold weather we felt that it would be better to let them alone. To rectify my error I waited until the sun stood above the steep conical hill across the harbor which, according to my compass and after making the necessary allowances for the variation due to our proximity to the North Magnetic Pole, was due south. I therefore knew that it was midday and set the clock accordingly. When the whaler arrived six months later we were just nineteen and a half minutes fast by the ship's chronometer.

The closing days of the year were bitterly cold. On December 30 the thermometer outside registered thirty-one degrees below zero while in my room it was only two and a half degrees above zero and my hot-water bottle was frozen at the foot of my bed when I awoke in the morning. On New Year's Eve I was allowed the usual weekly fire in my room and the temperature rose to nine degrees above freezing.

It was only now, early in January, that we were able to complete the building of a snow wall round the house and a snow porch at the door. These proved invaluable in keeping out the terrible drafts and in preventing the snow from seeping in through the chinks in the boards that formed the walls of the house.

We were so busy that we seldom felt lonely. After school, I would take my gun and, accompanied by one of three lads, Yarley, Matto or Senaleocktok, find fresh food for the larder. There were flocks of ptarmigan in the district and the boys were always keen to be with me. After I had shot the first bird, I handed my gun to my young companion and so we had it turn and turn about. This added zest to our trips and the boy was free to choose whether he wished to take the birds he shot home to his family or to barter them with me. As the Eskimo were well supplied with fresh food at this time they often liked a change and preferred to have some of the things which we could supply. In turn Bilby and I were always glad to buy from the people fresh meat and fresh fish which we froze for future use. When it became known that we made these purchases we ran into a curious and rather difficult predicament.

A man named Pit-soo-lak, a powerful angakok or conjurer, had been for some years the "boss man" for Captain Murray of the whaler *Active*. Pit-soo-lak was, of course, a pagan and was without doubt the most influential hunter in the region. He now came to us and proposed that he and his family should have their dwelling near the mission house and that he would see to it that the people brought us all the fresh meat that we required. Then there would be no need for us to leave the station to visit the villages, he said.

To his surprise we politely but quite definitely declined the offer. But Pit-soo-lak was not so easily defeated. He had set his heart on this scheme so he went on to explain that on board the whaler he was the captain's "voice." The captain told him what he wanted and he, Pit-soo-lak, then arranged for the Eskimo to carry out the captain's commands. He explained that he would act in the same way for us, which would be best for everybody.

This was my first experience with a situation that was to repeat itself many times over during my years in the Arctic. An angakok has nearly always attained his position by virtue of his force of character and his ability to control the people. Being human, he enjoys the prestige of his position and in the "teacher" who sets forth a different way of life he recognizes a rival if not a foe. Rather than evince open enmity he often feels it better to maneuver himself, if possible, into the advantageous role of interpreter and general manager. At this juncture the missionary is faced with a delicate decision. If he refuses the offer and offends the angakok the whole tribe may be influenced against listening to the Gospel of Love. If he accepts the offer, can he trust the sincerity of the man? We did not minimize Pit-soo-lak's great influence with the people but we decided that to agree with his suggestion would not be in the best interest of the work. In taking this stand with Pit-soo-lak we knew that the matter was not concluded and that a struggle lay ahead. He was obviously anxious to keep us away from the snow villages. But we had promised the people that we would come to them and teach them and this we intended to do.

Soon after Christmas most of the Eskimo went away, the population at Lake Harbour dwindled and by mid-January it was time for us to begin our journeyings. Bilby felt that before we went far afield he should visit the nearest snow village and find out what arrangement could be made for us. We agreed that it was necessary for me to stay at Lake Harbour in case any Eskimo stopped in to see us on their way to or from the hunt. So for one week I was left alone without even one of the dogs to keep me company. To be for seven days without the association of any living thing is quite a test. My forced privacy was frequently broken when the boards in the walls of the house creaked and groaned due to the contraction caused by the intense cold, or a "bang" from the attic overhead indicated that a precious jar of fruit had been broken by the frost, or the wind howled a mournful song down the stovepipe. Sometimes as I sat at my desk there came an almost soothing sound caused by the snowflakes as they flipped gently on the windowpane thickly covered with "fernwork and lacework and filigree in endless variety."

The quietness of the house and the stillness of the air often filled me with a strange and wonderful peace so that I seldom grew weary or lonely. In fact that week proved to be a very happy one. I was able to give myself more completely to the study of the language without the constant interruptions from callers.

When first the winter came with its cold and bitter winds, I had looked forward with considerable trepidation to life in a snow village. But now my ideas had changed. I had learned that it is the common necessities that have priority value—food, shelter, light, heat, useful work, and friendship. I was not ignorant of the physical drawbacks of the life lived by the Eskimo in tents and igloos but I had become aware that there were compensations. I also realized that only by living their life and thus meeting them on their own ground, could we accomplish what we had set out to do. Besides, I had already come to love the people and now I was to have the opportunity to share the most demanding part of their life.

Bilby returned on Friday, January 21, and the following morning, being on duty as cook, I arose at six o'clock to begin a very busy day. While the coffee was brewing on the stove we had our devotions together. Now came our last breakfast at the base—oatmeal porridge with condensed milk, coffee, pilot biscuit.

While the world was still shrouded in darkness and with the help of our Eskimo driver, the team that had brought Bilby back from the camps was made ready. Bag after bag was carried out to the sledge, boxes containing food supplies, some pots and pans, books and school equipment, two suitcases of personal belongings, sacks containing our extra caribou-skin stockings, boots and mitts. When the sledge had been fully loaded, strong thongs made from the skin of the square flipper seal were lashed over the irregular mass of bundles to keep them in place.

Bilby now called our driver into the house and there, kneeling on the kitchen floor, commended us and our undertaking to God.

On his way out, our driver walked close to some small round heaps of snow and gave the nearest heap a sharp kick. A dog rose up and shook itself free from its thatch of snow. This was repeated at each of the other mounds and after some stretching and growling the dogs were harnessed and their traces attached to the bowline of the sledge. We were off.

Where were we off to? In a sense, into nothingness. In that vast land of ice and snow there were no familiar landmarks, no signposts at a crossroad. Nothing but cruel, cold, blinding blizzards. Yet in that nothingness were the Eskimo, warm, loving, human people held in the bondage of pagan fears. We trusted to our guide to take us to them in their villages of snow, and we trusted that our common Heavenly Father would enable us to show them the uplifting and redeeming vision of His Love.

☆ 4. Snow Village ☆

IT WAS WITH considerable difficulty and only after much
labor on the part of men and dogs that the heavily laden
sledge was maneuvered over the rough jagged ridges to reach
the level ice on the sea. To reach the sea ice is much more
difficult at Lake Harbour than at many places on the coast
because of the fluctuation of the tide. Here the rise and fall
varies from twenty-eight to forty feet. All during the winter
the ice between the high- and low-water marks is broken up
twice each day and this forms a thick barrier around the
shore line. Once there, however, we found the surface of the
ice in splendid condition. The wind, also, was in our favor
that morning. Light though it was, it came from the north,
driving us and the snow in a southerly direction.

This was my first journey by sledge and dog team and I
found everything interesting. Daylight broke through at last
and while we saw little of the sun the light was a beautiful
grey. In spite of the apparent desolation there was something
indescribably impressive about the scene. We were soon
traveling at a fair speed. The three of us took turns sitting
on the sledge while one walked alongside and the other in
front of the dogs to break trail. No sign of life appeared all
day except once when a large raven passing overhead gave
two hoarse croaks. His black coat showed up most clearly

against the whiteness of the world around and the dogs answered his call with sharp yelps, while Bilby hurled some strong epithets at him. My companion had an amazing dislike of "these robbers," as he called them because of their persistent and successful raiding of our meat larder near the mission.

For some time we traveled near the shore but as we reached the mouth of the fjord we were often far out from land, sometimes skirting an island enveloped in a blanket of snow, the ruffles of broken ice round the edge the only perceptible evidence of its existence. One island looked exactly like a bed covered with a white counterpane and frilled valance. Towards evening as we rounded a point of land projecting from the rest, we saw a tall stone or pile of stones standing on top of a small hill. "Au-lat-se-vik," shouted our driver. "Au-lat-se-vik," we echoed.

The driver halted the dogs. "Aulatsevik," he continued, "means the place of parting. It is our custom after leaving Lake Harbour to spend a few days here before separating, some to go west and some east to our winter hunting grounds. The dogs," he added, "know that the end of the journey is near. They will exert themselves. Therefore you can both sit on the sledge. The day has been long." Most willingly Bilby and I climbed on. With a crack of the whip we were away, the driver running alongside but still finding breath to keep up a continuous chatter to the team.

My excitement mounted when I saw the cluster of igloos, a whole village of them, and realized that I was about to become a member of that community. In my exhilaration I felt it a glory to become one with the people and "to sit where they sat."

As we drew near, the men of the village saw us and with a clamor of welcome hurried out to help us drag the sledge over a formidable mass of broken ice that separated us from our destination. After much hard work we reached the lake around which the igloos were built. Before the people could greet us the local dogs came upon us like a pack of howling

wolves and there were angry altercations between them and
the members of our team.

Once the snarling discord was put down, what a warmth of
welcome was ours. With ejaculations of pleasure each Eskimo
came forward to shake hands in courteous greeting. The men
helped us to unload the sledge and then led us to two small
igloos which Bilby had previously arranged that they should
build for us. Each was about eight feet in diameter at the
base and had a double porch, common to both, with a snow
wall at the entrance to protect us from the drifting snow.

Three women quickly spread a warm caribou skin on top
of the snow sleeping bench and brought us each a small
kudlik, or stone lamp, and a quantity of blubber. These
lamps were made of soapstone obtained in different parts of
the country and were simply a hollow saucer with one edge
straight and the other crescent-shaped. In this receptacle the
women placed the seal blubber, which had already been well
smashed with a bone or stone beater. In Bilby's igloo they
hung pieces of blubber on a little bar over the lamp but in
both cases the oil from the blubber found its way into the
bowl of the lamp. Dried moss gathered in the summer from
the banks of the streams was rubbed down as a man rubs his
tobacco before placing it in the bowl of his pipe. The moss
was then mixed with the white bloom of the little cotton-
weed which grows profusely in the marshy places in the val-
leys. These together constituted the wick, which was laid
along the straight edge of the lamp and lighted. Burning with
a yellow and blue flame, it emitted a strong, pungent smoke
and threw grotesque shadows dancing round the walls.

Over the lamp the women placed a frame made out of two
wooden barrel hoops with a crisscross network of thin sealskin. On top of this frame, which was supported by several
stakes thrust into the snow, our fur stockings, mitts, and skin
boots were placed to dry. Then our teakettle was filled with
broken pieces of ice and hung from the frame over the lamp.
After the cold journey we were both very hungry and blessed
a woman who, having anticipated our need, brought us a

steaming pot of seal stew. To this we added some pilot biscuit and found it most satisfying.

As soon as the meal was over I went out to have a look around the village. When I appeared the people, old and young, greeted me kindly with smiles so I felt that in spite of my very limited vocabulary they welcomed me to their midst. I recognized one woman named Er-kak-tah-lik, who had been my seamstress and made all my skin clothing. Later Bilby told me that during his previous week at Aulatsevik when I had been left by myself at the mission, Er-kak-tah-lik had wanted to send her son with his team over to fetch me because she thought I must be feeling very lonely.

The day had drawn to a close, the sky had cleared and I felt that after all the stimulation it would do me good to be alone for a time. Although the temperature was below zero there was no wind; as I walked I was surprised to find that because I was not familiar with the landscape and in spite of the brightness of the light, it was impossible to judge distances accurately; the shadows on the snow made walking treacherous.

When I returned to the camp I discovered that the young people were playing games and wrestling. They were all dressed in thick caribou-skin clothing and looked like balls of fur as they ran and tumbled in the snow. One of the games was a modified form of football. In place of the regulation pigskin they had a bladder from a seal filled with caribou hair. While I was watching them some of the men and women joined in the fun. They charged at one another freely and it was not an uncommon sight to see a woman with a baby in the hood on her back sprawling in the snow. Before reaching my igloo I came upon five young girls sitting together in the snow, singing hymns which they had learned from me at Lake Harbour.

This was the first time that I had spent a night in an igloo and I fully expected to have a good sleep after my long and tiring day. Alas, it was not to be! I found the igloo cold and damp and the lamp soon went out and left me shivering in the darkness. To say that I was thankful when old Pah-Ne came to light the lamp in the morning is an understatement. She soon had it burning evenly along the edge, giving forth light and warmth. As I watched her haggard and wrinkled old face my mind became filled with thoughts of all the struggles, privations, and sorrows that had been her lot. There was something wonderful about that old grandmother. I liked her and her family and we became good friends not only then but through many years.

Pah-Ne had hung a small kettle over the lamp and filled it with broken pieces of ice. When they had melted I quickly put on my clothing and took half the water over to Bilby. In this way we were able to wash our faces and hands and teeth. Bilby's kettle of water was used to make coffee which, with pilot biscuit, butter and marmalade, constituted our breakfast that morning. Our midday meal was much better—a large bowl of steaming caribou stew flavored with dried onions, pilot biscuit, and a plateful of corn starch with condensed milk.

It was Sunday and the usual services were scheduled to be held in the largest igloo. When the time came, fifty adults, with numerous babies in their mothers' hoods, were able to squeeze inside. Many others packed themselves into the porch, while still more sat on the snow outside the igloo where they could hear all that was said or sung. As usual Bilby gave the instruction but I was responsible for the hymns and some of the prayers, which I could now sing from memory or read with ease.

Until we came to live with the people at Aulatsevik I had been so engrossed with the many problems connected with this new and strange life that I had not given time to the careful study of Bilby. Now we were thrown together in the closest possible manner day by day and almost each hour of the day.

It was as a teacher of the Eskimo that Bilby was at his best. When he described some Biblical scene his listeners felt as if their teacher had actually been there and was relating what he had seen and heard. It was all done with such simplicity and sincerity that he held his audience from beginning to end. In imagination they had left Baffin Land and were living in the days of the prophets and apostles. How often have I watched him at work when neither cramped quarters, cold, heat, nor mosquitoes could spoil the interest of the pupils gathered around him.

By nature he was kind, generous, and honest to a degree, being meticulous concerning all expenditures from our common stores. At the same time he was a constant enigma to me. His whole nature tended towards friendship but he seemed to have an instinctive fear lest he should appear too possessive. This almost amounted to a phobia. He also suffered from bouts of congenital nervousness.

Although our ideas did not always synchronize I was very conscious that he was my superior officer, a feeling enhanced by my own ignorance of life and work in the Arctic. Not only did we never quarrel but we soon learned to appreciate each other and as the months passed an understanding and affection developed between us that lasted until his death.

At Aulatsevik Bilby decided that I was able to begin regular day school with the younger children and thanks to his initial guidance the effort was not without success. Eighteen youngsters were enrolled and, except occasionally when the older boys were off hunting with their elders, it was seldom that we did not have 100 per cent attendance.

My school equipment might be described as the minimum. I had lead pencils, scribblers, a few Sunday-school picture rolls, a small rack with colored wooden balls that moved on wires for use in teaching arithmetic, and a piece of wood from a small packing case to which I had given a coat of black paint and then painted in white a set of the Eskimo syllabic characters representing the vowel sounds with the additional consonants. Our efforts must now appear crude and feeble but we had to make the best of conditions as we found them.

Eskimo life is entirely dominated by weather and hunting conditions. Time, as we understand it, plays very little part in the daily routine. When we first went to Baffin Land many of the Eskimo had cheap alarm clocks purchased from the whaler and two of the men had good watches, but not one among them could tell the time. They liked to hear the tick and generally placed the clock or watch inside an open tin in order to increase the sound. If it ticked then it was alive but when it stopped it was dead.

Under such circumstances we could not tell the children to come to school at a given hour each day. Instead we told them that they would be called soon after the sun was highest in the heavens. This arrangement gave me a chance to devote my mornings to the study of the language. The people displayed great patience and gentleness and would repeat their words and sentences slowly to enable me to catch each syllable. Here at this settlement I learned much from some of the more intelligent boys and girls. Indeed these were happy times for us all. For me, because it was easy to get the correct pronunciation of the words from the lips of these younger people who spoke so much more clearly than the older men and women. Happy for them, because they liked the idea of teaching their teacher. In return for their help I spent some time each week showing them pictures of the white man's country. These never failed to interest them. Then, too, they enjoyed the small donations of sweet biscuit which I presented to them at the close of the last session of school each week.

Bilby and I had our frugal meal at noon and then I made it my custom to read some English author until two o'clock. At two o'clock I went over to the igloo belonging to Now-yak. School was held here because that particular igloo was large and clean. Immediately I sent two children to call the others. They would dash off over the snow and at the entrance of each igloo call out in their own tongue, "Come ye. It is time for teaching." Then my lively young pupils would come racing across the lake towards Now-yak's igloo. Before entering they would take a small wooden stick, kept inside the porch for the purpose, and beat out the snow from their fur garments and skin boots.

When they had gathered on the sleeping bench I would stand at the inner doorway and with bowed head ask God's blessing on our efforts that day. The children were quick to learn so that each week we added to our repertoire of hymns. This was also true of the prayers and Bible verses. Finally, we studied the syllabic characters, and arithmetic.

At this stage of the Eskimo's development neither the children nor the adults had much use for arithmetic but it seemed necessary for them to become familiar with the English method of counting. It put them at less of a disadvantage with the white men in the country.

So great has been the evolution of the Eskimo since 1910 that the syllabic system of reading and writing which was then such a boon to them has almost outlived its usefulness in Arctic Canada. The syllabic system, in which sounds are represented by little hooks and crooks resembling shorthand, was devised by the Rev. James Evans for use with the Cree Indians and later adapted for the Eskimo. It is an excellent means of teaching an illiterate people to read and write an unwritten language, but for the most part today the Eskimo are no longer illiterate. However, to my eager little pupils at Aulatsevik all those many years ago learning the syllabics was a high adventure. By the time the whaler *Active* arrived in July the older children could read, write, count, repeat prayers, collects, and goodly portions of Holy Scriptures without error and sing over twenty hymns.

Then and always I have found the Eskimo children delightfully natural and honest. By many engaging ways these happy youngsters at our camp showed their affection. Naturally they warmed my lonely heart and made me doubly anxious to lead them to Him Who said, "Suffer the little children to come unto me, and forbid them not: for of such is the kingdom of God."

One evening at Aulatsevik just as Bilby and I had finished

our evening meal (on that occasion it consisted of canned sheep's tongues made in Australia and very good they were too), two hunters came into the igloo. One brought us a nice piece of seal meat and the other some seal liver of which we were both very fond. While the men were with us a girl brought me a pair of caribou-skin stockings which her mother had made for me. "Kee-now-veet?" I asked—"Who art thou?" "O-blo-re-ak," she replied—"My name is Star."

This reminded me that Mr. F. F. Pain of the Dominion Meteorological Office in Toronto had told me to be on the lookout at about this time for the coming of Halley's Comet. I therefore asked Bilby to request the men to let me know if and when they saw it in the sky. Our friends smiled incredulously. "How can the teacher know this?" they queried. "He is very young and not like our angakoks who have unnatural powers." Nevertheless a few nights later we saw this long-tailed phenomenon flashing across the heavens. It was a dramatic spectacle but the Eskimo were even more affected by it than we were. They clamored to know how I could foretell its coming. They were sure I had not seen it ahead of time! This incident raised me to a level far above the native conjurer and contributed greatly to the willingness of the people to listen to my teaching then and in the years to come.

Life in an Eskimo snow village is almost continuously exciting, but there are also unpleasant conditions to which the stranger must adapt. I was always cold, incessantly hungry, and permanently uncomfortable. It was trying to discover that it was impossible to get away from the observant eye of the Eskimo unless one went clear away from the village. Sanitary arrangements were simply nonexistent. Except for the shelter of a friendly rock, one had no protection and it was not possible to avoid the bitter cold (sometimes 50° below zero). Even worse, whatever one did and wherever one went two or more hungry sledge dogs trailed along behind. As a matter of safety and defense it was a prime necessity to be armed with a good stout stick or ski pole. It was vehemently true that we were reduced to the ultimate simplicities and became thoroughly acquainted with life in its most primitive form.

Often the picture of the glowing stove in the mission-house kitchen came as a torture to my mind. I wrestled with myself. Deep in my soul I knew that the deepest strength of any teacher comes from being able to say from the heart, "I sat where they sat." In a marvelous way once I had conquered my weakness and become freed from the restless complexities of civilization I was able to enjoy primal peace. Many another Arctic man will testify to the truth of this statement.

After we had been at Aulatsevik about four weeks the Eskimo, who are from necessity nomadic, told us that they were going to move along the coast nearer to the floe edge where they hoped to get seal and walrus. On hearing this Bilby and I decided to return to the mission for a clean-up, and to collect further supplies. We needed these both for ourselves and to pay the Eskimo for the seal and walrus meat with which they would supply us.

The week we returned to the mission was very cold with the temperature hovering between forty and fifty degrees below zero. We found everything in the house frozen solid. The house was much colder than the igloos at Aulatsevik! These, after all, could be brought up to 32° Fahrenheit before the roof began to melt! We lit the kitchen stove at once and before long that room warmed up. But Bilby decided that no extra coal could be spared to heat our bedrooms. When I went to bed that night it was fifteen and a half degrees below zero in my room. I was angry and it required all my self-control not to light the fire in my bedroom when I knew from Bilby's own calculations that we could well afford to burn a little coal for our comfort. As I have already said, we had decided to spend half of both summer and winter living with the people until the supply ship came in 1911, and we had rationed our allotments accordingly. This drastic and quite unnecessary economy combined with severe discomfort brought my annoyance with Bilby almost to explosion point. I knew that there was enough coal for a bedroom fire, and I wanted it. I shut myself in my own room for a time and wrestled desperately for self-control. I am not ashamed to say that it was a hard fight! Through God's good grace I won the victory. To have lit my bedroom fire would have seemed to Bilby a revolt against his authority. I would have spoiled the good fellowship which had been established with some effort. As it was, the bond between us was strengthened and I experienced peace in my own soul.

It was agreed that we should cook as much food as possible each day, then freeze it for use at the camps. Over a blubber lamp cooking is reduced to a minimum. Everything has to be stewed or boiled and there are no suitable means by which bread and the like can be made.

In addition to replenishing our supplies during these days I completed my first address in Eskimo and submitted it to Bilby for his criticism. He seemed pleased with my effort and gave me helpful advice regarding idiom. For various reasons the address was not delivered until almost a month later but then, to my delight, the people understood every word I said.

One night at about eight o'clock we were surprised to hear the howling of dogs. Outside we saw two sledges struggling over the rough shore ice. These Eskimo proved to be strangers from the west. After the briefest of greetings they set to work to build their igloos, which they did with extraordinary speed in spite of the semidarkness and a heavy snowstorm. They erected their dwellings near the mission house and it was only after they were completed and put in order and their dogs fed that they accepted our offer of a meal. We provided them with hot coffee, hardtack biscuit, and corned beef. After this had been eaten noisily and with great appreciation they began to talk.

From their home base on the east coast of Hudson Bay just opposite the Ottawa Islands they had traveled north along the coast to the west end of Hudson Strait and spent a winter on the mainland near Cape Wolstenholme. The following summer they had crossed to Nottingham Island by open umiak. Then as weather permitted, they pressed on to Salisbury Island and Mill Island, finally reaching King Charles Cape. There they spent the next winter but when summer came they moved east and met some of the local Eskimo who told them that a whaler called at Lake Harbour each summer. This determined them to journey there in the hope that they might obtain such necessities as gunpowder, matches, and rifles as well as tea, tobacco, and other luxuries which the white man was known to bring. At Amadjuak Bay they learned that white teachers had settled at Lake Harbour and they decided not to delay their arrival until the summer but to come on to us. If the reader will trace these journeyings on the map he will see what an astonishing distance these families had covered.

Neither they nor we got much sleep that night for our visitors had much to tell and many questions to ask. They had visited Whale River and either seen or heard of Peck and they knew of Blacklead Island Mission which they had hoped someday to visit. Their interest in us was intense and their leader, a man named O-hi-tok who seemed a very shrewd fellow, was determined to learn as much as possible now that they had at long last reached a mission. They said they planned to stay in the district for a year or more so that they might better understand "the new way."

They proved to be a very virile group who were most successful in their hunting and trapping. This was all the more remarkable since they did not know the country. They were delighted that we were able to supply them with copies of the four Gospels and the Book of the Acts of the Apostles but greatly disappointed about the shortage of service books. They kept us busy making stenciled copies of portions of Morning and Evening Prayer and hymns, which they prized highly. They memorized most of these, as well as many portions of Scripture, and by the time they left the Lake Harbour district two years later they were better taught than some of our own people.

In 1914 when I again met O-hi-tok near Cape Dorset, he

told me how much their visit to Lake Harbour had meant to them and brought me a finely carved walrus tusk as a thank offering. For this he refused any recompense.

O-hi-tok's people decided to go with us to Kinguckjuak, where the next snow village we planned to visit was located. After we had waited for several days, two sledges came from Kinguckjuak to take us to the village. It was a slow journey. Heavy snow fell all day, and darkness had descended long before we saw the faint glimmer of yellow lights in the igloos of the settlement. Our guide went ahead to rouse the people to help us drag the sledges over the rough shore ice and we were soon in the center of the village. When the usual exclamations of welcome and enthusiastic handshaking had subsided one of the leading hunters, At-se-ak, invited us to enter his igloo. His wife offered us each a mug of hot tea which was most welcome although it had a strong flavor of oil. Due to the shortage of blubber for the lamps, no igloo had been built for us but instead we were to be accepted as paying guests with the people. When I first heard this I must admit that my heart sank within me. I thought that at Aulatsevik we had reached the ultimate in primitive living but I knew that worse was now in store.

At first I found it very difficult to adapt myself to a milieu which was not only unfamiliar but often most nauseating. Yet I was fortunate in having a place in one of the largest igloos where our friends, Noo-voo-le-a and his brother-in-law Sai-mo-nilk lived. Noo-voo-le-a had a wife and two children while Sai-mo-nilk had a wife and three children. Life in a crowded hut had many obvious disadvantages. The foetid atmosphere was sickening and the acrid smoke from the blubber lamps was not an aromatic disinfectant, though when it caused us discomfort the hole in the roof was cleared and a better circulation of air was created. Then, too, the Eskimo smell pungently of blubber and perspiration since it is impossible for them to have baths during most of the year. What Commander Peary wrote of Eskimo dwellings was true: "A night in one of these igloos, with a family at home, is an

offense to every civilized sense." It is unnecessary to describe
the contents of the mysterious vessels emptied out on the
snow directly in front of the igloos or the unpleasant and evil-
smelling odors within.

The life we lived was austere and comfortless but I discovered that it had its rewards. The adults were kind and
solicitous and I could not fail to be impressed by their neigh-
borliness and the love they had for one another and particularly for their children.

During this, my first time in residence with an Eskimo
family, I remember my interest in watching Noo-voo-le-a's
wife engaged in making a pair of sealskin boots. How skillfully she sewed the soles to the uppers and how proud I was
when she told me that the boots were for me. Later she prepared a raw seal hide for boot soles by letting it soak in uric
acid in order to rot the black outer skin, that it might be
made thinner and more pliable for use in the cold weather.
The stench of ammonia in the igloo nauseated me and induced frequent coughing spells.

Yet in the long evenings as a member of this household
watching the doings of young and old under the flickering
flame from the blubber lamps I knew that I had come a long
way from the River Clyde. I had learned to sit where they
sat. I had found the peace I had sought in serving this once
remote people who had now become my friends. I was glad
that I had obeyed the Master's command "Go tell."

☆ 5. Famine at Kinguckjuak ☆

THIS FIRST VISIT to Kinguckjuak proved to be one of the most profitable experiences in all my years with the people. Kinguckjuak was a big settlement that winter and try as we might we could not get all the adults into even the largest igloo when Bilby conducted the teaching services each weekday evening. It was therefore arranged that I should take the older boys in another igloo at the same time and do the best I could for them. I laid no claim at this time to speak the language, but I had succeeded to some extent at least. So although the junior missionary's ignorance of the language might be termed colossal, yet there was progress.

The lads were keen and eager but the Eskimo have the typical Mongol characteristics, one of which is politeness. When they are in the presence of a white man who has won their respect they are not only anxious to please but even more anxious not to give offense. This inherent trait made most of these young hunters appear to agree with all that I said. But among them was one who, although reticent, had courage enough to indicate that he either did not understand or did not believe. His name was Joseph Pudlo. At first I thought he was an Eskimo edition of St. Thomas, but it soon became clear that this sturdy lad of just five feet, with his grave face but sparkling eye, was a doubter only because it was too serious a thing for him to accept something lightly, whether it was the sound of a syllabic character, or a religious truth. He, like the disciple of old, wanted to "see." He would exclaim in his blunt staccato fashion, How? or Why? and the point had to be made clear before he would consider himself free to proceed. He was a patient seeker after truth, and once he had cried, "My Lord and my God," he never wavered nor doubted. I learned much from him and owe much to him and he holds a special place in my heart. Pudlo's life and mine were interwoven unto the end.

It had been our intention to stay at Kinguckjuak for a week or ten days and then to visit the settlements farther east. Under favorable conditions this would have been an excellent plan but unfortunately, owing to constant bad weather, there was a great scarcity of both seal and walrus. With tireless patience the hunters went out each day over the ice to the floe edge only to return weary and sad from their fruitless expeditions. This also meant that the people had little or no blubber for their stone lamps. As the supply of blubber decreased, the people only lighted the lamps when melting ice for water. It was a trying experience. The dirt, the grease, the sights, the sounds were often excruciating but these were not the worst of our experiences. We soon had something infinitely more distressing to reckon with.

As supplies dwindled we all reached the bare subsistence level. The meager rations of Bilby and myself did not go far when they were shared among the people. Slowly but with fearful certainty we were all faced with that most horrible of specters: slow exhaustion and death from hunger and cold. I now learned for the first time, but not the last, that one of the terrors of life for the Eskimo is this omnipresent menace of starvation.

The scenes that confronted us daily were heart-rending in the extreme. The despairing looks on the faces of the people, old and young, as they crouched in their cold unlighted huts of snow; the sledge dogs dying by the dozen after having gone mad; the sight of the living dogs devouring what remained of the ones that were dead. Bilby and I thought of taking a scratch team to the mission in order to bring back food to the settlement, but the wretched animals were so weak that we decided they could not make the long journey there and back. It was a testing time for us all, and not least for Bilby and myself who had come to tell the people to have faith in the Great Spirit, the Creator and Lover of all people.

Our hearts ached as we gathered together each day. How proclaim the love of God to people with empty stomachs, to children crying for food, "weeping and watching for the morrow"?

With the wind raging and blizzard after blizzard sweeping the snow across the ice it would have been madness for the hunters to venture out. Yet death would soon be our fate unless we got food, and every man, woman, and child in the settlement knew it. The children sang with me, "Jesus loves me, this I know"—but did He? The men and women sang the Twenty-third Psalm, "The Lord is my Shepherd, I shall not want"—but we were in want, desperately in want. Would He, the mighty Creator of the universe, cause the blizzard to cease so that the men could hunt the seal and walrus at the floe edge? Would He do something in time to save us?

But when we were confronted with the sternest laws of nature, there arose the clearest evidence of a spiritual influence that brought us, both pagan and Christian, nearer to one another.

Early one morning, before the sun had actually risen, we awoke to find the wind had changed. To the south we could see a dark line indicating that the broken masses of ice along the floe edge had been blown offshore. This brought hope that the hunters might be able to reach the walrus. Immediately new life stirred in the camp.

The men, along with the remnants of their emaciated teams, were all harnessed together and pulled the sledges towards the open sea. Shortly after they had reached the sea ice and while we were still watching their movements a pallid streak of light shot above the indigo of the eastern sky. As the sun rose higher, its welcome rays tempered the cruel clawing grip of the wind and as the wind became warmer vapor rose like white smoke. From the vapor we could judge where the water ran open in the channels. This increased our excitement and our optimism. Once during the morning the sky became overcast and a heavy fog settled down on the ice and drifted over the land in a sullen fashion. Our buoyancy became again despair, crueler perhaps because of the respite we had had. But soon after midday the sun broke through the clouds. Again our spirits rose. Everyone was restless, and it was one of the longest days I have ever spent. Hour after hour a watch was kept but it was not until the light was fading that someone cried, "The sledges!" With that one word, every man in the settlement ran with a kind of crazed eagerness down to the shore ice. More shouts were heard—shouts with such a tone of triumph in them that we knew the hunters had met success. With the whole settlement jostling, pushing and pulling, the sledges heavily laden with their precious load of walrus were dragged to the center of the village.

Without delay the people gathered in the open for a feast. They were so hungry that they gulped their food like the sledge dogs. In the excitement the fear that had hung over the settlement vanished, and the spirits of the Eskimo were ravished with delight.

Before going to bed Bilby held a service of thanksgiving which all the adults, including the conjurer, attended while the younger people kept watch lest any prowling dog might attempt to raid the igloo where the surplus meat was stored.

It had been a strange and searching experience, and for days I found it difficult to throw off the memory of that sorrowful time. But because we had been so closely linked with the people in their days of strain and adversity, and because we had helped them to the limit of our own resources, we discovered a brotherhood of feeling and action which drew us together as nothing else could have done and made us feel an at-one-ness which we had not known before.

In later years we were to discover that the agonies we had endured were transmitted into deep and lasting affection.

These experiences could never fade from memory and the ensuing fellowship never failed to warm our hearts in the days to come. Indeed, I do not think I am wrong in supposing that for the Eskimo and for ourselves it changed our whole attitude towards life's values.

It also became clear to me then for the first time in my life that however much we may desire to be rid of fear, it is not without its value. When the hunting is good the Eskimo gorge themselves with food and some become indolent, frittering away their time during the fine warm days. Then when the weather changes or the wild life migrates along the coast, they have inadequate reserves of food and become a burden on the community. Good hunters, knowing that there will be times when it will be impossible to hunt, seize every opportunity to lay in reserves when game is plentiful. They cache their surplus stores of seals and walrus in caves or under rocks at strategic points on the land against the lean winter months. Why do they go to all this trouble when things appear to be so propitious? As Aeschylus put it, "It is good that fear should sit as a guardian of the soul, forcing it to wisdom . . . else how should they revere the right."

Even without the threat of starvation, the misery and stultification of life in this and other snow villages might have been difficult to bear except that I was so busy. My work gave me neither the leisure nor the inclination to be depressed. Indeed I was so happy in the work that I frequently sang by myself hymns in Eskimo or in English and some of the old familiar songs of boyhood days. With St. Paul I could say quite honestly, I have learned both "to abound and to be in want." It was here at Kinguckjuak that I delivered my first address to the people in their own tongue and I was delighted to find that my hearers found no difficulty in understanding me.

It was here also that I first attempted to take photographs while away from the mission. The reason for this delay was the difficulty in changing the old-fashioned glass plates. In order to meet the need I got an Eskimo to patch up an old disused and much-buried igloo. He was surprised that I should want every crack carefully packed with snow and then have the whole roof covered with caribou skins to shut out any possible ray of light. This improvised darkroom proved satisfactory except that my fingers got so cold that I found it difficult to change the plates in their containers. I did have film packs but in cold weather the film cracked and when they were developed innumerable fine lines spoiled the negative.

Owing to successive blizzards our igloo had been completely enveloped in ten feet of snow and steps had had to be cut through to enable us to reach the outside world. Late one evening after we had all retired into our sleeping bags, three dogs surged into the igloo. It was pitch-dark so that we could not see them but we heard and felt them. They rushed around like mad animals, lapping up the oil in the blubber lamps and growling and tearing at one another in their efforts to reach the walrus meat on the ledge beside the door. Noo-voo-le-a grabbed a spear but in the darkness and confusion it was difficult to use it effectively. One of the dogs snapped at him and its fangs tore his naked thigh. Noo-voo-le-a now knew exactly where the beast was and in a paroxysm of pain struck his assailant with the sharp spear. This was followed by the most bloodcurdling cry that faded off into groans and moans from the dying animal.

The blubber lamps could not be lighted because there was now no oil in them but I had a candle and lighted it. (In these days we had no electric torches.) This gave Noo-voo-le-a a chance to fetch some blubber from a neighbor's igloo. Once the lamps were lighted again, I bathed the wound with water, soaked it with peroxide and then bandaged it carefully.

Whether it was the result of the snowstorm or the burglary or both I do not know, but it was decided that a new igloo must be built. I was considered too ignorant to be of use but I watched the erection of our new home with more than ordinary interest. First my host had to find a suitable location. The snow had to be of sufficient depth and beaten hard by the wind. If the snow is not of the right consistency the blocks will either be too hard and difficult to work, or too soft and collapse as the building proceeds. Noo-voo-le-a took his seal spear and thrust it, here and there, into the snow. When he had discovered the right place, he cut a hole with his knife at the center of the proposed building. The blocks as far as possible were all cut from within the circle of the house. Noo-voo-le-a worked entirely from inside the dome; then when the igloo was all but finished he went out and, climbing up on the dome, filled in the chinks between the blocks with soft snow. This last act always proves the skill with which a builder has done his work. When it is remembered that nothing but blocks of snow have been used in the whole process of construction, it will not be questioned that the Eskimo has developed his art to great perfection. The ordinary arch was a relatively late development of civilized man, but the Eskimo of the Arctic, using only the material at hand, and that not the easiest to work with, has developed the use of the spiral arch, which is much more difficult than the ordinary arch.

When an Eskimo intends to spend several weeks in an igloo, the interior has to be glazed before the family settles in. Noo-voo-le-a did this by lighting two lamps in the igloo and allowing them to raise the temperature inside so that the whole inner surface of the snow walls began to melt. The tiny quantities of water thus formed on the surface hermetically sealed all the air holes in the snow. The lamps were allowed to burn for a short time only. When they were put out the temperature, which had risen a few degrees above freezing, quickly fell again and on the inside of the igloo a glassy ice surface formed, making the building tight against the fury of blizzards that sweep over Arctic lands.

In Noo-voo-le-a's new igloo we lived happily until early in May. Then, when the spring sun began to show its strength, our roof of snow collapsed. This did not worry Noo-voo-le-a who simply covered the top of the igloo with the sail of his whaleboat. This served as our roof until we were ready to move on.

It is interesting to note that the nomadic tribes of Central Asia, the Mongols and the Turks, who inhabit the vast tracts near the Russian border, build their homes dome-shaped very like the snow hut of the Eskimo of Arctic Canada. Like her Canadian Eskimo sister, a woman on the Russian border also uses the same kind of oval wooden platter for her meat tray.

Living for weeks as I did in this village and as a member of Noo-voo-le-a's household, I was able to understand the Eskimo economic system and to appreciate the relative value of things from the native point of view. An Eskimo works in order to live. He takes no particular interest in accumulating wealth and he would be considered, according to our standards, improvident. When food is abundant he often eats to excess with very little thought of the morrow; when it is scarce he carries on uncomplainingly.

The man is the hunter and brings home the trophies of the chase. It is the woman's task to prepare the skins, to make the clothes and to perform all the household duties. The woman paddles the umiak but it is the man's privilege to steer; the man feeds the dogs but the woman feeds the children; the man builds the igloo and the woman keeps it in order; the man drives the team but the woman breaks the trail in the snow.

On stormy days when hunting is impossible and in the long evenings, the woman is kept busy attending to her domestic duties while her husband reconditions his sledge equipment. Although the woman is regarded as the property of her husband so that he can exchange her for another woman, or lend her to another man, or send her back to her parents if he so desires, yet the Eskimo woman is generally able to hold her own and is by no means the browbeaten, dejected female that we might assume. It is true that sometimes her "lord and master" is lacking in sympathy and treats her with contempt and cruelty, yet I have had enough experience with these people to know that it is no uncommon thing to find that the wife is the real dictator.

On one occasion I was most anxious to obtain Now-yak to act as my guide on a difficult trip because his team of dogs was in fine condition and he was a particularly reliable man. Knowing both the man and Pe-ta-lik, his wife, I was aware, to quote Harry Lauder, that she was "the boss of the hoose," so I schemed a bit and approached her first, getting her advice. In her opinion who would be the best person to take with me on this particular journey? As we sat in their igloo discussing the matter, her husband stayed quiet, smoking his pipe, while she suggested first one man and then another. In each case I raised some objection such as, his team was poor or his wife could not be left behind alone, whereas I wanted to travel light with a guide only. Finally I asked her if she thought by any chance she could persuade her husband to go with me. In my judgment he was just the man, but of course I knew he would not want to leave her, etc., etc. A moment's silence, a glance at her husband, and I got my guide!

In the long dark evenings my Eskimo friends did their best to amuse themselves in spite of the cramped conditions in which the entire family lived. I spent hours watching them make string figures. They used a light thong of soft seal or of white-whale skin about six feet in length and by deft manipulation created symbolic figures. The women were extraordinarily proficient at this, and I discovered that it was not only a pleasant occupation but quite purposeful. They illustrate the stories they tell by means of these representations and once you understand the art you have no difficulty in seeing the hunter stalking the caribou or the seal popping into its hole or the boat in the water or the bird hopping over the land. Years later I found that some of the string figures made by the Eskimo are identical with those made by people who live in far distant parts of the world such as New Guinea.

The children and sometimes even the grownups enjoyed the cup and ball game. Instead of the conventional cup and ball the game was played with a piece of bone carved to look like a bear, but perforated all over with holes. One end of a thread of sinew was then attached to the bear and on the other end a sharp pointed piece of ivory was fastened. The bear was tossed up and the trick was to succeed in impaling it on the point of the ivory stick. Sometimes instead of a bear the skull of an Arctic hare was used in the same way.

A somewhat different form was adopted in which a piece of flat bone perforated with many small holes was slipped under a piece of sealskin having but one hole to represent the breathing hole of the seal. A boy took a diminutive spear made of a pointed piece of ivory or bone, while another moved the perforated piece of ivory underneath the sealskin. The trick here was for the boy with the spear to impale the ivory underneath.

In another game a thin skin line was suspended from the roof of the tent or igloo with a stone or bone disc tied to the end at shoulder height. The disc had a hole in it and swung to and fro while players threw darts at it. Whoever was successful in sending a dart into the hole gained a point.

The winter inevitably seemed long but on the morning of April 16, while walking on the hill overlooking Kinguckjuak, I was surprised to see a flock of snow buntings fluttering among the rocks. This was the first sure sign of spring. For the first time since autumn, I heard again the chirping of these tiny puffballs of feathers. To me it was music unutterable and released an intensity of pent-up feeling of which I had not been aware. Their little chirps seemed an assurance that in spite of all our trials faith was not an illusion.

On the eleventh of May the temperature rose during the night. To our great surprise we had a heavy shower of rain that lasted for an hour and a half and the surface of the snow became soft. Bilby and I had expected at about this time to move on to the Saddleback Islands, carrying out in the settlements there our same program of instruction and worship. But in view of this change in the weather and the deteriorating condition of the ice, the leading hunters advised against it. They thought that travel by sledge and dog team now would be both dangerous and difficult. They urged us to wait until the ice had broken up sufficiently for us to make the expedition by boat. So not unwillingly we returned to the mission house. An elderly man named Ing-mil-ayo and his wife Ite came with us to tend our needs, and for a brief time we reveled again in the comforts of civilized living.

Soon after the arrival of the snow buntings, the Arctic silence was broken with the whirr of the wings of thousands of migrating birds. At times the air was filled with the quawks and plaintive whistles interspersed with low uk-uks of duck busily feeding along the margin of the now melting lakes or at the floe edge. Frequently we heard the wild calls, the maniacal laugh, and the weird piercing cry of the loons. I never wearied of watching the great flocks of duck and geese flying tirelessly like arrows across the sky. We had further evidence of spring when the little Icelandic poppies raised their pale yellow heads above the snow as if to confirm us in the hope that winter was past.

The weather was now fine and, refreshed with our respite of civilized living, we returned to Kinguckjuak. The walrus had been seen in an open stretch of water, some ten miles away to the east, so one morning I took advantage of the opportunity to go with the men. When we reached the floe edge we could see the walrus rise to the surface and perform a feat that always made me laugh. With head and shoulders showing above the water, they opened their cavernous mouths and spit out, high into the air, a great quantity of broken clam shells. They dig up the clams with their two big ivory tusks, then having crushed them with their strong teeth, suck the edible parts away from the shell and swallow them. While continuing to dig up more clams they store the broken shells on either side of the mouth until it is necessary to come to the surface for breath. They then expectorate the indigestible elements into the air.

That morning the walrus came near to the floe edge but not near enough and it was most tantalizing to see them splashing around, just out of reach. The hunters knew that it

was futile to try to make a kill; even if successful they would
not have been able to secure the carcass. Not only would it
have been out of range of their harpoons but the wind, being
offshore, would have blown it away and it would have been
lost. For more than two hours we sat practically motionless.
Suddenly a young walrus, more curious than its parents,
broke water within a few feet of the ice where a man named
Noo-na was waiting. A shot rang out and the harpoon, thrown
with all Noo-na's strength, secured the quarry. The other
hunters hurried to his assistance and all was excitement while
the heavy mammal was dragged out of the sea and landed on
the ice. Next it had to be cut up and loaded onto the sledges,
but without waiting the men and dogs drank its blood and
ate part of its entrails. When this had been accomplished we
returned to the camp and were received with much jubilation.

Earlier in the year when the unbroken ice covered the sea
for great distances out from the land, some of the Eskimo had
their igloos right at the floe edge so as to be more conveniently
placed for hunting. In one way this is the natural and logical
procedure, but it is extremely dangerous and may be disas-
trous. During the month of March a number of families from
Blacklead Island had risked building their snow village out
at the floe edge on the ice of Cumberland Sound. A storm
rose and on the fateful evening, towards midnight, the ice
around and beneath them began to break up so that their
plight became very desperate. Enveloped in Arctic darkness,
the people struggled against the piercing wind and bitter
cold in an endeavor to reach the land and safety.

It was a cruel business and one poor woman named Lydia
It-tu-kak-sak, while blundering on in the darkness over the
crashing ice, fell between the heaving blocks. With difficulty
her husband succeeded in rescuing her from the water only
to see her speedily freeze to death through sheer exhaustion.
Two others likewise perished.

An account of the disaster, sent to Peck by one of the sur-
vivors, a Christian woman named Eve Noo-e-yat, could hardly
be excelled for simplicity and pathos. It shows, too, how some

of these erstwhile pagans had grasped the fundamental meaning of the Christian evangel and were sustained by God in their time of gravest peril.

Here is the translation made by Peck himself:

While we were on the ice a great storm arose. The ice did not break up in the daytime, but at midnight, when it was very dark. When the ice was breaking up we fled from our snow houses. We were separated in the darkness, one party from another. We could not see a sign of land anywhere on account of the darkness. When I left my house I took nothing with me and had to leave some of my clothing behind. Now, when it began to dawn, we (the party with me) saw a small land, to which we fled, passing over broken masses of ice. When we reached the shore the waves and large blocks of ice were driven up on the beach.

As we tried to get on to the land, on the cakes of moving ice, my father-in-law fell into the sea; but as I was close I laid hold of him and helped him out.

We reached the land, which was only a very small uninhabited island. Here we remained for two days when we were finally rescued by people from Blacklead Island.

We were very thirsty, as we had but little water; we had something to eat, however, as a seal was caught by one of the men while we journeyed over the ice. I did not see Lydia It-tu-kak-sak who had been baptized and had given evidence of true faith but I saw Omingmuk, a poor girl who was also finally frozen to death in the morning, and her flesh was frozen very badly. Kingmealuk, another girl who perished, I also saw when we were close to the land.

I was not in much fear as we passed over the blocks of ice, for I was thinking of God, and I prayed much to Him. I feel thankful that I was taken in safety to the land, for Jesus delivered me. While I passed from one pile of ice to another jumping from block to block with the sea between I wished to be guided to a place of safety by the Spirit of God. These things I write to you, from Nooeyat.

It was my practice at Kinguckjuak to try to have one day a week free from my regular routine of duties—no language study, no afternoon school with the younger children, no evening classes with the older boys. Since weather could never be counted upon, Bilby had agreed that I should take time off whenever a fine day occurred and have school on the Saturday following.

Frequently I went hunting with one or other of the men and so became better acquainted with them as well as observing their various methods of hunting. On one occasion I left the camp at dawn with a man named Ma-lik-tok. He was a pagan and refused to attend our services, but through his children we became friends and I liked him very much. We traveled over a wide expanse of ice at the mouth of a fjord in the hope of locating the breathing holes of some of the seals known to be in that area. Like the walrus the seal is, of course, a warm-blooded mammal and must come to the surface every fifteen minutes or less in order to breathe. Unlike the walrus, it does not always keep to the open sea but when the water begins to freeze over it makes a series of breathing holes near its feeding grounds and travels the rounds of the holes quite methodically. It keeps them open by scratching away the newly formed ice that would otherwise soon firmly close them up again. Since the air space in the breathing hole above the water is relatively small, a kind of pocket of air is formed of the seal's breath which filters through the light covering of snow above.

Following the usual practice of the Eskimo, Ma-lik-tok took one of his dogs with him, leaving me to look after the rest of the team. The animal's keen sense of smell soon enabled it to locate one of the breathing holes. Ma-lik-tok built a small pillar of snow to mark the place and then they moved on to discover the other breathing holes in the series.

Finally, Ma-lik-tok returned to the sledge, having chosen the hole that he would try. Quietly we moved nearer to it. Here he built himself a small shelter of snow, placed his spear on two little pillars of snow, and sat down on a block of snow, first covering it with a piece of bearskin to make it less chilly. His feet were tucked into a foot bag of caribou skin and the line from his spear was carefully arranged so that no kinks or tangles would be found in it when the time for action came.

It might have been many hours after Ma-lik-tok had taken up his position before the seal returned to the breathing hole the hunter had selected. Great patience has to be exercised. I have known a man to remain at a breathing hole ten hours. The Eskimo also told me that sometimes a hunter has fallen asleep and been found frozen to death at his post. On this occasion my friend did not have to wait long. Eventually he heard a scratching sound and knew that the crucial moment had arrived. Silently he grasped his spear and kept it poised in the air ready for instant lunge. After the scraping there was a pause, then the seal put its nose above the water to expel the air from its lungs. That accomplished, it slipped quietly back to the side of the hole. At this point I was almost overcome by excitement—waiting! After a moment or two the seal returned, evidently unafraid, and putting its head well above the water, proceeded to inhale the fresh air. It was at this point that Ma-lik-tok thrust down his spear. The stroke was true, the movable barb at the point of the spear was buried deep in the seal's neck. Immediately it dived and the line ran out, but the end was held by Ma-lik-tok. Now a battle developed between the seal and the hunter, but there could be only one end to the fight. The more the mammal exerted itself, the quicker its lungs emptied. It was then forced to return to the surface for air, there to receive its final thrust from the spear.

But Ma-lik-tok's work was not yet completed. The sharp iron-pointed butt end of the weapon was used as a chisel to enlarge the hole in the ice so that the seal could be pulled out.

There were other hunters in the vicinity so the signal was given that a catch had been made and in no time a group had gathered round to join in the feast. The seal was ripped open from tail to neck, the liver and ribs dripping with fresh warm blood were cut out, handed around, and eagerly consumed. Ma-lik-tok offered me a piece of the still-quivering liver. I took it and swallowed it bravely and thus pleased my friends.

It is not usual at this juncture to eat the whole of the seal but to have merely a taste. The skin over the rest of the carcass was drawn together and secured by small ivory pins like skewers. In this way the flesh did not freeze as it would have done had it been left open. Also, the blood was preserved.

This seal was what is commonly called the jar or ringed seal and weighed about three hundred pounds. The hair on its skin is a silver grey with dark rings and markings. When cleaned, stretched and dressed, it provides the Eskimo with valuable material for clothing, tent and kayak coverings. Between the flesh and the skin there is a layer of white blubber about one inch in thickness.

From time to time, four other varieties of seals were secured by the hunters: the fresh-water or harbor seal, the hooded or bladder-nose seal, the harp seal of which we had heard much from the men on the *Lorna Doone,* and the square flipper or bearded seal which is the largest of all and weighs some six hundred pounds. The hide of the last is prized for use as boot soles, harpoon lines, traces for sledge dogs and coverings for umiaks.

While we were staying at Kinguckjuak that spring I was horrified to find that the father of a family of six had exchanged one of his sons for a whaleboat. The child's father was a decent fellow but a poor hunter who lacked initiative. During the winter he had found it very difficult to provide for his family so he thought that the whaleboat would be more of an asset than an extra mouth to feed. Later I decided that it was, perhaps—not such a bad idea. The childless couple who received the boy in exchange looked upon him as their very own son, training him with skill and wisdom so that they had good reason to be proud of him. He was, of course, the surest guarantee of provision for their old age. The father of the family was tremendously pleased with the whaleboat and when within a year his wife presented him with another son he felt he had all the good fortune anyone could ask for! In spite of his lack of success as a hunter—or was it because of it?—he had the good sense to go into partnership with a somewhat younger man who was an excellent shot and quite aggressive, so thereafter prosperity replaced adversity.

From the first I had loved the Eskimo children and I became particularly interested in a small orphan girl named Bah-ta. I found her exceedingly shy and as I watched her in class and in the village with the other children I came to the conclusion that her excessive timidity was the result of an inferiority complex. She had been adopted by an aunt and uncle who already had three children and while they did not mean to be unkind or unjust they allotted all the distasteful tasks to Bah-ta. She was really an Eskimo Cinderella. My heart went out to this child and I tried to encourage her not only in school but also by asking her to come to the house where she liked to perform small chores. I paid her according to the agreed standard and gave her little presents, which helped more than anything else to establish a feeling of confidence and friendship. Eventually she chattered freely to Bilby and me as if she had known us all her life.

It gave me great satisfaction, when I returned from furlough in 1913, to find that she had developed into a very attractive young woman who, while still reserved, took her place naturally and effectively among those of her own age. The following summer she was married to a fine young hunter and the next year they came to see me, radiant with happiness and good health. After the usual greetings they showed me their four-weeks-old baby and asked for baptism. They told me how grateful they were to God for all the blessings He had bestowed upon them and said, "We love Jesus truly."

☆ 6. Journeys by Umiak and Kayak ☆

DURING THE LAST weeks we had been looking forward to making our long-delayed visit to the Eskimo living on the Saddleback Islands. Almost every day I climbed the hill behind the settlement and scanned the area to find out if the ice was breaking away from the shore line. Finally, on June seventh, the men said that the attempt might now be made. The boat was dragged to the edge of the ice ready to be launched in the morning and all our equipment that could be dispensed with was hidden among the rocks in a ravine to await our return.

We awoke at three o'clock on Wednesday, June eighth. As the sun climbed into the sky, the clouds glowed with warm tones of bronze, then changed to gold as the dying night gave place to the newborn day. The tide was rising so the boat was easily launched. The glare from the water and the ice forced us to wear our snow goggles as the sun gathered strength. At first there was no wind and the women plied the paddles chanting their songs amid much laughter. From time to time the children were restless, asking for food or drink, but the dogs, curled up under the thwarts, slept peacefully most of the long day.

The boat in which we were traveling was an old umiak and was in very poor condition. It leaked so badly that a young girl and her brother took turns all day bailing out the water. An umiak is a family boat, large enough to accommodate an entire household, and is at best clumsy both in design and in construction. Its wooden framework is about twenty-four feet in length, four feet in width, and three feet in height. It is almost rectangular at the gunwale, being only slightly tapered towards the bow and stern, but on the waterline the tapering forward and aft is more pronounced so that it comes to a blunt end. The frame is covered with skins of the large ground seal or square flipper which are sewn together in the same way as the smaller sealskins are sewn for the kayak.

This umiak was really an open boat propelled by paddles instead of oars but had a small mast with a square sail made out of the split intestines of the seal. Because intestines vary in size, the woman had sewn with sinew the broad and narrow strips alternately to offset difficulties due to shrinkage! Every night after the day's journey one of the women poured water on the sail to avoid the possibility of its splitting. The men wore jackets made of the same material, and for the same reason they too were dampened each night.

Kuk-saub and O-ya-rak, who were the joint owners of the boat, preceded us in their kayaks and I was allotted the task of taking the steering oar while the men did some hunting. It was not hard to guide the boat between the scattered pans of ice, but I had to remain at my post for eight hours and at the end of that time I felt stiff, cold, and very hungry.

The men arrived back in their kayaks at about two o'clock, having been successful in securing one seal, three eider duck, and one loon. Two of the lads were then sent off in the kayaks to try their skill as hunters while Kuk-saub took my place at the stern. Just as the boys were returning at about five o'clock a light offshore breeze sprang up. Their kayaks were quickly fastened to the umiak, the sail was set, and for some hours we made wonderfully rapid progress. At about eight thirty the tide being high again, we were able to draw the boat onto the floe edge for the night. Bilby was so tired that by the time we had set up our small tent and made a mug of tea, he crawled into his sleeping bag with his clothes on and was asleep before I had even cleaned myself up.

The night was cold, the tent draughty, the rock on which we lay seemed to be unusually hard and bumpy, but we both slept well and awoke at about six o'clock in the morning stiff and very hungry. Bilby soon made a pot of coffee while I packed our gear and carried it down to the boat. We ate our simple breakfast ravenously. Soon we were on our way once more, but it was not until four o'clock the following afternoon that we arrived at a place called Kooneyuyet on one of the Saddleback Islands.

We were delighted to find fifteen sealskin tents on a rocky ledge below a dreary-looking cliff. The tents looked like barnacles that had grown there. The people came swarming down to the water's edge to greet us and the warmth of their welcome offset the piercing chill of the southeast wind which had arisen. With the help of two men we had soon pitched our little tent and stowed away our scanty provisions. A woman kindly brought us a pot of boiled Arctic char, which is like trout. The fish had been boiled in salt water and we felt we had had a wonderful feast.

The Eskimo had a feast of their own. They all sat in a circle on the rocks and with much laughter and exchange of news ate huge quantities of raw seal meat and eider duck. When the feasting had come to an end, Bilby asked Lei-ta, the conjurer, if we could have a service. To this he readily agreed. There was no tent large enough to accommodate all of us but people crowded into one that was somewhat sheltered from the wind while others, including Bilby and myself, stood just outside. I took the service and Bilby gave a simple but effective address, at the close of which each Eskimo in turn shook hands with us and told us how thankful they were that we had come.

The previous October, before these people left Lake Harbour, Bilby had paid two of the men to take with them in their boats two boxes of biscuit and two other boxes containing a variety of food supplies. These were to be stored in a safe place until we arrived in the spring. We had made this arrangement because it was much easier to carry the boxes in the umiaks than on sledges where every added pound is an added handicap. As was our custom we were planning to use these provisions to pay the people for the fresh food they brought us. When the men were now asked to bring the boxes to our tent, they produced them but they were empty! Artlessly they explained that during the winter they had been hungry for the white man's food and knew that we had plenty more at Lake Harbour.

This seemed to me an understandable defection but Bilby was greatly upset and told them that this meant he could not trust them. Of more immediate discouragement was the fact that we could not now remain with them as planned. We had counted on the supplies for both our use and theirs and we were too far from Lake Harbour to go back for more. The Arctic is a cruel land and one of the cardinal laws of survival is that each man must depend on himself, not on others. If you have not food with you then you move on to where you can get it. Otherwise you become a burden to the Eskimo community.

As though to make up for this incident the people insisted on our accepting gifts of seal meat and seal liver, eider duck and eider duck eggs. Nevertheless Bilby was not satisfied. Perhaps he was right in thinking that Lei-ta the angakok was at the bottom of the trouble. I was then, and later, greatly interested in Lei-ta. His face indicated intelligence and force of character. There was a Mongolian droop in his mouth that gave him an unpleasant, sullen look, but his movements were those of a healthy, vigorous man. Like all conjurers he had become the recognized leader of his particular group of people. In order to maintain his prestige he wrapped himself in sacrosanct mystery and with clever subtlety deluded those around him when it was to his personal advantage. His passive leathery face with its small, slightly slanted eyes gave no inkling of the temper and determination that smoldered behind the mask.

Bilby was also annoyed when he found that our tent had been pitched near Lei-ta's, for he felt that this had been done deliberately in order that our every movement might be watched. In turn we inevitably saw a lot of him and his family, a proximity that bore fruit later on. His wife, Noo-tow-la, some nine years younger than her husband, was a comely little woman, intelligent and hard-working. She dressed well and was always clean and tidy. Her smooth black hair fell in two plaits that hung round her ears and were tied at the back of her head with a cord of colored wool. Sometimes she would sit outside in the sunshine, her soft docile eyes intent upon her sewing as she made sealskin boots for her lord and master or for the other members of her family.

Their little son Se-ko used to come and watch me in the mornings when I was busy preparing for the teaching services. There was a shy yet open friendliness about this small lad that appealed to me. He had many attractive ways and I soon discovered that he was a combination of his father's courage and his mother's gentleness. He liked to go for short walks with me and was ever eager to show me something of special interest. During these days Se-ko and I became great friends and it was to the children that I felt my message of the Saviour's love was best conveyed.

On our return journey to Lake Harbour via Kinguckjuak where we had left our equipment, we traveled in the well-built boat of our friend King-o-wat-se-ak. With the mainsail and jib set we skimmed through the water at considerable speed and had an uneventful voyage until the afternoon of the second day when the sky suddenly darkened and King-o-wat-se-ak, touching my arm, said in Eskimo, "It is very bad."

Even I could see that a storm was coming but we all mistook its speed. Before we realized what was happening it burst upon us with demonical fury. In a moment's time we were enveloped in a swirling darkness. Then we heard the sound of rolling thunder, followed by crashing peels and lurid flashes of lightning. The wind swept down upon us, accompanied by rain that seemed to come not in drops but in torrents so great that it raised splashes on the water of the sea it-self. Spray and sea water slopped over the bows so that bailing had to be continuous and quick. The dogs howled and whimpered. The children cried in fear while the women tried to cover them with part of a tent. First we rose to the crest of a wave and saw the black rolling clouds in the sky and the spume on the water, then they were lost as we sank into the trough. To avoid being thrown into the sea we had to grasp the gunwales as tightly as we could. The knuckles of King-o-wat-se-ak's hand on the tiller showed white from the strain.

By the time we reached Kinguckjuak the storm had blown itself out and, having been sixteen hours on the boat without adequate food or rest, we were all exhausted. As rapidly as possible hot food was got ready, and prayers of thanksgiving were said for our deliverance from the perils of the deep. Picking up our gear, we finished our journey back to the mission house by sledge and dog team. Just after we had rounded Hawk's Head, at about nine o'clock in the evening, we saw the little house standing out against the rocky hillside. Suddenly the amenities of civilized living seemed supremely to be desired. Bilby and I would be able to get clean and warm at last. We were home.

Scones that we had baked and frozen for this very occasion were brought out. I set the table in our little dining room with a clean white cloth and our best napkins and as a finishing touch added a vase of artificial flowers as a centerpiece. Our main course was eider duck eggs fried in bacon fat, and canned potatoes also fried, but to make the meal complete I opened one of our few tins of apricots and made after-dinner coffee. As the heat of the house and the good food attractively served did their work, the grim look of determination faded from the face of my companion and was replaced by smiles. Our tongues were loosened and while we ate and chatted in the dining room our Eskimo companions did full justice to their own meal, indicating their approval with the usual gustatory noises.

Darkness soon closed in, and we lighted the coal-oil lamps

and rejoiced in our content for perhaps an hour before we were ready for the two large pots of hot water which had been steaming on the stove. One for Bilby and one for me. What an inexpressible comfort to have a soft flannelette sheet, clean pajamas, and warm blankets! I was so exhausted mentally and physically that I am sure I would have slept around the clock had I not been awakened in the morning by the voices of the Eskimo who were now anxious to start on their return course back to the Saddlebacks.

When I stepped out in the bright sunshine to wave farewell to our companions of the journey, I was surprised to see the changes that had taken place during our absence. The great masses of ice and snow on the land had largely disappeared. Our little stream, that had meandered so quietly when we arrived the previous August and had been frozen into silence since November, was now a turbulent river purling down from the hills above and rushing between its grey boulders in small cascades on its way to the sea. Its banks were covered with grass, lichen, and heather as well as dainty Iceland poppies. Truly spring was here.

The last week in June found us back at Aulatsevik with our small canvas tent pitched beside the sealskin tents of the Eskimo. My knowledge of the language was steadily improving and by now I was able in a limited degree to express thoughts and ideas. I no longer hesitated for words of everyday use and felt happy confidence in teaching the children. I enjoyed my daily visits to the tents, trying to carry on prolonged conversations and to understand all that was said to me. I found that without undue stumbling I could talk with the people about their hopes and fears and tell them the stories of the Bible which, despite a background incomprehensible to them, were understood because of their essential truths.

Towards the end of June tension increased in the Eskimo and in Bilby and myself. Our thoughts turned constantly to the whaler *Active*. At any time she might appear. Uncertainty in all its forms has ever been, and even with modern ameliorations still is, one of the most trying features of Arctic life—and this was before the days of radio and wireless. To the Eskimo the arrival of the *Active* meant the excitement and profit of the whale hunt. To Bilby and me it meant contact with the outside world. We had seen no other white men now for almost a full twelve months. It also meant mail and parcels. A year is a long time to go without recent word from family or friends or any news of events in the world that had once been ours. But foremost in our minds was the question of coal. If we could buy even a moderate amount of coal from the captain of the *Active,* then our second year in Baffin Land could be spent in at least occasional comfort.

These days of waiting and suspense were among the most difficult and nerve-racking of the year and to add to the strain myriads of mosquitoes appeared, causing us much pain and annoyance. No one had warned me beforehand that these noxious insects existed in the Arctic so I had not provided myself with netting, and, my skin being sensitive, they poisoned me quite thoroughly.

During the ebb of June a sharp lookout was kept for the ship from five o'clock in the morning until ten o'clock at night. On the fourth of July, I had taken my turn at the lookout and was scanning the horizon with my telescope when I noticed a tiny black speck far out to sea. After watching it carefully for a quarter of an hour I was satisfied that it was moving and shortly afterwards, when it must have changed its course as it threaded its way in the ice fields, I knew it was a ship. Involuntarily I breathed a prayer of thanksgiving and ran back to the camp to tell the joyful news. The sleepy village suddenly came alive. The excitement was intense, and everybody seemed to be running to the vantage point shouting, "O-me-ak-juak! O-me-ak-juak!" ("The ship! The ship!")

When eventually we were ensconced in the captain's cabin, replete with a fine meal of fresh food, the captain said that he must prepare us for bad news. I could feel my inmost spirit freeze. A year of isolation leaves one in a state of peculiar susceptibility. "Let us have the worst bit first," I said, scarcely recognizing my own voice. The captain looked at me with understanding. He cleared his throat before speaking as though his message were difficult to convey. "I am afraid, gentlemen," he said, "that your colleague in the work, Mr. Greenshield, has been lost. The ship on which he sailed north last summer has not returned. We fear she has been crushed in the ice."

There was silence. Bilby had worked with Greenshield and had a great admiration for him. It was Greenshield who had replied to my first letter of inquiry four years before.

The captain cleared his throat again. "Also, gentlemen," he continued, "the owners of this ship in Dundee gave me no reasons, but they would not let me carry anything but first-class mail."

Again there was silence. No newspapers, no magazines, no parcels! What a stinging blow.

"Knowing what this disappointment meant," the kindly man continued, "I questioned their decision." He smiled ruefully. "They were adamant. So there it is."

Then Bilby brought up the question of coal. The captain uttered some very emphatic exclamations over our plight but alas! with all the good will in the world he could not help us out. He himself was faced with a shortage. This year the ice had been exceptionally heavy and from Resolution Island on he had been forced to buck it, which had used far more coal than allowed for. With the long cruise into Hudson Bay and the return voyage to Scotland still ahead of him he dared not cut down on his supply.

That night back at the mission house Bilby and I were in sore distress of mind and spirit. Why could we not have coal for our minimum bodily needs? We had prayed about the matter for twelve months and we believed that God answered prayer. Yet here was that which seemed a complete denial. Some shameful thoughts crept into my mind and I seemed to hear the serpent's voice: "Where is now thy God? Is not this proof that prayer is an unreal thing and purely subjective?"

When, at evening prayer, on the twenty-fifth of the month, I read Psalm 119:75: "I know, O Lord, that thy judgments are right: and that thou of very faithfulness hast caused me to be troubled," I asked myself if I could honestly say that. Certainly we were troubled, greatly troubled, but had God anything to do with it? In which sense could I believe that out of faithfulness He had allowed this thing to come upon us? I meditated long and often upon this passage and it was not until much later that the true meaning penetrated the error of my thinking. At this time I entered upon a spiritual aridity, "the dark night of the soul," as St. John of the Cross calls it. I could not pray as I had done before with unquestioning faith. Night after night I knelt upon my knees but no prayer came save, "Lord, I believe. Help Thou my unbelief."

It was not until much, much later that I came to realize that these experiences were the stamp and signet of the pioneer and that prayer is intercourse with God, not simply petition for something that we want. Prayer inspires hope but it may also be the occasion of great disappointment, because in our ignorance we forget that while we may have boldness to make our request known to God we can only ask for that which is according to His will.

But very gradually, as the result of our experiences with the people in their own villages, it dawned on me that our prayer had been more abundantly answered than we had originally dreamed of. Had we received an ample supply of coal we would not have spent so much of our time living with the people. Therefore we would not have made the same advance in our knowledge and understanding of the Eskimo, their customs and language, nor would they have come to know and trust us.

Eight days after the whaler left, the Eskimo arrived and then a very busy summer began for us. We breakfasted at seven o'clock each morning and our routine was the same as at the camps except that we spent many hours working on the house to make it more wind- and weatherproof. The eaves were filled with heather to help insulate the walls. Bilby termed it a "frill" when I erected a flagpole so that we could run up a flag to welcome visitors and fixed a pennant to indicate the direction of the wind. Actually this was a help to me when recording the weather conditions twice each day.

Most of that summer an old Eskimo named Johnny Penny had been seriously ill. He had been born and brought up in Baffin Land on the Davis Strait shore and he told us that his mother had called him Johnny Penny after the captain of one of the many whalers that cruised in Baffin Bay. Bilby was much more versed in doctoring than I and generally attended to the sick and suffering, but Johnny was a great friend of mine and it was my practice to look in upon him each day to cheer him up and bring him some small portion of food with which to tempt his failing appetite. The old man lingered on and seemed not too uncomfortable. But early one morning a girl came to say that Johnny Penny was in pain and would I come. I hastily snatched some things from the little medicine cupboard and followed her. Johnny was breathing with difficulty but seemed to recognize me. I administered something to ease his pain and was rewarded with a smile. Feeling that the end might be near, his relatives joined with me in a very brief service of prayer asking God to prepare him for what seemed inevitable. To our astonishment Johnny said "Amen" quite loudly and smiled again. When I reported this to Bilby he said, "Yes! Yes! There's life in the old boy yet!"

I could not settle down to language study that morning because Johnny was constantly in my mind, and in less than an hour I went over to see how he was doing. I was horrified to discover that his relatives had already sewn him up in his shroud, which was his own sleeping bag of caribou skins. I found them dragging him to a place under a cliff where there were piles of loose stones to cover the body and to protect it from prowling dogs, foxes, and wolves. When the Eskimo saw me coming the procession stopped and they told me quite unemotionally that the old man had died shortly after I had left them.

While they were speaking a loud moan came from the corpse. I ordered the sewing to be undone and found that Johnny's heart was still beating, though faintly. After a small dose of stimulant he not only opened his eyes but in an audible whisper asked that he be buried in a wooden box like the white man. He did not want the wild animals to eat his body. He lived for about two hours more and then with a sigh breathed his last. His dying request was granted and he was put into a rough coffin and received a Christian burial.

In the Arctic, where everyone is known to everyone else, the passing of a soul into the Unseen is a very real loss to all. I was interested to find that the Eskimo had rejected the idea of annihilation but had a very definite belief in the trans-migration of the soul. They believed that the spirit of a human being can take up its abode in some animal or bird. After death the spirit of a hunter may enter a wolf and live as a wolf on earth until the wolf is killed, and then it may enter a lemming, but it is possible it may return and enter a child about to be born.

When Johnny was dying, Pit-soo-lak, the angakok, bent over him and putting his two hands together cup-shaped placed them on the dying man's mouth. Then as he breathed his last the angakok caught his "spirit" in his two hands, took it away from the body and was able to pass it on to a child just born. This incident suddenly made me understand why the Eskimo were so particular about taboos in connection with the killing of animals.

For three or four days after Johnny died his immediate relatives were not allowed to wash, to cut their nails or to comb their hair. The tent in which a death occurs has to be destroyed and for this reason when Johnny was taken ill he had been put into a small separate tent. If he had died in the family tent, his people would not only have lost their tent but all of its contents as well.

In the old days the implements used by the dead were laid alongside the grave just as the Anglo-Saxons and Jutish invaders of old England buried their warriors with shield and spear by their side. In the case of an Eskimo man, his kayak and hunting weapons; of a woman, her stone lamp, pot, and sewing materials; while the toys of a child were placed nearby. They also placed a dog's skull beside the child's toys at the graveside, the explanation being that the spirit of the dog would be able to act as guide to the child in the spirit world. Johnny Penny was an old man and had already given away all his hunting equipment so they laid his pipe and a knife beside his grave. Owing to the scarcity of all materials in the Arctic, the custom had developed of replacing the actual implements after three days by models, the idea being that the spirit of the departed would require only the spirit of the implements in the realms beyond.

One explanation of the undue haste on the part of the Eskimo in burying their dead was their dread of touching dead bodies. The corpse was carried out through a hole in the wall so that the spirit might not re-enter the abode as it would if the body were carried out through the door. I have also known the clothes and other possessions of the deceased left in the house at death to be thrown out of this hole in the wall.

After Johnny's corpse and his belongings had been taken from the tent, three old women entered to "make fire" by striking the fire stones. They lighted the kudlik and said, "There is nothing more to be had here." This was to inform the spirit that everything had been removed. For three days after the death the relatives slept in tents other than their own and did no work. Thrice daily during this time they came together to weep and lament for the departed.

The Eskimo do not mince matters and often use the crudest language. The advantage of this is that one is not left in doubt as to the meaning their words are intended to convey. It is hard for people who have been brought up in civilization to realize many of the painful experiences common among primitive pagan people. In the Arctic everything is frozen solid in winter, and it is not possible to dig a grave. Even in the summer the ground is frozen to within a few inches from the surface. It is not unnatural, therefore, that when faced with such conditions the pagan sometimes removes the dead only a little way from his dwelling, leaving it exposed in order that the animals may feed upon it. In the summer, however, the stench from a corpse is horrible and it was not easy to bear patiently with people who had so little regard for the remains of their beloved ones.

From east to west, in spite of differing conditions, the same fundamental religious principles were to be seen among the Eskimo. Behind a great variety of rites and prohibitions, there lay the fear of the unseen. In order to propitiate the spirits which were ever hovering close around and ever ready to be offended, the mediation of the angakok was sought. The angakok possessed remarkable powers and was really the high priest of the tribe. He had been trained for his task and by study of the natural forces of nature and the migration of the birds and mammals, he was able to sustain his position as a man possessing magical powers. Taboos, spells, charms, and incantations all had their place in the religious life of the Eskimo, whether in the barren lands or on the shores of the Arctic Sea.

During this short summer I sometimes borrowed a kayak and with one of the older lads paddled down the fjord to explore. The Eskimo kayak is designed and built with great skill out of the materials at hand to meet the need of its originators. Then and later, I have examined dozens of kayaks in Baffin Land, Hudson Bay, Labrador, the Western Arctic, and Greenland and found them all very much the same. Kayaks vary in length from twelve to twenty-two feet and all have relatively flat bottoms. The framework consists of one central strip of wood with upright frames ten to twelve inches apart, bound together by two curved lateral strips, one at the gunwale and the other at the bilge. The frames and strips are held together by fine lashings made of skin, sinew, or gut. The kayak varies in width up to about thirty inches. It is well tapered towards the bow and rounded towards the stern where the deck rises slightly. Just aft of amidships is the cockpit in which the hunter sits. The framework is covered with the skins of seal or caribou put on while raw and carefully stretched and sewn together by the women with sunken stitches in a lap seam. Sinew is used for thread and the stitching makes the vessel absolutely watertight. In front of the cockpit a round wooden receptacle is placed to receive the harpoon line. The harpoon with its long sealskin or white whaleskin line is kept on the deck while the harpoon float, or bladder, is attached to the end of the line and placed on the deck immediately behind the hunter. The bird spear with its throwing stick is sometimes tucked in under the cockpit. The harpoon and the bird spear are kept in position forward and the hook and the lance in the rear. Finally, there is the paddle with its long, narrow, ivory-tipped double blades. At a distance of about two feet from the center on each side a ring of skin is fastened to the paddle, which keeps the drip from the blades of the paddle from running down to the man's hands.

The kayak is both efficient for its purpose and smart in appearance. Even the ivory fittings and the general arrangement of the weapons on deck are most attractive. It was described by Sir Clements Markham as "the most perfect application of art and ingenuity to the pursuit of the necessaries of life within the Arctic Circle."

Nansen claimed that the Eskimo kayak "is beyond comparison the best boat for a single oarsman ever invented." Its lightness makes it well designed for speed and it can be carried over ice or land by one man, but that very factor weighs against it in rough weather and makes it very vulnerable when attacked by a walrus with two heavy ivory tusks. I marveled to see the dexterity with which the Eskimo handled it in the chase and when heavy seas were running. Nevertheless a high percentage of deaths each year are caused by drowning in or from the kayaks. This was why Bilby was so reluctant to agree to my venturing in them and why, in fulfillment of a promise made to him, I never took a rifle or gun with me on these expeditions. A hunter will seldom—and then usually under very great stress of circumstances—lend his kayak to a stranger. It simply is not done, so I felt specially privileged when A-va-le-sak offered me the use of his.

I generally spent more time, however, walking over the land than paddling on the waters of the fjord. The weather was fine now and warm and it was a delight to discard all our heavy winter clothing. My favorite haunt was a sheltered corner among some black rocks high up on a hill overlooking a long lake called by the Eskimo Big Lake. Here a tapestry of green grass and brown and purple heather afforded me a comfortable resting place from which I could view the vast expanse of the country. The nearby hills were rich green and russet red where they bordered on the lake, then they were somber beside the overhanging cliffs, but higher up their snow-capped peaks sparkled in the sunlight. One day as I sat there I was amazed to see a small swarm of bees busily engaged investigating the blooms beside me, although the heather and the flowers seemed to me quite void of perfume.

The summer sped by all too quickly and on September 8, 1910, the morning of my twenty-seventh birthday, I recorded four and a half inches of snow on the ground—a warning to us that all necessary preparations must be made for the winter.

The following day we got a great surprise when we saw a strange ship come sailing up the fjord and drop anchor opposite the mission. She proved to be the Dundee whaler *Earnest William* which had wintered at Cape Fullerton and was on her way back to Scotland. Captain Connon told us that she was leaking so badly that the pumps had to be manned every half hour. At low tide the next day the hull was examined, and to his relief it was found that the ship had been only slightly damaged at the bilge on the port side. The mate and one of the sailors had been talking rather noisily about refusing to cross the Atlantic on the ship but changed their minds when they saw that proper repairs could be made. Unfortunately icy gales swept down the hillside, bringing a tempest of sleet, and their work was delayed. Because of the forced inactivity the sound of laughter was seldom heard and a spirit of depression settled on the men of the whaler. It became my custom to visit the ship each day to try to rouse them from their heaviness of spirit. They were dejected not only because of the damage to the vessel, but because the voyage had not proved very profitable. They would get their regular pay but not the anticipated bonus that meant so much more.

On Sunday a heavy gale was blowing and I had to struggle against wind and sleet as I clambered over the slippery rocks at low tide to reach the whaler. The captain had asked me to hold a service on board. All the members of the crew were present and soon the old ship rang as they joined together in singing the familiar Presbyterian and Anglican hymns. It was with regret that I had to decline an invitation to stay to supper but I had to get back for the service at the mica miners' house. By coming to the ship I had left Bilby alone to take the afternoon service with the Eskimo and could not fail him with Ross and Brown.

The mate of the *Earnest William* kindly took me ashore in the ship's boat and as we moved across the harbor he told me a strange and interesting story. Back in 1901, when he was sailing for another whaler, they had landed on an island in Davis Strait and there found a house built by Sir John Franklin more than fifty years earlier. It had withstood the winds and snows and was in good condition. In it they discovered an assortment of articles including a case of canned sausage which they tried and found to be tasteless, some rum and whiskey in casks which, he said, were excellent, and two pairs of cork-soled boots. The latter proved to be most comfortable and useful to the men who found them. The mate said that one of the men put on two pairs of heavy woolen socks and used the Franklin boots constantly during the remainder of the voyage.

At dawn on the morning of September 27 the *Earnest William* departed for Dundee. Nine hours later the *Active* dropped anchor. It seemed strange to us that these two ships should have just missed each other.

Ross and Brown had their gear ready and as soon as the Eskimo had been paid and the mica taken on board, the *Active* sailed away and left us alone once more to settle down to the work committed to us.

That night Bilby and I could settle down to nothing.

7. Pagan Life

DECEMBER SECOND FOUND us once more living in a snow village on the coast east of Lake Harbour, where we remained
with the people until the New Year. Except for the gales,
silence had fallen over the world as the earth now lay under
a heavy quilt of snow. Ice covered the fresh-water lakes and
the small coves and bays of the sea. Even at this time of the
year the scene was fair and full of splendor. Sometimes at
early sunrise the sky became a sheet of gold and the sun sent
forth a great shaft of fire within the nimbus of which every
hummock of ice was revealed in the most striking shapes and
colors. At night the moon rose early and as it came above the
horizon it bathed the world in a silvery light that caused
these same hummocks to cast long dark shadows like evil
specters. Fascinated, but shivering, I was always glad to return
to the relative comfort of the igloo.

All unwittingly we had arrived at the time when the
Eskimo were about to celebrate the Feast of Sedna. Pit-soo-lak,
the conjurer, was in great spirits because he had been most
successful in securing the largest number of seals, including
four square flipper or bearded seals. When we reached the
settlement he, with the assistance of several of the men, was
building a very large igloo for the festival.

Two days later all the necessary preparations had been
completed and there was great excitement among the people.

Few attended our services, and this was most unusual. Bilby felt that we were facing a very crucial problem. Should we as missionaries attend this exhibition of pagan magic and dancing? He was sure that Peck would not approve for he had shunned all such meetings at Blacklead Island. On the other hand, if we absented ourselves, Pit-soo-lak might well claim that we were afraid of his powers since he attended our services and allowed his wives and children to attend. After prayerful consideration, we decided that we should attend and see the feast for ourselves, not as critics but as interested observers.

In spite of the size of the building, which measured some twenty-five feet in diameter and was supported in the center by a pillar made of blocks of snow, it was difficult for all the people to find room. A curtain of sealskin had been set up in readiness to separate the conjurer from the audience when the seance began. After the people were seated the blubber lamps were extinguished and, since the sky was overcast, the hut lay in semidarkness. Pit-soo-lak's attige (inner skin coat or shirt) was removed, leaving his trunk bare, and he wore a mask made of thin white sealskin with strips of dark sealskin sewn on to indicate the markings of the local tribe, similar to the tattooing on the faces of the women. Standing under the curtain, Pit-soo-lak sang several songs in a strong voice and with fine spirit. I was disappointed that I could not follow the meaning and asked Bilby about it at the end of the first song. To my surprise he admitted that many of the words were unknown to him. It was not until four years later, when I had returned to Baffin Land, that this mystery was solved.

Pit-soo-lak now sat down and two men tied his hands behind his back with thongs of rawhide and lashed his head to his knees. At this point the curtain was dropped and the people sat in silence with eyes closed. Gradually low, gurgling sounds were heard. These became louder and louder for a time, then died off to a whisper. Suddenly piercing shouts rent the air and a prolonged blood-curdling howl that ended in a peculiar wail was followed by a sound like the rushing wind.

Then once more all was silent. Pit-soo-lak's soul had now departed to the spirit world and would converse with Sedna. After a time the silence was broken by groans and moans, and finally the spirit of the conjurer returned to his body. The curtain was drawn aside, the lamps lighted, and there before us sat Pit-soo-lak freed from the thongs that bound him but with foaming lips and flushed face as he awakened out of his stupor. He had returned from the spirit world where he had seen and heard strange things about which he would speak privately in due course. At the moment he was tired and thirsty so he was given refreshment—a drink of seal blood.

The singers, two men and one woman, each wearing a mask similar to that worn by Pit-soo-lak, now began to sing. They addressed their songs to some old man or woman in the tribe, to the moon, to the sun, the stars, the aurora, the fog, the spirits in the unseen world, the mammals in the sea, the birds in the air, the caribou, the wolf, the fox, the lemming, and the bear; yes, and to the fear of loneliness, or the fear of hunger, or the thought of man's impotence, or the spirit of the glacier, the mountain, the lake, the floe edge, the air. To all these and to others the songs were addressed. Among the most popular were the songs to the very old people, or to those who had departed this life. Sometimes a song referred to an able hunter long since dead, but whose name had been handed down to succeeding generations and who was remembered only because it was he who originally sang the song.

The music of the Eskimo was monotonous. Their one instrument was a drum made of a piece of raw caribou skin stretched across a hoop of wood or whalebone and struck with a stick. In their singing they seemed to employ five notes only and their songs were mere dirges. That night, the final and most important song was addressed to Sedna, the mother of all sea mammals, in whose honor the feast was given. Since these coastal Eskimo are dependent for their very existence upon the seal, walrus, white whale, and narwhal, this submarine deity had powers above those of any of the other spirits. It was of vital importance, therefore, that the people should keep on good terms with Sedna, so now the conjurer had visited her and by combing her hair and paying her other attentions was able to gain her favor.

When the singing finally stopped, some of the women by squeezing, elbowing, and climbing worked their way to the entrance and disappeared. Bilby and I, who were near the door, followed them, for we had no desire to participate in the feast that was to follow. It was not until later that we discovered that part of the ritual connected with the Feast of Sedna was that, as old Ang-er-nilk bluntly put it, "no man sleeps with his wife for three nights but always with some other woman."

There was a curious legend regarding Sedna: When Sedna was a girl, she refused to marry according to her father's wishes. One day when she was traveling alone with her father in a boat, a storm arose when they were a considerable distance from the land. The man became afraid and felt that his daughter's disobedience was the cause of the approaching storm. He therefore threw her over the side of the boat into the sea. The girl, however, held on to the gunwale and would not let go. Her father in desperation seized a sharp knife made of slate stone and chopped off the first joints of her fingers. These fell into the sea and became whales. The girl still clung to the boat so the father chopped off the second joints of her fingers, which falling into the sea became seals. Before the scene was finished, the father struck the girl with a paddle and put out one of her eyes. Then she sank to the bottom of the sea and there she lives to this day with only one eye!

Later when I visited the Coppermine, Bathurst Inlet and Perry River districts, I discovered that the inland Eskimo have a belief that the caribou have a mother or one who might be termed the "mistress of the caribou," even as the coastal Eskimo believe the mammals of the sea have Sedna who dwells below the dark water.

Many of the Eskimo beliefs are crude and false or a combination of myth and error, but as I lived with the people I constantly asked myself, Who are we to judge their value? We have inherited from our forebears some knowledge of truth because they, in their day, had struggled to find answers to the problems of life. We had never been urged to discard our set of beliefs and to accept another, nor had we ever been faced with the soul-searching decisions that now faced these primitive people.

The second evening of the Feast of Sedna was similar to the first except that Pit-soo-lak did not go into a trance but was master of ceremonies. Instead of a spiritualistic performance there was a trial of strength similar to that which took place when strangers arrived in camp. Two men, Oo-nah-pik and Noo-voo-le-a, went to the end of the igloo. They were stripped to the waist and I was impressed by their fine physiques. Oo-nah-pik placed his right elbow on a small bundle of sealskins which had been set in position between the contestants. He clenched his fist so that his biceps stood out. Noo-voo-le-a then struck the biceps with his closed fist. Things were then reversed and Oo-nah-pik had his turn. At first it seemed to me that the men did not put much strength into the game, but very soon the blows were powerful and caused the receiver to wince. The audience was quite impartial and each time, quite irrespective of which man had dealt the punch, redoubled its vehement applause. Finally Oo-nah-pik said "Na-muk-tok" ("It is enough"), and Noo-voo-le-a was considered to have won the event.

Two other contestants, Noo-na and Koo-tak, now came forward, but this time the blows were struck, not on the biceps but on the shoulders, and must have been more painful. Again, the contestants and the audience displayed the greatest good humor. It was Noo-na who was victor.

After these two exhibitions of strength there was singing and dancing. I found it difficult to follow the words until Bilby explained that at every second line the singer deliberately left much to the imagination of his hearers. Sometimes the plan was especially successful when, by the use of irony and sarcasm, the vocalist was able to annoy and even to insult someone in the audience against whom he cherished enmity in his heart. At other times there was a rhythmic abracadabra which aroused the people into a state of emotional excitement. Generally they were simple songs made interesting and suggestive by the mimicry of which the Eskimo are masters. The singing was followed by dancing, after which two men brought in a fine fat seal. The third evening was similar to the second and so ended the Feast of Sedna.

There could be no doubt that the festival was a success. Certainly the Eskimo loved to dance and there was much laughter and excitement. Individual men and women did not dance together. Sometimes the men danced around in a circle and the women in an inner circle in the reverse direction. At other times one man or one woman would be alone in the ring, sometimes two or more men. When they danced there was really a threefold movement since the tremolo of the body was quite independent of the beat of the drum or the syncopated rhythm of the song. This struck me as remarkable and suggestive of the primitiveness of their dances.

From observations made then and later I think the Eskimo dances could be divided into two groups: ceremonial dances which are carried out according to custom and performed, as on this first occasion, in a large igloo or tent especially built for the purpose and pantomime dances or action songs done for amusement and without religious significance.

The excesses of the Feast of Sedna, the obvious hearty delight with which most of the Eskimo joined in, the power of Pit-soo-lak and the other conjurers over these pagan minds, the dark fears that controlled the native life, all gave Bilby and me much to think about. After this experience we took further stock of our teaching methods to make certain we were using the most effective way of bringing these dear people into the light and liberty of the Gospel of Jesus. We had worked on the principle that in all thought one must pass from the known to the unknown, and we had not argued with the Eskimo about their religious beliefs. We listened carefully to what they told us of their customs and folklore so as to increase our own understanding and on that foundation we hoped to build because God does not leave any of His children without some glimmer of the truth.

In general their position might be summed up in the words of the hunter A-oo-la who said, "Our fathers told us many things both wise and good. They did not lie to us but there were many things of which they were ignorant. If you can tell us more we are willing to hear your words."

We also took care not to get at cross purposes with the angakoks, nor did we openly question their powers or their magic. Rather we concentrated on teaching that there was one Great Spirit whose name was Love and who ruled Iso-ham-i-to-mit–Iso-ham-i-to-mut, "from everlasting to everlasting."

Gradually, slowly, testing step by step the authority of our message, the men and women were wooed and won by the Saviour's Divine Sacrifice and they began to leave behind their old ways and to walk in "the Jesus way" as they called it. Quietly and persuasively the tidings of salvation transformed their thoughts, their ideas, and their inner life. The transition stage was—and still is—difficult for all. On their part it was not easy to give up their inheritance, superstitious as it was. Supposing, they said, the teachers should be wrong. Then by this change they would offend beyond redemption the spirits of which their fathers told them. Also as one man or one woman took the step and came forward to be baptized, it often wrought unhappiness in the family group, a husband avowing the new allegiance, the wife holding back; a son or daughter following in "the new way," the parents staying in the old. It takes courage and conviction to forsake all and follow Him.

On our part this period took patience and wisdom, for it is a delicate task to lead searching souls to the Eternal Father. Once the step was taken and they had declared their faith, the difference became evident in their faces and bearing, a peace and a radiance appeared, not seen before. Eventually even many of the Baffin Land conjurers became earnest Christians. I would like to be able to say that this was the case with my friend Pit-soo-lak. Unfortunately one cannot deck a tale and keep it true, so that with sorrow I have to confess that he continued crafty and indomitable, holding to "the old way" and died, as he had lived, a pagan.

One day as I was returning from a brief walk over the sea ice, I found a poor girl named Noo-nah-pik pushed into a small unheated snow hut without proper caribou skins to keep her warm and with only a tiny stone lamp and very little oil to cook with. When I asked why the girl had been segregated and punished in this fashion, I found that it was because she was suffering from a simple female malady. Then and on other occasions we had to insist that such cruel practices must be abolished. It was not easy to say much because the Eskimo were quick to resent our interfering with matters which they felt did not concern us. But as they got to know and to trust us and became increasingly interested in the Christian message, it was less difficult to bring them to an understanding that these practices were harmful and that it was better to help and comfort those who were ill.

When a child was expected great precautions were taken. First of all, the woman was set apart from the people and lived in a newly built igloo or tent—according to the season. She dressed her hair most carefully and wore various amulets. Until the child was born, no one was allowed to do anything for her except to supply her with food and water. Once the child had arrived she was received back into her home, but it was important for her to remember various taboos in order that the spirits might be pleased with both mother and child.

One of the most common practices of the Eskimo has been the use of amulets and charms. During my travels through the Arctic I have seen a great many of them, and it is almost impossible to believe that the people put such value on these things, but they do. I have seen anything from a loon's head or a polar bear's tooth to a bird's claw attached to the clothing. Underlying this use of amulets is, of course, the idea of mystical power that brings good luck, that saves from disaster, that gives strength, that brings warmth, that cures sickness, that protects the loved ones. Nearly always the children wore them—the boys that they might be helped to become great hunters, and the girls that they might bear a man child in due course. It was all merely a childlike groping after the infinite.

I claim that the pagan Eskimo—and, mark you, I say *pagan* —are neither moral nor immoral. They have their own code of ethics and according to these they may be considered good or bad Eskimo, but from our point of view they are simply amoral. When first we went to Baffin Land monogamy was the common relationship among them, but polygamy and poly- andry were permissible. Several of the conjurers had two wives; Pit-soo-lak had three, and one very able woman had two husbands. The marriage of two young people was generally arranged by the parents, or more particularly by the mothers of the children. Among some tribes I met in the Central and Western Arctic the children were betrothed almost at birth and were married between the ages of eight and twelve. Other tribes did not allow their children to be married until they had reached maturity. Yet many of their marriage customs are no more foolish than our practice of throwing rice and confetti.

I was particularly interested in the traditional celebration that followed the union of a young couple of whom I was fond. The young man, Ta-pah-ne, whose people were living at a camp about nine miles along the coast, was to marry a girl in our village named Ag-pa. This was in December 1910. On the appointed day Ta-pah-ne arrived by sledge and dog team and having been greeted by the people, called at the bride's igloo. After some delay the girl's baggage, in the form of various skin bundles, a stone lamp, and other things which were the equivalent of a trousseau, was carefully lashed to the sledge with thongs of rawhide. If anything should drop off during the impending journey it would be an ill omen. Ag-pa then came out dressed in a fine new set of caribou-skin clothing and helped her husband to get the sledge over the rough ice barrier near the shore. When they reached the smooth sea ice, the groom and his bride climbed on the sledge, she sitting behind him, and they started toward the new home. Suddenly, while the groom was whipping up the dogs, the bride slipped off the sledge and with haste ran back to our village. The groom took no notice of this for a time and thus the girl had a sufficient start to enable her to reach her parents' igloo before he appeared to notice her absence. Finally he stopped his team and after a delay returned to the camp. It now appeared that a vigorous protest was being made by the aggrieved groom. Eventually Ag-pa came out once more and departed. When I asked the meaning of this little bit of play-acting, I was told that it was the Eskimo custom, in order to emphasize the fact that the girl was quite independent and was doing the man a great honor.

The bride was received into the home of her husband's parents with very little ceremony and soon settled down contentedly as an assistant to her mother-in-law. If after eighteen months no child had arrived Ag-pa would have been sent back to her parents. This would have been a supreme insult from which she could not recover until such time as she bore a child to another man.

In Baffin Land, as elsewhere, young people fall in love. The romance of Pudlo, the once doubting Thomas I have already mentioned, shows how even in the Arctic true love can conquer almost any obstacle. Pudlo came to us across the mountains from Frobisher Bay and promptly fell in love with Sarah, the youngest sister-in-law of the conjurer Pit-soo-lak. Because of Pit-soo-lak's exalted position Sarah was considered a very eligible partie. Pudlo had no blood relations in the Lake Harbour district, no financial backing because his parents were dead, and he was, as yet, an inexperienced hunter. In short he had little to recommend him as a husband for a young girl who was regarded as an heiress.

When it became known that he aspired to Sarah's hand Pit-soo-lak gave Pudlo his congé and told him to move on. He took his dismissal in a courteous manner and went away. One afternoon about six months later he reappeared and there was a repetition of the former experience. In the meantime Pit-soo-lak tried his very best to marry Sarah to various young hunters in the district, suggesting to her first this one, then another, but all his efforts were of no avail. Sarah only shook her head and reiterated with finality, "I love Pudlo."

With the turn of the season there was Pudlo again back in our midst. This time he gave an accounting to Pit-soo-lak of his progress, his record in hunting and a list of his material possessions—a new tent, a good kayak, etc. Pit-soo-lak capitulated. What else could he do? The two were married and no finer illustration of true love could be found than that displayed by them throughout the years. In prosperity and in adversity, in joy and in sorrow, they were happy together. As children came to bless their union it was touching to see Pudlo watch over them with tenderest care, carving them toys from bits of wood and ivory, helping them to repeat their lessons for school, and teaching them by precept and example to love their Lord and Master.

One night in the second week of December, as I was taking the meteorological observations, I heard a prolonged blood-curdling howl that ended in a peculiar wail. After silence the howl was repeated. Pit-soo-lak the conjurer came out of his igloo, listened, and said simply, "A-ma-rook" (wolf). In the morning wolf tracks were found near the fox traps of a man named Muk-ki-ti-tok. The wolf destroyed one fox, leaving only its tail. That evening Muk-ki-ti-tok spent a long time making a weapon with which to kill the marauder. He took two pieces of fine whalebone and tied them together in the form of a cross, the end of which he made very sharp. He then bent the ends together and held them in place like a ball with a very light thread of sinew. With great care he wrapped around this horrid invention a thin piece of seal meat with a little blubber and then set the whole on the roof of his igloo to freeze. He explained to me that the wolf grasps hungrily at the meat. Once the ball of meat and fat is swallowed, the light threads of sinew disintegrate so that the sharp points of the whalebone pierce the walls of the stomach and kill the animal.

The next day, Muk-ki-ti-tok had caught two wolves. After skinning them he performed a curious rite which neither Bilby nor I had seen before. He placed all his hunting equipment on top of the snow porch of his igloo and then, carrying the wolfskins in his arms, he walked around the dwelling seven times. When this was done he handed them to his wife, who also walked seven times around the igloo.

Muk-ki-ti-tok said that in the early days before the whalers came and gave them steel traps his father caught wolves and foxes in stone pits and falls. The animal was lured into the pit by means of scraps of meat leading to the entrance. Once the beast went inside and snapped at the bait a heavy slab of stone fell upon it and killed it. Years later, during my visits to Greenland, I discovered that this old method was the only one allowed by the Danish Government.

One day a woman named Me-tik came to give us some seal liver. When addressed as Me-tik she said her name was now Noo-nah-pik. This puzzled us because we had noted that from time to time some of the other Eskimo had changed their names. At first we had been inclined to think that it was a trick to confuse us, for the Eskimo delight in practical jokes. But now we discovered that when an Eskimo had a run of ill luck he besought the conjurer to give him a new name in the hope that he would thereby gain new physical powers and more success. Pit-soo-lak was quite willing to tell us about this. He said that the new names were those of departed Eskimo and that was why the dead were never mentioned by name but always referred to as "his father, her mother, his sister," and the like. He explained that the name of the dead one was no longer valid since it had passed into some other person, animal, or bird, and he said that there was no connection between sex and the name. This last matter had been a source of confusion to both Bilby and me.

Through years of study of the Eskimo I found that conceptions of the supernatural varied from individual to individual and that, like all primitive peoples, they conceived of nature as animate throughout. A man has not only a body and a spirit, but also a name which is always with the man just like his shadow when the sun is shining, only it cannot be seen. When the man dies, his name is held in great reverence and is not mentioned until it has been transferred by the conjurer to a child. The name perpetuates the memory of the dead and the important thing is not the sex but the relationship of the individuals. A boy may be named after a great hunter, it is true, but equally he may be called by his grandmother's name. I also found that the Eskimo did not like to tell you their own name, but preferred that you should ask somebody else because it is unlucky for a person to speak his own name. In all this they are like other primitive races throughout the world.

About half past one o'clock on Wednesday afternoon, February first, while we were living in another village east of Lake Harbour, an Eskimo lad burst into our igloo to tell us that several sledges were arriving. This was exciting news so I hurried out to meet the newcomers, who proved to be Eskimo from Frobisher Bay and Cumberland Sound. They were led by a man named Kidlapik.

When the hubbub of welcome had subsided, a still greater surprise awaited us: we were presented with two letters written in English. One was from a Mr. O. C. Forsyth Grant who owned a whaling station at Cape Haven on the Davis Strait and of whom we had never heard. The other was from our fellow worker, the Rev. E. W. T. Greenshield. Bilby and I were literally trembling as we read his pages. As I have said, the previous July the captain of the *Active* had given us bad news about the almost certain fate of Greenshield's ship. We had assumed that he had perished.

In this letter Greenshield told how the vessel had been crushed in the polar pack but all had escaped to safety. Unfortunately all their food supplies had been lost with the vessel. He and the crew had experienced a year of great hardship but were thankful for many mercies and were even now in a few hours leaving for the south on board a Scottish whaler that had picked them up.

The letter from Mr. Grant brought a further surprise. It was couched in the most kind and generous terms and offered us both hospitality and plenty of dog food should we care to visit the Eskimo in that part of the country. The people were constantly asking him to bring them "a teacher" and he had explained to them that he did not trade in teachers but would be glad to do everything possible to get them one. He had heard from an Eskimo who had come from Frobisher Bay that we were at Lake Harbour and while he did not know our English names he hoped we would accept his invitation in the spirit in which it was given.

When Kidlapik and his companions were asked how long it would take to reach Grant's place they answered "many sleeps." The Eskimo reckon distance by the number of times they sleep on a journey and since that number depends on the weather, the surface of the ice, the condition of the dogs and the time of the year, their information is seldom more than relatively accurate. Bilby then asked me whether I would consider making the journey. He could not go because he had promised to visit some Eskimo in the west but he felt, as I did, that the call had come so unexpectedly and yet so clearly that the question should be faced. Another cogent reason for going was to study conditions in the hitherto unexplored region of Frobisher Bay which would open up the possibility of work there in the future. Against my going was the fact that Kidlapik's team was really no good. His dogs were in a pitiful condition, having been practically starved coming up from Blacklead Island because of the scarcity of seals. Also the journey was reported to be difficult with dangerous and treacherous mountains to be crossed and I had never undertaken such a long and arduous expedition by sledge and dog team. Then I was also needed by our people in the Lake Harbour district. I faced the problem all that night and prayed for wisdom to do what was right. At last I slept and in the morning I felt there was but one answer, for in my mind were the words, "This is the way, walk ye in it"; "as thy days so shall thy strength be."

For this trip I dressed in a double suit of caribou skins. The inner coat and trousers were made of summer skins because the hair is finer and less bulky than that of autumn skins. The fur on the inner garments was turned towards the body while the outer garments were worn with the fur outside. Similarly, double caribou-skin mitts, knee-high boots made of skins from the legs of the caribou with thin sealskin soles, caribou-skin stockings worn with the fur inside, and a slipper of thin caribou skin, seagull skin, or hareskin worn between the stocking and the sole of the boot protected my hands and feet. The trouble with this outfit was that it weighed twelve pounds. In bitter weather it was ideal but in the hard going over the mountains, or when I dragged the sledge over hummocky ice, it was a burden and I frequently removed the outer coat.

Kidlapik's sledge, the type used by the Eskimo of Baffin Land for long-distance travel, was about fourteen feet long and relatively easy to maneuver over hummocky ice or across crevasses. The runners were curved up at the front so that they were less apt to catch in the projecting ice barriers. Unlike the short light sledge used for hunting near a village, the runners of this one were long and narrow, of solid wood with separate crossbars lashed to them by thongs of raw walrus or white whale hide. The runners were shod with strips of bone cut from the ribs of a whale. These measured about two and a half inches in width and about three-quarters of an inch in thickness. Each piece was attached to the runner with wooden pegs.

Every morning before the sledge was loaded it was turned upside down and the runners were given a coating of ice. Kidlapik got a mug of warm water and taking a mouthful, blew it in a fine spray over the surface of the runners. He then took his caribou-skin mitt and rubbed down the quickly forming ice as it solidified. In this way it made a smooth glassy surface on the shoe of the sledge which reduced friction to a minimum.

At the outset of our long journey I suffered greatly from the extreme physical work. One night, after a particularly trying day when we had to climb a terrible hill, I was so exhausted that I lay down on the snow where we stopped and remained there until the intense cold began to freeze the moisture on my undergarments. Then of necessity I pulled myself together and by beating my hands and feet on the sledge runners revived the failing circulation until I was able to take my share in building the igloo. So overwhelming was my fatigue that, hungry though I was, I crowded into my caribou sleeping bag without waiting for anything to eat or drink.

On another occasion I was helping Kidlapik to relash some of the crossbars of the sledge and, having foolishly removed my fur mitts in order to do the work better, got the fingers of my right hand frozen. Thanks to Kidlapik's ready help, this did not prove serious but the pain caused by the returning circulation was considerable and my fingers were very sensitive for some days afterwards.

The second day out we very reluctantly threw off more than half of our dog food in order to lighten the sledge. This was an extremely serious matter and we suffered for it later, but had we not done so we would never have reached the summit of the mountain range. That day Kidlapik and I were harnessed to the sledge along with the dogs. We each had a heavy thong of walrus hide passed crosswise over the chest and one shoulder and attached to the afterend of the sledge. I found this method difficult and uncomfortable because it brought the center of effort much too high. But we were able to help the dogs up the hills and over the rough ice. It was hard work and the thong felt like a red-hot bar searing the flesh.

Each day had its special difficulties but when the weather cleared, the monotony of the dreary wastes was forgotten. One

day there was a brilliant blue cloudless sky and as we worked
our laborious way up a long steep hill we saw the bleak rocks
jutting out of the glittering snow like the heads of some wild
prehistoric creatures watching our poor efforts. At other
times we marched onwards through a deep valley with overhanging cliffs or along a frozen stream bed or across a lake.
There were frequent delays when a dog's trace or harness
broke or became entangled. Each dog had its own single trace
attached to the bowline of the sledge and thus it could jump
from side to side, interlacing itself with the others and causing
confusion.

When we descended a steep hill, thongs of skin were lashed
round the forward end of the sledge runners to retard our
progress, while others were fastened to the front so that each
man could pull back as the descent was made, acting as additional brakes and also helping to steer the sledge on its
downward course.

Each evening I watched for the coming of the stars. As
Coleridge said, "God comes to us with every day, with every
star that rises." It was not the Pole Star that I was especially
interested in at this time for I had come to take it for granted.
No, I watched eagerly for Capella's appearance high in the
northwestern sky and for Arcturus low in the east. Their
coming seemed to give me a feeling of security.

Nearing Frobisher Bay we came to a gully that led to a
frozen waterfall. The dogs were unhitched from the sledge
and taken down first. Then, when the heavily loaded sledge
was being lowered, we had what might have been a very
serious accident. Kidlapik had preceded the sledge in order
to guide it as it descended. Suddenly he lost his footing and
went sprawling down the icy slope. It seemed certain he
would be crushed between the rocky cliff and the sledge but
he escaped as by a miracle.

Before setting out on the journey our equipment had been
reduced to the minimum and I had bravely but foolishly cut
out the sugar ration. Later when we had been reduced to
eating raw frozen seal meat I, like Esau of old, felt "faint"

and would have sold my birthright for a pound of sugar!

When new snow had fallen it was generally necessary for us to take turns breaking trail. This is difficult or easy according to the amount of snow lying on the surface. You focus your eye on some particular object in the distance and then "keep on, keep on going." I found it a good plan to repeat to myself some poem, hymn, or passage from Shakespeare or the Bible. Whatever one did was helpful if it enabled one to forget, for the moment at least, the hardness of our circumstances.

My lips became cracked and bleeding with the cold. Driving ice particles stung my face like slugs from a shotgun. My breath froze on my mustache and clogged both mouth and nostrils. Then, when we were going over hummocky ice and had to exert ourselves to the limit in order to move the sledge over the rough barriers, I coughed incessantly because the chill air tortured my lungs. Often I stumbled on in the darkness with my nose and cheeks well-nigh frozen. Again, owing to the exertion I became very hot and thirsty, and this presented the greatest temptation. It is easy to suck a piece of ice or to swallow a handful of snow as the dogs do, or to drink through a hole in the ice on a lake over which you are passing, but to an experienced Arctic traveler all are taboo. The shock to the system is too great. Kidlapik had a very simple answer to my craving. He carried a water bag made of the skin of a seal flipper. He filled this skin bag each morning with broken ice, tied it at the neck with a thong of fine sealskin and then slipped it down his back, between the shoulder blades with the thong coming out of his hood and fastened to his belt. The heat of his body melted the ice in the bag and later on a drink of warm water was secured without any difficulty.

The natives are wonderfully clever in the way they notice everything that comes within range of their vision on the trail. Not only do they recognize the tracks of the various animals in the snow, but they can tell what they were doing, whether hunting for food or traveling in haste, as well as their sex and many other significant details. I was also astonished by Kidlapik's ability to continue in a straight line towards his destination over the snow-covered wastes without a single mark to guide him. He could not depend on the wind because it varied constantly. There were no trails—nothing. It seemed as if he traveled by instinct.

When we finally reached Frobisher Bay we found it to be a very large fjord running in a northwesterly direction from the Hudson Strait. On the east coast the rocky hills rise some two thousand feet, and the spectacular Grinnell Glacier constitutes the west side of the Bay. I have described our journey there in detail with deliberate intention. There have been of late many accounts of Arctic life remarkable for their inaccuracy and I have wanted to put on record a true account of sledge and dog team travel in these frozen realms. While admittedly this trip was taken many years ago, the conditions in our land of ice and snow have not in essence changed. The hazardous journeys undertaken by various of our missionaries today are often made in the same fashion and under the same austere conditions.

In my time I was considered something of a "fair-haired boy" because I traveled two thousand miles each winter by sledge and dog team visiting the people. But Canon Turner and Canon Webster, of Pond Inlet and Coppermine respectively, year after year in their turn far exceeded my early record.

☆ 8. The Grant Episode ☆

WHEREVER WE ENCOUNTERED Eskimo on this journey we held services with them, Kidlapik and I taking turns with the preaching. Thanks to the teaching that he had received from Peck and Greenshield, Kidlapik had a wonderful knowledge of the Gospels, as did his little wife Rhoda.

It was dark when after eighteen days we reached the broken barriers of ice in front of Grant's station. Kidlapik went ahead to coax the dogs while I was harnessed to the sledge.

Very soon the local Eskimo heard us and came running to our aid. Among them I noticed a tall well-knit figure in caribou-skin clothing who wore an Eskimo hair fillet. He came to Kidlapik's side of the sledge and after the customary greeting asked him if he had visited Lake Harbour and if and when a teacher would come. Kidlapik replied that the teacher was here and pointed at me. Grant—for it was he—swore in astonishment and then stretched across the sledge and shook me warmly by the hand. I was soon to discover that we had not been expected for at least another week and that to Grant my arrival earlier than anticipated was considerably embarrassing. The truth was that he had an Eskimo concubine, a fact which he would have liked to conceal from me.

Grant did everything to make me welcome and I was glad to enjoy even a feeble attempt at civilized life. But my head nodded long before he was ready to stop talking. The next

morning my host showed me over his place. It made me recall the Fenimore Cooper stories that had once stirred my
boyhood imagination: The walls of the house were covered
with racks on which rested firearms of every description—
from the latest British army rifle to the old Martini Henry
and American Springfield. When I entered the large trading
room I gasped for it held everything that the heart of an
Eskimo could desire, not only tea, sugar, and molasses but
delectable luxuries as well. There were clocks and musical
instruments, bolts of brightly patterned cloth, towels, and
fancy combs.

In one of the warehouses there were kegs of gunpowder,
iron bars for seal spears and strips of hardwood for harpoon
and spear handles. In yet another building hundreds of white
foxskins and some blue foxskins hung from the rafters, dried
and ready for the British market. Wolfskins and polar bear-
skins of all sizes were stretched over racks, while the hides of
walrus, white whale, and seal were stacked in separate piles,
salted and ready to be dispatched to the big manufacturing
centers in Scotland and England. In a corner lay a heap of
walrus tusks. Outside stood great barrels filled with frozen
walrus flesh for dog food; whaleboats, masts, spars, oars, and
sledges lay around in disorder; and beyond these were the
Eskimo igloos.

Grant's personality dominated all else, however. He was
kindness itself and willingly arranged for me to have regular
teaching services with the people, but I felt that he was watching my every word and action with a critical eye. On Saturday
he invited me to travel with him along the coast towards Lady
Franklin Island where an Eskimo had reported that he had
seen the tracks of a bear in the snow. We left the house soon
after breakfast, discovered no signs of a bear, and returned to
the post after dark. Having had nothing to eat for eight hours,
I looked forward to a fine meal of roast caribou.

Instead, when we sat down at the table, Grant's Eskimo
woman brought in the heads of two caribou that had been
boiled in water. One was placed on a plate in front of me and

one in front of Grant. These were ghastly-looking objects for, while they had been skinned, the heavy lips had much hair on them and the eyes were bleached and staring. Seeing the shocked look on my face, Grant asked me if I did not like haggis. Then before I could answer his question he added, "Caribou brains are much better!" I noticed that the half-cooked brains were oozing through a crack in the skull onto my plate. My host dug his fork into the skull and extracted some of the brains and began to eat. I followed suit. Only with the greatest possible difficulty did I succeed in swallowing a small portion and then I quickly asked to be excused from the table. Outside I was soon relieved and would have liked to have remained in the fresh air because I had developed a violent headache. But the intense cold forced me to return. Grant made no reference to my absence but there was a flicker of a smile on his lips as he suggested that I should have a cup of tea and a pilot biscuit with Tiptree English jam. I went to my bed in the attic wondering what further treatment I should have to face. Two days later Grant apologized and said he was just testing me to see how I would react.

The next morning, Sunday, I was fully occupied since I had three services, two for the adults and one for the children. That evening Grant and I had the first of a number of long talks about all manner of subjects. Grant was unlike the usual Arctic trader. He stood about six feet in height, had a clearly chiseled profile, searching eyes, slightly hollow cheeks, sensitive mouth expressive of both wit and sarcasm, and a very determined chin. I learned that he was the son of a Scottish landowner and had been educated at Rugby. He had entered Sandhurst in preparation for a career as an officer in the British Army but had what he called "a slight difficulty" with a superior officer and bought himself out of the army. After a visit to Canada and a voyage on a Scottish whaler to Greenland and Baffin Bay, he returned to Scotland so enamored with life in the Arctic that he bought the whaler *Snowdrop* and the whaling station on the Davis Strait. The

Snowdrop was wrecked on the Baffin Land coast in 1908 and was replaced by the brigantine *Seduisante*. The name of this second ship had a subtlety characteristic of my host.

When I visited Grant he had no white companion and was living in quasi-Eskimo fashion, apparently enjoying the life of freedom. His favorite saying was "Fools make rules for wise men to break." After the caribou-brains episode he became most friendly and confidential, expressing his opinions freely. A man of very positive convictions, he did not hold the Christian belief in God but recognized that there must be an author of some kind behind the universe. This mind, he claimed, was in no sense personal nor had it any interest in the doings of mankind. But it was necessary for men to discover the laws that were eternal for if we failed to obey them we were punished or destroyed ourselves. He felt that life was not something to get excited about but that a man should try to get as much pleasure out of it as possible. Immortality was a natural hope but without foundation unless we held that our immortality lay in conceiving children who would inherit from us minds and bodies that would enable them in turn to enjoy life. Grant claimed that we were immortal in the sense that our influence for good or evil upon those with whom we came into contact would continue down through the generations. For him there was no hope beyond the grave. He believed that this was the inevitable destiny of all living creatures.

Grant was an intense man; intense in his love of justice, equally intense in his hate. There was something arrogant in his handsome head, in the sensitive mouth that could curl into a sneer, and in the piercing light that came into his eyes. I was sure he would be dangerous if thwarted. As he spoke of honesty and justice I claimed that the difficulty of most people was to be found in the proper motive and that it was here that Christ's teaching meets the need. It provides the motive to do the thing that is right. When men let God be their master their conscience is like the needle of the compass so that, while it may tremble through spiritual infirmity, it finally points to the Pole Star and they see more clearly the difference between right and wrong, truth and falsehood; then conscience develops accordingly. In turn, this means blessing to the individual and through the individual to others.

When I claimed that the realization of the consciousness of God in the heart of man throughout the ages could not be lightly brushed aside, he agreed. His most constant theme was justice so I insisted that it was difficult to believe that the creature had a higher standard of justice than the Creator and quoted Immanuel Kant's words, "Two things fill me with ceaseless awe, the starry heavens and man's sense of law," and followed that with Job's question, "Shall mortal man be more just than God?" Grant was greatly interested and asked for the reference: Job IV:17.

When I told him about my own spiritual pilgrimage and of those dark days when I endured the doubt of ever finding an answer to the riddle of existence, he shook me by the hand and said he was in that very position now and only wished he could follow me through. Then after a silence while he puffed at his pipe he added, "Maybe—someday!"

When Grant spoke of the Eskimo he seemed just as anxious to help them as I was and a gentle look came over his hard face as he discussed those he loved and admired. He was particularly interested in a hunter named Ar-a-ne whom he had employed around the trading post. Having great confidence in him, Grant gave him unusual authority until it was discovered that the man was taking things from the store without permission. Ar-a-ne was recalcitrant about the matter, refusing to admit that he had done wrong, and consequently Grant was forced to dismiss him. Not long afterwards, Ar-a-ne went to another district where he met Lukesi Kidlapik, my guide and companion on this journey and a staunch Christian. After several months Ar-a-ne returned to Grant, and told him of his experiences, saying that from Kidlapik he had learned "the Jesus way." Lukesi had taught him the Ten Commandments and each day he said to himself, "Thou

Shalt Not Steal." He promised that if Grant would give him another chance he would be completely honest and that he was deeply sorry that he had been a thief.

Although the man seemed sincere, Grant was not convinced of the reality of his conversion and it was with hesitation that he decided to re-employ him, putting him on the whaler and not in the trading store. He had him carefully watched and, being Grant, frequently put temptation in his way. But from that day on Ar-a-ne gave abundant proof of his integrity. At the close of his tale Grant said, "I don't pretend to be a Christian but I acknowledge that you fellows have done a lot for the Eskimo and I shall always be glad to help you."

Grant went with us for the first few miles of our return journey to Lake Harbour, breaking the trail and thus encouraging our dogs. Then we parted never to meet again. It was not until three years later that I learned of his death. It was characteristic of the best that was in him. The *Seduisante* was wrecked in a gale. When he saw the end coming Grant ordered all the Eskimo ashore in the small boats, saving their lives at the expense of his own.

After our farewell to Grant our journey was fraught with many difficulties. During the previous ten days there had been several heavy snowstorms so that the traveling in Cyrus Field Bay and the Countess of Warwick Sound was slow and laborious. As the weather worsened we were very pleased to come across my friend Shar-ko and his companions, and finally stayed out a blizzard in his encampment. Early on the third day the fury of the elements diminished although it was not yet suitable for us to travel. That afternoon Shar-ko walked over to a nearby island and brought me back what he assured me were the remains of the Aborigines of Baffin Land—a thigh bone and part of the occipital, or head. Certainly they were ancient relics but at the time I could not say more. Three years later I took up in serious fashion the study of the pre-Eskimo people. According to Shar-ko's account the pre-Eskimo were smaller than the present Eskimo but very powerful and lived inland, seldom coming to the coast. His father had told him that his grandfather had actually seen one of these inland dwellers who, having trapped a bear in a pit and then killed it with a spear, carried it away on his back. This was proof of their strength, said Shar-ko, for an Eskimo could not do that. Across the years I talked with old Eskimo, not only in Baffin Land but in the Hudson Bay and Western Arctic areas and found that almost every group had tales of these people in some form or other. Sometimes the inland dwellers had two eyes, sometimes only one. One old man on the Foxe Channel coast told me that they were larger than the Eskimo and had hair on their bodies and tails like dogs!

What does it mean? Who can tell. Like so many of the Eskimo stories they seem mythical but may well contain a residue of historical truth. We might conclude, however, that they refer to contacts made by the Eskimo in the distant past with an earlier race of immigrants from Mongolia or with the North American Indians.

Another Eskimo brought me some bullets he had made out of iron pyrites—sulphide of copper—which he had found in the rocks close to where we were encamped. He had made these bullets the year the whaler *Snowdrop* had been wrecked because he could not get lead. He assured me that there were plenty of pyrites around but these came from a place he called "White Man's Island." The name was given because there the Eskimo had found many things including pieces of iron and wood which indicated the one-time presence of the white man. He further stated that from their fathers the Eskimo had heard that long, long ago white men had lived there and on a rocky ledge had beached their ships at high tide so as to be able to work at the under parts when the tide went out. After much questioning of some of the older men and women then and later, I was persuaded that this was where Frobisher and his ships spent the winter in 1578 and by oral tradition the facts had been kept by the Eskimo for over three hundred years.

At this same camp while we were waiting for the blizzard

to abate an incident took place which moved me more deeply than any experience that had yet been mine in Baffin Land. It showed so clearly the redeeming purpose of the Christian message. We had just finished our evening meal when two Eskimo came in, a man Ah-ling-ah and his wife Ke-ma-lo. I had met them on my outward journey but did not know them well. After a brief chat the others in the igloo went out, and I was puzzled to find myself so obviously left alone with this couple.

With hesitation they asked me to read the fourth chapter of the Gospel according to St. John, which I had read when they had met me before. They said I had spoken about the woman at the well of Samaria and I repeated it for them. After a silence Ke-ma-lo spoke and I listened as she told me her story.

Years before Ke-ma-lo had been married to a man named Matte. At that time she must have been a very attractive young woman and she lived happily with her husband, who was an angakok and the chief of his tribe. Matte, because of his local importance, had been made the right-hand man of the captain of an American whaler. The captain issued his commands to Matte and Matte passed them on to the other Eskimo.

After the custom adopted by the white men at that time, Matte's wife became the favorite concubine of the captain. She was always in attendance in his quarters, and from the time of arrival of the ship on the Baffin Land coast until it left at the finish of the whaling cruise, Ke-ma-lo lived with him. When the ship departed she received many valuable gifts and went back to her Eskimo husband. This was the accepted practice and no one resented it.

One year the captain decided that he could not part with Ke-ma-lo and so when the ship sailed south it took Ke-ma-lo with it. All winter the whaler was tied up in the harbor of New London, Connecticut, but for obvious reasons the captain would not let Ke-ma-lo go ashore. The dragging months were desperately lonely for the poor woman, virtually a prisoner in the captain's quarters, and her heart was like lead until the ship returned to the Arctic in the spring. She said that she was very happy to be back again with her husband.

Meanwhile Matte had unfortunately been in trouble with his tribesmen. They complained that he had told the whaling captain more than he should regarding the number of pelts in their possession. This forced them to trade everything with one man instead of trading part with him and part with the captain of the Scottish whaler. The hunters were very angry and warned Matte that unless he refrained from giving information to the American captain they would kill him. On the arrival of the ship, Matte was so filled with his own importance that he forgot his promise of silence and told the captain all that he wanted to know. Nothing was done at first and the Eskimo proceeded on the whaling cruise as usual. In the autumn after the ship had sailed for the south, this time leaving Ke-ma-lo with her husband, the men held a council and decided that Matte had violated customs of the Eskimo and must pay the penalty. One morning four men accompanied Matte on the usual hunt, but after they had gone out of sight of the village and while they were going over some rough ice, one man tripped Matte while two others instantly seized his arms and pounded him on the snow. The fourth man, Ah-ling-ah, who was sitting with me now, stabbed him through the heart with a knife and threw his body into the water through a crack in the ice. That night, according to the established custom, the man who struck the blow took Ke-ma-lo to wife and from that day on Ah-ling-ah and Ke-ma-lo had been living together as a married couple.

They had both been much touched by the story of the woman at the well of Samaria and as they grasped the truths of the Christian message they realized the enormity of such a crime. They knew now that through the redeeming love of their Saviour, their sin would be forgiven.

Years later I was visiting the people at Cape Dorset and to my surprise found Ke-ma-lo installed as cook at the Hudson's Bay Company post while Ah-ling-ah was the trusted handy man. The post manager spoke in the warmest possible terms of them and asked what I knew of their past history. I merely told him that I had known them at Frobisher Bay in 1911. I did not betray their secret.

At another encampment on the homeward journey I stayed with a man named Too-loo-gak whose wife had previously received some medical help from me. They were both most appreciative and did all in their power to make me comfortable. After supper the Eskimo crowded as usual into the igloo and in the course of the evening the conversation turned to adventures with bears. A man named Johnese whom I had not met before told me the following tale, the veracity of which was vouched for by frequent grunts and ejaculations from the others.

In those days the Eskimo were supplied with old-fashioned muzzle-loading rifles. Johnese went out one morning with his seal spear and food bag slung across his shoulders and carrying his rifle under his arm. All his dogs had died and the people were "very hungry," so he was determined not to return to the village until he had secured some food. After trudging for hours he came upon the footprints in the snow of several polar bears and proceeded to follow the tracks. These led to very rough broken ice.

While clambering over a hummock he came suddenly face to face with a large bear. Fortunately his rifle was loaded and it was the work of a moment to slip off the sealskin cover, take aim and kill the animal. Full of joy at his success, he began to skin his trophy. Hardly had he commenced when he heard an angry roar and to his consternation discovered another bear hurrying over the ice straight towards him. His muzzle-loading rifle was empty and there was not time to reload. Quickly he reached for his seal spear which was lying on the snow. As this bear drew near it rose on its hind legs to strike, but Johnese was waiting. With perfect aim he thrust his spear through the great creature's heart and it fell limp at his feet.

As he was examining this second animal, he was startled

to receive a blow from the rear which sent him sprawling over the snow. To his horror he discovered that without either rifle or spear he was facing a third bear. Quickly, he did the only possible thing. He took refuge behind an ice hummock. For a time the live bear sniffed around his dead brother beside which lay the spear. Getting no response to his sniffs, he uttered a roar and then passed on to smell the first bear. In doing this he drew farther away from the spear. The Eskimo was quick to take advantage of this opportunity. He slipped forward, recovered his lost weapon and dispatched the third bear with a swift thrust through the heart.

Three years later some Cape Dorset Eskimo told me of an even more remarkable experience. They were traveling westward after a visit to Lake Harbour when they passed a deserted snow hut. One of the men thought he saw something moving and almost immediately a large polar bear came out of the hut. Sniffing the air for a moment, the animal sensed the men, rose on his hind legs, uttered a roar, and made direct for the loaded sledge.

The attack was so sudden and unexpected that the Eskimo were unable to reach their rifles which were lashed to the sledge, and so they fled before the onslaught. When the bear reached the sledge, which was fifteen feet long and heavily laden, he walked around it, deliberately turned it over and carefully examined the load. Lashed to the rear he found fresh seal meat, which he immediately tore away and proceeded to eat. One of the Eskimo crept stealthily back towards the sledge hoping to secure his rifle. Each time he drew near, the bear stopped his feast, growled and appeared ready to attack. After having driven the man back repeatedly, the creature seemed to lose his apprehension and allowed him to get close enough to the sledge to grab his spear. With this weapon, he drove the bear off sufficiently to be able to unlash his rifle. Then the end was swift.

A yet more extraordinary tale was vouched for by Mr. C. Harding whom I had first met in James Bay where he was district manager for the Hudson's Bay Company. At a later date we met on the Mackenzie River and renewed our acquaintance.

A widowed woman and her son lived alone in a tiny wooden shack and maintained a meager existence by hunting caribou, foxes, rabbits, and ptarmigan. One winter during the long night there was a succession of terrible blizzards making hunting impossible. At last their small reserve of food gave out and starvation stared them in the face.

In the morning the old woman told her son that she must go out and visit her rabbit snares but would return as soon as possible and then he would be free to visit his fox traps. In this way she hoped that the lad might have a rabbit for his breakfast before starting off on the long day's trail. In an incredibly short time she returned and told her son to "hitch up the dogs and go and bring in the bear."

The boy was startled by the news and unbelievingly asked what she was talking about. When the mother replied that she had killed a bear, her son was seized with a horrible fear that the privations of the last few weeks had been too much for his mother and that she had now gone mad. "How could you possibly kill a bear," he asked her, "when you had neither gun nor axe?" Without explanation his mother insisted that she had killed a bear and again urged him to hurry and bring it in.

Still unbelieving but deeming it better to humor her, the boy went out and followed her footprints in the snow. Within a short distance from the shack he was amazed to see a large polar bear lying across the track. It seemed impossible that it should be dead so he approached it cautiously until he was sure that there was no sign of life. He was very puzzled because he could discover nothing to indicate how the animal had been killed. There was neither a wound nor a trace of blood.

The truth was this. When the old woman started off to visit her snares, she ran right into the bear at a quick turn in the trail. The bear stood up and seized her and all she was conscious of was trying to push the bear away with her hands. Then she fainted. Without being aware of doing so she had pushed her rabbitskin mitten into the bear's mouth before she had blacked out. The mitten had stuck in the animal's throat and choked him. Unconscious, woman and bear had lain side by side on the snow! When the woman recovered, she hastened back to tell her son and to offer a prayer of thanksgiving to God for this wonderful replenishing of their larder.

My return journey from Frobisher Bay across the mountains did not seem so wearisome until we were about to leave the sea ice and begin the long climb around the north end of the Grinnell Glacier. The Eskimo explained that a very powerful spirit dwelt in the glacier which they called An-yoo-e-tok, meaning "that which does not melt," and this spirit always objected to people coming near it; hence the storms of wind and snow that blew down upon us. It was their custom to placate the spirit by placing a token offering, such as a small piece of skin line or a woman's ornament, in a crevice of a big rock protruding out of the ice. When they had to cross open water in the bay past two large glacier outlets, they made a similar act of reverence, trusting that because of the spirit's anger the glacier would not shed an iceberg at that particular moment and capsize their boats.

The air in the uplands was crisp, clear, and cold, while the magic light on the snow-clad mountain peaks might be described after the fashion of Plutarch "as of spun-silk"—the ice-blue hush so different from the cruel terrifying blizzard that had come down from the Grinnell Glacier when we were traveling across the ice at the head of Frobisher Bay only three days before. At other times there was something awesome about the wild mountain gorges and scarred rocky slopes as we watched the snow clouds settle down upon them, blotting out everything from our view.

One menace always threatens the Arctic traveler in the spring of the year, when the sun is high in the heavens. The dazzling reflection from the snow quickly produces blindness which is exceedingly painful. The white man is not immune to this any more than is the Eskimo. On the advice of an oculist in Toronto, I wore a pair of amber-colored glasses and found them most helpful but I discovered that the Eskimo used two effective methods of their own for protecting their eyes. They rubbed some lampblack from the blubber lamp on the sides of the nose and around the eyes or they wore protectors of bone or wood with slits cut for the eyes. This protector has been praised by many Arctic and Antarctic explorers because, unlike those made of glass, it does not become fogged.

When we finally arrived at Aulatsevik the Eskimo gave me a grand welcome. That night, after evening prayer, they told me that they had a new name for me. I was no longer to be called "the young teacher" but In-nook-tah-kaub, that is, "one of the family." Of all the honors that have been accorded me during the course of my life, none has been more cherished than this tribute from my children by adoption.

When I got home I found Bilby quite unwell and it was some weeks before we were able to visit the camps again. However, June found us both at a place called Pumeooyang near Icy Cape. Here the Eskimo took me to the foundations of some dwellings of the Too-neet, the pre-Eskimo. These buildings were in very fair condition except that the roofs had collapsed. The walls were still standing about two feet above the level of the ground and the floors about one foot below the ground level, while the rib bones of whales were lying inside the walls and the shape of the outside porch was clearly visible. Two of my guides lay down inside the houses to show me that they were too small to accommodate present-day Eskimo. Since the Eskimo himself is small by our standards, the Too-neet seemed to have been of diminutive stature.

The people were in good health and spirits and attended the teaching services most faithfully. Since I was going out on furlough in September, I was anxious to find out how much progress the people had made as a result of our teaching. I told them that before I left there would be examinations, and prizes for those who did well.

They all seemed genuinely anxious to prove that they had been able to master some of the things that had seemed so strange and difficult to them when we had first arrived in their country. The results were most encouraging. They also showed that the Eskimo were no different from their neighbors to the south. Some were very quick and intelligent, some were slow and dull-witted, but among those who had received careful teaching great progress had been made and in this lay our hope for the future.

As the summer passed the thought of furlough was increasingly in Bilby's mind and mine. Each day of July we looked for the whaler *Active* which would almost certainly bring us news. Each day she failed to appear. No one who has not experienced it can realize the tension caused by this sort of waiting, nor the devastating effect it can have upon mind and spirit. It takes a stable and controlled nature to avoid display of unchecked emotions just before "ship time" in the Arctic. The Eskimo thought that since the ice pack was so heavy she had probably gone on into Hudson Bay after whales and walrus and would try to get in to us on the return voyage. Then suddenly on the tenth of August the *Active* came. From Captain Murray's viewpoint speed was the need of the hour and before the clock went round, the mica miners and their supplies had been landed, eighty Eskimo taken on board to help with the whaling and about three hundred dispatched for caribou, seal, or for work at the mica mine. The captain did not have time to talk much with us but he promptly gave us a letter from Peck. What excitement was ours!

Peck said that two men to replace us and all the supplies were being sent north on the schooner *Burleigh* due to arrive about the middle of August. This meant that the schooner might arrive at any moment. We ourselves were to have all in readiness for departure as soon as she came in. Peck also stated that from mid-August on we were to keep a pilot stationed somewhere at the entrance of the fjord to take the ship up the channel to Lake Harbour.

Despite this happy news Bilby was overcome with gloom.

He had a dark foreboding that the *Burleigh* would never arrive. Indeed he was so convinced that he insisted on asking Captain Murray then and there if we could get passage back on the *Active* when she returned from Hudson Bay! He reasoned that since the *Active* was a steam auxiliary vessel under a skilled and experienced captain and had only got through the heavy ice after weeks of battle, it was not likely that a small sailing schooner from Nova Scotia under a captain not familiar with Arctic navigation would be able to succeed. But I tried to reason otherwise and to relieve Bilby's depression by playing records for him—almost the only interest we shared outside our work.

We chose Noo-voo-le-a as pilot since he had so successfully guided the *Lorna Doone* to Lake Harbour two years before. His vantage point was an island at the mouth of the fjord and there he was established with two other families to keep a constant lookout for the vessel. Bilby stayed at the mission getting all in first-class order while I divided my time between the watchers on the island and the Eskimo who came in to Lake Harbour for supplies on the week end.

September arrived and still there was no sign of the *Burleigh*. The weeks dragged on. It was now the middle of the month and when I returned to the mission on the second Tuesday of September with seal meat and some wild fowl for our larder, but had to report "no ship," poor Bilby looked at me with sad questioning eyes and replied simply, "I told you so."

Finally, on Sunday, September 17, we were startled to see a black speck on the southeastern horizon and still more surprised when a whiff of black smoke appeared above it. This could only mean a ship. But it could not be the mission vessel for Peck had written that he was coming on a schooner. What did it mean?

The excitement was intense. Quickly we launched the whaleboat. Noo-voo-le-a sat at the tiller while the others rowed and soon we took up the position he wanted the oncoming steamer to head for. Slowly but steadily the vessel drew near us. With our glasses we could see men walking on the bridge and on the deck. Then we could read the name on the bow—*Stella Maris*. Suddenly we saw Peck with his white hair and whiskers standing at the rail and waving his hat. Beside him stood two young men also waving.

We had hardly clambered aboard the ship and presented Noo-voo-le-a to the captain before there was further excitement. Another ship rounded the east end of Big Island and ran up a signal in flags: "Send me a pilot." After a hurried conference the *Stella Maris* ran up the answer: "Follow me." After the quiet weary vigil of the past weeks I found it hard to believe that now *two* ships had actually arrived. When I asked Peck why he had been delayed and why the *Burleigh* had not come, what a story of frustration and disappointment and ultimate success he had to tell!

The *Burleigh* with Peck and the new helpers, Broughton and Sainsbury, on board had left Sidney, Nova Scotia, just two months before. After the usual encounters with stormy seas and ice fields, the schooner was found to have developed a very serious leak. From six to ten inches of water flooded into her hold every hour so that the hand pumps had to be worked continuously day and night to keep the ship afloat. There was no choice but to return south. The mission cargo, however, was landed at Okkak on the Labrador coast where the Moravian Brethren had a mission. They kindly arranged to store the supplies and give hospitality to Broughton and Sainsbury while Peck took the mail boat back to St. John's, Newfoundland.

Because at that time of the year the cod fishing was at its height it proved impossible for Peck to charter a schooner. Not knowing what else to do, he approached the Minister of Fisheries for the Newfoundland Government. The minister most kindly agreed that the *Stella Maris,* which delivered mail to the few settlers living north of Nain on the Labrador, could make the trip to Lake Harbour after completing her regular work. But she must be back at Nain in time to meet the mail steamer on its return from St. John's.

Hard astern came a motorboat from the other ship and we were naturally overwhelmed with curiosity as to her business. We all thought that it must be a Canadian Government ship on its way back from Fort Churchill on Hudson Bay. But what brought them into Lake Harbour? When the launch came alongside the *Stella Maris* we saw no sign of government officials and no gold braid. To our amazement they proved to be officers of the Hudson's Bay Company and their ship, the *Pelican,* had seventy tons of cargo to be landed! It was their intention, they said, to establish a fur trading post at Lake Harbour. This too was most exciting and almost unbelievable news.

Noo-voo-le-a went off with the H.B.C. men in their motorboat and in a few hours the *Pelican* dropped anchor near the *Stella Maris.* The representatives of the Hudson's Bay Company bombarded us with questions about conditions in this part of the country. Mr. Ralph Parsons, who seemed to be in charge of the operations, kindly suggested that since time was of the essence the boats from the *Pelican* could help to take the freight from the *Stella Maris* to the shore, and so speed the discharging of mission cargo.

Bilby and I had little sleep that night and we were up and dressed at four o'clock in the morning. After a hurried breakfast we went the rounds of the tents to ask help from the people. By six o'clock, every available Eskimo, young and old, men, women and children, was at work. All day long we toiled carrying the supplies from the water's edge up over the rocks to the misson house. As a result of this magnificent co-operation it was a record in unloading. By five o'clock that same afternoon all supplies had been landed and the *Stella Maris,* with Peck, Bilby, and myself on board, weighed anchor leaving Broughton and Sainsbury to carry on the work. Bilby hoped to return in a year's time; I when my necessary theological studies were completed.

The new Hudson's Bay Company's post was under the management of a Mr. and Mrs. Ford of Newfoundland and Labrador. They both spoke Eskimo fluently, loved the people, and showed much interest and sympathy regarding the evangelization of the Eskimo. They kindly promised Peck to give our replacements all the help they could.

Noo-voo-le-a piloted the *Stella Maris* safely out into the Hudson Strait and then left us. I shall never forget that parting. I had come to know and love the Eskimo. I had stayed in their villages and as a paying guest in their igloos. I had been with them in days of plenty and days of near starvation. I had shared their personal joys, sorrows, and disappointments. They had proved themselves to be true and devoted friends and had named me "one of the family." I felt towards them as such. When I was standing on the deck with a big lump in my throat, Peck put his hand on my shoulder and said that he understood how I was feeling, adding, "I have often told audiences in England that while the Arctic is a cold and cruel country there is nothing warmer than the clasp of an Eskimo's hand." How often in after years I was to remember the words of this old white-haired veteran.

The trip south was both pleasant and interesting. At Hopedale Captain (afterwards Commander) McMillan came on board. He had been with Peary on his last trip to Greenland when he (Peary) claimed to have discovered the North Pole. McMillan was a most fascinating traveling companion. Among other things he was able to tell me about my young Eskimo friend Mene Wallace. McMillan said that Mene had been very unhappy on his return to Greenland and had found it most difficult to adapt himself to life with his own people. When he described the skyscrapers in New York as high as the hill beside the Greenland village; the sledges that traveled with great speed without dogs; the street lighting and all the other wonders—he was dubbed "the big liar." In less than two years poor Mene had died of lung trouble.

At Hawke's Harbour we met Dr. Grenfell. I had just read his Nobel lectures and was thrilled to meet him there in his proper setting among his beloved fisherfolk. The thing about Grenfell that impressed me then, and on several later occasions when he stayed with us, was his sympathetic understanding of human nature and his genuine devotion to Jesus Christ as Lord and Master.

When at last we entered the harbor of St. John's the twinkling lights brought a nostalgic rush of longing for all that the word civilization implies. The syncopated noises of the city—the rattle of horse-drawn carts over the narrow cobbled streets, the puffing, whistling, and clanging of the bells in the freight yards and along the water front seemed to us sweet music.

From St. John's, we traveled across Newfoundland on the twisting and narrow-gauged Reid–Newfoundland Railway. Then on board the S.S. *Bruce* from Port-au-Basque to North Sydney. I was strangely pleased to find that the vessels on which I was returning to civilization had all come from the Clyde in Scotland. It was as if old friends guided me home. At last we reached Toronto. Twenty-seven months had passed. As I thought of what I had left behind I hoped that what I had done in those months had been acceptable to the Lord God.

INTERLUDE I

As soon as I reached Toronto I was plunged into a multitude of activities, the most important being the completion of my theological studies. It had been arranged that I should be ordained to the diaconate with little delay and priested before I returned to the Arctic twenty-two months later, in the summer of 1913. Mine was, I think, the first ordination to be held in the present chapel of Wycliffe College which was then just completed.

My time was fully occupied. It was difficult to do justice to my studies because of the pressure of speaking and preaching engagements, and I found that my mind turned constantly to the land and to the children of my adoption as I tried to assess with candor and honesty our successes and failures in the work.

Bilby and I had begun our task by accepting what religious beliefs each Eskimo already had, and from that premise we had tried to lead them out of the darkness of paganism and fear into the light of Him Who is the Light of the world. Of necessity all growth that is sturdy is slow and the adjustment of spiritual values gradual. Only as they yielded their wills to their new-found Master could we hope for permanent results. As I pursued my work in Toronto I was reassured by the conviction that to win these pagan people for the Christ of God had not been a haunting chimera. It was *a continuing challenge, requiring a strong venturesome faith. That faith I had.*

On April 13, 1913, I was priested and only two months later, in June, 1913, I was married to Miss Helen Grace Gillespie who had long lived with her cousin Miss Julia Greenshields at 2 Elmsley Place, Toronto. Ever since my arrival in Canada both Miss Greenshields and Miss Gillespie had been extraordinarily kind to me and had taken every interest in my welfare and success.

I shall not attempt to describe what it cost to face, only six weeks after our marriage, two years or more of separation. Little did we realize at the time that this was but the prelude to a life spent more apart than together, but one in which my dear wife always gave me willing and prayerful support, since I was absent on "the King's business." The desire of her life, as of mine, was that I should keep this tryst.

☆ 9. Return to the Arctic ☆

ON THE AFTERNOON of Thursday, July 17, 1913, I found my-self standing on the bridge deck of the S.S. *Nascopie* as she steamed down the mighty St. Lawrence, leaving the great city of Montreal wreathed in a haze of heat and smoke. As I had already learned and was to continue to learn throughout my Arctic career, one of the most trying aspects of northern travel is the uncertainty of one's movements. Delays, unex-pected and hurried departures, last-minute rearranging of plans and itineraries are unavoidable because of ice, wind, and weather, but no Arctic traveler will deny that they are vexing to the spirit. I suppose one should add that they are developers of adjustability and patience. At any rate, this July there had been a forced delay in the *Nascopie*'s sailing, dragging on a day or two at a time until it stretched into a fortnight and all the while the *Nascopie*'s passengers were required to stay in or near Montreal with bags packed. So it was now a relief to know that we had actually started on our voyage to Baffin Land.

In contrast to the *Lorna Doone* of my first trip, a fifty-two-ton sailing schooner with no auxiliary power, this icebreaker of some 2,500 tons carrying capacity was fitted with electric light and all modern conveniences.

In the early afternoon on Tuesday, July 22, we cast anchor opposite the Hudson's Bay Company's post in the spruce-bound harbor at Cartwright, Labrador, and within three hundred yards of the company's ship *Pelican*. Almost before the captain of the *Nascopie* rang down "Finished with engines," boats of all kinds came alongside bringing the H.B.C. district manager Swaffield, Captain Smith of the *Pelican*, Dr. Paddon, who was in charge of the Grenfell Hospital, the Rev. J. Kirby, the Anglican missionary for that part of the coast, and many others.

We were told that two vessels passing through the Strait of Belle Isle in the fog two days ahead of the *Nascopie* had collided and sunk. It was with all sincerity that, on the Sunday following in the little church, we returned thanks for journeying mercies and prayed for all who travel by land and sea.

For thirteen days the crews of both ships were kept busy exchanging cargo. When all had been completed, I was transferred to the *Pelican* and on Monday, August 4, the two ships parted company—the *Nascopie* for Hudson Bay and James Bay, while the *Pelican* was to call at the various H.B.C. posts on the Labrador coast, Hudson Strait, and Ungava Bay.

After traveling on the *Nascopie*, the *Pelican* seemed cramped, though more convenient than the *Lorna Doone* except that we were allowed only one gallon of fresh water each day for cooking and washing. The *Pelican* was a three-masted barque with small auxiliary power, originally built for the British Admiralty as a frigate. Her guns had been removed except two small brass cannon used for signaling purposes. The ship had square yards on the fore- and main-masts but not on the mizzenmast. The wooden-stocked iron anchors hung from catheads on either side of the bow as if to protect the finely carved figurehead of a handsome female in flowing draperies. The brass fittings and teak deckhouse with skylight all gave a superior touch to the appearance of the old ship. In the saloon the marble-topped sideboard with brass guardrail; the small English coal-burning stove with brass andirons; the narrow alleyway from deck to saloon beautifully paneled in mahogany; and doors of dark highly

polished mahogany with cut-glass handles were all suggestive
of the early days when she was commissioned as one of Her
Majesty's men-of-war. The rooms were lighted by small port-
holes and hanging wax-candle lamps. Although her speed
without sail was not more than four or five knots she could
make nine knots with all sail set and running before a strong
breeze.

It brought a surge of pride to my heart when five years
later the *Pelican* won great distinction during the First World
War. In 1918 when crossing the Atlantic on her return from
Hudson Bay with a cargo of fur valued at one and a quarter
million dollars, she was attacked by a German submarine.
Owing to the skill of her captain "she was able by means of
zig-zag and the effective use of her defense gun to reach port
safely." Not so the German submarine; and the Admiralty
bounty was given to the captain and crew.

Captain Smith, the first mate Edmund Mack, and the crew
all received me kindly. There were four young Scotsmen on
board who had joined the company in Aberdeen as apprentice fur traders and were en route to various posts in the
North. Their names were Cantley, commonly called Jim;
Stewart, known as "Lofty" because of his great height; Livingstone, who was tall and slight in build and wore very tight
trousers, and McGibbon, who had a trick of standing with
his hands in his pockets, smoking his pipe and making quiet
caustic remarks when the others were at work. They became
quite popular on board ship and two of them gained speedy
promotion in the fur trade, and have remained my good
friends to this day.

After we left Cartwright we ran into a stiff wind and it was
a thrilling experience to see the crew led by the bosun
McPhail hasten up the rigging with catlike dexterity to the
fore-lower tops'l and shorten sail.

Every Sunday throughout the voyage, whether on shore or
at sea, we were able to hold services for the crew and the
smallest attendance was twenty-two officers and men.

Each port of call had its points of interest but Rigoulette,

Labrador, was outstanding because it was here that the famous Scotsman, Donald Smith, afterwards Lord Strathcona, began his career with the Hudson's Bay Company. I sat at the desk where he had worked for thirteen years so long ago and was allowed to write at it letters to be taken south by the coastal mail boat. Here, too, Mr. Swaffield and his wife arranged a concert and dance in order to celebrate the arrival of the *Pelican*.

Our next port of call was Davies Inlet. Here I was asked to visit a dying woman who had been indisposed for nearly five months and, with the exception of one visit from a Moravian missionary, had seen neither doctor nor clergyman during her illness. The shack in which she was living was typical of those on the Labrador. On the outside it looked cheerless and bleak but the inside was scrupulously clean. Captain Smith, who knew the sufferer well, introduced me and knelt with us as we prayed and, after commending her to the ever-loving and merciful Saviour, I gave her the Blessing. It was an inspiration to find this poor lonely widowed woman unafraid of death and calmly content to leave all in the hands of her Creator. I had been impressed by Captain Smith's attitude to this woman and during this voyage came to appreciate the fact that there is a virility and attractiveness about men of the sea that is seldom found in those who dwell in the seething rush of the cities.

At last the red-letter day came on August 21 when we arrived at the entrance to the fjord leading to Lake Harbour. Noo-voo-le-a was again on hand to take in the *Pelican*. It gave me an indescribable joy to see him and the other Eskimo with him. Three hours later we cast anchor in the harbor and it was with genuine pleasure that Bilby and I shook hands. He welcomed me most cordially back to the land and the people of my adoption.

Almost at once the tragedy of Broughton came up and Bilby was able to give me the full details of the story. It will be remembered that Percy Broughton was one of the two young men who had come out in 1911 to replace Bilby and myself. The following year, 1912, Broughton was returning from a visit to the Eskimo at the Saddleback Islands and hoped to reach the mission before nightfall. It was a glorious spring morning in March when he started out from a camp about thirty miles east of Lake Harbour. Broughton, who had tremendous vitality, thought that by proceeding ahead of the sledges he would save time, since his tracks would encourage the dogs to press forward. So while his Eskimo guides were loading the sledges and harnessing the dogs he set out. He believed that he knew the way and trudged along calmly and contentedly. After traveling for some hours he became conscious of the fact that the others had not overtaken him.

Although he scanned the vast expanse of ice carefully, there was no sign of the sledges. He had been following various sledge tracks on the snow and had felt sure that he had taken the right direction, but now his confidence was shaken. He decided that it would be best to continue to follow the sledge tracks and after several more hours of walking they brought him to an igloo, but it was deserted. As the slanting rays of the evening sun told plainly that darkness was approaching, he decided to spend the night in the deserted dwelling, although he had neither sleeping bag nor food. After a fitful slumber he awoke in the early morning when the moon illuminated the landscape. There was no wind and the whole world was shrouded in silence. Again he tried to sleep but it was useless, so he arose and started on his way once more. Soon he became entangled in great hummocks of ice along the shore. The tide was rising and the flood water had come up through the cracks in the ice and made great pools between the ice ridges. As he was working his way over the ice, the wind began to rise, the moon was clouded, and he stumbled and fell into the water. That morning the temperature fell to twenty degrees below zero and, hungry and cold, the wretched man had to make the best of it. He sat down, took off his skin boots and stockings to empty them of the water, but before he could get them on again they were partly frozen, with the result that when he started to walk both his boots and his clothes split open, resulting in severe frostbite. All that day he stumbled and crawled on hands and knees, but neither saw nor heard any sign of a living soul. How he passed the second night he never could tell, but the following day he drew near a settlement and on being welcomed by the Eskimo fell into a faint from which he did not recover for twelve hours. His feet and other vital parts were frozen, but the Eskimo thawed them out against their own warm bodies. However, three weeks later his toes had to be amputated and an emergency operation was performed by his companion Sainsbury on another part of his body. The following autumn he returned to civilization. In spite of the efforts of the most skilled doctors in Toronto he died in the spring of 1916. It was a tragic end to the promising career of a brave young man.

Even after all these years words fail me when I think of the warmth of the greetings that I received from the Eskimo at this time of my return. The memory of this day often cheered me in times when my pathway seemed lonely and desolate.

I was sorry but not surprised that Bilby was again in poor health. Because of his unsatisfactory physical condition he had done very little traveling by sledge and dog team but he had been unremitting in his efforts to teach the people whenever they came in to trade at the Hudson's Bay Company post. He had held special classes for those who wished to present themselves for baptism, and thirty-one adults had been baptized. Later when I was able to talk with them individually I saw that the reality of their faith as shown in their daily living fully justified Bilby's belief that they were ready for baptism. The first fruits of our labor had appeared to be slow in coming, but here was the beginning of the harvest.

My joy, however, was not unmixed with fear. I knew well some of the difficulties and dangers which would beset them. They would need to be steadfast and strong in their attempt to lead Christian lives amid the paganism that surrounded them.

And what of baptism for the children? This question vexed me and after Bilby sailed away on the *Pelican* I had no one with whom to discuss it. I longed to have someone more experienced than myself to tell me what to do. As I turned the question over and over in my mind I came to understand the necessity for the children to be baptized and received into the family of God. The children of Christian parents were either members of Christ's family or they were not. Christian or pagan—which? There was no neutral ground. So hereafter when I baptized the father and mother of a family I baptized their children too.

With the departure of the *Pelican* the curtain fell over the outside world for another year. I applied myself with all diligence to building a little church and attending to the spiritual and also the physical needs of the Eskimo. There were a great many cases of what we called "ship's cold" due to the fact that each year after the annual visit of the supply ship the natives develop bronchitis. This meant that every day I had to make one or more visits to the Eskimo tents with medicine and food.

I made arrangements to leave the mission for a nearby camp on the third of December. There was little sunlight at that time of year and on that particular day the sky was overcast so that the coast line seemed sullen and uninviting, while the air was hushed as in the sleep of death. After six hours' slow traveling I was feeling hungry, tired, and depressed when I heard a chuckle from Noo-soo-pik, my driver, and saw the faint yellow lights of the settlement showing just above the level of the sea ice over which we were moving. What a welcome sight it was with its suggestion of warmth, the companionship of the Eskimo and food and drink.

At this camp I was able to get into close touch with the people not only at the services but when visiting them in their own dwellings. Our simple friendly talks there were of untold value because questions were asked and answered, and a deeper fellowship established.

One of the things that moved me deeply was the affectionate trust they placed in me. They never seemed to doubt but that I wanted to do everything possible for them. They came to me with their joys and sorrows, their aches and pains, their successes and failures, their problems and, yes, their private quarrels, and seemed content to follow my advice. The companionship was mutual for I enjoyed visiting them and appreciated the smiles with which I was welcomed. I came to realize how little a human being requires to meet the fundamental needs and how content one can be with that little. I do not mean to say that I took delight in every aspect of life among the Eskimo. When I saw the family squatting on the skin-covered sleeping bench at mealtime pulling and tearing at the raw flesh of a recently killed seal, the blood oozing out between their fingers and dripping from their hands and chin, I felt nauseated and repelled beyond measure. Yet I asked myself, Was not this the way our Anglo-Saxon forefathers in Britain ate only a few centuries ago? They, like my Eskimo friends, had to wage a perpetual war with nature, with wildlife and with enemies known and unknown. Such thoughts kept me humble and helped me to look upon my people with sympathy and understanding.

Before leaving this camp and returning to the mission I gave a party to express my appreciation of all the kindnesses I had received. First, everyone had a dish of rice mixed with canned boiled beef served hot. Then hardtack biscuit and steaming coffee sweetened with molasses were handed to each one coming forward with mug or bowl. When the food had been consumed I set up a small mirrorscope given to me by a friend in Toronto and began the entertainment with photographs taken during my first sojourn among them. They were amazed to see themselves, their friends, and the places they knew. I then took them for a trip in southern Canada, the United States, Great Britain, and the Continent. This was followed by a series of views showing foreign sledges, from a milk cart drawn by a dog in Holland to the latest Pullman trains and flying machines, as airplanes were then called. I hoped with these pictures, many of which were in color, to open the minds of the Eskimo by giving them some knowledge of an outside world so different from their own.

On Sunday December 21 the little church at Lake Harbour was formally opened. It was far from being complete but the intense cold had made it impossible to do anything more to it for the present. Even in its unfinished state it represented to me the fulfillment of a great desire. I had longed for a place of worship that should be clean and attractive, where services could be held amid surroundings conducive to reverence and devotion. I had talked seriously with the natives about the purpose of the new building, emphasizing that it was God's house, and they conducted themselves with exceptional decorum during the first service which was held that morning for both Eskimo and white.

Robert F. Flaherty was present at the opening. He was in charge of a mining and photographic expedition wintering more than a hundred miles to the west. He was to become famous as a motion picture producer of such unusual films as *Nanook of the North*. At the time, however, we thought of him only as a vivid, entertaining guest, an excellent violinist, and an incomparable raconteur.

As was to be expected, Christmas Day was a busy one. Mr. Parsons, district superintendent of the Hudson's Bay Company, breakfasted with me at the mission house, a pleasant change for me from my usual solitude. So also did over eighty Eskimo. Then we all crossed the harbor to the little church where a special Christmas service was held with its message of the Father's Love for all "the inhabitants of the world." After church each Eskimo received a small present and what was left over was distributed in the form of a scramble, which always has had such charm for these unspoiled children of nature. Afterwards we went down to the H.B.C. post where games and contests continued until the dinner bell rang. Mr. Parsons had kindly invited me to dine with him and it was a great pleasure to sit down to a meal regarding the preparation of which I had taken no thought. We were a merry party as befitted the occasion.

Finally we had another service with a full turnout of Eskimo and white, and at this I showed lantern slides. At about ten o'clock I returned across the harbor to the mission house, physically tired and quite alone but full of thankfulness and contentment for the privilege of being God's messenger to these dear people. After reading and rereading my letters I went to bed.

That winter I made a three months' trip along the Baffin Land coast to King's Cape at the extreme west end of Hudson Strait. Up to the time that I set out on this journey I had had the help of my faithful friend Ing-mil-ayo, his wife Ite, and a boy. Between them they had taken care of most of my domestic needs and we had been happy together. Now a heavy shadow was falling upon us because cataracts were forming on Ing-mil-ayo's eyes. We realized that he could not accompany me on this proposed trip, and the grief on both sides was heartfelt because our companionship was true and real. In the dark days when life must indeed have been dreary to the old man he was very wonderful. "I have so much," he kept reiterating. "Soon I shall see the King in His beauty. I shall be able to see Jesus and the Apostles and Moses and Abraham and all the others."

I remembered the first day I had met him four years previously. Then he was a pagan but I had liked him and we soon became friends. I called all the old men "father" but had come to refer to Ing-mil-ayo as "my father" and he called me his "material for a son." As long as he lived our friendship remained deep and strong. Would God there were more Christians with the faith of this erstwhile heathen.

Before Ing-mil-ayo left me, I secured the services of Joseph Pudlo, who has already come into this story. That former doubter whose teaching I had begun had been baptized by Bilby when I was on furlough and had since shown himself a sincere Christian as well as a diligent and successful hunter. At one point I wrote in my diary, "Pudlo returned today from the interior. He secured twenty-two caribou."

Our friendship that lasted through many years was broken

only at his death. He had the honor of being the first full-time native catechist in the service of the mission. Together we traveled far and wide by sledge and dog team in order to reach hitherto unvisited tribes. It was on such expeditions, sometimes extending for three months on end, that I came fully to understand and appreciate my fellow worker. It is sufficient to say that with each expedition my love and admiration for him increased. From time to time he was perplexed as new vistas of truth opened up before him through the study of the Scriptures. It was then he waited and prayed, and prayed and waited until clear light was given. Later when he prayed aloud, the curtain that hid from my gaze the deep wells of his soul was drawn aside, and I became conscious of the richness of his spiritual experience and of the depth of his nature.

After leaving Pudlo's wife and child with some of her relatives, we started on our journey west which proved long, hard, and physically exhausting with the usual sordid discomforts. Traveling when the temperature is sub-zero necessitates the expenditure of much energy because the heart and organs of respiration and circulation are taxed to the limit of their capacity.

It was our practice on this and subsequent trips to make an early start each morning. When the illuminated hands of my watch pointed to somewhere between four and five o'clock we climbed out of our sleeping bags to begin the day's work. First we turned our caribou-skin clothing inside out and beat it with a stick so that the accumulated body moisture which had frozen during the night now dropped to the floor of the igloo in a foamlike powdered snow. While Pudlo harnessed the dogs I cooked breakfast. After morning prayers the sledge was again loaded and, aided by the combined strength of the men and dogs, plowed its way across the hummocky ice once more.

There is nothing, I think, more monotonous than journeying steadily day after day over the vast fields of ice and snow with little to relieve the white sameness save perhaps occasional outcroppings of windswept rocks. There is no glamour about such travel. It is extremely hard work.

When the surface was difficult, we adopted the plan already referred to of attaching a thong of walrus hide to the rear of the sledge and passing it over the shoulder. In this way, it was possible to add considerably to the motive power, but the arm and shoulder muscles suffered terribly from the unaccustomed strain. The thong seems to cut through the clothing and the skin becomes bruised and blistered so that the shoulder feels as if it were being seared with a red-hot iron. At the end of the day agony was completed when the perspiration froze between the shoulder blades.

When a settlement was not reached by nightfall, we built a little hut of snow big enough for us to crawl into but not high enough to stand upright in. After the dogs were fed, we then closed the entrance hole with a block of snow, spread our sleeping bags on the snow floor, and began preparations for the first meal we had had since long before sunrise. A small primus lamp I had purchased in Toronto was put into use and soon the ice in the kettle was converted into boiling water for a warm drink of cocoa. A few hard biscuits were produced, while some boiled beans were thawed out in a frying pan. When these simple preliminaries had been completed, Pudlo and I knelt and gave thanks to God for the food He had given. In a very short time the cocoa, ship biscuits, and beans had disappeared. We then rubbed our plates, mugs, and spoons in the snow so that they might be relatively clean and in a few minutes curled up in our sleeping bags.

It was a common thing to start out in the morning with the stars shining brightly overhead in a clear sky only to find by noon that the sky had become sulky and overcast. Then with all haste an igloo must be built, for traveling during a bad storm is impossible. Gradually the wind increased in fury, driving the snow before it and shutting out both sun and landscape. Then there was nothing to do but wait until the storm had spent itself, which generally meant two to three days.

There is something terribly vindictive about an Arctic blizzard and one has great sympathy with the pagan Eskimo's feeling that some malevolent spirit is angry and seeking to destroy both man and beast. When one watched the snow driven madly by the gale across the landscape and swirling around the hut, or listened to it as it pounded on the domed roof and howled its weird song in the tiny ventilator, there crept into the heart a prayer of thankfulness that one was safe in a warm place, and another was offered for any unfortunate traveler who might be caught on a journey and unable to find shelter. In the Arctic nature seems to take a fiendish delight in making things as uncomfortable as possible for the invader. After a few years' experience the newcomer finds the strength to respect and accept the cruelty of these conditions, for it forces him to consider the eternal values more deeply.

On this trip there were many wonderful displays of the aurora. My diary at this time also contains frequent accounts of mock suns and coronae. In civilization there is a common belief that the aurora borealis is something largely peculiar to the Arctic regions and it is supposed that the farther north one goes the more spectacular will be the display of this phenomenon. Both of these suppositions are wrong. In old Chinese writings dating back some three thousand years, accounts of the occurrence of northern lights have been found. At least it is difficult to believe that they can refer to anything else for they speak of observing "red vapors arising in the northern heavens," and "sometimes the fiery sheen was circled by a large white bow and flaming rays pierced the vapor." Aristotle and others also described the appearance of what must be considered the aurora borealis.

The ancients made many attempts to explain the phenomenon but without success from a scientific aspect. Even today the whole question of the aurora borealis arouses strong differences of opinion. Some years ago the *Journal of the Royal Astronomical Society of Canada* contained a series of letters written by men who had been in the northlands of the Dominion and who claimed to have heard the aurora. They described it in varying ways as a "rustling of silk taffeta," a "crackling sound," and the like.

One of the earliest statements I have read describing the sound of the aurora in Canada is that made by Samuel Hearne in 1771. In that year he made his historic trip from Fort Churchill across the hinterland to Coppermine River and back, and in his journal he goes into detail about the aurora and its sounds. We see therefore that the claim is by no means new. If it is asserted by an observer that no sound can be heard, then he is told that is simply due to his defective hearing, and of course it is exceedingly difficult, if not impossible, to prove a negative. Scientific men first tried to discover the nature of the aurora by considering its general appearance and it is certainly one of the most fascinating phenomena connected with the Arctic. The strange clarity and the iridescent pale greens and blues of the night sky make the aurora look like a supernatural searchlight throwing beams across the vaulted dome.

No two displays of the aurora are alike either in the glory of their colors or brightness of their form. Sometimes they arrange themselves into fluttering folds with colors ranging from violet to pale yellow and deep gold with touches of crimson; now they dissolve and disappear, now they rush madly back in wreaths of glorious brightness. The rapidity of the number and the brilliancy of the flash lights cause the observer to stand in hushed and solemn awe. It is a thrilling display but with the thrill there comes something of an ominous feeling, and in this the modern spectator finds himself akin to the ancients. In a lecture some years ago Mr. Gar Elson of the National Research Council of Canada demonstrated that most of the colors of the aurora can be obtained when a discharge of high-voltage electricity passes through glass tubes filled with nitrogen, helium, and oxygen. In this way the colors can be accounted for.

The aurora borealis has for long been associated with sunspot activity and it has been claimed that the aurorae are caused by electrically charged particles from the sun which enter the atmosphere and cause the luminescence of the upper rarefied atmosphere.

Experts seem to agree that there is a close relationship between magnetic storms and aurorae and since magnetic storms and sunspots are also closely correlated, it would appear that there is a connection between sunspots and aurorae. It is also believed that the particles emitted by the sun, or at least some of them, are electrons. The aurora is also supposed to play pranks. Some nights in the Far North when the aurora is brightest, the static puts the radio out of commission while on other occasions when the aurora is equally bright, there is little or no interference.

A very logical theory of the cause of the aurora has been given by Dr. Hulbert of Washington who regards the aurora as produced by the discharge of high-speed electrons of terrestrial origin caused by eruptions on the sun "which produce a tremendous release of ultraviolet energy." He shows that "the field of the lines of force which lead back to the earth is about twenty-five degrees from the North Magnetic Pole. As soon as the electrons enter a region of atmosphere which is sufficiently well condensed, the phenomena known as aurora borealis is produced." When traveling in the North, particularly in the Eastern Arctic, we have found practical verification of Dr. Hulbert's theory regarding the field of the lines of force. Once the traveler gets north of the field of the lines of force, the aurora is brightest not in the north but in the south.

The white man is inclined to smile at the explanations of the aurora given by the Eskimo but it seems to me that since we ourselves cannot successfully explain this mystery of the upper atmosphere we might well refrain from criticism.

To return to the story of our journey from Lake Harbour to the west coast of Baffin Land, Pudlo and I were always welcomed as "much longed for friends." At a village called Itinik, of which Mary Er-kak-tah-lik was the head, we accepted the offer of hospitality in a new and very large igloo. Here Mary, her two married sons, and their children dwelt

but they made room for Pudlo and me and their thoughtfulness for our comfort could not have been greater.

A few months before our arrival Mary had been left a
widow and was mourning the loss of her beloved. Her husband had been a powerful conjurer and in her early days
Mary had been one of the singers at the pagan festivals. Now
in spite of her age she was a woman of high spirits and vitality
and appeared to be the undisputed head of a large, influential, prosperous, and obedient family. Bilby and I had met
Mary the day we arrived at Lake Harbour in August 1909.
She had come with other members of her clan to meet the
whalers and to join in the excitement that surrounded its few
days in port. It was she who had made the winter clothing
for us and proved herself to be an excellent needlewoman.
She frequently came to the mission house and after her business had been transacted would sit in the kitchen silently
watching us as we attended to our regular household duties.
Her small quizzical eyes, following our every movement, suggested that, in spite of her apparent innocence and her lack
of knowledge of the English language, she was greatly amused
at all we were doing. When some other Eskimo entered, Mary
became talkative to a degree so we concluded that she was
giving the newcomer a lively picture of the way we did things
in what was to her an exceedingly large igloo.

At Itinik things were reversed and it was I who watched
the movements of Mary, her family, and her friends. One of
the things that attracted me to them was that they were so
perfectly natural. As a rule, they were remarkably free from
resentfulness and seldom, to my knowledge, harbored malice,
even though intensity of temperament and character was not
unknown. Because they lived a nomadic life they were often
crude and primitive in their ways, yet, as I studied them,
there was something noble in their simplicity. Their in-
born courtesy had to be experienced to be understood and
appreciated.

Mary was a true daughter of a race that had never come
close to civilization as we understood it. Yet this elderly

widow woman had great dignity, was highly intelligent, a born organizer, and a kindly and sincere spirit. Outside her family circle she was looked upon with respect and admiration. On one occasion when I complimented her on the excellence of her sewing her tattooed face, which had a myriad of wrinkles, lighted up with a flush of pleasure, her eyes sparkled, and smiling at me without embarrassment she replied, "Certainly, I sew well for you because you are my own adopted son."

When I first asked her to tell me the meaning of the tattooing on her face and wrists, she said, "I am as one who has forgotten." At first I thought she had said, "I have forgotten," and knowing that this could not be true I repeated my question. When she said again, "I am as one who has forgotten," I felt rebuked as I realized that with the acceptance of the Christian faith Mary had put away the old beliefs and practices and had indeed become "a new creature." My stay at Itinik was made effective largely because of this remarkable woman.

The highlight of this visit was the celebration of Holy Communion on the Sunday morning before I left for the west. This was, as far as I have been able to discover, the first time that this holy sacrament was celebrated in an igloo.

So that we might do all things decently and in order, the Eskimo first cleaned the dwelling of all rotten meat, blood, blubber, and dirt. Then fresh snow was brought in and tramped down until the whole interior was white and clean. The floor was then covered with caribou skins so that the worshipers might kneel with less discomfort. A sledge box was placed in a suitable position and acted as the Holy Table. When it had been carefully covered with spotless white towels, the sacramental linen and vessels were arranged on it. Two flickering stone lamps filled with seal oil gave a subdued light, just sufficient for reading and quite suitable for the service.

The communicants were ten in number, six men and four women, the first fruits of the harvest. As I looked into the round tattooed faces of the dumpy little women and the bronzed, weather-beaten faces of the men, I was filled with an unspeakable longing to serve them.

My diary best records the tremendous significance of the occasion:

After some moments of silent prayer together, when no noise disturbed our devotions save the rustling of the snow outside as it whirled round the hut, the service began. It is no exaggeration to say that in almost a literal manner the experience of the disciples who walked to Emmaus was repeated at this time, and the Lord was made known to His disciples in the breaking of bread. I could only pray that through this celebration these people might learn that "all life is a Sacrament, and that God is all and in all." After the service the people did not wish to go away. For nearly ten minutes no words were spoken. It was as if we all with one accord felt in our soul that it was "good for us to be here," for we had seen the Lord.

When the silence was broken at last, we quite naturally spoke of the gathering of the other Eskimo into the fold of the Good Shepherd. They said they would pray for the Eskimo "in the beyond" who had not yet been visited by a missionary that they might have hearts prepared to receive "God's words."

I shall always consider myself most fortunate in having had the privilege of helping them, in some small way, to find the key that unlocks the door to peace and brings strength to the soul.

PUDLO DID NOT know the country to the west and since there were no trails and the people were constantly on the move in pursuit of the wildlife, it was necessary to secure the services of two experienced men to act as guides. One was a man named Chartie and the other was his cousin. Chartie not only possessed a fine team of dogs but was an exceedingly good hunter, an earnest Christian, and a nephew of Mary Er-kak-tah-lik.

Later he became one of our most influential native catechists. The missionaries who followed me at Lake Harbour have written in glowing terms of his great devotion and influence for good among the people, and the officers of the Hudson's Bay Company have often expressed their respect and admiration for him as a man, a hunter, and a Christian.

Thanks to Professor Cotton at Wycliffe College, I had given some thought to primitive religions. The reading of Sir James Frazer and other outstanding writers on the subject had excited me and also opened my eyes to the importance of the relation between the religion of a people and their economic life. I was soon to realize through close contact with the Eskimo that religion was the chief lever of this, and I assume of every other, primitive society.

It was on this journey that I first heard freely many of their songs and tales of folklore, almost all of which have religious significance. It was of considerable importance that we should gain such knowledge so that we might go from the known to the unknown in presenting the Christian faith. God does not leave any of His children without some glimmer of the truth and on whatever glimmer these dear people possessed we must build. Like the rest of us the Eskimo are shy about speaking of their religious beliefs to strangers. To them as to us their religion is a sacred thing and they hesitate to share its mysteries. This reticence has been responsible for much misunderstanding on the part of white men who have visited them and sought to discover the thought of the Eskimo. Also, most white men have not had the kind of training that would enable them to grasp the significance of what the Eskimo might tell.

I shall always feel indebted to an Eskimo named Neparktok for the help he gave me in this matter. He had been an angakok and had become a Christian only after much travail of soul. We were sitting in his igloo at a place called Arnaking at the close of day. His wife was out gossiping in one of the other snow huts so he and I were alone. I do not recall how our conversation began but very soon he was telling me about the days of his boyhood; then gradually he spoke of some of the old customs which had a definite religious meaning. It was a wonderful revelation and I sat entranced, fearing to interrupt the flow of his ideas and words. There, with the flickering light from the blubber lamp illuminating his wrinkled, weather-beaten face, he seemed to forget my presence and to get lost along the road to yesterday.

The sun, he said, is a big ball of fire which moves around the hill [the world]. In winter it is very greatly weighed down by the cold and frost and so cannot rise up into the sky. Or sometimes, he continued, our people think that the sun and moon are the snow huts of certain big spirits who dwell in the upper world. The moon is a disc of ice which follows the sun and turns about of itself so that sometimes it looks big and round and sometimes thin.

The stars are little holes in the floor of the upper world

and the reason why they twinkle is that the spirits of the upper world are passing and repassing or that the wind is blowing. Or, again, each star is the eye of a spirit looking down and the twinkling is due to the winking of the eyelid.

Story after story he told me of animals in human form, of sea mammals marrying human beings, of a fox and hare being married, of a conjurer changing himself into a woman, of a woman who adopted a bear, of dwarfs and giants and fairy folk, and of human beings who were turned into birds and beasts.

As I studied the religion of the Eskimo it seemed to me that although their thinking was confused the people were conscious of their own limitations and the universal need of help from higher powers. In the face of the mysteries of life they had a sense of awe and of the infinite. There was much about which they were, understandably, ignorant and they often did not distinguish between the spiritual and the material world.

Rivers, mountains, lakes, glaciers, and other inanimate objects all had their spirits and to them the people offered reverence and worship. Why not? Do not these things have tremendous influence upon the life and well-being of the race? Also, many animals and birds such as the polar bear, the wolf and the raven, had powerful spirits and these must be treated with deepest respect or trouble would ensue.

The soul of man and his breath were spoken of sometimes as identical and when a conjurer had taken part in a seance he had for all practical purposes been "dead," since his spirit had for a time departed from the body to visit the unseen world. Thus it will be seen that the pagan religion of the Eskimo was a simple animism akin to most primitive religions. There was much more in it, however, than a mere belief in powers superior to man which directed and controlled the course of nature and of human life.

Their religion was personal in that the unseen spirits were aware of the individual, ready to bless or curse, according to whether they had been propitiated or annoyed, and from this tenet of their faith has developed the system of taboos. As in all primitive religions the ritual connected with taboos is magical, mystical, and sacred and the terms used by the angakok during his incantations were not those commonly used in the language of the people.

Sir J. G. Fraser in *The Golden Bough* explains that generally the taboo is instituted because the animist believes that by doing the thing which is taboo evil results will follow automatically. This was certainly the case as far as our Eskimo were concerned. They also considered that when a taboo had been broken and evil results followed, then the mere confession of guilt must inevitably stop the continuance of evil.

For some years as a missionary I did not understand this fact and because on this point I had not entered into the mind of the people it caused a serious obstacle to my work. Once I grasped the situation, my teaching met with greater success.

The Baffin Land Eskimo believed that there were at least fifty spirits or gods, and of these two were very powerful. One was the spirit of the land which bore to the land animals somewhat the same relationship that Sedna bore to the sea mammals, since it controlled the caribou, bears, and wolves. The other was the spirit of the lakes. This was the spirit that told the conjurer "the things he wishes to know."

The workers of evil magic were called "il-le-silk-se-yak." These people held secret communication with supernatural powers and were often guilty of grave misdeeds. They operated by means of magic and could kill or bring disease upon the unsuspecting members of the community.

A study of world faiths shows that religion is fundamentally the same craving of the heart, from the primitive people of the world to the most highly developed Christians. As the primitive mind is brought into relationship with Christ, it becomes more integrated and shows itself to be as "logical" as the more "advanced" minds in civilization. Were it otherwise, it would be futile for the missionary to "preach the Gospel" to primitive peoples.

It cannot be too strongly emphasized that the moral nature of man is as fundamental as any other part of him—hunger, thirst, self-assertion, or sex. It is only as men follow Christ that human nature is revealed in all its fullness. Aristotle said that in order to understand anything you must study it in its highest development. Of nothing is that more true than of religion. The pagan is unhappy in the power of evil spirits and uses magic in an effort to control them, whereas true religion aims at union and communion with the Unseen.

While the message of the great Evangel is essentially that of God's sovereignty over the individual, yet Christ does violence to no man. He appeals to the highest in man's nature and helps him to realize his personality. Religion is a quickening influence in every part of a man's being. The truth of this has been abundantly manifested by our Christian people all over Arctic Canada.

The soul of the Eskimo reflects the free moods of hostile nature—silent like the stillness of the frozen sea at one time, then restless and hilarious like the rushing spring floods at another. He is endowed with wonderful gifts of imagination and humor and because of his primitive views his humor often takes the form of coarseness.

It would not be correct to state that the Eskimo are always in dread of evil spirits. They have their periods of happy freedom from dull care. When seals are plentiful and the weather is kind, the Eskimo abandons himself to the joy of living. He accepts the good things that have come to him, enjoys them to the full, and is thankful.

It is when adversity overtakes him and he cannot understand that his heart is filled with fear. It is then that the angakok enters the picture and becomes the mediator between the people and the unseen powers that control the forces of nature. It is accepted that access to the spirits is only possible through the angakok. Behind all the ritual with its excesses of ejaculations, groans, and mutterings, there is the desire to discover what is wrong and to put it right. That there are excesses cannot be denied. That the angakok resorts to magic is all too true but in fairness to these men, some of whom I first knew more than forty years ago and for whom I conceived a profound regard, it is only right to state that magic was resorted to because the angakok believed it essential to their religion, since by this means he could obtain the aid of his "special helping spirit."

Sometimes, it is true that magic was employed for the angakok's own private advantage, but so far as I could judge this was because in his mind he apparently did not differentiate between what he considered vital religion and the need to bolster up his own prestige. This has been a weakness found among leaders of every religion and is not unknown even among exponents of the Christian faith!

The angakok had various methods of divination, but one of the most peculiar was that of head-lifting, practiced in the case of serious illness. At a place near Cape Dorset I saw Kad-loo-e-tok, the conjurer, lie down on the sleeping bench alongside a man named Noong-ar-lo who was running a high temperature. A cord of sealskin was then placed round the head of the sick man and attached to the end of a stick in the hands of the conjurer. Then incantations began and the spirit of a departed friend was summoned by Kad-loo-e-tok. After a pause he asked if a certain spirit were present. The head was so heavy that it could not be lifted so the visiting spirit was now asked for advice regarding the disease and its cure. Again there was a pause, somewhat longer than the other, after which the weight went out of the head and thus Kad-loo-e-tok knew that the spirit had departed. The seance was closed with the promise that the sick man would get better.

At this settlement an amusing incident took place. For nearly five weeks I had been living largely on seal meat—stewed or raw—and had become very tired of it. One morning I spoke to my hostess, a fat little Eskimo woman who was busy scraping a sealskin, and told her that I was hungry for a change of diet. She asked me if I liked caribou, and when I assured her I did she said she was very sorry that they had no caribou! To my astonishment she then said that she had some clams and asked if I would like some for my next meal. I accepted, of course, but a little later when I got to thinking about it, I was puzzled as to where my friend was going to find the clams. The sea ice was at this time anywhere from six to twenty-five feet thick and at best clams are only obtainable at low tide in the summer. But by and by my hostess entered the igloo with the inverted lid of a can in which I was amazed to see a quantity of shelled clams. My hostess exclaimed, "Taika," meaning "Here they are!" and there they truly were. I expressed my profound gratitude to the old woman as I thought of the delicious stew I was going to have that evening and then I made the mistake of asking, "Mother, where did you get the clams?" She replied, "From the stomach of the walrus." That evening I again had seal stew! On my return to civilization I recounted this incident to my friend Dr. Malcolm Cameron, and was told that I had made a bad blunder. He assured me that the clams would undoubtedly have been tasty and easily digested.

When I arrived at Cape Dorset the Hudson's Bay Company men, Hayward Parsons (brother of Ralph), S. J. Stewart (Lofty of the *Pelican*) and Johnny Hayward, all gave me a very warm welcome. We then went on to the extreme west end of Baffin Land where there was an Eskimo encampment of thirty-seven people. At the daily services here one man, named Sun-e-yet, listened so intently that his bronzed and haggard features became transformed, and seemed to me to take on a spiritual radiance.

Before our visit was ended I learned his story. The previous autumn when the Eskimo were hunting at the floe edge, this man and his wife found themselves adrift on a pan of ice. Although their friends kept a sharp lookout all hope of their survival had been given up because the weather was bitterly cold. Several days later a hunter saw two black specks on a pan of ice and concluded that they were seals. He had his rifle loaded and ready to shoot them when the pan of ice, driven by the wind, came within close range. Suddenly one of the black figures stood up and the hunter realized that it was not a seal but a man. In telling me about it the people said that Sun-e-yet and his wife had been adrift "many days" so that they had "no flesh on their bones" and were hardly able to crawl on their hands and knees when at last they were rescued.

At this encampment as well as at many of the others I gave myself with diligence to teaching the people the fundamentals of the Faith. We did not begin with some theory of inspiration or with the authenticity of the Scriptures. Revelation is not doctrine—it is history, the story of the manifestation of the mighty acts of God. When the mind has grasped something of the truth then by experiment it gains the assurance needed to go forward in faith and so discovers that the teaching remains true independently of the revelation. Many were anxious to be baptized but, while this was encouraging, I remembered Pascal's words that "there is a vast distance between knowledge of God and love of God." It raised a perplexing problem. Only after having tested the knowledge of each individual and finding out from separate witnesses whether the applicant had given clear evidence of having forsaken the old pagan traditions and following the "Jesus way" was I willing to receive them into the Church. Then before the sacrament was administered intensified instruction was given.

Some appeared to me to be in need of further instruction before they could be baptized. The reason for this delay was my anxiety that the standard of Christian living should be high. At the same time I had to admit that they had heard the story of the Great Spirit Who was made clear to them in the life and teaching of Jesus Christ. This, in turn, had stirred within them a sense of gratitude, especially when they learned that Jesus was not of the same race as either themselves or their teachers. I had reason to believe that within the limits of their knowledge they were earnestly trying to give up whatever in their old mode of life was not "like Jesus."

They were still only half-instructed, however, and not fully prepared for the Sacrament of Holy Baptism. Were these converts not "regenerate" because they had not been baptized? I felt that this was a problem for the theologian rather than for the missionary, and I was thankful that I was not called upon to settle the doctrines of the Church.

For the people who wanted to be baptized, I drew up a system of preparation and arranged, wherever possible, for one or more of their number who had been instructed to act as mentors. In order to make the schedule for study and preparation effective I had to provide a calendar which I mimeographed at Lake Harbour. It showed the dates of the Christian festivals, the new moons and the probable time of the arrival of the annual ship. The calendar was necessary because the Eskimo take little account of time except in a very general way; their movements are all subject only to weather conditions and to the period of daylight. Yet even before the advent of the white man they reckoned the seasons with considerable accuracy.

They divided the year into thirteen periods of twenty-eight days each, according to the moons. Beginning with the January moon their calendar ran thus:

1. *Kah-pid-rah*—It is cold
2. *Hir-ker-maun*—The sun returns
3. *Ik-ke-ar-par-roon*—The sun is rising
4. *A-von-eve*—The baby seals are born
5. *Neoh-e-a-ler-roon*—The seals take to the water
6. *Kav-ah-roc vik*—The time the seals shed their coats
7. *Nook-rah-hah-le-yoon*—The fawn of the caribou are born
8. *Mun-cha-le-yoon*—The birds are nesting
9. *Ich-yah-yoon*—The young birds are hatched
10. *Ah-mer-ral-yoon*—The caribou migrate
11. *Noo-le-ah-le-yoon*—The time to have a wife
12. *Se-koot-se-room*—The ice is making in the bays
13. *Sik-ker-ne-loon*—The sun disappears

When I revisited these people in the western section on my way to Foxe Channel, I was greatly comforted to find that my plan had worked most successfully. Indeed, I was astonished at the progress made in the study of the Bible, the Catechism, and the Prayer Book, and at the care with which they had been taught by those of their own group who had been appointed by me the previous year.

On the return journey from King's Cape in 1914 we visited all the camps we had missed on the way west. One of these was at the head of Amadjuak Bay. I had heard that the people there were under the influence of a very powerful angakok and that all the old pagan practices and festivals were retained. Although the trip took us far to the north, it was clear to me that I must visit these people. Unfortunately the weather was very bad, with constant and heavy snow falling, but at the snow huts we received the usual kindly welcome from all the people and not least from the angakok, whose name was Anil-me-oob. Almost before Pudlo and I knew it, our equipment had been unloaded from the two sledges and we were sitting in the conjurer's large igloo enjoying a delicious caribou stew served by his wife, Ah-no-re. Our host had already given orders about our accommodations— Pudlo and I were to stay in one dwelling, the two guides in another. This was a great help to us since it avoided the necessity of building a new igloo. I also noticed that both dog teams were given a plentiful meal of walrus meat. Altogether I felt that the reports about this angakok must have been grossly exaggerated since he had done everything possible to make us welcome.

As soon as Pudlo and I had got settled and had chatted with our host and hostess and their children, I sent some gifts of biscuit, tea, and sugar to Anil-me-oob's wife. Then I asked Pudlo to arrange where we might hold a service since it was now dark and the men would wish to start off to the hunt as soon as daylight returned.

We gathered in Anil-me-oob's igloo and there was an overflow congregation in the porch and around the walls on the outside. Pudlo assisted me as usual and I gave a carefully prepared address stating the reason for our coming to Baffin Land. The people responded with ejaculations of approval and after the service was over thanked me most warmly for coming and for the message I had brought.

After Pudlo and I had shaken hands with them all we were invited to remain and have more food, which we did with thankfulness. I had explained that we would stay in the camp a week if the people could supply our dogs with food, for which of course we would pay. As we were saying good night and starting over to our own igloo Anil-me-oob thanked me for coming but said it was not a good time for us to stay. The people, he announced, were short of dog food and planned to separate on the morrow. Some would go south to hunt the walrus at the floe edge; some would go to a place near the mouth of the river coming out of Amadjuak Lake where seals were frequently to be found; while yet another group would go into the interior to hunt for caribou. Then, as if it were an afterthought, he added that he had dog food to spare and would let me have some to help us on our way back to Lake Harbour.

It was a wonderful exhibition of quiet determined opposition. He was the conjurer and he had no intention of allowing his people to forsake the old way, the way of their fathers, for the new way. This pagan leader intended to retain his power over the people, but no Christian could have acted in a more courteous or gentlemanly fashion. I listened very carefully to all that he had said. I was aghast at the sudden turn of events and for a moment I could not speak but, pulling myself together, I expressed my thanks for the kindly welcome we had received and admitted that it was a great disappointment that we could not stay longer at this time. Next year, I said, I hoped that things might be better. I added that I would pay him for the dog food before we left in the morning. Then we shook hands and I retired from the contest grievously disappointed and yet unable not to be amused. The words of the Newfoundlanders came to my mind: "That'll larn ye!" I would have to plan more carefully for the next year.

In the morning when the people discovered that we were leaving them, they were greatly surprised and showed their disappointment in a number of ways. Some of the men spoke to me while others spoke to Pudlo expressing their desire for teaching and asking if we would come to them again. We were much touched by the number of mysterious bundles handed to us—caribou tongues, two haunches of caribou and eight caribou back steaks which they knew I particularly liked. Anil-me-oob himself gave us two sacks of walrus meat which had been carefully cut up into small pieces and was the best possible food for the dogs. When I thanked him and asked him what he wanted in return, he said with a lordly air, "Nothing. It is a gift, but if you wish you can give something to my wife." Needless to say, I did give her a present and so we parted with warm handshakes and good wishes. For the time being, this angakok had defeated us.

Our next stop was at an island where my old hunting companion Ma-lik-tok and a group of Eskimo were encamped near the floe edge hunting the walrus. Ma-lik-tok had not been an easy convert, but he and his clever little wife had eventually found peace through simple obedience to the will of the Great Spirit Whose name is Love. We spent a most useful and happy week with them. They had a superabundance of walrus meat and blubber for people and dogs and we were not a burden. Most of all I was delighted at the progress made by both adults and children since I had last visited them.

The day we left Ma-lik-tok's camp we were caught in a blizzard. Unfortunately Pudlo and I became separated from our guides and got hopelessly lost. Our misfortune was increased by the fact that the food box and oil for use in the primus stove were on the guides' sledge so that we could obtain neither light nor heat. To complete our misery we had wandered among some small rocky islands around which we could find no suitable snow for building an igloo.

Nothing daunted, my loyal companion set to work to prepare for the night. First, the sledge was set crosswise against the drifting snow. We then made a loose wall of snow to act as a windbreak and when this had been done crawled into our caribou sleeping bags fully dressed. Unfortunately the wind veered round while we slept and when we awoke in the morning we were nearly smothered by the snow that had drifted over us. Thanks largely to Pudlo's skill we suffered no ill effects from our night in the open in sub-zero weather. By noon the following morning the blizzard had spent itself but unfortunately the wind continued strong and swept a heavy drift of snow several feet high along the surface of the frozen sea. This made it exceedingly difficult for us to see any distance ahead. Indeed, it was so bad that from time to time Pudlo climbed to the top of some of the small islands in order to decide which direction to take. Had I been alone on this journey I am quite sure the story would have ended there. However, thanks to Pudlo, more than a week later we arrived back at the mission.

During this long trip I had called at every camp between Lake Harbour and King's Cape and made a note of the people —their names, sex, approximate age (if below twenty), and location. It was the first time that such an attempt had been made to find out the exact number of people in any one area. I was much surprised to meet some eighty Eskimo scattered along this coast line whom I had met in Frobisher Bay four winters previously. This showed that a census should be made in the various districts during one and the same year. After my return to Lake Harbour, with the help of our Eskimo who had visited Frobisher Bay and Davis Strait that winter, I was able to make a complete census of all the Eskimo living south and west of Blacklead Island. At ship time I sent a copy of the census to Ottawa.

It was a tremendous relief to be again in my own quarters with so many of the comforts of civilization. Each evening my Eskimo clothes were discarded and replaced by my dinner jacket and patent-leather pumps. I simply took this opportunity to remind myself that there were other ways of living than those I had become accustomed to in the snow villages and on the trail.

Early in May after Pudlo had left for the seal hunting, Lukesi Kidlapik arrived with Rhoda his wife and their adopted son Noah. They brought the welcome news that Greenshield had spent a very successful time among the Eskimo in the Cumberland Gulf area. As it was now too late in the season for Kidlapik to return overland to Blacklead Island, he agreed to stay with me for the time being.

Once more the problem of feeding the dogs loomed large. Therefore, when Pudlo returned after a fortnight's absence with a double load of seals Kidlapik also went off to hunt. In this way we were able to have the dogs well fed and to lay up caches of seals for use later when the hunting would be poor. The plan worked very well. The men enjoyed being with their own people, hunting and teaching; then they worked on the final construction of the church during the following two weeks. Without their help the building of the church would have been delayed considerably. Pudlo in particular became an excellent carpenter and took great delight in that work.

On Sunday, July 26, the ice in the harbor broke up and the following day the people from all along the coast both east and west arrived back from their hunting and trapping districts. Our quiet settlement now rang with shouts and laughter.

A week later the church building was finished. The bell was hung in the little spire, and the gleaming paint inside and out gave it a very neat appearance. On Sunday, August second, the Eskimo crowded into it for services of thanksgiving and dedication. It is impossible for me to tell what it meant to us to have this little place of our own in which to worship God. The work had been done almost entirely by the Eskimo themselves; I merely gave them the necessary guidance. It was only a rough little building made from the material sent out for two small storehouses but it seemed to me, and I believe to the Eskimo also, a little piece of heaven on earth. It had a seating capacity of fifty but could accommodate seventy or eighty people when occasion demanded.

On August 24 the *Pelican* arrived. The captain and other members of the crew were most cordial in their greetings. I was greatly torn between accepting their kind invitation to dine with them, and getting my mail and going ashore without delay. The captain suggested that I should come to lunch the next day. It was indeed the thrill of the year. When I entered the salon and sat down at the captain's table I got at first the impression of sophistication. Before the meal was over that impression had entirely passed away and I realized how quickly we react to our surroundings. Then we exchanged news. They wanted to know how I had survived the winter and whether I planned to leave with them. Then they gave me their news.

While on the Labrador coast, they had heard rumors that war had been declared against Germany and that a number of British warships had been sunk in the North Sea. This, of course, was the beginning of the First World War.

Then I was not surprised to be told that Bilby had been advised by the doctors in England not to return to Baffin Land. I was greatly disappointed that a new worker had not been sent to join me, but it could not be helped. I would simply have to face another year single-handed. However, Bilby had been extremely kind in arranging with the Hudson's Bay Company in London to ship out to us several boxes of books containing the new and revised Eskimo Prayer Book. There were also other supplies which had been kindly accepted by the captain and the chief officer after the ship had been considered fully loaded.

The next few days while the *Pelican* remained in harbor life became pandemonium. We had constant visitors from the ship and greatly appreciated their coming but it gave little time for answering letters or for checking the cargo as it was carried ashore.

When a whole year's supply of food and fuel is unloaded,

the Arctic dweller must be prepared for bitter disappointment. You can imagine how upset one can be to discover that
out of a case of fifteen dozen fresh eggs ten dozen are cracked
and broken. Always some of the cases containing jams and
fruit have been ruined, and the fresh vegetables so eagerly
looked forward to are entirely rotten. Yet the Arctic man
must try to overcome his self-pity, and discipline himself to
stay silent. It all happens so quickly that by the time the ship
sails away the brain is in a muddle. I remember one time on
board the *Nascopie,* when a man asked a trader if he was
glad to have the ship arrive. He received the surprising reply,
"Yes, glad to see her come and glad to see her go!" Nevertheless a feeling of bleakness crept over the settlement when the
annual ship weighed anchor and slipped swiftly out of the
harbor. We were alone again.

☆ 11. Where No White Man Had Gone ☆

As I ENTERED upon a new year of work I realized that the establishment of Hudson's Bay Company trading posts at Lake Harbour and Cape Dorset had changed many things. When I had first gone to Lake Harbour there were no white men wintering on the coast between Davis Strait and Hudson Strait. Except for the annual visit of the whaler *Active* we were alone with the Eskimo.

Captain Murray of the *Active* was such an outstanding personality and left such an impress upon the North that I would like to say a little more about him. I have already mentioned how kind he was to Bilby and me. But he was more than a good man with a warm heart. He was the old-time whaling captain at his best. The principle on which he worked was very simple and in its way beneficial and effective. He looked upon himself as the father of all the Eskimo with whom he came into contact and they accepted him as such. Years of experience had given him a detailed knowledge and understanding of practically all the individual Eskimo at the ports of call. He was a shrewd Scot and knew who were the good, reliable hunters and who were not, and whether to trust this seamstress or that. When the ship arrived the natives came swarming on board, bringing their fur, ivory and blubber, and with the innocence of children, handed these to Murray. They had complete confidence that he

203

would supply them in turn with all they needed for the ensuing year. Nor was their confidence misplaced. He gave each family such things as he felt they required, and not necessarily in proportion to the quantity of fur which any individual hunter had brought in. If dissatisfaction arose, the captain simply pointed out that the hunter in question had ample supplies to go on with and that any balance that might be due to him had been given to his dependents, such as his aged parents or the less successful members of his family.

There were weaknesses in this system, of course, but it must be put on record that the best of the whalers did much that was good for the Eskimo.

Now that the powerful Hudson's Bay Company had come, there was an immediate change in the entire method of trading. The whole effort of the H.B.C. was to redirect the thinking of the native. They were not interested in securing whalebone and made little or no attempt to hunt the large whales. Instead they began at once to train the Eskimo to think in terms of foxskins and instituted a very carefully worked out system to encourage this. Among other things they substantially advanced the price of fur, carefully explaining to each native that they were now working on a definite business basis; i.e., so many foxskins would bring so much return and no foxskins would bring no return. The Eskimo now became a trapper more than a hunter.

Also since the company's officers remained in the country twelve months of the year, the Eskimo were able to trade their fur throughout the year instead of having to keep it until the whaler arrived in July. Like all other systems this had its advantages and its disadvantages. But I am convinced that the old whaling plan could not have been continued with advantage either to the Eskimo or to the companies operating in the North. The whalers made their contribution but times had changed and new days require new ways.

As winter approached I arranged for Kidlapik to spend "two moons" with the Eskimo at their hunting grounds in the vicinity of the Saddleback Islands to teach them while they supplied him and his dogs with fresh food. Other Eskimo were leaving to hunt at various points on the west coast and I arranged with them to transport and store certain supplies for me so that when I visited their camps early in the New Year I would find them on hand. They were the usual items to pay for my keep, dog food, and some of my own food.

Early in November I got a chill and for ten days felt miserable—so miserable that I told Kidlapik that if I should die before he returned he was to tell the white men that they were not to take my body home in the ship. Kidlapik very sensibly said, "You will not die; soon you will be very strong." He was right but for a time I lacked my usual energy. Both Kidlapik and Pudlo also complained so we all took cod-liver oil and by November 20 had regained our normal health.

One Sunday evening when Kidlapik was returning from the house to his igloo, he found the H.B.C. clerk, John Eaton of Edinburgh, huddled in the snow beside a rock. Rushing back to the house, Kidlapik called me and we found the exhausted lad's feet and hands were frostbitten. We aroused Pudlo and together we carried Eaton into the house. Then I sent word across the harbor to the H.B.C. Needless to say, Mr. Parsons was greatly disturbed but in two days' time Eaton was able to return to the post quite restored and not a little frightened by the experience.

We were much encouraged at this time by the number of seals that came up out of the water and rested on the ice. The hunting was very good, and on November 24 Pudlo shot thirteen seals and Kidlapik eleven. This was the greatest possible help since it enabled us to store food for our dogs against the time when hunting would be impossible.

Early in December we all moved to a camp at a place called Tesseyooakudlung. Here I stayed as a paying guest with my old friends Simeon Ing-mil-ayo and Ite his wife, and here I was surprised and delighted to have a visit from James Cantley. He was on his way to Frobisher Bay to gather information for Parsons regarding the condition of the Eskimo in that area.

For some days before we broke camp the weather had been clear, cold, and invigorating, so that I felt it was good to be alive. One morning when I went out of the igloo before sunrise, I saw the opaque masses of clouds in the east slowly become flushed with red until the whole sky looked like a vast conflagration of fire that might sweep down and destroy us. Gradually the angry colors faded and the refraction of light soon transformed the heavens into a dome of dazzling beauty. To me the amplitude, the order, and the sublime beauty of the universe were a constant source of wonder.

It was not only the morning sky that thrilled me. In the evening the stars shone with marvelous brilliancy. There in the icy stillness of Arctic night they seemed to be living things and I understood why the pagan Eskimo believed that they were windows in the house of the spirits who dwelt above the earth.

The Hudson's Bay Company had invited all the Eskimo in the district to come to Lake Harbour for Christmas so that they might have "a time of rejoicing." So when I returned to the mission a few days before the festival, I was accompanied by a score or more of sledges, a hundred Eskimo, and one hundred and fifty dogs.

That Christmas was a memorable one. In the first place, the services in our little church were a bright joy to us all. So many more Eskimo had come forward into the "new way" and those who had followed it had been marvelously strengthened and guided by God. It seemed to me that the Love that came down to earth on that first Christmas shone in the face of every bronzed child of the Eternal Father.

My plans for this winter were somewhat different from those of the other winters because both Bishop Holmes and Mr. Peck were anxious that I should find out if there were Eskimo living on the Foxe Channel coast. Intelligent planning of future work depended on knowledge of what groups were still unreached. It would be a momentous journey for no white man had ever gone to Foxe Channel and come back alive.

Peck had sent some press clippings about a German named Bernard A. Hantzach who was the first white man to visit that area. Hantzach had been a passenger with Greenshield on board the ill-fated *Jantina Agatha* when it was crushed in the polar pack off the Baffin Land coast in 1909. He had traveled north in order to make ornithological investigations and seven months later left Blacklead Island accompanied by some Eskimo and made the journey up the fjord at the head of Cumberland Gulf to a great lake named Netilik and then down the Koukjuak River to the Foxe Channel coast. Hantzach was devoted to his work but by February of the following year he and his companions were starving. They found the country sterile of wildlife and consequently ran out of food. Hantzach wrote in his diary: "Death knocks at our door." A little later he stated that he was reduced to eating a sealskin boot sole cut up in little pieces while his Eskimo companions ate "caribou dung smeared with oil." On April 23, he wrote: "Hot head—shivering. The will can no longer overcome the body." He died early in June.

Kidlapik told me that he had known Hantzach at Blacklead Island and that the three Eskimo who had accompanied the explorer had all been friends of his.

With Hantzach's experience in view I realized that I must make exceedingly careful plans or his fate might be mine. My problem was to try to estimate how long the trip to Foxe Channel would take and how much food, if any, could be obtained en route. I could get no information on either subject from the Eskimo around Lake Harbour but I felt confident that those in the Cape Dorset district would have reliable knowledge. So the first step would be to work my way westward to Cape Dorset.

With the purchase of two more dogs to strengthen my team the first preparations for my great journey were complete. It was a sobering thought that I was attempting to go where only one other white man had gazed upon the endless wastes and to know that for him it had been the land of no return.

At a quarter to five on the morning of January 25, I

aroused Pudlo and Yarley and by seven o'clock we were off with Foxe Channel as our ultimate goal. When we started the light of the full moon cast long shadows on the ice and created in the mind an indescribable feeling of loneliness.

In my diary I noted that this first day's trip was a great success because the team was strong and Pudlo had been able to get it into good working order. We spent only two days at the first village since the people belonged to the Lake Harbour district and had already received much teaching, and we were anxious to push on. In the valley up which we were traveling that day the shadows looked as if they had been roughed on the snow with charcoal. We were kept busy guiding the dogs and sledges as we wound our twisted way around the rough boulders that projected through the snow and ice of a river bed.

Our dogs worked on contentedly for hours at a time as long as progress was being made and they knew their driver was in control. But the moment the sledge stopped trouble began. The dogs would then turn around to see what was the matter, or lie down in the snow as if to say, "Let the fool who stopped the sledge get it started again."

In rough ice there were, as usual, frequent stops when the runners or the traces were caught in a jagged piece of ice. Then we had to strain at the traces and shout ourselves hoarse in the hope of getting the team on the move once again. At the crucial moment a dog would not infrequently break its trace and then gleefully come nosing in among the other dogs. This always started a fight and the confusion was complete. On the second day two of our dogs ran away, presumably back to Sabooyang, but the heavy drifting snow made it impossible for us to search for them. A blizzard now overtook us so we settled down to make the best of our enforced delay. The men went over the dogs' harness and the sledge lashings and we had some rewarding talks.

When we eventually reached Itinik I was happy to find that everyone had carefully followed the course of study which I had set out for them before they had left Lake Harbour in

September. They had many questions to ask about the meaning of this Biblical passage or that, but the one that puzzled them most was St. Matthew V: 29-30. What, they asked, did Jesus mean when He spoke about "plucking out the right eye," "cutting off the right hand"? To answer with lucidity took great care and thought on my part.

On the Sunday we had three services including the Sacraments of Holy Communion and Baptism. That evening Pudlo, Yarley, and I had our evening meal with Mary Er-kak-tah-lik and her family. Before we said good night to our friends I asked Pudlo to express our thanks and to offer a special prayer. I shall never forget what followed. There in that igloo we all knelt with bowed heads while Pudlo said a prayer that obviously came from the depths of his heart. He thanked God that the people in the south had sent the teachers to tell the things they needed to know, and for God's goodness in calling them, the Eskimo, to be His children through faith in Jesus. He remembered the needs of the people all along the coast. He then asked God's blessing on Lukesi Kidlapik as he visited the people in the east and that he and I might have wisdom granted to us to understand what God wished us to do and where to go.

When the silence was broken the people thanked Pudlo over and over again. For me it brought a double blessing because it not only indicated the sincerity of my spiritual children but the deep spiritual understanding of my friend and fellow worker, Joseph Pudlo.

Life with the Eskimo is seldom dull and this was specially true at Itinik. One day when I visited in a tent I saw a tiny, muckle-mouthed infant being suckled at its mother's breast. The baby had a peculiar dark spot like a birthmark on its buttocks. Its mother told me that many Eskimo children had these dark spots at birth. She said that they varied greatly in size and position and that they gradually faded completely away. They were not what we call "birthmarks" but the famous "Mongoloid spot."

This sacral pigmentation, which apparently can occur in

the young of all races, appears most often among people of Mongoloid stock. The mark I saw on Eskimo children was exactly similar to that commonly found on Japanese and Chinese children. The argument is not that it only occurs among those of Mongolian race, but that it is seldom found among other races. The fact that it is so pronounced among the Eskimo suggests that it is a "telltale" spot and points definitely to a common origin. It is one of a whole series of factors which indicate the probability that once the Eskimo lived in Asia.

I had sent ahead to Itinik in September boxes of provision and supplies and these were brought to my igloo on my arrival. In one bundle were papers and magazines to be read as opportunity allowed and among the illustrated magazines there was a picture of a young English mother with her twin baby girls. Thinking to interest my hostess, I showed her this picture. She was not pleased and I was soon to learn that the Eskimo had nothing but contempt for a woman who produced twins. I then made a further mistake by telling that a white woman in Italy had given birth to triplets. Her only comment was, "The white women breed like lemmings!"

It was an unexpected point of view because the Eskimo are greedy to have children; they are the only security parents have when old age overtakes them. Later, I learned that the conjurers insisted that only a woman possessed by an evil spirit bore twins and that of the twins one was the true child and one the evil spirit of that child. No human could tell which was which. Therefore the people deliberately let all three starve to death. I have read that this same belief is held by other primitive peoples.

This question of spirits was ever in their minds. One day I spoke to an Eskimo mother about the destructive naughtiness of her little boy but she only smiled at me and said, "He will learn." The grandmother, however, spoke up and explained that it was not the custom of the Eskimo to interfere with a child at play lest by so doing they drive away the spirit after whom it was named and who lived in the child sometimes if not always. She also told me that it was a grievous thing to raise one's voice since that indicated anger and anger led to quarreling and to other evils. Again I realized that many white mothers could learn a great deal from the Eskimo women.

Between Itinik and Cape Dorset we called at as many of the camps en route as possible and at every camp the people gave evidence of having followed the plan of instruction I had given them the previous year. I was delighted to find them relatively free from the fear which had burdened them in the pagan past.

At one snow village after a very happy but all too short visit we left at dawn. The people were up and helped us to get the sledges over the heavy barrier of hummocky shore ice. Then while Pudlo, Yarley, and Chartie were busy straightening the traces of the dogs, the chief called the people to prayer. We knelt on the snow while he thanked God for having sent the teachers and asked that we might be given "the sundry things" we needed; and that the Holy Spirit would bless the people to whom we went. He then repeated the Lord's Prayer in which all joined. Once more we shook hands all round and went our way while the people returned to their igloos. This spontaneous approach to God in prayer made a deep impression upon me and upon Pudlo, stirring our spirits and confirming us in the belief that our efforts were not in vain.

At another camp called Arnaking it was necessary to have three services each day because, in spite of the men having built a very large igloo for use as our church, it was unable to hold all the people at one time. At Arnaking I renewed acquaintance with a grizzled old man named Kilk-re-apik whom I had met when the *Lorna Doone* first brought us to Lake Harbour. Being old and unable to hunt, he was dependent upon his relatives for the bare necessities of life. Like the other old men, his voice had been made rough through shouting at the dogs in the sub-zero weather during his long life and it was not always easy to understand the words he spoke. I grew very fond of this old pagan who had lived a hard life and passed through many joys and sorrows. His children were all dead but he and Matte, his wife, were together still and devoted to each other.

One day my friend made me a present of three little sledge dogs carved out of the molar teeth of the walrus. I was surprised that they were so well made for he had no tools other than an old jackknife. The next day Matte brought me a small figure of a man that she had found beside an ancient Eskimo grave. It was of ivory but so old that it was stained amber color and pitted by exposure. She explained that since the child's grave from which this doll had been taken was very old the spirit of the dead child had long ago passed into another and she was free to appropriate the figure.

I studied the old ivory figure and realized that it represented the ancient forerunner of the little dogs that her husband had brought to me and the excellent models of animals, birds, sledges, and weapons which Bilby and I had encouraged several of the men to make.

Every morning Kilk-re-apik and Matte would come to my igloo in the hope, which was never disappointed, that they would get something to eat. The previous summer, the summer of 1914, I had received a letter from Dr. Franz Boaz of the Museum of Natural History, New York, asking me to obtain for him translations of over three dozen Eskimo songs which he had gathered during a visit to Cumberland Sound some years before. I had already spent a considerable amount of time on this project, getting my best help from the conjurers, but I decided to consult Kilk-re-apik also. He and Matte sang a number of the ancient songs in their funny cracked voices but their words were so indistinct that I could not always catch them. Consequently I asked a very intelligent boy named Sookso and his sister to come into the igloo and listen and then they repeated to me the words that were not clear until I was able to understand all except those special words used only by the conjurers.

Later Kilk-re-apik told me a terrible story of a woman he

knew who had eaten part of a child because she and another woman were left alone at a camp and were starving. He said that the woman was alive at that time but he would not tell me who she was.

On February 22, after eleven days in this village, we said farewell to all our friends and continued our journey westward. We now changed guides, Chartie returning to Itinik, and King-o-wat-se-ak and Naglikgeanilk took us on to Cape Dorset where we arrived five days later. My greatest problem now was to find guides who knew where the Eskimo would be living on the Foxe Channel coast at that particular time in the year. Inquiries were made but not a single man in the district had ever been there. This was disappointing but not altogether unexpected. I decided to send Pudlo and Yarley on to King's Cape, the most westerly camp on the Hudson Strait, to see if they could obtain a guide there. In addition to this mission Pudlo was to conduct services and to secure walrus or seal meat with which to feed our dogs on the journey. At Cape Dorset we were also able to purchase a limited quantity of dog food. Before many days they returned. They had found no guide but they brought a fine supply of dog food.

Then, quite unexpectedly, two strangers with one sledge arrived at Cape Dorset and to our joy they were from Foxe Channel. This dispelled my chief anxiety and my spirits rose accordingly. These men had exhausted their supply of dog food and expected to get walrus meat from the Cape Dorset Eskimo. This they were unable to do, so we ultimately agreed to chance the future with the understanding that if they would guide us to Foxe Channel we would share what dog meat we had.

On March 9 we set out on the memorable expedition which was later to be recognized as a piece of exceptional exploration by the Royal Geographical Society, London, which made me a fellow of that society. In the face of the heavy drifting snow that swirled against us and blotted out the landscape we plodded on our way. After we left the sea ice we were faced with a gentle climb up a valley so filled with hard wind-beaten snow that the actual river bed was hidden from our view. Then we crossed mile after mile of frozen lakes and undulating stretches of snow-covered tundra. For a time it was as if some mysterious evil thing were closing in around us in order to blur our vision and in the end destroy us. Later the drift ceased and there was a sharpness in the air that seemed to quicken the flow of blood in our bodies, giving us new strength.

That night while we slept the weather changed. The temperature had risen above zero and several inches of snow had fallen. This made it necessary for us to break trail all day. Pudlo, Yarley, and I took turns and found it exceedingly hard work. As soon as we had done our share of tramping ahead of the dogs, we were then harnessed to the sledge in order to help the team to go forward.

Just before midday we reached an Eskimo camp and were overjoyed to find that we could buy some dog food. True, it was frozen caribou but we had it cut up, put in a bag and sunk in water under the ice on the lake, in order to get it thawed out. We troubled to thaw it out because at best the flesh of the caribou is a poor substitute for walrus or seal and it was better thawed than frozen. These people also kindly supplied us with a hot meal, after which I took a brief service and explained why we had come and where we were going. We greatly benefited by the food and the short rest. When we resumed our march the temperature was falling steadily and a bitter wind sprang up which caused the newly fallen snow to drift furiously.

Some idea of conditions that day may be understood by the fact that Yarley and our two guides all complained of frozen cheeks and on several occasions we were completely lost. It was not the fault of our guides. The visibility was impossible and at times the drifting snow so deep that we could hardly see our leading dog only some thirty-five feet ahead of the sledges. We were greatly relieved to reach a camp near a lake.

The people were surprised to see a teacher in their midst for the first time and each family brought us gifts.

On leaving this camp two days later we made splendid progress. The surface of the snow was now both hard and smooth except where the wind had swept it into crisp rhythmic ridges. In the lee of protruding rocks it had been formed into the most lovely contours as if some modern artist had been at work. As I surveyed that great white land without any sign of living creature except ourselves, the stillness caused a feeling of depression until some little fugitive clouds drifting southward caught my attention and broke the spell.

We traveled hard all day for there could be no delay. Even the aching of my legs drove me on in order to reach the camp known as Kimil where the Foxe Channel natives were staying. It was very cold but there was no wind or drifting snow as we pushed our way forward. On and on we went. By midday the sky had become overcast and the dreary expanses seemed more cheerless than ever. Darkness fell and on we plodded. My thoughts were busy. Here I was at last in the Foxe Channel region! Hantzach and I, separated by years, interests, the only two white men ever to have reached this place. Would I get back? Would I fulfill my mission among the Eskimo? Being young, I was thrilled with the adventure of it; being a missionary, I felt the urgency of my mission.

Suddenly there loomed before us in the darkness the yellow glow of the tiny windows of the Eskimo igloos. They seemed to be standing in mid-air surrounded by the inhospitable wastes of ice and snow. Again we received the kindly welcome I had learned to expect from these strange and wonderful dwellers of the Arctic night. The head of this family group was an old conjurer named Luk-ta, but his nephew Silah was much more virile and was evidently the active leader.

Times for services were soon arranged, and Pudlo, Yarley, and I sang hymns and were delighted to find that the people not only liked to hear them but were eager to learn them.

This took the best part of an hour. Then Pudlo read the Ten Commandments and I talked to them about our Faith. The congregation listened most attentively, including Luk-ta and Silah, so we went to rest with happy and contented spirits.

The next morning my first call was made on Luk-ta the angakok, who was most cordial but also quite frank with me. He thanked me for coming to visit them, hoped we would stay "many days" and assured me that the people would supply me with food. He then said that he considered me a good man for he had heard much about "the teachers" and knew that they were friends of the Eskimo. On the other hand, while the laws they had heard last night were doubtless good laws for the white men the Eskimo had different laws. He and his people were followers of the *old way* and would continue therein. This was said quietly as a statement of fact.

There was in this man that which I had observed in many of the Eskimo, a dignity and honesty that was most disarming. I explained that the Decalogue was not good for the white man only but for all men and after we had talked Luk-ta said, "Perhaps you are right. When I know more I too will understand why our fathers had the customs we keep and how many of the laws of the Great Spirit we should keep also—probably! I heard that you were young but had wisdom and could tell the coming of a great star [Halley's Comet at Aulatsevik]. Now I know that you have wisdom and I am glad that you have come."

When I left Luk-ta's igloo, the temperature was about fifty degrees below zero and in the frozen silence my breathing sounded like a whistle, but the sky had turned a glorious turquoise blue.

A new igloo was built by the men in which to hold our services. Since there was room now for all the people to congregate, we had only the children in the afternoon and the men and women together in the evening. I was anxious that Pudlo should develop as a teacher, and since he was devoted to children I decided to let him take school with them. He was very happy with this arrangement as he was anxious to share more fully in the work, and in turn this gave me more time for personal contacts with the people in their own igloos.

One day Silah asked if I wanted to go down to the sea ice with him. He needed to fetch some walrus meat and blubber which he had cached near his whaleboat just above the high-tide water mark. I was anxious to understand ice conditions in Foxe Channel, so quickly accepted his invitation, taking Yarley with me. Silah's team was in excellent form, and as the surface of the snow was hard and smooth, and the land was almost flat with a gentle slope towards the sea, we all sat on the sledge while the dogs raced forward. It was a new experience for me to travel thus and I was never able to repeat the performance.

At the shore we visited Silah's boat which was just as he had left it, except for a great drift of snow that hid all but the mast and part of the bow. Standing on the deck and with the aid of my Zeiss binoculars, I could well understand why the whalers complained about the heavy ice that came down into Hudson Bay from Foxe Channel each autumn. For miles out the water is shallow since the earth continues to slope very gently to the west. This means that when the cold weather sets in, the ice forming around the shore becomes ever thicker with the rise and fall of the twice-daily tides. Then, according to Silah, it often happens that when the autumn tides are at their height the heavy ice pans that come down the Channel from the north get stranded on the coast. There they remain until released the following year. During their months of imprisonment the movement of the tides causes them to roll over and over, becoming ever greater in size. Silah declared that many were "twenty-thirty, forty-fifty feet in thickness."

One evening after service Silah came into my snow hut. He said he did not want anything in particular but just to talk to me. First he asked some question about what I had said at the service and then we drifted into local affairs. He gave me much information about the topography of the country and the wildlife throughout the different seasons of the year. He did more. There in that igloo with pencil and on paper that rapidly became wet from the perspiration that fell from his face, and with the poor light from a flickering blubber lamp and two candles, Silah drew me an excellent map of the coast line. At my request he kindly made a fresh copy in the center pages of my diary. This was less smudged than the other and has been carefully preserved. It differs considerably from what was shown on the maps issued at that time. I concluded that the differences were because he was not drawing to scale. In this I was wrong, for later when the Government at Ottawa made a survey of the coast, Silah's map was proved to be much more accurate than our maps. The most striking discovery was when Silah told me that had I crossed to Foxe Channel Peninsula from the north end of Chorkbak Inlet it would have been a shorter journey than the route I had taken. This seemed strange since the printed map indicated that the distance would have been much greater. When I showed Silah my map he examined it very carefully and then said quite frankly that the man who had drawn it was "completely ignorant." That was a rather devastating statement, but it proved to be nearly the truth. I pressed him for further information. He then said that when hunting the caribou he had often walked from the head of the Chorkbak Inlet to the hills overlooking the sea and that the distance was not great. Reference to this matter was made later in the Canadian Government publication *Exploration of Southern Baffin Island,* published by the Department of the Interior, Ottawa.

However, my task was primarily to meet the Eskimo, not to correct government maps. What to me was of even greater importance was that according to Silah there were no Eskimo living on the coast north of Kimil. He said that there were ruins of old dwellings at various points along the Foxe Channel but he did not know whether the Too-neet (pre-Eskimo) or Eskimo had built them. From his description I gathered that they were similar to those I had seen on the Hudson Strait east of Lake Harbour.

Silah was fascinated with my pocket compass, having seen the big compass on the whaler *Active*. He knew that it was of considerable importance to the captain of the ship, but had thought it was some kind of clock. He now asked me to explain its use. It was not difficult to show that the needle pointed to the North Magnetic Pole and thus we could know the direction of our travel. He was puzzled as to why the needle swung east and west before it finally ceased to vibrate and why it pointed in one particular direction, no matter how we turned the face of the compass. It was more difficult to make clear how to set the course of a ship at sea when out of sight of land.

At the service that night I told the people that the compass needle was like our conscience. Sometimes it trembled because of the contradictory desires within us. But, I continued, if we are willing to be guided by our conscience, then we do the things that are right and have peace inside us. This was true, I said, whether we were pagans or Christians. It is thus, I told them, that our lives become rooted in God Who is the Great Spirit and we are glad to follow that which is true. I then tried to interpret Henry Van Dyke's words: "Life is divine when duty is a joy." I also told them at this service that the time had come for us to leave them and to turn our faces homeward.

On Monday, March 15, Luk-ta and three other hunters called and expressed their thanks to me for making the long journey to their land. The people hoped, they said, that I would come again soon. Later in the day Pudlo handed me a caribou-skin bag, which he said the men had asked him to present to me after we had started our journey south. The reason for this unexpected maneuver was that they did not wish me to pay them since it was a gift. In the bag were a fine pair of caribou-skin mitts to replace the worn and shabby ones I was using; some sinew from the jumping muscles of the caribou to be used for sewing skin clothing; several strips of meat from the back of the caribou which they knew I liked best of all, and finally three caribou tongues to be divided between Pudlo, Yarley, and myself.

Conditions were so favorable that we made rapid progress back to Cape Dorset where we received a rousing welcome. Lofty Stewart seemed as glad to see me as if I had come back from the dead. While we ate an excellent dinner my host plied me with questions and when the table was cleared we talked on into the wee small hours. It appeared to give Lofty peculiar pleasure that a Scot was the first white man to make the overland journey to Foxe Channel and get back alive.

On the journey back to Lake Harbour we had to travel up the great Chorkbak Inlet to a point where it becomes a two-armed fjord running a considerable distance inland to the north. Here we stayed at a camp called Akooleroon. From thence we proceeded south again on the east side of the Chorkbak to a camp called Tekoon where we spent two nights before traveling east again.

The season of Lent had now run its course. Easter morning was dull and the frosty halfhearted daylight revealed an apparently endless stretch of snow and ice until it reached some distant ice peaks, yet in our northern Easter celebration of the Holy Communion we remembered that we were joined with the vast multitudes all over the world who rejoiced that the Lord had risen. On Wednesday of Easter week we worked our way to Amadjuak Bay past many islands and across great barriers of rough ice. I wanted most particularly to approach again A-nil-me-oob the angakok, for I knew his people wanted to be taught. But A-nil-me-oob was as determined as ever that I should not instruct his people and used the same courteous and effective technique that had proved so successful the previous year. As I studied his strong face, his thick black hair falling almost to his shoulders, his piercing brown eyes and the arrogant set of his head when he spoke, I reminded myself that I was dealing with a man of superior quality. I felt that, perhaps with good reason, he had not a high opinion of the white men he had met and had no intention of allowing his power over the people to be lessened by them. I tried to put myself in his position and ended by admiring him very much even while I knew that he was the greatest obstacle to the progress of the work to which I was committed.

When we were about ten miles from Itinik I witnessed one of the most interesting hunting scenes in my life. Dotted here and there on the ice we saw seals basking in the sunlight near their breathing holes. Our sledges were stopped lest we should frighten the seals for we also saw two Eskimo stalking them. The seals took short sleeps extending from a few seconds to about one and a half minutes. After each nap they raised their heads and looked around. Seeing nothing of a suspicious nature, they dropped off to sleep again. But seals have quick eyes and move swiftly, so the hunters were exercising great care and much patience.

One of the men adopted the plan of impersonating the seal by looking and acting like one. In this way, he was able to come within easy firing distance and was successful in shooting a fat male. The method employed by the other hunter was different. He sat on a very small sledge about two feet long, propelling it over the ice with his feet and holding in front of him a screen of white cotton cloth with a peephole. He crept slowly to within range, then waited until the seal raised its head. Suddenly we heard the crack of the rifle and a seal lay motionless on the ice. In shooting seals it is absolutely essential to obtain a head or neck shot that kills the mammal instantly. Otherwise, it will wriggle, slip into the hole in the ice and be lost.

The average white man who goes to the Arctic shuns seal meat, probably because he so often sees the freshly killed corpses piled in the native boats or around the huts. Moreover, the flesh of the seal is like that of the walrus, the whale, the white whale, and narwhal—dark, chocolate-colored. This becomes black when cooked or exposed to the air and at first sight appears rather repulsive. Nevertheless, seal meat is good eating and is rich in vitamins. It has also other valuable properties. In the North during the dark period of the winter, it is hard for white men to get sufficient exercise to keep themselves in good shape physically, and a diet of seal meat will do more than anything I know to relieve constipation.

With Abraham, son of Mary Erkaktalik, as our guide, we left Itinik at eight o'clock on Monday, April 12, but because the snow was soft and deep we did not travel more than nine or ten miles before the men and dogs were so tired that we gave up when we came to an abandoned igloo and there we spent the night. At two o'clock the next morning we were awake and by four o'clock were on the move once more. During the night the wind had been blowing from the southwest, causing drifting snow to sweep across the ice. By ten o'clock the wind moderated and veered round to the north, the weather cleared and we continued on our way until about midday when the temperature quickly rose above freezing and the surface of the snow became soft and sticky. At Abraham's suggestion we stopped to rest for an hour and a half and ate some raw caribou meat. There were now three things in our favor—the wind had ceased, the loads on the two sledges were light, and the dogs were in good condition—so we determined to push on until we reached a camp called Katang at the mouth of the Lake Harbour fjord. This we did at half past eight, having traveled about seventy miles in fifteen and a half hours with an hour-and-a-half rest. This was a remarkable feat.

Our arrival caused great excitement in the camp. Everyone wanted to know what had happened during our three months' absence and whether we had met their relatives along the way. Pudlo rejoiced to find his wife and little family at Katang and it was with gladness that I greeted old Ing-mil-ayo. The trip to Lake Harbour the next day was easy and after we had had a hot meal I sent Pudlo back to Katang to be reunited with his people. Yarley and Abraham remained with me.

After living for three months in igloos with my Eskimo

friends, it seemed to me that the mission house was the height of luxury. I frequently rose from what I was doing just to move from my room to the kitchen and on to the little dining room and back again merely for the pleasure of contemplating it. To be the first white man ever to return alive from Foxe Channel had been an exciting experience, but already my mind was turning again to my people at Lake Harbour.

12. Farewell to Baffin Land ☆

A☆

At about eight o'clock that first evening back at the mission house two Eskimo arrived with a note from Parsons to bid me "welcome home." He had also sent along a leg of caribou. As he rightly suspected, my stock of fresh meat was low. I acknowledged both letter and gift without delay but did not cross the harbor to the Hudson's Bay Company on the morrow. Neither did Pudlo return to the mission as planned because the weather, which had been so beautiful during the last week, changed completely.

All the next day the storm raged, but I made good use of the time. Yarley and Abraham helped me to clean the house and to check my remaining food supplies. I was to leave Baffin Land on furlough in August or September and I wanted to have everything in order for my successor. It was difficult to plan for the continuation of the work when I did not know whether the mission would be manned or whether I would have to rely on the native leaders. Two men at Wycliffe College, Fisher and Gillett, had volunteered for the work the previous year. Would they arrive or would one of them be sent to Blacklead Island and the other come here with Greenshield?

I was also disturbed to hear that one of the white men in the country had tried to force Chartie and Abraham, against their expressed wishes, to make the round of their fox traps on a Sunday. This was very upsetting because these men were

two of our strongest Christian leaders and had been author-
ized by me to conduct Sunday services. They were also the
two best hunters in the Erkaktalik district. Later, I found that
the incident acted as a boomerang, for the Eskimo, of their
own volition and without consulting me, decided that they
would keep God's Word as they understood it and that they
would not work on Sunday unless it was a case of necessity or
mercy, which trapping was not. The trader said he did this
in order to test whether or not these leaders could be relied
upon to continue with the H.B.C. should Revillon Frères
establish a post between Lake Harbour and Cape Dorset. His
reasons for this trial balloon may be understandable but his
ethics need no comment.

At Port Harrison on the east coast of Hudson Bay and at
Wakeham Bay on the south shore of Hudson Strait the French
company had been in complete control until a few years previously when the English company erected trading posts in
opposition. Because of this the H.B.C. men had a strong feeling that competition would develop immediately in Baffin
Land. As a matter of fact their fears were groundless and it
was not many years before Revillon Frères sold out all their
trading posts to the H.B.C.

Two days later Pudlo and his family arrived from Katang
and with them five other sledges. This increased our Lake
Harbour population and meant greater activity in the
settlement.

Suddenly on May 26, Pudlo's little daughter, Pit-soo-lak,
took ill. When I went into the tent I found her mother sitting on the sleeping bench with her feet sticking straight out
in the usual Eskimo fashion. She was busy making a pair of
dainty sealskin boots for the child and as I entered the doorway she looked up and said simply, "She is not well." There
beside her covered with the skin of a caribou lay the child,
asleep but flushed and hot. In her arms she clutched a little
woolly rabbit I had given her at Christmas that had been sent
to us by the Women's Auxiliary of the Church of England in
Canada. The rabbit's color was many shades darker than

when I had first seen it and its long ears had been well chewed, but Pit-soo-lak's two little chubby hands clasped it to her breast. At the sound of our voices the little girl opened her eyes and looked at me in solemn silence, then she recognized me and with a faint smile turned to her mother and whispered my name, "In-nook-tah-kaub." The mother bent down, took the small face between her hands and murmured endearing terms while kissing it passionately. With a piece of the soft white skin of an Arctic hare she very gently wiped away the perspiration and gave the child a sip of warm condensed milk and water, after which Pit-soo-lak closed her eyes and seemed to sleep. The Eskimo's love for their little ones is unequaled. With the tenderest devotion, they give generously of those things that constitute true wealth.

In view of little Pit-soo-lak's condition, it was impossible for me to leave the mission except for brief visits to nearby camps to take services. Pudlo now needed me, as I had so often needed him. This was a time of bitter trial for him, and our friendship was deep. Indeed there had grown up between us a devotion and a mutual intuition that was at times startling and almost unbelievable.

On Trinity Sunday I preached at the morning service and Pudlo was to speak at the afternoon service. After my midday meal I had just begun to read when there was a knock at my door and Pudlo entered. In his very direct way he said that he did not understand how there could be three-in-one. Was it that the Father, the Son and the Holy Spirit were a family of three? Realizing the importance of this question to him and to me and knowing that whatever transpired would in time echo through the Arctic, I said that I was grateful to him for coming to me and suggested that we first ask God to help us to understand. We knelt together and prayed God to guide us into a knowledge of this truth. As we rose from our knees my eye caught sight of some artificial roses in a vase on top of my bookcase and in that moment I felt our prayer had been answered.

Taking one of the roses, I gave it to Pudlo to examine,

explaining that it had form but was not like an Arctic poppy; that it had color which was quite different from the wild heather; and that it also had smell. (I explained to him that because it was made of cloth the perfume had to be sprinkled on and that the real roses that grew in the lands far to the south had their own fragrance.) To these statements Pudlo readily agreed. I then asked: Is the form the rose? No. Is the color the rose? No. Is the smell the rose? No.

Yet, I pointed out, these three—form, color and smell— together make up the complete flower and no one of the three is more important than the other. Again, I said, in the white man's country it is common to have many roses in vases in the houses where we live. When you come in at the door you know because of the sweet perfume that there are roses in the house even when you do not see them. So it is with God the Holy Spirit. We don't see God but we know He is near. If we follow Jesus, then the Spirit speaks to our hearts and we do the thing that is right. Pudlo's face lighted up with a smile and he said, "How wonderful!"

I shall never forget that afternoon service when Pudlo stood before us as one filled with the Spirit of God and quite simply told his people of our interview and what he had learned from the rose. Then he appealed to them in the most eloquent, inspiring fashion to put aside all—yes, *all* the old pagan practices and beliefs. He pleaded with them to follow only the Great Spirit Who is Iso-ham-i-to-mit—Iso-ham-i-to-mut, that is "from everlasting to everlasting"—since now they had learned of His love in Jesus and had been given His Holy Spirit to guide them day by day.

There was a rush of words as he poured forth his thoughts. It was like the waves of the sea surging upwards because of the force behind them. No one hearing Pudlo could doubt his sincerity or his understanding of human need and his communion with the One of Whom he spoke. I thought of the difference between this converted Eskimo and the icily cold words of some preachers I had heard in the south. Here in this lonely land of bitter cold the warmth of the Spirit of the

Man of Galilee was manifested by an erstwhile pagan, for he spoke the language of Heaven.

In that simple service of common worship a feeling of peace and happiness swept over us as we discovered with new freshness our at-one-ness in Him Whom we adored. Pudlo's message had caused us greatly to desire to be channels of the strength of God to each other. It was an unforgettable experience.

It was evident that the faith of these Eskimo burned ever more brightly and was gradually changing their whole outlook. It was one more demonstration of how character is itself a precipitate of belief. I remembered how I had once wondered if these wild and ignorant people would ever be willing to leave the *old way* and follow the *new*. Although I was conscious that there was much to be done, my hopes and prayers had been gloriously answered.

As I studied some of our converts it appeared to me that their awareness of God was seen in their daily living. They had discovered that obedience to His known will, which involved sacrifice and service, was not simply their duty but their privilege. The fear, the bondage, the abysmal shadows had given place to a new-found liberty and a deep inner joy not known before. One hunter expressed it quite simply: "Before you came the road was dark and we were afraid. Now we are not afraid for the darkness has gone away and all is light as we walk the Jesus way."

At five o'clock one morning soon afterwards Pudlo's little daughter Pit-soo-lak was breathing heavily and, though we did everything possible for her, she just quietly stopped breathing. Later, it was sad to see the child lying in the small neat coffin made so skillfully by her father, lined with soft flannelette and covered with white calico which we used for making screens for the spring seal hunting. As I looked at Pit-soo-lak for the last time, I noticed that her little hands were clasped to her breast. I went back into my room and took one of the red artificial roses, cut the stem to make it shorter and then quietly slipped the flower under the clasped hands. I did not know until weeks later that the Eskimo had seen my action or how pleased he had been. Pudlo said he recognized the rose as the one I had shown him on Trinity Sunday and said he thanked me "a big one."

Little Pit-soo-lak's passing into the Heavenly nursery left an ache in our hearts but her parents, especially her father, were wonderfully upheld because of faith in their God. Nevertheless, "the heart knoweth its own bitterness."

The day after the funeral I thought it would be wise to leave Pudlo in charge at Lake Harbour while Yarley and I went off to Kinguckjuak to visit the people there over Sunday. It was at a service here at Kinguckjuak that for the first time I delivered my sermon without notes. This was a great step forward. During my first term with the people I wrote out my addresses in full and read them to the people. Later, I had been speaking from notes, but now I left my notes in my Bible. It involved more labor for it meant that I had to go over my notes repeatedly ahead of time, but I felt it was worth the extra effort.

The weather was very changeable on this visit of ours. Early in the morning of June 16 the wind had risen. By eleven o'clock thunder growled and rumbled. For a time there was silence, then suddenly flashes of lightning leaped across the darkened sky and then vanished, leaving us in what seemed the blackness of night. Unconsciously a shiver ran through me. There is something elemental and frightening about an electric storm as it sweeps over the Arctic hills and ice. It makes one feel very insignificant and I longed to be back in my own snug little room at the mission house with something more substantial than a wall of eight-ounce duck between me and the elements. In contrast to this the following day, Thursday the seventeenth, presented a complete change. At dawn the sky was silent. It was such a morning as John Masefield must have had in mind when he wrote:

> *A grey mist on the sea's face,*
> *And a grey dawn breaking.*

Gradually the open water beyond the floe edge became green while blue shadows lay on the ice. Soon a pale yellow light appeared in the sky low on the horizon. This took on a tinge of amber giving an exquisite combination of coloring. Overhead through rifts in the clouds we could see the cobalt dome of the sky stretching to infinity. My soul was filled with thankfulness and I resolved to give myself more unreservedly to the service of the people.

Yarley and I went for a walk which we enjoyed after having been restricted as far as exercise was concerned during the recent stormy weather. On our return I stopped to speak to an elderly man named Sow-ne-ah-lo. He was bending over an old corned beef tin in which he was boiling a concoction of bones, moss, seaweed, and blubber in order to make a glue with which to smear the seams of a leaking kayak.

We spoke of the weather and I remarked that Kinguckjuak seemed to be a place where there were many thunderstorms. Sow-ne-ah-lo said that it was evident I did not know that a powerful spirit lived in the hill overlooking the camp and that was why we had so many thunderstorms. This led us to speak about religion. As always, I found this man quite definite in his opposition, not to me personally for we were good friends, but to the message I had come to bring the Eskimo. With a simplicity and straightforwardness characteristic of his race he stated that he was an angakok and that he had no intention of changing his beliefs. He said that he knew "God's Books" were wise and that I spoke good words but that they were not for him. This attitude of outspoken directness never failed to command my respect.

That was the last occasion when I had any serious conversation with Sow-ne-ah-lo. He was a shrewd man, having great influence with his own particular group. It was not until twelve years later that I learned more about him. When in 1929 I asked about Sow-ne-ah-lo this is the gist of the reply given me:

"After you left us for the white man's country, Sow-ne-ah-lo gathered his family and friends together and departed to the land beyond the glacier [i.e., Frobisher Bay]. There he kept the feasts [pagan] and lived as the Eskimo used to live, for you remember he was never a believer 'in God through Jesus.' Last winter he died, but before he died he called the young men of the village into his igloo and spoke to them after this fashion: 'You who are young have wisdom and learn from me who am old and about to die. All my days I have kept the customs of our fathers. I have met the teachers but I have not believed their words. Indeed I have always endeavored to forget their teaching because I wished to follow the words of our fathers only. Now I am as one who is greatly weighed down and it is not good. So this is my advice to you who are young. Do not refuse to believe in God through Jesus, but cross the glacier and arrive at the teacher's and learn the commands of God and the words of Jesus, and believe. Then, like the other Eskimo who believe, you will be happy inside, whereas if you do not, then when you are old as I am you will be very heavy.' "

Am I wrong in thinking that Sow-ne-ah-lo believed more than he knew and was not far from the Kingdom of God?

That same day I had a long chat with my old and greatly loved friend, Ing-mil-ayo. During the six years since first we met my esteem for this man had deepened with each succeeding year. He had been a good pagan and was now a good Christian, but even I was not prepared for the faith which he displayed that day.

As I write, I seem to see him sitting on a box at the door of my tent. Cataract had blinded his eyes, yet his face was beaming with joy as he told me how God had blessed him and cared for him. Because his children were followers of the "new way," they were always kind to him, gave him the best of food, good clothes, and told him all the news. He could hear his grandchildren's voices as they played, and feel their faces when they came to tell him something.

He then said that he was very happy because God loved him and gave Jesus to be his Saviour and Friend. I expressed my great sorrow that I was not "a complete doctor" but only "the material for a doctor" because there were clever doctors in the south who could take away the veil from his eyes so that he could see again. Before I had time to continue he interrupted me by saying, "Yes! Just like Jesus did to the blind man!"

He then went on to say that because he was an old man he knew he must soon die but he was not afraid since his spirit would go to be with Jesus, with Him he would have new eyes and would be able to see the prophets and other believers. Then, with a smile, he added, "And you also, you will become an old man and you will die and be with Jesus and I will look out for you and together we will serve Him in the beyond." Need I add that my heart was full to overflowing and that the remembrance of his words still inspire my own faith after all these many years?

On June 30, Pudlo, Yarley, and I were early astir for we were to bring back to Lake Harbour a load of twelve seals shot by Pudlo.

The ice was in wretched condition—soft and sticky on the surface with multitudes of wide cracks and treacherously deep holes of water. We had hard work to keep the dogs on the trail, even with one man forging ahead and two walking by the sledge to help the dogs when added power was required. However, all went well until we came to a barrier of rough ice just at the south side of Hawk's Head. Here in order to see what lay ahead Pudlo climbed to the top of one of the larger hummocks and having decided which would be the best route for us to take, pointed it out to me. It being my turn to go ahead, Pudlo then returned to Yarley and the sledge while I started on, shouting to encourage the dogs and to guide them through the perilous and broken masses of ice. When the team finally reached the level ice their traces became snarled and had to be disentangled. It was then suggested that I go ahead again to pick out what seemed to be the best line of advance.

The ice in the narrow channel at Hawk's Head appeared

to be in good condition so I was encouraged and as soon as I rounded the headland I was thrilled to see the mission house on the hill about a mile away. I saw that the ice at this particular point was thin but carefully picking my way and prodding the ice ahead of me with my ski pole, I made slow but satisfactory progress. Suddenly the ice gave way under me and I found myself floundering in the water. I had no difficulty in stretching my arms out on the ice around me but each time I struggled to lift myself out of the water the ice gave way under my weight. The tide was strong and kept pulling my feet under the ice. I knew that I must exert every ounce of effort to avoid being sucked under and drowned.

Realizing the seriousness of my predicament, I shouted for help and fortunately the cliffs caught and magnified my cries. Pudlo and Yarley heard and guessed what had happened. Yarley was the first to see me. He tried to throw one end of his belt to me but I was too far away and ordered him to keep back. Then Pudlo came and threw me the end of the thirty-seven-foot whip. The twelve-inch wooden handle proved useful and Pudlo, after two unsuccessful attempts, landed it within my grasp. I managed to pass the thong round my back and under my armpits, a rather difficult task under the circumstances, and this gave my friends a chance to keep me above the water. Both men were petrified with fright and for a time little progress was made. Poor Yarley whimpered like an unhappy dog. Finally, after much effort on their part as well as on mine, I was dragged onto solid ice, bleeding, cold, and exhausted. The men quickly removed my drenched garments, rubbed me down with a towel and then helped me into some dry clothes, and into my caribou sleeping bag for a brief rest. When I felt able to go on six of the seals were unloaded from the sledge in order that we might make greater headway. Before we started we offered a prayer of thanksgiving to God for His great mercies and for giving Pudlo and Yarley the courage to risk their lives for my sake.

Up to this point we had all been very serious, but now,

without the slightest reason, we began to laugh. It was, of course, relief from the terrible tension. We were seized by a nervous convulsion of merriment and Yarley, blessed with an irrepressible buoyancy, alternately doubled up with laughter and shed copious tears.

An hour later three thankful men entered the mission house knowing that in this accident the shadow of tragedy had brushed very close.

Each day now we worked hard getting the mission ready for the coming of the man or men who would relieve me. The rowboat and canoe were repaired, scraped, and painted; the kitchen, porch, and the outside of the house cleaned and painted. The dog food required careful attention also. First, Yarley returned for the seals which were skinned, the blubber stored in barrels, and then the solid flesh was packed into the stomach linings of the large flipper seals, after which it was carried up the hill and buried in suitable places at the foot of one of the cliffs. Knowing that when the ship arrived we would all be pressed for time, we labeled the boxes and cartons of food supplies in the attic since these would be left intact for my successor and it was important they should be arranged in such a way as would make it easy for him to check them.

By mid-July the ice in the harbor broke up, the Eskimo came in and Parsons went off in his motorboat hoping to visit Wakeham Bay, Cape Wolstenholm, and Cape Dorset. I ran up the flag and fired a salute to let him know that I wished him a safe journey.

Each day more Eskimo arrived so that I was glad that I had got the affairs of the mission in good order earlier. Now I could devote myself wholly to the needs of the people. It was very pleasant to meet old friends and to note their pleasure at being with me again. I continued with daily school and daily teaching. I shall never forget Na-luk-tok's rubicund face streaked with sweat as he bent over his exercise book in an effort to master the multiplication tables and calculate how many .303 rifle cartridges, pounds of biscuit, and plugs of tobacco could be purchased at the trading store in return for a given number of white foxskins.

But their chief anxiety was to receive "more teaching." Our teaching services were now conducted in the church because there was not room in the house. This meant that I had to cross the harbor in the canoe each afternoon and evening which, in turn, meant that I did not have much free time. Nevertheless I was very happy. The Eskimo never seemed to tire of asking questions, and I encouraged them to do so, but my problem was how to answer them in such a way that they would understand and be satisfied. Some of their questions would have tested far wiser men than I. It required considerable perseverance and frequent repetition, since so many things common in civilization had no counterpart in Eskimo life. Besides that, it is not easy to answer even in English questions about God.

On many occasions I have heard individual families singing their evening hymn and closing with a simple prayer of thanksgiving spoken as if the Master were present in the igloo or tent. They were speaking to Him as children to a loving Father. "This is the confidence that we have in him, that, if we ask anything according to His will, He heareth us."

By now the warm weather had reduced the hillside to tears and the melting snow poured down in torrents and dropped from the glistening icicles which still fringed the cliffs at the back of the mission house. The sledge dogs, having nothing to do, lay about with tongues hanging out of their mouths, panting in the heat, while the poppies lifted their heads to the sun.

One night after I had returned from the evening service in the church I stood watching the afterglow of the sunset. On dull black nights this same scene could make me feel so terribly desolate, aloof and unsociable that I found it hard to throw off the feeling of utter loneliness. Knowing that I would soon be gone from the scene that had become both familiar and dear, I felt a great yearning to visit once more my old haunts beside the Big Lake. When I started out the sky was overcast and the barometer was falling, but I hoped that there would be no change until noon. For the first two hours all went well and I enjoyed the clean air and the feeling of the springiness of the moss under my feet. The tundra was now in full bloom.

Soon scattered low-hanging rain clouds that looked like mist came rolling down the mountain slopes and before I realized it I was enveloped in a downpour that seemed to penetrate into my very bones. There was no place where I could find shelter so I returned home drenched. Before entering the house I noticed that the wind sang among the cliffs and had whipped the waters of the harbor with such fury that curling waves crashed and boomed on the rocky shore sending spray high into the air. That meant that I could not use the canoe but would have to walk around the head of the harbor when I went to school in the afternoon and service in the evening. Yet when I lighted the fire in my bedroom, and thought of the furlough to come, I knew that I would miss such hardships. And sitting there I knew too that the Arctic was my true home.

On August 6, 1915, a two-masted ship was sighted far out at the mouth of the fjord, evidently stuck in the ice. This caused great excitement and I was confident that it was the mission schooner! For the next five days there was confusion at Lake Harbour until Parsons managed to get out to the ship in his motorboat. On his return he reported that she was an American schooner bound for Hudson Bay. Parsons was told by the men on the American ship that a great war was raging and the *Lusitania* had been sunk by the Germans with hundreds on board. It will be remembered that I had taken part in the designing and building of this ship. Not to hear of a major war until a year after it had begun seemed incredible and all this news was most disturbing. Parsons also announced that he had seen two other ships but that the ice was so thick he could not get near them.

Early on the morning of August 12, the *Nascopie* arrived. How can I describe the effect upon me of the news that she brought? It was a terrible shock to find that no man had been sent to take over the work. Somebody had blundered badly and I had to face the fact. Furthermore, Kidlapik had not returned from his trip to Blacklead Island. I was bitterly disappointed, for I had wanted to leave my work in the best of hands. Then, after prayerful consideration, I decided that the native Christian leaders must be used, and with speed I revised my plans. I felt sure that Lukesi Kidlapik had been delayed only by difficult traveling conditions and that he would reach Lake Harbour in the near future. I had every confidence in him as an outstanding Christian. So I arranged with the Hudson's Bay Company for him to receive the same food and pay allowances as Pudlo. Kidlapik would live, travel and teach the people east of Lake Harbour, while Pudlo would do the same for those between Lake Harbour and Cape Dorset.

I received another shock when Yarley told me that since there would be no missionary at Lake Harbour he wanted to go to the Amadjuak district where his married sister had invited him to stay with her family. Knowing how adamant Anil-me-oob, the angakok, was in his opposition to our work, I was filled with concern and wondered how this dear lad, so full of life and vitality and as yet without a wife, could stand up against the dangers and temptations inherent in life as a member of a pagan community.

There was little time, however, for exhortation or the making of alternative arrangements. Two days later after the farewell service in the church and just before the *Nascopie* sailed, I said goodbye to Pudlo, Yarley, and the others with a great ache in my heart.

The following morning as I leaned over the rail watching the ship slice its way through the green waters of Hudson Strait, we passed close to a huge iceberg. I felt that for sheer beauty nothing could compare with this floating mountain of ice whose magnificent pinnacles glistened in the sunlight.

The words of the Benedicte came into my mind and I cried, "O ye Ice and Snow, bless ye the Lord: Praise him, and magnify him for ever."

Suddenly I remembered that just as the ship was leaving Lake Harbour a letter had been handed me by one of the Eskimo. In the excitement of the moment I had forgotten all about it. I opened it now and discovered that it was from Ralph Parsons and was written on Hudson's Bay Company official paper. Here is what I read:

We are indeed sorry that you are leaving us, and we as well as all the Eskimo of this country will miss you greatly during this coming winter, not only in the good work you are doing, but because your cheery words and good advice to one and all of us have been the means of helping us to do our duty more than you have any idea of.

I read it twice, in surprise and pleasure. I could only ask God to make me more worthy of my opportunities and to keep me humble in His sight and in the sight of all men. My thoughts went back to the experiences that had been mine in the land we had just left. The journeys had often been perilous and physically wearisome. When I had been actually traveling in the winter, exercise had kept me in good health, but when held up by bad weather in cramped, cold, and uncomfortable igloos, I had constantly suffered from constipation, severe headaches and other pains due to wrong diet, irregular meals, lack of exercise, excessive cold, and the nervous strain inherent in that form of life. The lesson from these experiences was now all too clear. No matter how high my motive, I had ignored the needs of the body. The penalty was sure. The body has a way of avenging itself and its misuse was now affecting me in every way. I wondered how soon I could hope to recover from the toll these last two winters had taken. But even so, there were great compensations. Through association with the Eskimo, the traders, and the men on the ships my life had emerged richer, broader, and fuller than ever before. I felt that God had seen fit to use me as a channel of enlightenment to these people and especially to the copper-skinned children of my heart.

Twenty hours after leaving Lake Harbour, we arrived at Wakeham Bay, a beautiful cove hemmed in by bleak cliffs, on the Quebec side of the Hudson Strait. Here we found a very difficult situation as the result of the competition that had developed between the Hudson's Bay Company and the Revillon Frères. Fundamentally it was the old story of the white man's inability to grasp the fact that, while he may have advanced along one road of civilization unknown by the native, all men are in essence the same. The white men had come to this group of Eskimo very conscious of their own supposed superiority. They found the people good listeners and assumed that what they said to them, through an interpreter, was bound to impress them. In one way this was correct. The people were impressed but not always in the way that was meant! The Eskimo who has sometimes suffered as much as he has gained from the white man is likely to press an advantage when it presents itself. This was often true of half-breed interpreters who shrewdly played off one company against another. Perhaps as he grows up the half-breed has inwardly cursed the man who was responsible for his conception and for his mother's poverty. Neither does he feel disposed to like the white man even while he may envy him his "superior" social position. Only those with close and sympathetic understanding of him can assess his trend of thought or the accuracy of his interpretation. Most white men are not likely to outwit him.

At Wakeham Bay the half-breeds seemed to be sulky, unreliable, and lazy. But these generalizations must be qualified, for I have known many half-breeds who were cheerful, faithful, and courageous. Certainly the white man brought on his own troubles.

On August 25 we arrived at Churchill, and I was impressed

by the beauty of the big river with its strong five to eight knot tide. Above all I was thrilled to see again green trees even though they were seldom more than five to seven feet in height. The ship anchored in mid-stream, giving us a splendid view. On the north shore, near the sea, stood the ruins of Fort Prince of Wales which had been built by the Hudson's Bay Company in the eighteenth century.

A little farther up the river on the same side stood the Hudson's Bay Company trading post with our Anglican mission only a few hundred yards away. The church had been prefabricated before being shipped from London and was the gift of friends in England. It was similar to our other Anglican churches at York Factory and Great Whale River. On the south bank we saw a trim set of wooden buildings which housed the Northwest Mounted Police, now the Royal Canadian Mounted Police.

On our way back to the *Nascopie* from a courtesy call at the post and mission we ran into a school of white whales. It was quite exciting to be surrounded by these strange creatures whose white skin looked exactly like that of an automobile inner tube. They did not appear to be afraid of the launch in spite of the noise of the engine and propeller. They swam past us up the river at a much greater speed than we were capable of. I had seen and eaten white whale but had never got such a close-up view of them before.

At Chesterfield Inlet the captain and I went ashore and visited the Hudson's Bay Company. Then we called at the Roman Catholic mission and had a chat with Fathers Turquetil and LeBlanc. This mission had been established three years before and was their first among the Eskimo of the Eastern Arctic. Captain Mack invited them to visit the ship the next day and when they arrived sent word for me to join his little party. The priests were both from northern France but Turquetil spoke English quite fluently. We had a very pleasant time together. The captain drank gin, the chief engineer John Ledingham drank Port wine, the priests drank rum, and I drank water—which was doubtless the least appetizing because it had been in the ship's tanks for more than eleven weeks!

Before leaving, Father Turquetil asked me to visit them the following day. I did so and found them both interesting and affable. I was impressed by Turquetil's shrewdness and by LeBlanc's sense of humor. Somebody had told them that I was establishing a mission at Chesterfield and had forty tons of freight to be landed. This caused them great anxiety until I assured them that such was not the case. They agreed that we should not establish missions in opposition to each other at the same places since the Arctic was very large. But later it turned out that their authorities had different plans.

The last port of call that was of special interest to me was Fort Chimo, Ungava, which lies some twenty miles up the Koksoak River. Here I met our missionary, the Rev. S. M. Stewart, and his congregation of Eskimo and Nascopie-Cree Indians who came from the hinterland of the Ungava Peninsula. These Indians speak the Cree language with some dialectal variations and differ little from those who trade at Great Whale River and Fort George farther south but who are generally called Inlanders by the white men there.

I was interested to find that the Nascopie Indians and the Eskimo kept strictly aloof from one another. The Eskimo pitched their tents near the river while the Indians had theirs on the other side of the settlement. The Nascopies referred to the Eskimo as Est-te-mew, which showed that the old name given to them had been retained. It is recorded that more than three hundred years ago when a French trader from Quebec made a trip north along the Quebec-Labrador shore, he was surprised to meet a stranger whose appearance was different from that of his Indian guide. On asking who the newcomer was he received the reply, "Ies-chi-mou." It was a term of contempt and meant "an eater of raw flesh." The white man naturally called these northern people by that name, which the French spelled "Esquimau" and the English "Eskimo."

On October 19 we finally reached St. John's, Newfoundland, where I lunched with the bishop, Dr. Llewellyn Jones, before leaving for Toronto.

It was strange to be at home with the feeling of absolute freedom. To be able to speak to my wife of the loneliness and hardships was a sweet relief. Adventure, tragedy, joy had all been mine, and above all a deep satisfaction in the work committed to my charge. I felt proud yet humble for I was becoming increasingly conscious that "Power belongeth unto God."

INTERLUDE II

Yet the next few years were fraught with disappointment and frustration. To my amazement the doctors pronounced my health to be precarious—in fact, they feared that it might be permanently injured. They insisted first upon a year of complete rest. For a young man of thirty-two to be laid aside with ill health was not easy. I had sacrificed all aspirations of worldly success to preach Christ Crucified to the Eskimo, but here at the end of just four years of missionary work the door seemed shut.

During this year of idleness I tried my hand at gardening but found it was not my métier. Then to provide an outdoor occupation we purchased our first car, a Buick, and this gave me considerable pleasure and amusement. But all the while I was unhappy and discouraged and extremely restless. What did the apparent negation of my high endeavor mean? I prayed and pondered but found no answer. Doubts of every kind assailed me. At the end of the year the medical pronouncement was much the same, "Light work, no strain, a return to the Arctic out of the question." It was hard to keep my faith and not to let bitterness and self-pity take command.

But looking back now across the years I can see so plainly that this was a period of development and training. The very fact that I had to fight so strenuously against doubt and despair and that, by God's grace, I was victor gave me the

243

strength to pass more confidently through other trials. I think that I can say with complete honesty that after this experience I lived in perfect confidence of God's will, and never again cried out, "Why, oh, why?"

For the first year of light work, that is in 1916, I was locum tenens at Port Hope, Ontario, and in 1917 I held the same position at the Old Stone Church, Saint John, New Brunswick, it being thought that the sea air might prove beneficial. Again, as I look back I realize the inestimable value of these experiences. Heretofore, I had had no firsthand knowledge of parochial work and I knew little or nothing of the organization of a parish or of the many problems involved. My two assets were a genuine love of people and a passionate desire to win souls for Christ. All that I learned at this time bore direct fruit when God called me back to my chosen work.

By the autumn of 1918 my health was sufficiently improved for me to assume the post of chaplain and financial secretary at Wycliffe College, Toronto, and again, looking back I appreciate how necessary for my future responsibilities was this training in the handling of money and the raising of funds. When later the Church saw fit to lay upon my shoulders the burden of raising $15,000 new money each year as well as capital sums for the establishment of hospitals, schools, and missions, I realized that that task could never have been successfully accomplished had I not struggled with this earlier endeavor. I was happy in my work at Wycliffe, though my mind turned ever towards the North and my heart leaped with joy when in 1920 I was considered strong enough to return to Baffin Land for the summer. Bishop Anderson felt that if the work among the Eskimo was to proceed at all, the time had come when it was essential to have some report on their spiritual well-being. Peck was now too old to venture North, so Bishop Anderson asked that I undertake the mission.

13. The Rescue of Matto ☆

☆

It was July 8, 1920, and I stood again on the deck of the *Nascopie* as she steamed down the St. Lawrence River on her way to the Far North. The ship was under the command of Captain Mead, a young Englishman, while my friend Captain J. E. Mack was on board but as superintendent of transport of the Hudson's Bay Company. The chief engineer was my old friend John Leadingham, who had been trained on the Clyde and was a great favorite in the North because of his kindly Christian spirit and his ability to meet every emergency with motorboats.

In those days the *Nascopie*'s passenger accommodation was somewhat limited and I shared one of the four small four-berthed cabins off the saloon with Inspector Oakley-Reams of the Royal Canadian Mounted Police, Mr. Storker T. Storkerson, a Norwegian, and Brother Gerrard, O.M.I., bound for the Roman Catholic Mission at Chesterfield Inlet. It would have been hard to find a group of men holding more divergent views on life and religion or with such different backgrounds, yet we enjoyed each other's society in spite of the closeness of our quarters.

Storkerson was a pleasant companion until he purchased a pair of sealskin boots on the Labrador and insisted on putting them under his bunk. Thereafter, the cabin was filled with a strong aroma that called forth many equally pungent remarks from the inspector. Storkerson had been a sailor on the ships of the Canadian Government arctic expeditions and had also accompanied Dr. Vilhjalmur Stefansson on his long trip over the ice in the Western Arctic. He was now on his way north to investigate conditions in Baffin Land and to report whether there was adequate sustenance for large herds of reindeer. He was under the auspices of an organization that had just been formed, "The Hudson's Bay Reindeer Company," with Stefansson as chief adviser. Stefansson, never having been in the Eastern Arctic and being busily engaged in other matters, had recommended Storkerson for the task.

Inspector Oakley-Reams was a big square-shouldered man with a strong personality. He was not talkative, but even so the fragments that he related were an amazing revelation. Henceforth I had a new admiration and respect for the Royal Canadian Mounted Police. The inspector was traveling north to inquire into the case of two Eskimo who had been murdered south of Baker Lake. We had one of the so-called murderers on board in charge of Sergeant W. O. Douglas, R.C.M.P. This man Ou-ang-wak was of the tribe of inland or caribou-eating Eskimo called the Padlimute. The inspector allowed me to visit Ou-ang-wak in his little room at the stern of the ship and it seemed to comfort him to be able to speak to someone in his own tongue. I became much drawn to this poor lonely man who could not, or would not, understand why the white man took him away from his own people or why they seemed to think that he had done something wrong. He had merely followed the customs of the Eskimo and not the customs of the white man of whose laws he was ignorant. With the usual candor of the unspoiled Eskimo Ou-ang-wak freely confessed that he had killed two of his tribesmen named Ang-a-look-you-ak and Ale-cum-mik. His story as he told it to me on the *Nascopie* differed in no essentials from what he said at his trial:

According to Ou-ang-wak he had four dogs and the two men whom he had killed wanted them and were very angry with him because he would not part with them. He heard that Ang-a-look-you-ak intended to kill him in order to secure the dogs, so on the simple basis of doing first to others what they intend to do to you, he went out early one morning with his rifle and shot Ang-a-look-you-ak dead. Having made this statement, he added, "When I had killed Ang-a-look-you-ak I was afraid of his brother, so I ran over quickly to his tent which was nearby, opened up the flap and saw him sitting on his bed. I shot him and hit him in the right shoulder and he fell dead."

The bodies were left in their tents for five days, this being the custom of the tribe, but at the end of that time Ou-ang-wak buried them. They were laid on the ground and the three rifles, the ones owned by each of the murdered men and the one used by Ou-ang-wak, were laid beside the bodies and the tent of the first murdered man was used to cover them. Rocks were placed around the edges of the tent to keep it from blowing away. One of the customs of the tribe was that when an Eskimo kills a person, he must not handle rocks for a time, must eat only a little meat, and when he is doing so must be sheltered from the sun's rays. These customs Ou-ang-wak said he had observed. He added that he had traveled a lot with the two brothers, hunting the caribou in winter and going in summer to the trader's store at Baker Lake. During these trips he had always got along with them very well and there had never been any angry words spoken.

Actually the case of Ou-ang-wak had a strange ending. Apparently there was no suitable place at Baker Lake for the confinement of the prisoner and when Inspector Oakley-Reams left to hold inquest Ou-ang-wak fled into the night and is believed to have perished in a blizzard. No trace of him was ever found despite the fact that the R.C.M.P. gave chase. The concluding sentence in the official account compresses the matter into these words: "Arrangements for trial for murder were rendered nugatory."

But through the police record of this case runs an attitude that is of the greatest importance. They, the guardians of the law, recognized that the whole tribe to which Ou-ang-wak

belonged was pagan and that the accused had carried out or,
I should say, fulfilled the pagan practices relating to a murder. I think it a matter worthy of the highest commendation
that while that great force on the one hand uses all its
splendid organization to bring evildoers to justice, yet on
the other hand it is not unmindful of the primitive state of
the people with whom it is dealing and takes the limited
development of the Eskimo into its consideration.

Of course the first person whom we saw when the ship
reached Lake Harbour was Noo-voo-le-a the pilot. The little
community had been watching and waiting for the ship even
as we had done in other years and they had seen her from
"my" point. So when we reached the entrance of the fjord
there was dear old Noo-voo-le-a waiting to take us in. Up the
ladder he came, and in no time was shaking hands with us
all. He was quick to remind me of the coming of the *Lorna
Doone* eleven years before.

Behind Noo-voo-le-a came Joseph Pudlo, and I am not
ashamed to say that at the sight of him my eyes were filled
with tears. Suddenly the five years of separation were oblit-
erated and we were again as brothers. I was allowed to take
Pudlo to visit the murderer Ou-ang-wak and they were soon
good friends. Indeed, I had difficulty in explaining why the
prisoner could not be allowed to come ashore and visit the
Eskimo in the settlement. Pudlo's heart went out to him very
truly as we asked God's mercy for him.

As the *Nascopie* rounded Hawk's Head we were surprised
to see the *Pelican* in the harbor. She had broken her propeller when bucking the ice in the Hudson Strait and had
come into Lake Harbour to have a new one put in place.
Pudlo and I had only a very brief chance to catch up before
the *Nascopie* dropped anchor opposite the mission.

My hand clasped that of another true friend, Lofty Stewart, formerly of Cape Dorset but now in charge of the Lake
Harbour District for the Hudson's Bay Company. He and the
other company men greeted us heartily. Lofty may be a man
of few words but as I looked that day into his strong fine face

I felt again that there is a bigness about him that sets him above his peers.

Then the Eskimo clambered aboard and greeted me as only Eskimo know how. Again I realized the value of the long years I had spent in the struggle to master the language. It was a thrill to find that after five years' absence I could instantly change from speaking English to Eskimo and to hear from these friends the things I wanted to know about their welfare.

I had yet another welcome and an unexpected one. On stepping ashore I was greeted ecstatically by a big wriggling dog who jumped up at me and in his exuberance nearly knocked me down. I suddenly recognized him as my old sledge dog and companion whom I had called Mack after Captain Mack. After five years he had recognized my voice! As I patted him and talked to him he whined just as he had been wont to do when I first brought him to Lake Harbour as a small pup from Cape Dorset in 1914. Now he was one of the senior dogs in the mission team.

Thanks to Lofty's kindly interest, I found the mission house had been cleaned and put in order. In no time it was as though I had never been away and it gave me inexpressible pleasure to welcome at the mission house the many Eskimo who came to see me. Their warmth reinforced my own enthusiasm for the work. The first few weeks at the mission were very strenuous since there were so many Eskimo in the settlement. We had wonderful services but since the church was unable to hold all the people at one service, I had to adopt my old practice of having three services each day—one for the children, one for the women, and one for the men. Then the constant interviews took up much time because the Eskimo properly do not like to be hurried. They reported that the winter had been a hard one since seals had been scarce. At times a few of the less successful hunters had found it necessary to get government relief. Some of the people, however, had caught many foxes and for the time being they were well off. One of the things that cheered me was the way the Eskimo spoke of Stewart and his colleagues, indicating a fine spirit of co-operation and mutual respect. Lofty's innate common sense had much to do with this, I felt sure. It is axiomatic that no matter for what purpose a white man comes to the country he has to merit the good will of the Eskimo or he will not succeed. This applies equally to the missionary, the trader, the explorer, the policeman, the anthropologist, or any other.

Once the broken propeller of the *Pelican* was replaced, she sailed away, and the *Nascopie* left on August 12. After that we entered upon our regular routine, but there was much to hear and many decisions to make. I was confronted with a problem about Pudlo and my other helpers. I had to make some distribution of the territory to be covered during the winter and as yet neither Kidlapik nor Yarley had got back to Lake Harbour nor was there any word from them. It would have been much easier had we been able to discuss it all together. I finally decided to have Pudlo spend the winter among the people between Itinik and Foxe Channel.

Pudlo came constantly to the house and we both reveled in our long quiet talks. But one evening he told me a tale which I heard with a sad and almost unbelieving heart. The previous winter an Eskimo named David whom we all knew had become ill and his mind unhinged so that he developed into a homicidal maniac. David lived in the Lake Harbour district about fifty miles to the west. He had first killed his own family. Then he built an igloo on a point of land where in the spring the Eskimo had to cross on their way to and from Lake Harbour. Whenever travelers approached his point of vantage he fired at them. Some were killed while others turned back in terror.

It was a serious business and caused great alarm, for David had always been considered a quiet kindly man, very fond of his wife and children and on good terms with his friends before he had grown silent and sullen. After much consultation Joseph Pudlo, who knew him well but was in no way related to him, offered to make a final effort to speak to the madman.

But David had developed great cunning. When Pudlo came within sight of David's igloo, he quieted the dogs and overturned the sledge so that they should not follow him. With arms outstretched to show that he was carrying no rifle and therefore came in peace, he drew near. David shouted at him to stop. After a long-distance exchange of words the two men came closer to one another, but David still held his rifle under his right arm. Pudlo tried to reason with him but soon realized that the poor mind was deranged. David believed that all the Eskimo were against him although he admitted that Pudlo was a friend. He accused his wife and children of harboring evil intentions towards him and explained that was why he had killed them. He was certain that the other hunters were shadowing him, hoping to take his life. Therefore he would not let them pass.

Pudlo assured him that he was mistaken but failed to make any impression upon the madman. Looking at Pudlo with blazing eyes, he spoke incoherently of his enemies, linking them all up with a medley of old pagan tales and stories from the Bible. Suddenly he stopped, and gently Pudlo tried to quiet his shattered nerves. David listened for a time and then reiterated that he believed Pudlo was a friend who would not kill him. He then said he wanted to be alone. Pudlo, not knowing what to do, offered David his hand which was taken and then quickly withdrawn. Finally the voice of the madman growled something about shooting any of the others who came near his place. Returning to Lake Harbour, Pudlo was conscious of having failed.

When the people heard the details of the interview there was great sadness in the settlement. The men gathered together to take council. It was clear that something must be done and done quickly. The plan adopted was simple and practical. Nine men were chosen. Each man took his rifle and each promised to act according to the strategy agreed upon. They traveled by sledge and dog team over the ice until David's igloo came into sight. Then they left the dogs in charge of one of their number while the others cautiously made their way, stalking the igloo. There were many broken boulders and it was not difficult for them to spread out in a semicircle and creep close to the dwelling. Not until the sun was setting did they see David coming across the ice on foot from the floe edge. Before entering the igloo he climbed on top and for a time scanned the district. Then he got down and lighted the blubber lamp which threw his shadow on the wall so plainly that his every movement could be seen. The men drew closer with their rifles cocked but it had been agreed that no one would shoot until the word was given by the leader. Nearer they crawled. David was now sitting down, and it was difficult to be certain of his exact position. At last the madman stood up. His silhouette was clearly etched against the ice wall. The signal was given; the rifle shots rang out; the shadow fell.

Who shot David? Not one man but all the men. In each man's rifle there was one empty cartridge. For days after hearing this story I felt as if something cruel had been at work among these people whom I loved. I understood the belief in evil spirits.

The tribe bore no ill will to this man whom they regarded as friend and brother, but because of his derangement they had mourned the loss of twelve innocent lives. And was not their handling of the situation perhaps as kind and just and merciful as ours has often been under similar circumstances?

If the story of David caused me much pain and sorrow, another incident was to fill me with thankfulness:

One morning as the winter sun was sending its first shafts of light through the haze that enveloped the coast, a few Eskimo hunters could have been seen busily harnessing their dogs to the sledges. When all the men were ready, the signal was given and the sledges soon disappeared in the distance as they sped their way towards the floe edge. The people in the village were hard pressed for food, since the walrus in that section of the coast had not been as plentiful as heretofore. Every hunter was therefore determined to secure his prey.

On arrival at the floe edge, where usually there was open

water, the men discovered that young ice had formed. From long experience they knew that to venture upon it would be to take the most grave chances. After consultation, they decided to divide into two parties, one traveling east and the other west, in the hope of finding some place where the heavy currents had kept the water open. Just as this decision was reached, they were amazed to see a lad venture out upon the young ice, evidently determined to approach the point where the walrus were sporting themselves. It is not the custom of the Eskimo to interfere with the action of another, and so the hunters contented themselves with a look of mutual understanding. Silence pervaded the group as all eyes turned towards the lad Matto.

They knew why he was jeopardizing his life in this way. It was not because he felt himself to be more courageous than his seniors, but because he had fallen in love with a maiden in his village, whom he hoped someday to marry. That day would come only when he had proved himself a hunter. This he could do by securing one of the great walrus, with its ivory tusks, valuable skin, and a thousand pounds of luscious meat.

Steadily but with great care Matto moved forward upon the smooth young ice until he reached a point beside the open water where a broken piece of the floe edge had been frozen in. Climbing upon that piece, he prepared to attack his prey. When his harpoon was suitably arranged with barb and line and his float inflated he was ready.

With a spyglass the men on the shore watched the boy's every movement. To their horror they discovered that the pan of ice on which Matto was sitting had been torn away from the young ice by the changing current. The young adventurer now stood on a floating island. Worse, he was being carried steadily south by the current. A muffled groan came from Matto's eldest brother and there was murmured conversation among the little groups of men. It was a desperate situation because the boy had no power to control the movement of the precarious pan of broken and drifting ice. The Eskimo forgot their need for walrus. The one absorbing thought was for the safety of the lad they loved. As the pan moved farther and farther away the men became more and more silent until Matto was finally lost in the vapor cloud that arose from the open water.

Nothing more could be done and of necessity the men now turned to hunting. All day long, weary and sick at heart, they traversed the floe edge in twos and threes but their search for food and for some sight of Matto was in vain. Their misery only increased as they thought of their dependents. Towards evening they met at the original point of departure and each succeeding group brought in the same dismal story of no success—no sign of Matto, no walrus. It was a sad and disheartened little assemblage. Then quietly Joseph Pudlo said, "Let us pray." With one accord the hunters knelt upon the snow while their leader lifted up his voice, asking God that He might in His mercy spare Matto and deliver him from a cruel death—and also that seal or walrus might be sent to feed the hungry people. As soon as the prayer ended, the little band turned slowly homeward.

When they arrived at the village they were met by the women and children and the old men who had come out in welcome and in anticipation, for the community was close to starvation. At the sight of the empty sledges the faces of the spectators became empty also and who can say what passed through their hearts when the sad news was told that Matto had been lost somewhere in that dreary waste of ice and water. The boy's mother gave a terrible cry and was at once surrounded by her children and friends.

After the first wave of sorrow had swept the village and while the people were all talking one with the other, Pudlo again raised his voice and, standing in their midst, reminded them that they were no longer pagans but Christians who believed in a prayer-hearing and prayer-answering God. He urged his people to have faith that this same God would hear their cry and answer as He saw fit for the sake of Jesus, the Redeemer. He then called upon them to join with him in offering prayer to the Most High on behalf of the lad out there alone. The people knelt in the open on the frozen lake around which their igloos were built and Pudlo prayed to the Heavenly Father, beseeching God to deliver Matto and to bring him back to the people who loved him. When the prayer was over, they sang a hymn and arranged for continuous prayer to be made all through the silent watches of the night. Two people, who were relieved in an hour by two successors, knelt in the appointed igloo, and thus it continued until the first streak of dawn. Then the men were aroused and returned to the floe edge.

The hunters now distributed themselves for miles in either direction along the coast line, hoping somehow to see Matto on his pan of ice and hoping to secure seal or walrus to meet the urgent need of food. All day long the men stayed at the floe edge watching and waiting. Silence and stillness surrounded them and the hours seemed endless. Towards the close of the afternoon a cry rang out, breaking the silence like a rifle shot. Then cry after cry was passed from one hunter to another in each direction. Suddenly with excited shouts all urged their dogs forward to the point down the coast from which the original cry had come. There, still crouched on the pan of ice, was Matto being borne by wind and current towards the floe edge. But the young ice lay between the open water and the floe edge and even if the boy were still alive this again presented a desperate difficulty.

The men discussed the matter and it was suggested that Matto's two brothers should go out upon the young ice and try to rescue him. But they were not courageous enough to risk the danger involved and frankly admitted they were afraid that they might meet the fate of their brother. No volunteers came forward. Then, without saying a word, that true and great Christian Joseph Pudlo quietly slipped from the floe edge onto the young ice, bearing in his hand an extra-long seal line. Who shall say what thoughts passed through his mind from that Scripture he had learned so well? "Greater love hath no man than this . . ." "He that will lose his life . . ." "I know that my Redeemer liveth." With great skill and caution he made his way inch by inch towards the open water to the point where the pan of ice with its precious burden was seen to be approaching. Then, seeing Matto move and stand upright, Pudlo threw a line to the frightened lad with a word of encouragement, telling him to fasten it around his body. Gently, steadily, Pudlo pulled at the line. When Matto came nearer, he finally supported the half-frozen boy as they crept together over the young ice towards the floe edge.

The spectators stood breathless, intent. Anxiety filled their hearts, and perhaps self-condemnation too. But above all there was admiration for Pudlo's pure heroism. When the two once again stood on solid ice there was great rejoicing. It was at once discovered that thanks to the good condition of his clothing Matto was not seriously hurt as the result of thirty hours' exposure. He was only cold and numbed, but no part of his body was so badly frozen that it could not recover.

Once more Puplo's instinctive reaction was to give thanks to God. This time we took the order of evening prayer and then spoke, urging those who were still holding to their pagan superstitions to become true believers, to give their hearts unto God, and trust Him Who "Jesuse pivloogo" (for Jesus sake) had at this time so wonderfully heard and answered the prayers of the Eskimo.

It was not Pudlo who told me this story but the other Eskimo who had accompanied him. In the south I had met critics who had challenged me saying, "Are missions worth while?" Here was the answer.

All too quickly the time came for Pudlo to set forth with the Amadjuak Bay Eskimo. After he left, Adam Nowdlak, who had been instructed at Blacklead Island, agreed to stay for the time being. Before his departure this strong Christian leader helped me greatly and I knew would be a true witness and teacher among his own people. After Nowdlak's departure, Naglikgeanilk, one of my old sledge boys but now a married man, became my helper. I continued to think of him as a boy and called him, as before, "son" and his young wife "daughter." We were very happy together and he frequently expressed his delight at being with me again, showing great diligence in his work about the mission and in his studies with me regarding the meaning of the great truths of the Gospel.

One of the things that impressed me as I settled down once more at Lake Harbour was the effect of the clean cold air and the freedom from the rush and turmoil of life in civilization which I had found so enervating before I left Montreal. Joy in my beloved work and the freshness of the air combined to give me a buoyant and cheerful spirit. There is something irresistible about the limitless stretches of that vast country which has become my country.

One night as I sat in my room I was surprised to hear someone walk into the porch and then into the kitchen. I shouted in Eskimo, "Who art thou?" and got in reply, "Me." But I did not recognize the voice. Rising from my desk I stepped into the kitchen and came face to face with my respected friend Anil-me-oob, the angakok. It will be remembered that he was the one Eskimo in Baffin Land who had been most unyielding in his determination not to allow me to teach him or his people.

After we had shaken hands we sat down and talked about the hunting, the weather, and the people who live in the Amadjuak Bay district. As we talked I kept wondering what this shrewd man who had twice so successfully and so politely given me my dismissal could possibly want from me. As the hours passed I finally decided to ask him directly, for I was certain he had not yet told me the real purpose of his visit. "What is it?" I asked him in his own tongue. There was silence for a moment. Then he said quite simply, "Because I wish to be baptized!" I was completely taken aback and looked at him with incredulity and amazement. To my shame I must confess that I doubted the man's sincerity.

I asked for his story. He spoke of the past, of my two visits to his camp and of how he had refused to allow me to teach his people. Then he reminded me that after I had left the country Yarley had come to live with his people and had married a maiden who was related to Anil-me-oob. He went on to say that Yarley had been true to the "Jesus way," refusing to join with the others at the pagan festivities or to believe in the power of the amulets to ward off evil spirits. Instead, Yarley read from the Books and sang hymns. He told how his own son and daughter had learned from Yarley to read the Books, to sing the hymns and to "make prayers to the Great Spirit through Jesus." So he, Anil-me-oob, the great conjurer, had learned from his own children and from Yarley. Now he believed and he wanted to be baptized and to become a "complete Christian."

It was my practice when a pagan Eskimo wanted to become a Christian to have him bring some other Eskimo to testify that the candidate had given up the old pagan superstitions and was earnestly seeking to follow in the "Jesus way." When he was asked that night to name a witness Anil-me-oob replied, "My wife and children." My heart thrilled for they of all people knew exactly how things were with him. I told him to bring them to see me the next morning.

Anil-me-oob then unburdened his heart to me. It was a long story and threw light upon many things—not least upon his contempt and dislike for the white man who had often misused his people. As we talked I could not fail to notice that with this man there was not the rapture of emotion that I had seen in some converts. Instead it seemed to be a transformed mind and will that attested to the reality of the change. My old friend had at last discovered that in true religion love, not magic, is the foundation and that this is revealed in day-by-day living by courageous acts of self-discipline, sacrifice, and kindness.

Because of his intellectual approach I gave to this man and his followers an especially reasoned and thoughtful preparation for baptism and then they were received most joyfully into the Church. I shall never forget that great occasion. After the service the people waited outside the church until

I had unrobed and then thanked me most warmly and told me how happy they were. As I looked into Anil-me-oob's radiant face and listened to his quiet words I had no doubt about the reality of the miracle that had taken place in the heart and mind of this strong and honest man. All his life long the pagan belief in the transmigration of the soul had weighed upon him like an incubus. This was now annihilated and for the first time he felt himself a free man with hope and joy in his heart. In him the Master's words were fulfilled, "Ye shall know the Truth and the Truth shall make you free."

It was with a wonderful sense of the power, the presence and the peace of God in my heart that I crossed the harbor in the canoe to the mission house. In the quiet of my own room I knelt and offered the praise and thanks due to the Most High.

The summer sped by and soon we were into September. The thirteenth of September began like any ordinary day at the mission. From a black and lowering sky the rain, driven by a strong south wind, banged upon the windowpanes as if demanding entry and heavy seas raced up the fjord from the Hudson Strait. Our small rowboat, the gift of the officers of the Hudson's Bay Company, was riding at anchor offshore and everything seemed to be safe and in good order.

Unfortunately we had no proper anchor for the boat but instead attached a heavy flat stone to the end of the mooring line, allowing plenty of slack because of the thirty to forty feet rise of tide. This simple device of using a stone for an anchor is very primitive but had hitherto proved effective since the weather had been calm. But the storm grew steadily in force. Each successive wave lifted the boat high in the water, causing it to strain at the mooring. As the tide rose each pull edged the boat nearer to the rocky shore. We saw the danger. We also knew that the boat was much too heavy for just my helper Naglikgeanilk and me to drag up over the rocks beyond the high-water mark. We decided that we must wait until flood tide. This proved a grave error in judgment.

We failed to realize how quickly the daylight would fade. As we launched the sixteen-foot canoe in the brief twilight the rocks loomed out at us like ghosts and by the time we reached the open water, darkness had closed down upon us. With the setting of the sun the fury of the wind abated somewhat but great breakers were still rolling in from the south. The temperature had also dropped sharply and a nasty wet sleet swept down upon us. Then we were unable even to locate the boat. At last we reluctantly decided to abandon the search and to return to our little cove.

For a time we successfully worked our way against the oncoming breakers towards the lighted storm lantern that marked our landing beach. Suddenly the canoe upset. My companion gave a cry as we were thrown into the angry sea. As we came up, we clung desperately to the upturned craft while the waves crashed over us. Once more we were both thrown back into the sea. Again we clung to the canoe. There was another rush of water. Then only I remained grasping the gunwale. I heard nothing and when I called there was no answer. I knew that Naglikgeanilk must have been swept under and away. In the inky darkness with the wind, sleet and waves surging over me I wondered when my turn would come. I could feel my body fast growing numbed and exhausted. After what must have been only fifteen or twenty minutes but seemed to be eternity, my right foot struck a rock. It was as if an electric shock charged through my whole being, giving me new hope. The next waves swept me into deep water again but my determination to hold on was revived. Then I felt broken boulders under my feet and, backed by the breaking surf, I was washed onto a ledge where I hung half in and half out of the water. I was now relieved of the strain of gripping the canoe, and gradually I began to regain my breath and my heart pounded less furiously. I was chilled to the core. After a time I succeeded in dragging myself away from the water's edge. Then I collapsed. I have no idea how long I lay there before my strength returned a little. I wanted to look for Naglikgeanilk but when I tried to stand upright I immediately fell down and I also realized how hopeless such a search would be alone in the fury and the darkness of the night. After a further rest I managed to crawl on my hands and knees over the rocks to the mission house. On entering the kitchen I fell on the floor. To this day I do not know how much time passed before I was able to remove my drenching clothes.

I finally managed to light the fire. Then I secured a towel but the effort involved in drying my body tired me too much. Drifting between consciousness and unconsciousness, I lay on the rug in front of the stove. Over and over the details of the tragedy were re-enacted in my mind, causing me alternately to shiver and to perspire violently. It was a night of utter horror and anguish. At last the grey light of dawn filtered through the window of my room. The fire had burned itself out. I shivered and my ears rang. I cried out, "Naglik-geanilk, Naglikgeanilk," and the sound of my voice startled me. My mind was confused until I saw in pools of water the clothes I had cast off a few hours before.

I now put on clean, warm clothes and in the early morning light walked around the head of the harbor to the Hudson's Bay Company's post. Lofty heard my footsteps on the platform that ran around the house and sensed that something was wrong. As he opened the door, he asked, "My God! What has happened?" His face was grave and white in the pale morning light. As soon as he heard my story he aroused the other members of the household and, accompanied by some of the Eskimo, went to the scene of the tragedy. The tide having gone out, they found Naglikgeanilk's body lying face down with arms outstretched on the shore near the low-tide mark. Both the canoe and the rowboat lay on the rocks at high-water mark. When Lofty returned we had breakfast and then he sent me to bed until lunchtime while the Eskimo began to make a coffin.

My interview with the lad's family was especially painful. I could only clasp the mother's hands in my own. His young wife stood silent, cold and motionless in her grief. It was not

hymn and then with profound reverence praying to their heavenly Father. I, the unwitting eavesdropper, went back to my own quarters with a glowing heart.

In the Arctic, as in the south, some people, both white and Eskimo, live sordid and ignoble lives. No one knows this better than the missionary. At the same time I had abundant evidence that many of our Eskimo leaders both men and women had not only become what St. Paul calls "new creatures"—but more. Their fellowship in the Gospel had deepened with the experiences of the years and had resulted in the development of Christ's disposition in the mind of the people as a whole. This was my comfort and my exceeding great reward.

On October 7 the *Nascopie* returned. To my intense surprise and pleasure I found Dr. R. B. Stewart of Toronto on board. When the doctor came ashore I took him to examine those Eskimo who were or had been ill. I was thankful when he approved of the medical treatment I had given them.

After two days the ship weighed anchor and once more I was homeward bound. It was with a heavy heart that I parted with my many friends. From my own personal viewpoint this trip had been in one way most satisfying and in another way most upsetting. My heart was given irrevocably to my spiritual children yet my health, as even this short trip had proved to me, left much to be desired. What was my future to be? Was Arctic work to be denied me forever?

☆ **14. Archdeacon of the Arctic** ☆

UPON MY RETURN to Toronto I had again to accept the verdict "unfit for active service." Not yet understanding why the door of my chosen work in the Arctic had been shut, I had now to decide through what channel the Lord intended me to work. In due course I accepted the rectorship of the Old Stone Church in St. John, New Brunswick, where I had recently been locum tenens.

The next six years were among the happiest in my life for my dear wife was at my side and I threw myself heart and soul into the activities of the parish and the city. The rector of such a parish lives a very varied life and mine was no exception. To me the most satisfying of all the phases of the work were the discussions with individuals on the fundamental issues of life in relation to the Christian witness.

It was during these years at St. John when I was constantly preaching and speaking that I came to feel strongly that the Church should deliver a positive and not a negative message. In spite of the sin inherent in human nature it is possible for men and women to respond to the call of God and to rise to higher levels. Time and time again struggling souls unburdened themselves to me, knowing that they had not the inner strength to meet the conflict. Yet time and time again as they truly surrendered their wills to the strong Son of God I saw the power to conquer come into the individual life and with it peace. This being true it seemed to me that the Church should proclaim much more emphatically that Christ came not to destroy but to fulfill all that is worth while in human life.

Some of the congregation were what might be called conventional Christians and I realized that one of my tasks was to break through the heavily coated and starched propriety and rouse them to a deeper consecration. This pressed upon me the conclusion that it was the Church's duty to stress urgently the individual's personal responsibility to God for the life he led day by day. In my preaching I tried to make clear to my people what Christianity really is, apart from all our traditions, customs, and accretions. And often whether with rich or poor, the respectable or the down-and-out, the drama of human life pressed hard upon me.

During these years at St. John my health improved although I was plagued by migraine headaches which laid me low for about three days of every month. My interests were wide and I did some diocesan committee work and also some preaching in other cities. It was during this period that I received calls from a number of important parishes both in Canada and in the United States. The two that attracted me most were in Philadelphia and in Baltimore but all were declined because I felt that my creative work at the Old Stone Church was not yet done. It was my opinion then, and has continued to be, that it is in the best interest of both parish and priest for an incumbent to stay at least five years in one charge. A man cannot grasp the particular situation, get to know the people, and do constructive work in less than that time. So I declined the offers that came my way. To the best of my ability I was lifting up the Christ. I was often consulted on Arctic affairs, but so far as active participation was concerned I had put that behind me.

Therefore it came as something of a shock when it was suggested that I should leave St. John to become the Archdeacon of the Arctic and dedicate myself to correlating and making more effective the Church's work in the Far North.

Up to now the missionary efforts among the Indians and Eskimo had been devoted but unconnected. It was becoming increasingly evident that some degree of correlation and unity was necessary.

The proposition was bristling with difficulties. The work lay in the northern portion of four dioceses—Moosonee, Keewatin, Mackenzie River, and Yukon. How could a man hope to organize, finance and minister to such an enormous field, particularly when he was not free but must be subject to the authority of not one but four different bishops? I had the greatest respect for the four bishops but I found it difficult to believe that if I accepted the position I would receive much practical assistance from them, a fear that unfortunately proved to be justified. It was natural that it should be so. I would also have to work under a committee of seven to whom I could report but once a year, and experience had already taught me that committees had a way of "leaving it to George" to carry on without much help once a resolution had been adopted and "George" appointed. This committee further declared that it would expect me to raise $5,000 new money each year in Canada and another $5,000 in England. Moreover I would have to start from scratch. There was no organization, no headquarters, no staff. The only thing that I would inherit was an overdraft of $9,000 at the bank.

It was not easy for me to arrive at a right judgment in this matter and I refused to give a hasty decision. I was filled with a deep sense of my own inadequacy for such a task. Yet I had to ask myself whether before God I would be justified in refusing to undertake the work simply because it was difficult. Duty, not desire, finally prevailed. It was with reluctance and fear, rather than with joy that I accepted. From the standpoint of health the assignment was also a gamble but the doctors thought that I would probably be able to stand the summer Arctic trips and gradually build up a resistance to the winters. So in 1927 I became Archdeacon of the Arctic and bought my first pair of gaiters! I established myself at Church House in Toronto in an empty room, acquired some secondhand furniture and wondered how I could afford office help.

Once I grappled with the task, however, the way opened. From then on I approached my work not only as an individual missionary but as an administrator who must decide what was needed here, who could be sent there, and how the people could best be served. I continued to keep in touch with and to know individual Eskimo, but my thoughts had also to encompass the work as a whole. Then I had to put my plans into action by raising the money and finding the workers. It was not a sinecure.

From year to year I watched the different men in their lonely mission posts struggling, striving, succeeding, and sometimes failing. I observed their attitude towards the Eskimo and the white men, their devotion to their Lord—or the lack of it—and I gave great thought to the essential purpose of the missionary task. The most difficult part of it, then as now, was to secure workers sufficiently dedicated to the call of Christ. The missionary task, in whatever land, is a high challenge with its dangers and austerities, its isolation and temptations. I have frequently been asked how it is possible for a person to be happy in the face of the privations involved. Briefly I would answer that the realization of the need of the people for that which the Christian message alone can bring inspires the hours of each day. Only men and women with a glowing love of their Saviour and a pastoral heart stand up adequately against the hardship and loneliness. But even more searing to the spirit is the hostility of the white people who flagrantly transgress the Christian laws.

One of our most pressing needs is to impregnate the theological colleges with evangelistic fervor. Let the men be fired with spiritual enthusiasm for their Lord and Master and they will so witness in their daily life that other young men will be drawn to Him and yield their wills to His service.

But these reflections were not clarified in my mind when I started north in the summer of 1927 on my first tour of inspection as archdeacon. Accompanying me on this trip was the Rev. B. P. Smyth, who had bravely volunteered to establish a new mission at Baker Lake which lies 210 miles inland from the northwest coast of Hudson Bay. When we reached my old station of Lake Harbour my heart went out again to my dear friends there. I cannot enumerate them all but neither can I fail to mention Joseph Pudlo. We were not brothers in the flesh but we were brothers in the spirit and when I felt his hand in mine and looked into his eyes I knew that all was well. We were also greeted most cordially by the Reverend and Mrs. Blevin Atkinson, who were now in charge of the mission, and by the Hudson's Bay Company men. Mr. Atkinson then gathered all the Eskimo together for a service of thanksgiving.

Instead of giving a sermon I introduced Mr. Smyth to them and spoke of the need at Baker Lake. The Eskimo there were wild and pagan. Before Mr. Smyth could become a "complete teacher" to them he would have to learn the language and the customs of the people. Therefore for the first two years he must have the help of a Christian Eskimo. Who from this group would go? I did not minimize the sacrifice on the part of the one who would make the venture. He would have to leave his friends and the hunting grounds he knew, and although a dweller by the sea he would have to live inland where there were no seals, walrus, whales, or polar bears. He would have to accustom himself to caribou, fish, and birds. It was, I told them, "the call from Macedonia" over again. They knew that the time for decision was limited to the brief stay of the ship.

The following morning two of the hunters called on me at the mission house and said that after a meeting of prayer and discussion it had been decided that Joseph Pudlo would go. Quickly I sent for him. His answer was simple and brief. "I do not want to depart but I will go with Mr. Smyth because Jesus calls me."

Some of the white men expressed the opinion that I was making a great mistake since Pudlo was a stranger to the

Eskimo at Baker Lake. They prophesied that he would not be welcomed by them. In fact they said he would almost certainly encounter enmity and danger. But I felt that the decision was right.

Pudlo and his family were then lodged on the *Nascopie,* and with his help and in spite of the rush I was able to hold services with the Eskimo at every port of call. As always the time of the services had to be arranged so as not to interfere with the unloading of the cargo. They were usually held at low tide.

I discovered that Captain Berthier, the Revillon Frères inspector on board, also had to get to Baker Lake. We were both relieved to find that the *Nascopie* was to remain at Chesterfield Inlet for four days. There we were able to hire the high-power launch belonging to Mr. Ralph Parsons and, accompanied by Mr. Smyth and the Pudlo family, we set off without delay.

At Baker Lake both the representatives of Revillon Frères and the H.B.C. were most helpful in their suggestions as to the best place for the mission house. Once that was decided, and with the co-operation of the traders, we gathered the Eskimo together and explained why we had come to them. We were not traders, we said, nor interested in buying furs. We were teachers. There were hearty expressions of thanks and when Pudlo told them his story they seemed to be ready and willing to receive him.

I had a chance for a private conversation with the Revillon Frères post manager, Robert Stewart, a fine Scot whom I had met on board the whaler *Active* in 1913 and again at the Revillon Frères post at Wakeham Bay in 1915. From him I learned, among other things, that the young Eskimo chief Na-te-lah was an angakok and had great power over all the people. This was important news for in a sense our success or failure lay in his hands. So far, he had been friendly. He had the usual Eskimo features—a round, flat bronze-colored face and thick shiny black hair that covered his ears, but his alert expression also had in it a touch of aggressiveness. On the other hand, his ready, disarming smile and his evident desire to be on good terms with us was encouraging. I liked him but felt that if these caribou-eating Eskimo were like their chief we would not find it easy to convert them. Because I desired to understand Na-te-lah and to be understood by him and also because I wanted to gain some idea of the countryside, I asked him to take me for a walk. We climbed the hills overlooking the lake and when we reached the top we sat down on the heather to rest.

Now that we were alone my companion became communicative. He answered all my questions most willingly and in turn asked me about the Eskimo in Baffin Land. Then, as if we were old friends, he turned to other things, pointing out a wide valley with a small stream running through it which emptied into Baker Lake. He said that when the caribou were migrating in June they took three days to pass down this valley. In that tremendous cavalcade there were relatively few stags because before the arrival of the rutting season the strongest stags chase the weaker from the herd. These unwanted stags then form separate herds and pass on their way. For the caribou, as for all the other animals in the Arctic, the stern law of the survival of the fittest is operative. Na-te-lah described to me in detail how sometimes during a fight the antlers would interlock and both beasts, unable to free themselves, would weaken and die while the herd passed unheeding on its way.

By the time we got back to the tiny settlement I felt that in Na-te-lah I had made a friend and that Mr. Smyth would encounter honest opposition but not craftiness or double dealing. As it turned out later I was correct. For a long, long time Na-te-lah kept to the "old way" and it was not until eighteen years later that he was baptized by Canon W. J. R. James who was by that time the missionary in charge of St. Aidan's Church, Baker Lake.

There was another angakok, A-ka-la, who attended the services regularly while Mr. Smyth was there although there was no conversion. One day he came to Mr. Smyth and said that the police were going to take away his wife because he was a wolf! "I am not a wolf," he added, "though I was before."

The H. B. C. carpenter very kindly started the building of the mission house and Mr. Smyth and Pudlo finished it. Pudlo did outstanding work here with the Baker Lake people. Among those who came under his influence was a pagan named Tapatai. They both took advantage of their year together and to this day Tapatai is the right-hand man of Canon James.

As I returned to the *Nascopie* in the motorboat with Captain Berthier I felt that our new venture was off to a happy start. It had been arranged that at Port Burwell I should transfer from the *Nascopie* to the H.B.C.'s small schooner *Fort Garry* and continue north. The *Fort Garry* called at Pond Inlet, Pangnirtung and Blacklead Island, and at each port we had a busy time. Blacklead Island was of special interest to me because of my memories of the devoted Peck, Greenshield, and Bilby. They had endured privations greater than any I had known. They had also faced the diabolic opposition of the handful of white men in the settlement. These men willfully and deliberately had stirred up the local conjurers against the missionaries. Later with subtlety and malice they raped the first little group of Eskimo women who had been prepared for the Sacrament of Baptism. Then, like Mephistopheles, they jeered at Peck and his companions, saying, "We'll show you holy Willies that your preaching won't gain a foothold here." For a time it seemed as if all Hell had been let loose on that little island. But after a time by God's good grace two Eskimo were baptized, then more. The good seed was slow to germinate and much was lost because of the white men, but in the end rich fruit developed. Now I clasped the hand of one of the first converts, Peter Too-loo-ak-juak, who had been baptized by Peck twenty-four years before. Through the years Peter had been sorely tested and tempted by the white men but he had kept his complete trust in his Saviour.

Later that summer of 1927 I traveled on the *Larch,* a small cargo vessel that was bringing supplies and equipment north for air bases being built at Port Burwell, Wakeham Bay, and Nottingham Island. I mention this because, as far as I know, these were the first air bases in the Arctic. Now such bases are commonplace.

My return journey to Halifax was spent in preparing my report for my four bishops and the committee. Money—money—money. That was what was needed. The future I could see but not without money to put my plans into execution. And who would raise it? I knew the answer. If the Archdeacon of the Arctic wants more money, let him raise it. And I did.

Skill in money-raising as in everything else comes slowly and I learned by trial and error. From the start, however, two things were clear in my mind. The order must always be interest, prayer, and money; for I held then, as I do now, that if interest is aroused and sincere and devout prayer offered, the gift will follow. I have never believed that it is to the glory of God or His Church to "hold up" people for a donation. I also felt deeply that I must use every legitimate means at my disposal to keep the work not only before the members of the Anglican communion but before the public. The Eskimo were, after all, Canadian. Their welfare, it seemed to me, should be the concern of all. It has been said that because I took this stand consistently and at times aggressively through the years, my concern helped at least in part to arouse the belated interest of the Canadian Government. In 1927 there was none.

It would be tedious for me to recount in detail the various methods by which I raised increasingly large sums of money for the work. Once in the early days I caused a sensation by showing my colored slides in a movie theatre in Ottawa on a Sunday night! All the Anglican churches canceled their evening services at the request of the bishop so that their congregations might attend. We had a packed house but it was considered such an innovation that not all the comments afterwards were laudatory! The greatest "boost" I received at the beginning was when Governor Sale of the Hudson's Bay Company wrote in 1929 that his company would give a substantial sum each year to the work for a period of three years. Within three years of beginning the work I had been fortunate enough to wipe out the inherited overdraft of some $9,000 as well as to bring in the funds required over and above the amount allotted me by the missionary society of the Church.

My attainments at this stage were not spectacular but on the other hand as a peripatetic archdeacon I did not meet in Canada with the opposition that I found later when as bishop I launched a definite Arctic appeal within the Church. Then I discovered that some of the bishops and many of the clergy were obsessed with the idea that every dollar given to the Arctic was a dollar taken away from their diocese or their parish. Time and time again I encountered skillful attempts to sidetrack the appeal. The Church itself had laid upon me this task of money-raising and surely I had the right to expect sympathy and support from its leaders. Yet I was often confronted with intrigue quite unworthy of those in high places. I love my Church and hesitate to set down criticism of some of her less worthy clerics, but because this strong opposition caused my burden to be well-nigh impossible I feel that in truth and justice it must go on record. In contrast to this was the unfailing and ever-increasing generosity of the laity of the Church of England in Canada.

In the original agreement with the committee of seven it was understood that I would raise money in England in addition to what I raised in Canada. So in 1929–1930 I crossed the Atlantic for this purpose. I went again in 1930–1931 and after that it became my practice to go every other year, staying for six months and returning to Canada just in time to set off again on my summer trip to the Arctic. In England I spoke on the average of three times a day, seven days a week, for the six months of my sojourn there.

On my first visit to England I faced a situation that automatically spelled failure and defeat for the Arctic cause. Most of my preaching and speaking engagements were made by the Society for the Propagation of the Gospel, that venerable organization commonly known as the SPG. Unhappily the previous year the SPG had run with a large deficit which they were now trying to wipe out. Consequently at every service the length and breadth of England, or so it seemed to me, the collection was assigned to the SPG overdraft fund, and not to the Arctic mission. Time and time again I poured out my heart's longing in my sermon and could feel that I had moved my listeners to sympathy. With a glow of expectation I left the pulpit and returned to my place in the chancel. Surely there would be some £10 notes earmarked for the Arctic. Then on my ears fell the cold voice of the vicar, "Today's collection will be devoted to the SPG general fund." Poor Arctic! Poor mendicant archdeacon! As the weeks and months passed it was doubtful if I would even make my expenses, let alone raise any substantial sum. My discouragement and frustration increased to such an extent that I was almost ready to give up and sail for home. But after that first time things went well, and I owe to the SPG and to the loyal and generous supporters of the Arctic more than words can ever say.

Another exhausting factor the first winter in England was that I could not afford secretarial help. All the vast amount of correspondence had to be written by hand at odd moments or late at night, including the making of *duplicate* copies of important letters since I did not know how to type. I also found it extremely difficult to make the right decision on Arctic problems at such a distance.

During my early attempts at large-scale money-raising my heart and my body literally ached, and it was only my complete conviction of the value of the Arctic mission that kept me going. Then too I was encouraged by the kindness, generosity, and gracious hospitality of the people of England. I was welcomed to their homes, their churches, and their lecture halls and given the warmth of their Christian friendship.

There was another situation that I had not foreseen at the beginning of my English visits and which at first caused me great unhappiness. I refer to the question of churchmanship. It is far too easy to become so entangled in theological niceties that one loses sight of the vital issues of the Christian faith. Nevertheless, it will be readily understood that churchmanship is a matter on which every bishop must declare himself. The sifting of thought and searching of heart that I underwent in my few short years as archdeacon were of the greatest value after I was raised to the episcopate.

The SPG, at whose invitation I was in England, is the traditional high-church missionary society and since I was working under them most of the parishes to which I was sent belonged to the high-church party of the Church of England. On the other hand, from their inception the missions in the Arctic have been "low" church in practice and custom. Several of the mission stations had been founded and supported through the years by the English missionary societies that are traditionally as low church as the SPG is high. To the Colonial and Continental Church Society and the Bible Churchman's Missionary Society anything that savored of high church was abhorrent. The very fact that I was under the sponsorship of the SPG at once made me suspect in their eyes. Yet for these two societies I had the highest regard, and of course I had constant dealings with them concerning the stations they maintained. The continuation of their support was vital. Should they, because of my association with the SPG, withdraw that support the Arctic endeavor would be indeed hard pressed.

Under these rather exceptional circumstances, my evangelical upbringing and my training at Wycliffe College, Toronto, had to face the Anglo-Catholic position held by most of my friends at the SPG. At first I was confused and often upset, but gradually as the result of close personal contact with some of the finest, as well as some of the less worthy, representatives of the high-church party, I came to appreciate much for which they stood. This led me to a middle course which greatly displeased some of my evangelical friends and some of the extreme Anglo-Catholics as well. On the other hand I discovered that however much the extremes at either end may dislike the moderates, there are a vast number of sensible people who, while supporting one or another of the parties, abhor party politics and respect those with whom they differ. They are more devoted to the main issues of faith than to any "ism" within the Body of Christ. They felt, as I did, that we must try not to be obstinate in our opinions but with searching honesty to ask the question, "What is our ultimate purpose?"

Brought up in a Presbyterian home, I became in young manhood a convinced Episcopalian and I have been intimately associated with most of the other Protestant denominations, including the Moravians and Danish Lutherans. Is it strange that I perhaps see things from a different viewpoint than those of less wide experience? I was and am in agreement with the French Jesuit de Lubac who said in "Catholicism" "the Church which is not tarnished by our own sins is also not straitened by our artificial barriers nor paralyzed by our prejudices."

With my religious background and experience I was forced to take an incredulous position regarding some of the things which the Anglo-Catholics seemed to consider so important. At the same time I was convinced that fundamentally I had not changed my stand regarding those things which I believed to be vital to the Christian Faith. I came to realize that if I were to be true to that which was highest I could no longer be a party man even while I knew that it would cause much misunderstanding and cost me the friendship of many whom I respected and admired.

It was a wonderful experience in England to be associated with churchmen of every school of thought. As I took part in services ranging from the simplest ceremony to the most elaborate ritual, I soon learned that ritual was made for man and not man for ritual and appreciated the wisdom that lay behind the liberty inherent in our English church. To some the aesthetic is of tremendous value in worship, stirring the imagination and emotions; for them the ritual is a help and an inspiration. But the value of ritual is to assist the soul to soar upward in humble devotion. If it is too elaborate it tends to defeat this purpose and causes the mind to be so taken up with ceremonial that the spiritual effort is nullified. As Milton puts it, "The soul shifts off from herself the labour of high soaring." To others elaborate ceremonial destroys the spirit of worship and becomes a source of irritation and a hindrance. To meet the differing needs of our people it is necessary to have variety within the Church. We must have unity amid diversity. But unity does not mean uniformity. To attempt to enforce uniformity would be the surest way to prevent it and to destroy our unity.

It seemed to me that as an invited guest, as a Christian, and as a gentleman, I must adapt myself to the type of service I found in each church where I was invited to preach. I felt that this courtesy was laid upon me. At this time to wear full vestments was a grievous trial to my spirit even while I could see no fundamental objection to them. Alas, some of my dear evangelical friends did not agree.

And when I listened to all the heated discussions within the high-church party my heart was heavy within me. I was depressed by the thought that some appeared overconfident that they alone possessed God, and that all who would know and obey Him must of necessity know and obey them. The Church, as far as they were concerned, had taken the place of the Kingdom of God. On one occasion I asked a young priest who was most earnest and definite where in his theological thinking he found room for the Kingdom of God since our Lord Himself had taught us to pray for its coming. Without a moment's hesitation he replied, "Oh that is all right. It is only through the Church that the Kingdom can come." The arrogance and intolerance in his attitude, which were not uncommon, struck me as unworthy of a Christian priest and pastor. I found myself unable to accept the position that non-Anglicans who believe in God and acknowledge Jesus Christ as Saviour and who live spirit-filled lives are outside the mystical Body of Christ, His Church, here on earth. In all denominations I have known people who loved their Saviour and witnessed for Him in their daily lives. Episcopacy, church order, and the like have their important place but I was unable to believe that a theological tenet could be sound if it did not respect the conscience of others when the outlook was different. Such an attitude would inevitably lead to dogmatic domination which in turn would engender bigotry and baseness. To me the Gospel as set forth in the Scriptures is fundamental love—the Love of God to man, calling upon man to love God and his neighbor as himself.

My difficulty was not with orthodox theology but with an increased dogmatism in what appeared to me to be speculative points on the Faith once delivered. I found that after listening to the theological wrangles, I could only maintain with Archbishop Temple that my earnest desire was to be a true Catholic not so much in externals as in devotion to the person of Christ Who alone is Head of the Church. The Faith once delivered I knew and believed. The doctrine of the Apostles was clear. But through the years men had built up superstructures which might or might not be useful within certain limits but they were not essential to the Faith. In fact they tended to obscure that which is vital to the believer. These superstructures were largely the cause of the Reformation. There are two tendencies inherent in the Church, Protestant and Catholic, but they are by no means irreconcilable. The Prayer Book is clearly a union of these two schools of thought, and it is our business, long after four hundred years, to perfect that union. We must not allow any class of extremists to destroy the effectiveness of the Church.

I felt that many of these good men were mistaking party spirit for a love of the truth and that the best contribution I could make was to counsel moderation and patience. Christians *must* obey the call of the Spirit of God and close their ranks. This is the most difficult as it is the most painful and humiliating problem confronting the Church today. What one section maintains as a conviction another calls only a prejudice without validity, and so it goes. Human nature being what it is, unity will only be achieved when in all humility the various denominations face the issue as in the presence of their Lord and Master.

To me the basic character of the Holy Catholic Church of Christ is clearly set forth in the New Testament as a belief in Jesus Christ as the Divine Son of God and the Saviour of mankind. I also believe that some things which are of great value in the devotional life, and which our non-Anglican brethren have not preserved, are to be found in the Church of England. Other Protestant denominations look upon these things as elements in the Christian tradition but not binding because not specifically set forth in Holy Scripture. Similarly the extreme Catholic view that the preaching of the word of God is merely an introduction to the Sacrament of Holy Communion, or that it is not recognized as a vehicle of the presence and power of God, is contrary to the teaching of the New Testament and the Church Catholic.

Our first call, surely, is to follow in the footsteps of the Master. By many my attitude has always been considered far too liberal but I cannot see how all this bitterness between brethren is related to the Man Whose name we bear and Who left us no indication that such things were of vital importance. To me it is imperative that we return to the fundamental simplicity of faith in Him Who said, "He that followeth me shall not walk in darkness but shall have the Light of Life." And being, all of us, near enough to the Cross of our Saviour to touch the wood, we are surely near enough to touch each other.

15. Epidemic

☆ ☆

AFTER THESE STRENUOUS months of money-raising it was almost with a sense of relief that I started North each summer. In 1928 when I was still archdeacon I made my first trip to the Western Arctic since that vast domain was also under my supervision. Had I been asked in advance what I expected to find I would scarcely have known what to reply. I knew how in 1789 the intrepid Scots trader Sir Alexander Mackenzie discovered the vast river flowing north which bears his name; that the native population were Hare and Dog-Rib and Loucheaux Indians and Eskimo down at the Delta. I was familiar with the self-sacrificing efforts of such great missionaries as Lucas, Bompas, Stringer, and Whittaker. I knew that as far back as 1861 the Rev. N. N. Kirby had made two visits to Fort McPherson on the Peel River and that the following year the Rev. Robert McDonald began his undying work. (Among his many contributions to the spiritual welfare of the Loucheaux was the translation of the New Testament and the Book of Common Prayer into the Takudh tongue, which is the language of these tribes. These translations are very complete and the treasured possession of the people.) I knew, too, that the mission at Coppermine had been opened in 1915 and that at Aklavik in 1919. All these and more I knew as *facts*, but I had no realization of the vast and complex river life and the intricate problems arising from a mixed population that was in many ways more "civilized" than that of Baffin Land and yet essentially primitive in its thinking. Nor was I in any way prepared for the thrill of all that I saw and heard and learned on that trip.

In those early days before plane travel, one had to go to the Western Arctic by rail from Edmonton to the end of steel at Waterways. The train bore the impressive name of the Northern Alberta Railway Arctic Express and it took twenty-three and one-half hours to cover 304 miles, an average of about 13¼ miles per hour. The two passenger cars were both so antiquated that by night they were lighted by coal-oil lamps that hung precariously from the ceiling.

When we pulled into the little station at Waterways on the Clearwater River, I was surprised and pleased to see Bishop and Mrs. Stringer waiting to greet me. A little later at the rather simple hotel, I had much helpful conversation with them. Early next morning the Stringers departed on the train for Edmonton but since the paddle steamer *Athabasca River* did not leave until afternoon, I had plenty of time in which to see Waterways and Fort McMurray, a few miles farther along the river. There I also met the proprietress of the hotel, Mrs. Coffin, who was one of the best-known personalities in the area. She was wonderfully capable, with a round face, ample bosom, and pleasant smile. Her technique in handling her guests who were mostly men left little to be desired. She took a sympathetic interest in the plans of the lonely men who stopped there and encouraged them to talk about themselves. This approach inevitably made them feel that they were wonderful men, she a wonderful woman, and the hotel the best in the North.

Half an hour before the *Athabasca River* was due to start, two shrill blasts of warning sounded from her whistle. Then came the final blast. The great stern paddle wheel began to thrash, and thus began the long voyage of approximately 2,514 miles by fresh water down the Mackenzie River to the Arctic Ocean.

The first few miles were on the Clearwater River but soon

that joined the Athabasca, the first of many "joinings," because the mighty Mackenzie is really the accumulated flow of
many rivers and many lakes which merge with it on its magnificent journey. We paddled down the Athabasca River and
across that great inland sea called Lake Athabasca, then down
the Slave River to Fort Fitzgerald, which is situated at the
southern end of the Pelican Rapids where each year the peli-
cans come to breed. These seven miles of turbulent water
that boil between Fitzgerald and Fort Smith are the only
unnavigable stretch of river between the end of rail and its
consummation with the sea.

The portage of freight and passengers entailed by the Pelican Rapids was successfully accomplished and at Fort Smith
we boarded the *Distributor,* which was similar to the *Athabasca River* though larger. Despite her renown the *Distributor* was simply a flat-bottomed wooden scow with two
superimposed upper decks that looked very much like the
verandahs of early Canadian and American houses. Stacked
around the locomotive steam boiler were lengths of wood:
the fuel for the furnace. Every eight hours during the entire
journey we stopped to take on a new supply. The location of
the new supply was marked by a "lopstick," which was usually
a tall spruce tree near the bank that had been shorn of all its
branches except those within a few feet from the top. There
the cords had been stacked by the woodcutters during the
winter. Day after day with the steam engine puffing and the
paddle wheel chugging, we slid north on the brown oily
waters that flowed sluggishly between ever-curving shores.

Attached to each side of the *Distributor* was a huge flat
barge and two more were pushed ahead. These were loaded
with freight. From my studies in naval architecture, the tow-
ing and pushing of these barges seemed an amazing feat in
view of the fact that neither the steamer nor the barges drew
more than four feet of water while floating over one thousand
tons of supplies.

As we approached each little settlement, the entire population swarmed the riverbank, for this was the biggest event of

the year. It made a gay scene in the summer sunshine with most of the men in colored shirts or in uniform; the white women with their light summer frocks; while the vivid cotton dresses and shawls of the Indian women added a bright accent.

From experience I knew I must not delay in arranging for church services along the way, for the *Distributor,* like the Eastern Arctic supply ships, did not dally. It was my privilege as well as my duty to get in touch with all the people and I deeply regretted having to work through an interpreter, because unfortunately I did not speak the Takudh language.

At our residential school at Hay River, I made my first contact with the Eskimo children of the Western Arctic and found them very like my little friends in the Eastern Arctic. There were sixty youngsters in the school, some Indian, some Eskimo, and the fact that we could have children of both races together in the school was in itself a testimony to the value of mission work. From time immemorial there had been warfare and bad blood between the Indians and the Eskimo, and while it was obvious that they did not mingle there was no longer much hostility. During the years of my Western Arctic service this interracial relationship has improved immeasurably.

In contrast to my happiness about the school at Hay River was my distress at the number of active tuberculosis cases among the Indians. The mission hospital there was overcrowded with them and I was to find this sad condition repeated all down the Mackenzie River.

There is constant travel up and down the great river. The *Distributor* dropped off and picked up a succession of transient passengers. Among those at Hay River waiting for a "lift" to Fort McPherson was a fine and handsome Loucheaux couple, James and Sarah Simon, who were to accompany me. Although they were young they were already outstanding church leaders, and from them I expected to learn much about the spiritual needs of the people and to gain some understanding of their race. My heart was full of expectancy. Yet at our first meeting I felt almost rebuffed. There was

none of the ready smile and responsive enthusiasm of the
Eskimo. Rather I felt a bit as though I were at the judgment
bar as their grave and unflickering gaze met mine.

Yet I liked them, and felt the sincerity and depth of their
character. During that summer I came to respect and to admire them more and more. And in a sense James and Sarah
Simon were typical of all Loucheaux Indians. Their somber
faces, slow to betray feeling, mask emotions that are intense to the point of anguish. The Indians are devastatingly
observant and are able to read and classify the human face
in the most unerring fashion. Any deceit or conceit on the
part of a white man is immediately noticed and remembered.
In the years that followed I grew to love the Loucheaux
people and respected the truth of one of their proverbs: "Let
me not judge my brother until I have walked two weeks in
his moccasins."

At about this time an outburst of influenza followed by
lobar pneumonia attacked the passengers on the *Distributor*.
Nurse McCabe, who was traveling with me on her way to All
Saints Hospital, Aklavik, was kept busy tending those who
were stricken. Since there was no doctor on board we were all
much relieved when we reached Fort Simpson and Nurse
McCabe could get help from Dr. Truesdale, the government
medical officer stationed there. At each settlement after the
steamer departed, the people succumbed and the epidemic
raged up and down the river, taking a final toll of more than
three hundred Indians.

At Fort Norman I first saw the government agent pay the
Treaty money to the Indians. The agent sat on a box outside
a small tent with an interpreter on one side and a scarlet-
coated policeman on the other, while he gave $5.00 in cash
to every Indian man, woman, and child. With each presentation he shook hands in token that the King wished them well.
Then he told them that all the King desired of them was that
they live in peace with their white brothers and with their
fellow Indians, the Dog-Rib and the Hare, and that they keep
the law of the land.

At Fort Norman the natural features of the landscape became much more beautiful. The Franklin Mountains rose in
the east and the yet higher Mackenzie range in the west, and
there was a remarkable change in the brown waters of the
river. Even the Peace and the Liard had been muddy at their
confluence with the Mackenzie, but as we passed the mouth
of the Bear River the water became a brilliant bluish-green
and clear as crystal. The source of the Bear is Great Bear
Lake where Gilbert LaBine and his brother discovered
pitchblende. The waters of the lake are deep and always cold
for they are fed by the melting ice and snow on the rocky
hills and on its westward journey the Bear River passes
through rocky country free from the oozing stretches of mud-
land such as that through which the Mackenzie winds its
circuitous way.

Nine miles north of Fort Good Hope we crossed the magic
Arctic Circle but the temperature both day and night seemed
to belie the fact. To add to our discomfort there was not a
breath of wind except that caused by the motion of the slow-
moving vessel. The saloon and cabins were so hot and stuffy
that the passengers lay on deck with handkerchiefs over their
eyes.

As we approached Fort McPherson on the Peel River,
James and Sarah Simon became much more animated, scanning the colorful crowd assembled on the high bank and soon
pointing out to me the man they were seeking. He was a full-
blooded Loucheaux Indian who had been educated and
trained by Archdeacon MacDonald until he was ordained. It
was therefore with particular joy that I clasped the hand of
the Reverend Edward Sittichinli. It is, of course, the ultimate
desire of every missionary to raise up in due course a native
priesthood that can minister to its own. With a primitive
people this can only be done little by little as first one man
and then another proves his capacity. The Reverend Edward
Sittichinli had proved his.

Fort McPherson is among the oldest settlements in the
region, the original fort having been erected in 1846. The

cluster of buildings stand on the very high bank above the river and command a panoramic view of the countryside. From the mission house with its trim garden and white picket fence one looks down on the busy river life with schooners, motorboats and little craft like sampans that dart about, and across to the fir trees on the opposite shore. Beyond stretch the Richardson Mountains.

As I entered the church it struck me at once how beautifully all was cared for. The hangings were in good repair, the communion vessels and linen spotless and the brasses well polished. Memorial brasses in the Arctic are somehow much more poignant than those in the south. I suppose it is because they represent suffering remote from the comfort of friends. Here in St. Matthew's Church this experience is told so eloquently and yet so briefly on three small brass plates each bearing the name of a child born to Archdeacon and Mrs. Whittaker. Two had died at Herschel Island and their bodies were carried two hundred and fifty miles by sledge and dog team to Fort McPherson for burial; the third died up the river. I knelt and breathed a prayer for all who had labored here since the mission was established in 1861. Because of their work the Indians (there are no Eskimo) are steadfast Christians.

As we continued toward Aklavik, influenza continued to strike down first one and then another of the passengers on the *Distributor*. Nurse McCabe was by now much overtired so she went off to her cabin hoping to snatch some sleep despite the heat, humidity, and mosquitoes. We came in sight of Aklavik in broad daylight almost exactly at midnight on July fifth. The bright sunshine, the soaring temperatures, the tall grasses, and the trees forty or more feet in height made it difficult to believe that we were now one hundred and twenty miles north of the Arctic Circle. Within half an hour we were shaking hands with Archdeacon Geddes (later Bishop of Yukon) and the Rev. and Mrs. C. C. Harcourt. (This charming and capable lady was the daughter of Bishop Holmes whose appeal in England I had first answered twenty-two years before.) As soon as possible the archdeacon escorted Nurse McCabe and me to the hospital where we met Nurse Hackett and Nurse Terry. It was past two o'clock when I went to bed and I was grateful that no one called me until half past nine in the morning.

Aklavik is really nothing but a mud flat exposed in clear weather to the intensity of the Arctic sun, and in wet weather it becomes an unspeakably slimy and oozy slough. Yet as the years went on I came to love it dearly and to choose it for the site of my little cathedral. But on this visit all impressions were blurred by the savagery of the influenza which, with the coming of the steamer, swept through the settlement like a scourge. The natives, of course, have no immunity to the diseases of "civilization."

Unfortunately the government doctor who had lasted only one year at Aklavik declined to stay to see us through and departed for the south on board the ship. We were left to battle the infection as best we could. It was a sad business and our hearts went out to the Eskimo, the Indians, and the half-breeds in their misery. They lay in their tents or in the cramped quarters of their boats with the passionless simplicity of sick children, too weak to attend to their own needs.

Somebody had to do something but because of the ever-increasing numbers that were stricken we could only provide makeshift care. Archdeacon Geddes, Mr. Harcourt, the Rev. John Martin (another ordained full-blooded Loucheaux Indian) and I came on in shifts twice daily, ministering to those in boats and tents. Each day we wondered who among us would come down with a fever. My three co-workers finally succumbed, but my turn had not yet arrived.

The little hospital had emergency beds in every corridor and corner and the nurses were heavily overworked. Then their native assistants succumbed and they had to take over the kitchen duties as well. Each day seemed to bring a heavier load for these gallant young women to carry. Yet they also willingly made the rounds of tents and boats doing what they could there. During these exhausting and discouraging days

I never heard a single complaint on the lips of any of our staff.

Convalescence was the time of our greatest disappointment. As soon as the people felt their strength returning they disobeyed orders and went outside to get something they wanted. Then they caught a chill which quickly went into pneumonia. Within a few hours they were dead. It was heartbreaking because we all knew that if there had been accommodation at the hospital their lives would almost certainly have been spared. On Sunday July 15 the nurses attended 175 patients.

I shall never forget how the Rev. John Martin and I toiled under the blazing sun digging graves. The ground was frozen solid less than twelve inches below the surface and the work was exhausting. As we were struggling to excavate a grave one day, three white trappers came and watched us. They offered to help us make coffins but by that time there was no cut lumber to be had in the settlement, so we had to bury the dead wrapped in a blanket or in a skin sleeping bag.

These three men were the typical spacious-minded type who find the law more easily evaded in the Far North than in Prince Edward Island, New England, or Scotland. The spokesman was a tall, lean man with stubble on his chin, commonly known as Slim. With considerable backing and filling he told me that they appreciated having the hospital at Aklavik for, as he said, "A man never knows when his turn may come." Slim said that he and his friends would like to help, without pay, wherever they were most needed. He assured me that he was a first-class cook, and suggested that he take over the hospital kitchen. The other two then spoke up and said that they were better able to dig graves than Martin or I. To this statement I heartily agreed!

Slim and I went together to the hospital where I spoke to the nurses. At first they were dubious but I persuaded them to give Slim a chance, and the tall unshaven man from the mountains with his bushy eyebrows and husky voice was installed in the hospital kitchen. The two others, Ted and Bill, undertook to dig graves, to remove the garbage twice daily, to split wood and to keep the water tank and iceboxes filled. When the R.C.M.P. men heard about it they lifted their eyebrows and smiled. I hasten to say that through the entire epidemic the Royal Canadian Mounted Police had been most helpful, but they had their own strenuous problems.

Our experiment was a great success and the three men never faltered in their kindness and support. There was a spontaneity about their attitude that seemed to make their help doubly welcome and when I ventured to tell them so they all declared that they had never been so flattered and appreciated.

By the end of the second week of this regime the picture began to look brighter. The pestilence had run its course. When the routine of the hospital was almost back to normal Slim and his friend, without being asked, split and stacked a fine supply of firewood, took down the tents that had been erected nearby for overflow patients, and generally helped to clear up the mess. Our benefactors would not accept any pay for their labors, so we decided to have a party for them in the nurses' living room and to present each with a small gift as a token of our very genuine appreciation. We kept the plan secret so they appeared in their working overalls; this, of course, embarrassed them not a whit. It was a happy experience for us all and provided much-needed relief after all the anxiety and sorrow.

Once the epidemic was over, I felt that I must push on to Shingle Point and Herschel Island for an inspection of those missions. We left Aklavik on the evening of July 22 under a hot and blistery sun. The river was like a mirror without a ripple on its surface. The twenty-eight-foot motorboat was covered over for about one-third of its length and under this cover was stored the baggage of the owner, his son, three policemen, a white trapper, Archdeacon Geddes, and myself. It, at least, would be kept dry if we ran into dirty weather when we entered the Arctic Ocean. The boat pushed ahead of it a light scow and on this craft were the owner's wife and six children, an Indian, eight dogs, and a large quantity of supplies. No one attempted to rest; the heat, the glare of the sun on the water, the vibration of the boat, and the cramped quarters made sleep impossible.

At four o'clock in the morning we landed on a sandspit at the mouth of the river where we put the kettle on to boil, fried some bacon and devoured the fresh-baked bread from the hospital. When the meal was over I thought that I would feel better if I had a wash, so I splashed water on my face from a battered tin basin. As I was wiping off the grime, Scottie the trader grinned at me and said, "Guid grief, maun, tak' it easy. A' that washin' fair tak's the life oot o' ye this warm weather!" Anyone who had sat beside Scottie on the little boat knew that washing was against his principles!

We now left the river and set a course parallel to the coast line at about a mile offshore. Soon we met another motor-boat on its way to Aklavik and from them learned that the influenza had struck the Eskimo at both Shingle Point and Herschel Island. After what we had just gone through our hearts were filled with dismay. When we arrived at Shingle Point at about noon we found all the Eskimo very ill and five dead. For these we had a funeral service in the little church and then carried them up the hill and buried them in the graveyard there. It was hard work to get the bodies of the dead up the rocky path of the steep hillside. The police and I did our part but Scottie took the heaviest burden. He also did most of the digging of the large grave in which we were forced to bury all five. Poor Geddes was still too weak from the flu to help with the physical work but he took the burial service.

The same unhappy situation prevailed at Herschel Island, which we reached the next day, but there Inspector Kemp of the R.C.M.P. and the H.B.C. post manager, W. G. Murray, had matters more under control. They were on the beach to greet us and Inspector Kemp invited Geddes and me to his house where we met Mrs. Kemp and their little daughter, Daphne. Nothing could have exceeded the kindness of their welcome and Mrs. Kemp gave us a most delicious meal, our first adequate one since leaving Aklavik. Geddes was now coughing so badly that as soon as dinner was over we excused ourselves and tumbled into our sleeping bags utterly exhausted.

The next day Geddes was worse so Mrs. Kemp and Mrs. Murray took over. Within an hour the two ladies had things well in hand. This left me free to arrange with the inspector about the welfare of the people. The first thing was to bury the dead, which we did in a large grave in the cemetery some distance from the settlement. There in the presence of five white men and one Eskimo I conducted the great service that had become all too familiar during the last few weeks.

We decided to turn the mission house into a temporary hospital and remove the ailing natives to it. The inspector gave a government order to the H.B.C. for all necessary supplies. Each of the white men took turns acting as orderlies and Mrs. Kemp and Mrs. Murray were more than guardian angels. As we were busy rearranging the mission house I thought of the noble work done there by Bishop Stringer's wife more than thirty years before. I thought, too, of how only ten years before, the Rev. W. H. Fry had fitted up the annex as a temporary hospital where Mrs. Fry nursed Stefansson when he was so ill that he begged to be moved from the R.C.M.P. barracks where he was lodged. The men there were doing everything possible for him but the barracks was a busy place so that the patient could not get the quiet he craved. Considering Stefansson's outspoken antireligious attitude, it must have cost him some inner humiliation to ask to be taken in by missionaries whom as a genus he despised and condemned. He made a complete recovery and in a recent letter to me Mrs. Fry says that his bark was worse than his bite.

Before going to bed that night, after my turn as orderly, I had a walk along the sandy shore. The temperature was that of a summer evening and I found it difficult to believe that this beautiful expanse of water with its lazy, rolling breakers was the Arctic Ocean.

On my return to the mission house I met an Eskimo carrying a can of fresh water from a little pool near the village. He told me that his wife had died so that he was now alone and sad at heart. He himself had been ill, but he assured me that he was now much better. Within two hours a policeman called at the mission to tell me that this man had died and that the inspector asked that he be buried as soon as a grave could be dug.

This whole summer was a sad and depressing time. It had also given me much to think about for the future. There was the nightmare of the epidemic. There was the scourge of tuberculosis. During my stay on Herschel Island I had considerable discussion with Inspector Kemp about how in the future the church and government, working together, could best meet the needs of the people. More and more often my mind was turning to the need for the establishment of hospitals and nursing stations. At the time such a program seemed far in the future. I had no money and the government was not interested. But I could see no other way to remedy the devastating lack of medical care. Since funds would be the first requirement, I decided to make this my chief appeal in England during the coming winter. In my dreams I saw fully equipped, fully staffed medical centers across the wastes of ice and snow. Some queried my ability to secure enough stalwart and self-sacrificing Christians to maintain such institutions in the Arctic even if I did establish them. But I walked in faith. I humbly believed that if I could obtain the necessary moneys, the call of God would touch the hearts of doctors and nurses and maintenance people. In this faith I have been abundantly justified. I left Herschel Island on board the *Bay Chimo* and for thirty-one days we sailed until we passed through the Dolphin and Union Strait between Victoria Island and the mainland, arriving on August 6 at Bernard Harbour where our missionary, the Rev. Herbert Girling, had been the first missionary resident in the whole area.

At Bernard Harbour two R.C.M.P. men came to see me about three Eskimo—one man was totally blind, another had a chronic ailment, while the third was a crippled lad. It was obvious that none could earn his living and that all were a liability to their kinsfolk. Left to their own resources these people would have starved to death. Not knowing what else to do, the police had taken them into their charge but they were naturally anxious that some better arrangement be made. We worked out a temporary solution but I knew that the ultimate care of the indigent and unfit was added to the many large issues that now crowded upon me as archdeacon.

From time immemorial the Eskimo had from sheer economic necessity but one solution to the problem of the aged and helpless: to wall them off during the cold of the winter into an igloo where death came quietly and alone. To us this seems cruel and terrible but in a land where constant traveling is essential and where hunger stalks each living thing, the burden of the handicapped makes an impossible demand. During the last thirty years conditions in the Arctic have so changed that this problem, the pity of which lay on my heart like lead, has been largely solved. I think it is safe to say that no Eskimo or Indian now needs to feel the death knell tolling when he has had an accident or exceeds the normal span of life.

At Bloody Falls near Bernard Harbour with our missionary, the Rev. J. H. Webster, I met three Eskimo families who were living at the falls where fish were plentiful. They welcomed us in the most friendly fashion, and, be it remembered, they were true pagans. In fact they still wore labrets, which are buttons made of ivory worn as ornaments and inserted into cuts in the lower lip on either side of the mouth. The man with whom I talked most was the angakok. Variation of idiom as well as of pronunciation made my account of the white man's country somewhat halting but despite this we were able to get along without too many interruptions.

The Hudson's Bay Company's Eskimo interpreter told me that he had met Knud Rasmussen and that he and I spoke "the same kind of Eskimo." Years later the correctness of this statement was verified in Greenland. This was the beginning of many years' association with the people who live in the Coppermine district. My new-found friends, however, did not become pillars of the church. The angakok was always friendly with our missionary, the Rev. J. H. Webster, and equally so with the Roman Catholic priest who arrived at Coppermine a year after we had established our mission. But he proved to be a crafty rascal who among other things murdered his two wives so that he might take younger women to be his companions.

That same year we were also establishing at Cambridge Bay, which we reached on August 18 and where I had the joy of meeting our missionary, the Rev. C. M. Hathaway, and his companion, Mr. Paul Likert. The mission buildings had just been completed and were in first-class order thanks in large measure to Likert's skill as a carpenter. Hathaway, who had previously been at Bernard Harbour, had gained a good working knowledge of the Eskimo language. He had also made a complete census of the people in the district.

The next morning we had a series of light snow flurries which acted like magic on everyone. The men had been working steadily at the unloading of the cargo, but now there was feverish haste and much talk about being frozen in for the winter. The captain set his course for Perry River, and we eventually reached Flag Staff Island at its mouth. Here to our great surprise the wireless operator on the *Bay Chimo* got into touch with the *Nascopie* in Hudson Bay. Through the kindness of the captain I sent greetings to Captain Murray, Ralph Parsons, and Bishop Anderson of Moosonee and when I received return messages it certainly seemed as though the Arctic vastness had been broken.

A major problem now confronted the captain. Perry River is about four hundred miles south of the elusive North Magnetic Pole. This meant that owing to the strong magnetic attraction the compass had become immovable. Under such circumstances the captain steers his course by sun and stars but unfortunately a haze overhead blotted out sun and stars. Because the season was far advanced and the *Bay Chimo* still some five thousand miles from her home port of Vancouver, the captain felt that he must not delay. As a makeshift, to get the direction of the wind, he tied a puff of feathers to a fine thread and attached it to an awning stanchion on the bridge. Knowing the geographical position of Perry River, he decided to steer a course accordingly but was well aware that the wind might change at any time.

After breakfast the next morning the first mate asked me to speak to the Eskimo, who with great excitement were pointing to the land on the port side. When I asked what was troubling them they replied that they wanted to go to Cambridge Bay and that the ship was going in the wrong direction. The captain asked me to find out why the Eskimo were so certain about the matter, and in answer to my questions they assured me that they had killed two polar bears on the smallest of these islands quite close to the *Bay Chimo*'s port bow. These islands, they said, lay off the coast of Victoria Island. They insisted that the land on our starboard bow was Lind Island. They also insisted that the ship was steaming in a northeasterly direction at the entrance to Victoria Strait. They were tremendously interested in the chart I showed them and seemed to have no difficulty in understanding it. When the captain heard what the Eskimo said, he changed the ship's course and we thanked God that the visibility was not worse. The weather was now stormy, the sky overcast with heavy clouds, and a cold and piercing wind was blowing. I record this incident because it shows the difficulties that used to confront the Arctic navigator. The answer for this particular problem was to have the ship equipped with a non-magnetic compass. The following year the *Bay Chimo* was fitted with a gyroscopic compass which could be relied upon when the magnetic compass was dead.

The rest of our journey back to Aklavik was not without incident but even a hurricane which had leveled most of the buildings at Baillie Island did not take first place in our thoughts. The all-engrossing question was, would we be back at Aklavik by September first? The arrangement had been that the *Distributor* would wait until that date but no longer. She too was afraid of being caught in the North and frozen in for the winter somewhere on the long slow journey up the Mackenzie River. From Shingle Point on, to save time, the Hudson's Bay Company party transferred to a motorboat and were kind enough to ask me to join them. We made a very quick run but it was not until 10:15 P.M. on the night of September second that we reached Aklavik. We were tense with excitement, and suddenly an audible groan of despair issued from the lips of us all. The *Distributor* was not there. Must we winter at Aklavik? What would happen to all our plans?

As soon as they saw us nosing in, Archdeacon Geddes, the Rev. C. C. Harcourt, and Nurse Terry came running down to the bank shouting, "You have made it. The *Distributor* is not yet in." It is difficult to explain the relief that this news brought us. Having had no sleep for two days and one night, I suddenly felt very tired so went to bed with as little delay as possible. In the morning I awoke with a splitting headache and considerable nausea, which has for most of my life been my reaction to strain. I stayed in bed until midafternoon when two of the incapacitated Eskimo from Bernard Harbour arrived—the crippled boy and the man with the ailment. A few hours later Nurse Terry wanted to speak to me privately. Did I know, she whispered, that the man was a murderer? I did. "But," protested Nurse Terry, "we can't keep a murderer here. We are all terrified. We have no man in the hospital!" "Well, you have one now," I replied. Then we both laughed.

At the same time there was a very sad and serious side to the matter for the man, named Uluksak, was one of two Eskimo who had brutally killed two Roman Catholic priests in 1914. The nurses were soon to learn all the grim details of the story: In 1914 a Dog-Rib Indian on the Mackenzie River told a queer tale to Inspector C. A. Rheault of the

Royal Northwest Mounted Police, asserting that Eskimo in the Coronation Gulf area had killed two Roman Catholic priests. It was well known, of course, that the Indians and Eskimo were frequently at odds with one another and as this seemed an unlikely tale it might have been brushed aside. But the priests, Fathers Rouvier and Leroux, had not been heard of for nearly a year, and the R.N.-W.M.P. sent out a patrol. At Coppermine they unfortunately found irrefutable evidence that the Indian had told the truth. The missionaries had indeed been killed by two Eskimo who, without the slightest hesitation, admitted their guilt. They were taken to Herschel Island, and from there to Edmonton, accompanied by several witnesses and an interpreter. The trial opened in Edmonton. One was found "not guilty" but this did not satisfy certain authorities. So on May 22 the trial was reopened in Calgary, when a verdict of "guilty" was passed on both men, but with the death sentence commuted to life imprisonment. On September 4, the R.N.-W.M.P. contingent, including witnesses and the prisoners, left for the North. One Eskimo soon died but from 1914 until 1928 when we arrived at Bernard Harbour the other, Uluksak, had been in the charge of the Mounties.

During his stay of ten months at All Saints' Hospital, Uluksak became a great favorite with the nurses despite their early consternation. He was fundamentally a peaceable, kindly, and intelligent person. Eventually he was considered well enough to be sent back to Coppermine where Canon Webster saw him daily. He came to realize the enormity of his crime and was filled with sorrow. In the end he died confident of God's love and mercy to him a sinner.

Where was the *Distributor?* There was still no sign of her. A heavy blanket of snow had already fallen and with every added twenty-four hours the possibility of having to winter at Aklavik became more nearly a probability.

On the evening of Monday, September 10, an Indian lad was sent by his mother to fetch a can of water from the river.

As the boy stooped down to fill his can his keen ears heard the thud of the paddle wheel through the water which acted as a conductor of the sound. Racing back to the tent he told his mother and quickly the cry sounded through the settlement. The people rushed to the bank and stood waiting for the steamer to round the bend. On it were Dr. Urquhart, the newly appointed government medical officer, and Nurse Bradford, both of whom we welcomed to the hospital staff. Greetings and farewells were hurried and I had no time to talk with either the doctor or the nurse for without delay the *Distributor* began her long journey south.

Adversity seemed to dog our footsteps all that summer, and not the least of our misfortunes occurred shortly after we left. We had endured the catastrophe of the influenza epidemic, the problem of the indigents, delay from fog and storm on the *Bay Chimo,* the hurricane at Baillie Island, the race against time in the motorboat from Shingle Point to Aklavik. And now for six mortal days the captain and his crew, with the assistance of Captain Smellie who was a passenger, battled unsuccessfully against the rushing waters of the rapids at the bottom of the Ramparts just south of Good Hope. Day after day we were tormented with disappointment. Again it looked as if we would be frozen in for the winter and would have to beg food and shelter. It was not until late in the afternoon of the seventh day that, with the help of a wire cable attached to some trees at the top of the rapids, the *Distributor* finally succeeded in reaching the quieter waters above the Ramparts.

During this trying week a fine spirit of comradeship developed among the passengers. Each time the ship failed to stem the swift-flowing waters; each time it grounded on a gravel bar; each time the wire cable, some two thousand, seven hundred feet in length, broke and was lost, necessitating weary hours of dragging to retrieve it; each time members of the crew and passengers carried fallen branches of trees on board with which to keep the fires burning; each time we learned that the river had dropped more than an inch in the last twelve hours—there was always good-natured banter.

It was during this restless week that I had an interesting talk with the eminent Porsild brothers, from whom I learned much about Greenland and its people. They were returning from a survey of the country that lay on either side of the Mackenzie Delta and were to give a detailed report to the government at Ottawa as to its possible use for the development of herds of reindeer.

Once above the Ramparts, we made good progress and navigated the Sans Sault Rapids without much difficulty. On our way to Fort Norman we passed three oil wells not in use, and little dreamed of the developments that would soon take place. Fifteen years later all the oil and gasoline used on the Mackenzie and on the Arctic coast was supplied from these derelict-looking places.

At Fort Simpson several prospectors came on board. They had been surveying the south Nahanni River which is a tributary of the Liard, and they spoke of a waterfall, which they estimated to be some two hundred and fifty miles west and north of Fort Simpson, that had a sheer drop of three hundred feet. They also reported a canyon through which the Nahanni flowed that was so high it was very dark at the water level. They said it gave them a terrible feeling of danger as they passed through it in their canoes. At one place they found some sulphur springs. I listened to these men as they talked about quartz, mica, pitchblende, feldspar, iron oxides, mispickel, pyrites, the outcroppings of the pre-Cambrian Shield, and what must be done to develop the North where untold riches were to be found. The remark that stuck in my mind was the statement that they had gone into the headwaters of the south Nahanni River by plane, a journey which took three hours, against the ten days it took to return by canoe.

"Next time," declared the prospector named Watson, "I will go both ways by plane." If he intended to do that, why couldn't I?

All went well after we left Fort Simpson until we reached Great Slave Lake, but at Hay River we were again delayed three days by stormy weather. We finally got away early on the morning of October second. The wind and rain had ceased and as the sun rose above the horizon there came a warmth that heralded what we believed to be the approach of fine weather. But by noon snow was falling and the temperature dropped below freezing. Owing to the poor visibility, we were unable to reach Resolution and spent the night at Buffalo River. After the evening meal the men were playing cards, when very quietly the saloon door opened and there appeared a funny old man, poorly clad and unshaven, with a violin case under his arm. Everyone looked up and he at once became the center of interest. We had seen no sign of habitation, no cabin, no rising smoke when the ship nosed into the shore, and were quite unaware that any human being dwelt in this isolated spot. But here was a man.

He told us that he had a shack in the bush not far away. Having seen the *Distributor* in the distance, he thought that it would be nice to visit it and perhaps get some extra food. We all gathered round him and soon he opened up his case and gave us, as he said, "an air." I shall never forget his crouching figure as he bent over his instrument and rasped out his tunes. His skill, like his repertoire, was somewhat limited. Nevertheless, he brought delight to our little company. He was able to express something that touched our hearts. When the hat was passed around it was literally filled to overflowing with dollar bills so that when the purser gave it to the musician his old eyes glistened with pleasure. The cook also gave him a carton containing three newly baked loaves of bread and some other eatables. Because of his coming we all felt in a better mood and for the first time in many evenings there was whistling and singing as we went to bed.

It seemed quite unbelievable that anything further could impede our homeward journey but when at long last we reached Fort Smith we found that the *Athabasca River* had sailed south the preceding day! As that was her last trip of the season it can be imagined with what consternation this news was received. Abuse was showered upon all and sundry by many of the passengers but while the grumbling was going on the men of the Hudson's Bay Company transport division were busy. Five days later we left Fitzgerald on two small scows pushed by motorboats.

The weather was now cold with wind and snow. Ice had formed not only in the small bays and creeks but in streaks across Lake Athabasca so we knew that winter had come. Had we been a week later we would have been frozen in until the breakup of the ice in the spring. There were now fifty-eight people on board these two small tarpaulin-covered scows and motorboats, and we existed under the most primitive conditions. Nevertheless, even when differences arose among some of the poker players, a fine spirit was manifested. Six days of traveling under such conditions are a strain, however, and when we reached Fort McMurray and found that we had missed the weekly train and were once more immobilized the lid of patience exploded. For five interminable days and nights we waited. There was never a more welcome sight than the great engine and shabby cars when they pulled into the little station at Waterways!

While I found this added delay as tantalizing as the rest, nevertheless it gave me a chance for much-needed sleep and to sift all the experiences that crowded in upon me. I tried to consider the work of the Western Arctic alone and also in conjunction with the Eastern Arctic. With the James Bay area I was not yet familiar. Our missions were well and truly established; our workers consecrated, capable, and energetic people. We needed more, of course, but whichever way I looked, medical care for the people seemed to be the most compelling requirement. There was pressure from the missionaries for schools which were also urgently needed, but there would not be money for both ventures to begin with. I had to choose and I chose hospitals. Funds for those would be my chief objective during my winter in England. I also determined from what I had heard of the prospectors' talk to investigate the use of planes for the future.

Hospitals and flying. Flying and hospitals. As these two projects turned over and over in my mind, I realized afresh the need for vision and faith—vision to look into the future and plan for the welfare of the people I loved and faith that funds and workers might be forthcoming to carry out the vision.

INTERLUDE III

As one reflects upon one's own life and observes the lives of others, it is remarkable how often periods of comparative tranquillity alternate with a compression of important events. This has certainly been true in my own case and now within a relatively short span of years my personal life underwent three major changes. First I was elected bishop of the newly formed Diocese of the Arctic with my ensuing consecration to the office of a bishop of the Church of God. Secondly my dear wife died. Then after a period of time came my second marriage.

The creation of the Diocese of the Arctic and my election as its first bishop were the logical outcome of the work that I had been doing as archdeacon. With the rapid expansion of the Church's effort in the Far North and the serious native problems arising from the unprecedented opening up of its great natural resources by the white man, it had become evident that such a step must be taken. With quickly changing conditions it was increasingly difficult and cumbersome to work under the jurisdiction of four separate bishops and the committee that met but once a year. Therefore it was felt by those in authority over me that if I was to carry the burden of the responsibility, both administrative and financial, then I must also be vested with adequate authority. To have the *one without the other is untenable in creative work. So the Dioceses of Keewatin, Moosonee, Yukon, and the Mackenzie River each gave up the northern portions of its territories and out of this was formed the Diocese of the Arctic which, so far as I know, is the largest in the world, comprising 1,204,697 square miles.*

The news that the Provincial Synod of Rupert's Land was meeting for the purpose of making this new venture reached me on board the Nascopie in Hudson Bay. I was requested by telegram to abandon if possible the rest of my journey and I arrived in Winnipeg in time for my election.

My consecration took place in St. John's Cathedral, Winnipeg, on Thursday, December 21, 1933, the Feast of St. Thomas, Apostle and Martyr. I shall not attempt to describe the service save to say that the ritual is simple and symbolic. The prayers combined with the laying on of hands is a moving act which indicates the Church's belief that the Holy Spirit of God is given to those who have taken the vows. Yet with all the beauty, dignity and solemnity of the occasion— or perhaps because of it—it is one of the loneliest moments in a man's life. When the words were spoken, "Receive ye the Holy Ghost for the office and work of a Bishop in the Church of God," I felt my whole soul stirring. I was conscious of my high desires and my many failures, of my unworthiness and of all God's graciousness to me.

Everyone showered the greatest kindness upon me and I was quite overwhelmed by the expressions of good will that flooded in from near and far. I was particularly touched that the Bishop of Alaska, the Right Reverend P. T. Rowe, came from his faraway diocese to attend the ceremony. He took part in the service, conducting the Litany.

My episcopal ring was given me by the congregation of the Old Stone Church, St. John, New Brunswick. My wife gave me my pectoral cross, and my pastoral staff was the gift of the Governor and Company of Adventurers of England Trading into Hudson's Bay. It was presented to me at a special service on Sunday, March 4, 1934, in Christ Church Cathedral, Mont-

real. It was given not only for my use but also for that of my successors in office, and for this reason is kept at All Saints Cathedral, Aklavik. It is a staff of more than ordinary interest since it is made of woods and metals indigenous to Canada, some coming from the shores of the Arctic and of Hudson Bay. The crook, ferrule, and end of the stem are made from Canadian silver that has been oxydized, and the stem is of native walnut. Six rosettes circle the base of the crook and they are filled with metals from northern Ontario, the Mackenzie district, and from Baffin Land, where the first Anglican communion service in Canada was held in 1578 during the third voyage of Martin Frobisher.

The centers of two of these rosettes are made of silver picked up at Gowganda and given me by a prospector. The centers of two others are of native copper given me by a pagan Eskimo at Bloody Falls on the Coppermine River, near Coronation Gulf, and the centers of the last two are made of iron pyrites given me by another Eskimo in Frobisher Bay. The communion plate used at my consecration in Winnipeg had been presented by the Hudson's Bay Company some sixty years before to the late Bishop Machray who was then chaplain to the company.

Of the death of my wife, Helen Grace Gillespie, I shall say nothing. Only those who have been called to walk through this particular valley know its meaning. To those who have not, mere words cannot convey the experience. She lived from day to day in close communion with her Saviour and something of His love, His presence, seemed to emanate from her pure spirit. I cannot express my gratitude to God for having had the privilege of companying with her along the road of life.

The gap that had been left in my life by her death was filled by my marriage to Elizabeth Nelson Lukens of Philadelphia. Our life together has been one of unclouded felicity and unbroken companionship. She has been at my side on my travels in the Arctic and on my journeyings across Canada and in the States. My first marriage had been so filled with

*separations that I determined such a condition should not
again prevail. My life heretofore, while richly blessed in many
ways, had been essentially a lonely one—seldom a loved one
at hand to turn to in perplexity; to share the burden. Now all
this was changed. Even with my fondest hopes I had not
realized what a difference the constant companionship of my
dear wife would make. I walked a new man and with this
unity has flowered a rich contentment of the spirit that has
crowned my life.*

16. The Flying Bishop ☆

☆

THE SUMMER FOLLOWING my consecration I traveled by rail, airplane, schooner, motorboat, and canoe to various sections of the Western Arctic and Hudson Bay. During these journeys I covered 14,422 miles, or more than halfway round the world, which, in that day, was considered quite an unusual achievement.

At Aklavik I was delighted to find that the additions to the hospital were proving most satisfactory. Indians and Eskimo were being cared for in greater numbers, and we were fortunate in having as nurse-in-charge at this time Miss Dorothy Bradford, R.N. She was a quiet, slow-spoken, reticent but very capable nurse. Her face was singularly beautiful and her fresh-colored skin showed up against her soft blond hair and white uniform. Professionally she was very highly regarded by the doctor and all the white people in the settlement. To me, her outstanding characteristic was her self-immolation for any native in trouble. It earned for her the respect and love (almost amounting to adoration) of all the patients.

We were equally fortunate in having as the teacher of our new day school a most unusual and attractive girl named Margaret Peck. At Miss Peck's own request no one at Aklavik knew that she was a graduate of Oxford University with honors in history, and came from a well-known family in Montreal. Few knew that only after much intellectual struggle had she attained the Christian position that allowed her to radiate love while performing the ordinary duties of life. Her faith, education, and culture enabled her by precept and example to interpret to the children, but even more especially to the older girls and younger mothers, what is meant by one's duty to God and to one's neighbor. As late as 1945 when I visited Aklavik, she was still remembered for her strength of character, her quiet dignity, and her good looks. To the natives, as to the white men, she gave the impression of unconscious grace and inner strength.

In addition to the day school run by Miss Peck I was by now also experimenting with a small residential school located at Shingle Point. The success of this pioneer effort made me determined that a new and larger school, in a better location and with the best of equipment, must be built as soon as I could find the money. The more intelligent Eskimo were themselves asking me to do so, and it was evident that we must try to meet the constantly increasing impact of civilization upon the people. In the south many opposed my plan and succeeded in making things very difficult for me. In Toronto one critic called me a gambler and prophesied that I would regret my folly. To this I replied that what he called a gamble I called Faith. However, there could be no question that for me it was a very serious adventure since it meant that I must first raise many thousands of dollars and that even then I would have to wrestle with church and government authorities about all the problems of buildings and securing suitable personnel.

During that summer planes began to come and go in the Western Arctic and with the words of the prospector still in my mind I made arrangements to fly "out" with Pilot W. R. (Wop) May of the Canadian Airways Limited. Shortly after six A.M. on Friday, July 6, we were looking down from two miles above the earth on a vast expanse of ice that covered the Beaufort Sea. The thermometer on the strut of the wing of the plane registered zero. As we turned back we ran into a heavy snowstorm but after that we were able to view the

Mackenzie River Delta as it stretched seventy or more miles from east to west.

At Coppermine our missionary, the Rev. John Morris, quickly arranged a service which began at ten thirty P.M. and ended at eleven forty-five P.M. Immediately after the service one of the wireless men lined us all up outside the mission and at the stroke of midnight took our photographs. This was the first time in history that a bishop in the Arctic had been photographed in his robes and with his congregation under the midnight sun!

Because of heavy storm clouds we could not remain the night but were forced to return to Cameron Bay on Great Bear Lake. We landed there under a cloudless sky with the flashing aurora borealis quivering high overhead. We had traveled 1,301 miles that day which, Wop said, was a record in those parts.

Because of bad weather in the south our departure was delayed until six o'clock in the evening. This gave us an opportunity to inspect the changes taking place in this hitherto isolated spot. The most startling innovations were a resident doctor; not one but two wireless stations; a woman insurance agent; a notice on a log cabin which read *Public Stenographer;* and two airplane companies, Canadian Airways Limited and Mackenzie Air Service.

With Wop I visited the various mining camps in the district, met some of the most famous mining experts and was shown rich samples of pitchblende. But I did not realize what an important role these discoveries would play in the years ahead.

The next morning we ran into dense fog and made a forced landing on a beautiful lagoon at Caribou Island in Great Slave Lake. It was a discouraging outlook but the men of the Canadian Airways were prepared for just such emergencies. In a short time a small tent had been erected, a fire lighted, and the mechanic landed a fine jackfish. At five thirty-eight P.M. we "touched water" at Fort McMurray and after a hurried meal I preached in the little church at evening prayer.

Then I went to bed for we were leaving at three thirty in the morning for Edmonton, where I actually arrived at the bishop's house before he was up. In spite of this he gave me a most kindly welcome. After I had a hot bath and change of clothes, we had a celebration of the Holy Communion in his private chapel. Then over breakfast we exchanged news.

That night on the Canadian National Transcontinental Express as we sped east, I wondered if the experiences of the past weeks were real or only a figment of my imagination. To have done so much in so short a time seemed impossible.

This, actually, was not my first flight with Wop May. Two years previous (1932) he had taken me the length of the Mackenzie. In those days flying in the Arctic was not only considered to be dangerous, it *was* dangerous. The air service in the North and in the Arctic was at this time in its infancy and the flying was over completely uncharted territory. No study had been made of the vagaries of magnetic attraction which made the early bush flying so difficult and there were no bases of reserve supplies. In case of accident there were no search parties to be sent out as there are nowadays. I often wonder if the young men flying today realize how much they owe to that *corps d'élite* of Canadian bush fliers who opened up the way—Punch Dickens, W. R. May, Berry, Britnell, Farrell, McMullen, and the others. It was Punch Dickens who carried in the first mail in 1929, and returned with a load of fur—thereby establishing a precedent. Dickens stayed in the North all that winter, not without adventures and misadventures, and the following summer made his flight down to the Delta almost exactly 140 years after Alexander Mackenzie's voyagers paddled through its waters.

This same summer Leigh Britnell made an outstanding reconnaissance flight covering the Mackenzie River area, the Yukon and the northeastern coast of British Columbia. It was Britnell who flew in Gilbert LaBine when he made his momentous discovery of pitchblende at Great Bear Lake and Punch Dickens who came some weeks later to fetch him.

But it was perhaps "Wop" May who most caught the public's fancy. To start with, during the First World War he had been in a dogfight with the famous German ace Baron von Richthofen. Then it was he who helped to track down the "mad trapper," as the newspapers called him. Actually Albert Johnson was neither mad nor a trapper. He was a petty scoundrel given to interfering with other people's trap lines, which in the North is a criminal offense.

Albert Johnson was a man of about thirty-five years of age. He lived in a lonely log cabin on the banks of the Rat River which flows into the Huskie River which, in turn, flows into the Peel River and joins the western channel of the Mackenzie. His cabin was about eighty miles west of Aklavik. When the Indians who hunt in the Rat River area came into Fort McPherson at Christmas in 1931 they reported that Johnson had been hanging up their traps when their lines crossed his. Since this man had not taken out a trapper's license, the inspector of the Royal Canadian Mounted Police immediately dispatched Constables A. W. King and R. G. McDowell to investigate the trouble. When the police reached the cabin they could find nobody about so they continued on to Aklavik to procure a search warrant. Armed with this, they arrived back at Johnson's shack on New Year's Eve to discover that in the brief interval of time its owner had barricaded himself in. He not only refused to let them come into his house but shot at them, seriously wounding Constable King. The temperature was 45 degrees below zero so Constable McDowell took the only course open to him. He put King onto the dog sled and brought him as quickly as he could to our hospital at Aklavik, where King made a good recovery.

From New Year's Eve until February 17 Johnson succeeded in keeping posse after posse of police at bay. He was both brave and skillful and had evidently spent many years in the North. He was adept at covering his trail and used all the low cunning of the savage to elude his pursuers. It was Wop May who finally located him. Flying low in his Bellanca, he saw Johnson's tracks in the snow. I will not recount the tragedy in full, but the R.C.M.P. "got their man," although one constable was killed and a second wounded. Twice they almost had him. Twice he escaped and even at the end he kept up a gun battle against all comers for fifteen hours, with the thermometer registering forty-eight degrees below zero, until he was finally shot to death. Contrary to newspaper reports, I was told at Aklavik that Johnson's body showed that he had been in excellent health. There was no surplus fat and every muscle was in perfect condition. May, who watched the fight from the air, told me that although Johnson had been wounded early in the battle death came quickly at the end. The police found that he had on his person $2,004 cash, mostly in U.S.A. currency—and the payment of a miserable seventy-five dollars for a license fee would have saved all this bloodshed and death.

While these events were in progress May was constantly flying in and out. He brought out the body of Constable Miller and took back food supplies for the police. He flew Constable Bowen out to our hospital where the doctor said that another hour's delay would have made the trip too late. And finally he flew Johnson's body out for burial at Aklavik.

It was a wonderful pioneer experience for me to fly down the mighty Mackenzie with Wop in June, 1932. We left from Waterways, Alberta, at half past eight in the morning. As I stepped on to the float of the small Canadian Airways Bellanca plane C.F.A.K., I was surprised to find the cabin packed with 850 pounds of first-class mail for Good Hope, Arctic Red River, and Aklavik. There was just a small corner beside the door where I had room enough to sit on a sleeping bag. No safety belt was required. After Wop had shut the door and climbed into the cockpit W. G. Nadin, the mechanic, spun the propeller. We winged our way North over the trees, spruce, poplar, hemlock, jack pine, and an occasional birch. With the ever-increasing altitude the rivers and lakes and great ranges came into view, all glittering in the sunshine.

Between Fort Smith and Resolution we followed the course

of the river but then cut across the land and skirted the shores of Great Slave Lake where the ice was massed and the thermometer on the wing strut now registered 43 degrees instead of the 84 degrees at Waterways. I was glad when we landed safely at the mouth of the Hay River and I was able to visit our mission, residential school, and hospital but as soon as the plane was refueled we were off again.

According to our original plans we were to spend the night at Fort Simpson but since the weather was perfect Wop decided to push on to Fort Norman, where we arrived at eight fifteen P.M. Thus it was that we had traveled 1,120 miles in eleven hours and forty-nine minutes lapsed time, or seven hours and fifty-five minutes in the air. This would have taken seven days by boat.

While at Fort Norman I learned much about the new activities in this area. One of the old wells situated about fifty miles to the north had been uncapped by the Imperial Oil Company and would now supply fuel oil for the newly established LaBine Company's plant at Great Bear Lake and our hospital at Aklavik. All around us there were evidences of the very considerable developments at Great Bear Lake. Groups of men were busy sorting out vast quantities of supplies and equipment that had been landed there eleven months before. These were waiting to be transported seventy miles up the Bear River and across the lake to what was to be known as Eldorado where pitchblende, from which radium is obtained, silver ore, and other metals had been found.

Friday began uneventfully and everything promised another day of fine weather. We were sure that we would reach Aklavik about noon. How little we knew! The air was so still that there was not a ripple on the surface of the river. After several futile attempts to rise, Wop asked me to change seats with Nadin since he weighed fifteen pounds less than I did. So I sat with Wop in the cockpit, from which I obtained a splendid view once the plane lifted.

Here was the country as I first saw it—aloof, uninhabited, immense, indifferent. Now its hidden resources have been bared, with the surety of more to come. It has also become the site of incredible military activity; and the limitless centuries of primeval silence have been broken by the sound of man. I am glad that I was part of it in the early days.

By the time we passed over the oil wells we were several thousand feet in the air and could not distinguish clearly how much progress had been made. In the east the Franklin Mountains only a few miles away looked barren and forbidding. Suddenly a great eagle appeared alongside the plane and after a brief examination "banked" and thus displayed to our astonished gaze something of its size. Then it wheeled to the rear and was lost to view. The bird came so near that we could see its eye.

Near Arctic Red River we ran into bad weather. The rain came down in torrents with a bitter wind from the north so that the plane "bumped" constantly. How Wop navigated against the blinding storm I do not know but we reached Arctic Red River safely at seven A.M. and gratefully accepted the kind invitation of Mr. R. W. Dodman, H.B.C. post manager, to stay with him until the storm abated.

We were storm-stayed at this point for three complete days and it was not until four forty-five P.M. on the Monday that we were able to leave for Aklavik. Even then our troubles were not over. Soon after we started we ran into heavy snow. Wop tried to evade it by climbing up to five thousand feet, only to find yet thicker cloud banks of snow. He then descended to escape these clouds, but finally decided that he could not face the storm and made a forced landing although within only a mile of our destination.

The day after our eventual arrival at Aklavik, May took off for the south with the outgoing mail. I was sorry to see him go for I respected and liked this man. He had created in my mind the utmost confidence in his skill as a pilot and he was always imperturbable and good-humored.

Before he left us another famous bush pilot arrived, Walter Gilbert, in the famous G-CASK Super-Fokker plane with a four hundred and twenty-five H.P. Wasp Engine. It was arranged that he should take me to Shingle Point. At that time this plane had probably the most interesting history of any flying machine in Canada.

S.K., as it was usually called, was one of the machines used by the Dominion Explorers Ltd. in 1929 when Lt. Col. McAlpin and others were forced down on the Arctic coast and saved from death by the friendly Eskimo who discovered them. These Eskimo supplied them with food and shelter, and guided them across the frozen wastes to the H.B.C. post at Cambridge Bay. The plane, which had run out of fuel, was staked down on the beach at Dease Point on the Arctic coast about twenty-five miles west of Ellice River. The machine was left unprotected except for a tarpaulin over the motor from September 8, 1929, to August 4, 1930, exposed to the fury of the Arctic weather—rain, sleet, ice, snow, blizzards, and the blazing summer sun. Yet in two hours and thirty-four minutes after plane G-CASK came with supplies, S.K. took off and flew faultlessly the thousand miles south to her home base Fort McMurray. It was this plane flown by Gilbert that made the historic trip with Major L. Burwash in 1931 to locate the remains of the Sir John Franklin Expedition on King William Island.

Gilbert and I left Aklavik in S.K. for Shingle Point on the morning of June 8 hopeful, but not without forebodings, for we had received contradictory reports as to the possibilities of landing on open water near the coast. At first the condition of the country below us was encouraging but soon a change took place which caused us alarm. The lakes no longer showed open water; the mountains in the distance stood out in purest white. At the coast we found the sea frozen for twenty miles out and no sign of water either in a lake near Shingle Point, which we had been advised would be open, or in the river itself. We circled over the school three times, coming down within two hundred feet. The staff and children were out on the snow waving to us. We dropped their mail and saw them run out on the frozen sea and pick it up. It was a bitter disappointment to me personally, but that was lost in the realization of what it meant to these gallant workers. Yet we were thankful that we had seen them and they us, and also that they had got their mail a month earlier than usual, as well as a few presents. They also got a little bag of mine containing my tooth paste, brush and wash cloth, which was not intended as a gift!

Our friends in civilization visualize the cold, ice, and snow, but in the field these are taken for granted, and are of little moment. It is the constant grind in the same place, doing the same things day in and day out with so little opportunity to get away from one's self and one's neighbors—it is this that constitutes the burden. It is this isolation that cuts deep like iron in the soul, that tests the reality of one's religion more than anything else. It is this that calls for real heroism, and only those who have truly surrendered their wills to Him can stand the grim test.

I flew with Gilbert in S.K. on out to Winnipeg. There I discovered that in the pages of the press I had become "the Flying Archdeacon." The following year this was changed to "the Flying Bishop" and it was by this name that I was known for many years.

☆ 17. Hospitals in the Far North ☆

As I LAID my plans now for a hospital in Baffin Land my mind often went back to the beginning of the missionary venture and I was strengthened as I realized how wonderfully God had prospered our efforts. When Peck first began his labors in Cumberland Sound, in 1894, he had been much impressed by the suffering and sorrow endured by the Eskimo because of their ignorance of medical science. He insisted that before going north both Greenshield and Bilby should each spend one year at Livingstone Medical College, London, England.

In a small shack at Blacklead Island those two young missionaries had spent long hours ministering to the sick and diseased, and from it many an Eskimo returned to his people restored to health and strength. That the pagan people had been willing to come to Bilby and Greenshield for treatment was in itself a great advance since they were in "competition" with the angakoks. There were many dangers inherent in the situation but at least confidence had been won and a beginning made. That little building had been the first hospital in Baffin Land. And now after several years of fund-raising, I hoped that, God willing, we would build another hospital in Baffin Land.

But when the time came to return to Canada from England where I had been raising money, only about half the total required for the hospital had been subscribed. With great disappointment I made up my mind that I would have to delay the building for a year at least. Then a strange thing happened. In a stack of mail awaiting my return in Toronto were three letters, two from the Director of the Northwest Territories, Ottawa, asking that the Church proceed with the erection of the proposed hospital in Baffin Land, and one from a lady in Montreal asking for information about the same project. The government at Ottawa agreed to give certain medical and surgical equipment, to carry the materials and supplies free of charge on their ship to Baffin Land, and to pay the usual per capita grants for the patients. But still the total guaranteed amount was not sufficient for me to feel justified in reversing my earlier decision. I told the government that I would give the matter prayerful consideration and return a final answer within a week. Before the seven days were up the friend in Montreal turned over to us the whole amount of a substantial legacy which had just come to her sister and herself, and a very generous check towards the hospital was also received from a friend of the Arctic whose headquarters was Churchill on Hudson Bay. His unsolicited gift was doubly cheering because it showed how the white men living in the North felt about this adventure. With all this in hand I felt that I was justified in giving the word to go forward.

From the beginning it has seemed to me vital that our Church hospitals should be first class scientifically and that the furnishings be not elegant but comfortable and agreeable. One could not ask doctors and nurses to come or expect them to lead contented, useful lives in such extreme isolation with inferior equipment and drab living quarters. Then surely the patients whether Eskimo or white were entitled to the best that could be provided. So the medical and surgical equipment was the very best and there was an attractive living room and solarium for the nurses. Most of the furnishings were provided by the Women's Auxiliary of the Church of England in Canada, whose loyal and consecrated service to the Arctic workers has never ceased nor ever been forgotten.

We agreed with the government and the H.B.C. to locate

the new hospital at Pangnirtung and the materials were all sent north in the summer of 1930. So was the builder, the Rev. George Nicholson, who had been especially prepared for pioneer work at the Missionary Training College, London, England. In order to fit himself more thoroughly for the task he had worked without pay for a firm of contractors in London and gained practical knowledge of housebuilding.

My first sight of the Pangnirtung hospital was the following year in the summer of 1931. The nurse-in-charge, Miss E. Prudence Hockin of Winnipeg, took me over the new building with as much enthusiasm as if it were her own property. When I had first interviewed Nurse Hockin for this responsible position I had not been favorably impressed. She had been shy and difficult to approach, peering at me in an odd way over the top of her steel-rimmed spectacles. However at the end of our interview I accepted her because her nursing qualifications were excellent and she was willing to commit herself to a four-year term. But, to my shame, I did so with misgivings and I herewith offer my apologies. Nurse Hockin has spent almost twenty-five years in the service of the people of the Arctic, and untold hundreds have risen up to call her blessed. In my opinion it is not too much to say that she is the epitome of what a white woman in the Arctic ought to be—efficient, self-reliant, generous of nature, good-humored and with an ever-increasing devotion to her Lord.

In 1931 Nurse Hockin had got everything into first-class order at Pangnirtung. Here there was none of the shyness that had come between us in Toronto. She talked quickly and freely and her face radiated something of the love for the people that she had in her heart. When the ship left after its brief stay I came away with a deep sense of gratitude that God had given us such a wonderful woman to begin this work in the face of so many difficulties. Her contributions have been outstanding to this day.

The most pressing needs were for electric light and X-ray equipment, but I simply did not have the $5,000 they would cost. Nor did I have an equal sum to meet the same deficiency

dead of winter in the Arctic, she ran to investigate. Her first thought was the kitchen but all seemed to be well there. On into the laundry she hurried. From behind the stove which she had tended just fifteen minutes before smoke was pouring. Quick as lightning she rushed to the kitchen for a supply of water and flung it over the wall which was already hot. Then she shook and shouted awake the slumbering staff. Nurse Hamilton ran to call the resident missionary, the Rev. George Nicholson, at the mission house. With an axe Nurse Harvey broke open the laundry wall and applied a fire extinguisher. The other two nurses concentrated on getting the patients out of the building.

When Mr. Nicholson arrived on the scene he found Nurse Harvey still in the laundry trying to battle the fire. Seeing that the flames had already got too far in that quarter he sent for help from other parts of the settlement. The temperature outside was 36 degrees below zero and patients and nurses alike wore only their night attire over which wraps had been hastily flung.

Meanwhile at the alarm the men of the settlement came on the run, hoping to rescue furniture and equipment. But the fire had taken possession of the wooden walls. As they crackled in the intense heat brave efforts were made to save the most valuable equipment. Ignoring the risk, two men climbed through the window of the operating theatre and got out one operating table and a cabinet of surgical instruments. They did not know it at the time but this case contained the majority of Dr. Urquhart's most necessary and cherished tools. After that the struggle had to be given up: the flames had won. The little band of workers stood and watched the fire burn itself out. There had been no wind. The sparks and embers fell back into the debris and not another building was hurt. Not a life was lost. Thank God for that. By 7:30 A.M. all was over.

I was immediately faced with the ultimate question. Should we rebuild at once this coming summer or not? This being April, I could not afford much time in which to make a decision if the materials and supplies were to go forward that season. If they did not, the minimum delay in building would be one year. During that year no care could be given to the injured, the sick, and the suffering. Yet the cold truth was that I had no funds in hand and the cost would run to many thousands. Moreover in certain influential quarters of the church I was already considered an unjustifiable gambler. On the other hand the confidence placed in me by my spiritual children was implicit. They knew the need. They believed that I would meet that need. Could I keep faith with the people of the Arctic or could I not? That was my terrible dilemma. After a night spent in much prayer the answer came to me: "And behold the word of the Lord came to him and said, 'What doest thou here?' " In the morning I telephoned the architects and said that we would build a new and larger hospital.

It soon became evident that among the members of the executive committee of our missionary society there was a great difference of opinion as to rebuilding and I was unofficially informed that I must not expect any grant from them. This was a serious blow although I realized that owing to other heavy commitments they too were in a difficult position. It meant, to put it bluntly, that I would have to assume the full responsibility and raise the money by special appeal. It was a time of great testing. I felt that if we were going to rebuild at all we must do so on a more adequate scale and so I planned and purchased for a forty-eight-bed unit. I arranged my appeal as best I could in the limited time and by God's grace the money did come in—gifts ranged from pennies given by small children to checks in four figures.

In this crisis I do not know what I would have done without the kind services of the Hudson's Bay Company. They could not handle so much additional freight on their scheduled runs but with their usual competence in the face of an emergency arranged to carry the complete "outfit" (their own term for a unit of shipping) on especially provided boats and barges. This was no light undertaking since the journey by water from the end of steel to Aklavik is 2,514 miles. Had the H.B.C. not helped us the whole scheme would have been held up for a year. I shall always be grateful to Mr. Ralph Parsons, now Fur Trade Commissioner, and his associates.

Exactly two months after receiving the news of the destruction of the hospital I was back in Aklavik once more. I arrived at an auspicious time as our new residential school for one hundred children had just been completed and was ready for the staff to move in. This meant that our master carpenter, Mr. Summers, was able to spend the necessary hours with me going over hospital plans and getting it started without delay and also that I was able to help in having the pupils from Shingle Point moved down to Aklavik.

On June 23 we laid the foundation post of the new hospital. We could not have a stone "well and truly laid" since there are no stones at Aklavik. The settlement is built on a deposit of silt from the river. Instead heavy posts were driven down into great holes dug at least five feet below the permanent frost line where they soon became imbedded in the mass of frozen earth.

We had a ceremony to mark the occasion and our little function was unique and colorful. Flags were flying from the flagstaffs and from the masts of the motor craft moored against the mudbank of the river. At two o'clock, fully robed, with my chaplain, the Rev. George Nicholson, and a full-blooded Loucheaux lay reader, I proceeded from the mission to the site of the new hospital. There we were met by a throng of Indians and Eskimo in their native dress, while the officers and men of the Royal Canadian Mounted Police and Royal Canadian Signal Corps added the bright scarlet of their uniforms. The Indian agent and the medical officer, Dr. Urquhart, represented the Department of the Interior and the manager of the Hudson's Bay Company was also present.

After a short service in English and Takudh the Eskimo sang in their own language "At even when the sun was set." Thus each of the three races took part. Then I called upon the five-year-old, Arctic-born daughter of Dr. Urquhart to drop a shovelful of earth into the hole where the foundation post was set. She was followed by a small Indian boy who, in turn, was succeeded by an Eskimo laddie. And so again the three peoples were represented whom the hospital would serve without regard to race or creed.

It is difficult for people "outside" where so much is taken for granted to understand the meaning of such an event as this beyond the Arctic Circle. It has an emotional and spiritual significance that moves one deeply.

Immediately following the laying of the foundation post of the new hospital, I left Aklavik by motorboat for Shingle Point. As the boat chugged along, I noticed the heavy erosion that was taking place. The Eskimo told me that they had often come across the bones of animals in the earth that fell to the shore level and that occasionally ivory tusks, very much larger than those of the walrus, had been found. One man said he had discovered such a tusk imbedded in the cliffs but protruding some two feet out. When he first noticed it he thought it was a piece of wood. I explained that it was probably the tusk of what the white man has named a mastodon, and made a sketch of what this animal looked like. The Eskimo were all greatly interested and assured me, with much gesturing as to size, that the tusks were as I had indicated. They added quite innocently that they had never seen such a beast. A few days after our return to Aklavik one of the men gave me a mastodon tusk that he had found near King Point less than one hundred miles from Aklavik.

Only a few weeks after this trip I visited the reindeer herd which was summering on Richardson Island at the mouth of the Delta. While yet two miles distant, the sharp eyes of my Eskimo guide spotted the tents of the herders. The Laplanders were camped on the shore at the north side of a little stream, while the Eskimo were nearby on the south side.

In order that we might not disturb the reindeer the speed of the motor was reduced and we headed for the camp as quietly as possible. About one thousand beasts were moving slowly along the sandy shore or were standing knee-deep in the salt water, while three thousand more were grazing quietly on the low-lying hillside. When we went ashore the herders welcomed us warmly. Then one of the Lapps took us over to the main herd, walking very slowly and with as little motion as possible. We could not but be delighted as we looked at these shy and beautiful creatures. It was surprising to note the way the whole vast company moved constantly in a wide circle, while the tramp of their hooves, the piglike grunt and the smell of their tawny bodies combined to make an unforgettable impression on me.

Although the Lapps were Lutherans, they had little difficulty in following the Anglican service that we had together and they knew enough Eskimo to understand the message I delivered. Previous to the service I had discovered three hymns common to both the Lapp and Eskimo books so the Lapps sang in their own tongue and the Eskimo in theirs. When the service was over the Lapps invited us to partake of a dish of fried reindeer steaks which we relished; we had had nothing to eat since our early breakfast at Aklavik. I was very pleased that from our boat stores we could supply these people with some provisions which they greatly needed since their annual supplies had not yet reached them.

Later that summer I traveled by motorboat to Tuktoyaktuk on the Arctic Ocean and then proceeded by whaleboat to Herschel Island. For various reasons it was rugged traveling and I found myself very tired. I looked forward to the arrival in two days' time of the schooner that was to take me east and I anticipated journeying in relative comfort along the 1,200 miles of coast where I would have services with the people at the various ports of call. But day after day after day dragged on without any sign or word of the schooner. On the sixteenth day the H.B.C. post manager handed me a wire. He smiled as he gave it to me and instinctively my heart lifted. I tore open the envelope. The message was from Ralph Parsons. He said that the ice conditions were so bad that for the time being all boats were frozen in. He offered to pick me up in his plane the next day and take me on with him to Coppermine, Cambridge Bay, and the other points which we both wished to visit. I wired a grateful acceptance.

We made the long trip together by air to Aklavik, Good Hope, Fort Norman, Cameron Bay, Coppermine, Fort Rae, Hay River, Fort Smith, Chipewyan, Stoney Rapids, Fond-du-Lac, Fort McMurray, and finally to Edmonton. This journey was not without its unexpected excitement and had it not been for the skill of our pilot, the famous Archie McMullen, I would not be alive to tell the tale. Sometime after leaving Fond-du-Lac the engine of the plane suddenly faded out. The situation was very serious since the plane was fitted with pontoons and consequently could not land on the open country over which we were flying. We were far from any habitation. Archie McMullen was fully aware of the gravity of our plight. As soon as the engine stopped he began to glide with twistings and turnings in a quick search for water. By a miracle he caught a silver gleam. As we came down nearer and nearer we saw a tiny river—very narrow and with its banks heavily lined with willow. It was, in fact, so narrow that to both Parsons and me a safe landing seemed impossible. However, thanks to McMullen's adroit handling of his machine, we came gently down onto the water. As we stepped out we saw that the wings of the plane had not more than a couple of feet clearance on either side.

McMullen explained that the engine itself was all right but that a vapor lock had developed in the pipe between the tank on the starboard wing and the engine so that gasoline could not flow through to the cylinders. For six hours Parsons and I watched the pilot and mechanic time and time again try and fail to turn the engine over. It was an anxious wait. When the lock was finally "released" all McMullen said was "O.K." When Parsons ultimately asked what would have happened if the two men had not been successful in both the landing and mechanical work, Archie McMullen shrugged his shoulders and replied, "You know the answer."

This incident was only one of many flying misadventures. Once, when the plane was piloted by W. J. Davis, we were grounded by fog and unable to radio our regular reports. The newspaper headlines sounded the alarm:

FLYING BISHOP MISSING
UNREPORTED FOR 8 DAYS

There was considerable concern until we could declare FLYING BISHOP SAFE.

On the present journey, it was a great pleasure to have again the intimate companionship of Parsons, my old friend and fellow sojourner in Baffin Land in the distant days of 1911. At Lake Harbour we had often discussed what was best for the Eskimo and while at times we differed very definitely, that did not interfere with our mutual respect for one another. He was the trader and I was the missionary. I loved the people for their own sakes, while he valued them primarily because they brought in the fox pelts which were the *raison d'être* for his being in the country.

Apart from some of the old men in the H.B.C. I probably knew Parsons better than anyone else and my regard for him grew with the years. Physically he was of more than average height, with a fine head, well-cut nostrils, and a rather tight-lipped mouth. His whole attitude was one of unrelenting vigilance. I delighted to watch him when he was in conversation with others. He was adroit in asking seemingly simple and natural questions. These would put the clerk or apprentice at ease and draw him out so that he revealed himself. Then if Parsons was not satisfied with the answers he got, he was liable to suggest the opposite of what he believed to be correct. In this way he obtained the desired information. I remember how on one occasion a youngster displayed considerable conceit so Parsons paid him a compliment but it was steeped in vinegar and quickly brought the victim to his senses. At the same time he had a way of making the men under him feel that he was not only one whose orders had to be obeyed but also a friend on whom they could rely. Thus he got the best out of them and became a fabulous image of power and fame.

He was naturally reserved, independent, self-controlled. He also had amazing powers of detachment and never appeared to be surprised no matter how unexpected or absurd a report or incident might be. These qualities enabled him to rise step by step in the company's service until he became Fur Trade Commissioner in charge of the whole extensive and complicated transportation system. There can be little doubt that the fur trade in Canada owes more to Ralph Parsons than to any other individual during the first half of the twentieth century. I do not make this statement because he established more fur trading posts than any four of his predecessors as commissioners, but because he raised the whole tone of the fur trade. He was ruthless in his determination to stop drunkenness and immorality, not perhaps because of any deep religious conviction, but because he knew that these spelled ruin to both trapper and trader.

It is not easy to sum up such a diversified personality. I think it would be true to say of Parsons what John Buchan wrote of Oliver Cromwell, that he had "the gift of forcing facts to serve him, of compelling men into devotion and acquiescence." He was a man of iron but his accomplishments indicated that he possessed that resiliency, initiative and ability so marked in Sir George Simpson and the other early fur trade commissioners of the oldest company operating on the North American continent today—"The Company of Adventurers of England Trading into Hudson's Bay."

☆ 18. John Buchan Opens the Door ☆

THE YEAR 1937 WAS outstanding in the annals of the Church's work in the Arctic. Early in June, as soon as the ice on the river broke up, I flew down to Aklavik. I had certain points to visit and many arrangements to make before the arrival of the Governor-General of Canada. Lord Tweedsmuir, better known as John Buchan the novelist, had graciously consented to officiate at the opening of the new hospital. His was the first visit of any governor-general north of the Arctic Circle.

When I arrived at Aklavik I found great activity in the settlement and it was with deep thankfulness to God and to each of our workers, white, Indian, and Eskimo, that I recognized the important and far-reaching advances that had been made: The large congregations (one hundred eighty-six at one service alone), thirty candidates presented for confirmation, the completion of the new hospital building with its X-ray, iron lung, electric lighting, and fully equipped operating theatre gave me a justifiable feeling of accomplishment. But they also made me very humble since I knew that it had all been achieved by the Spirit of God operating in the minds and hearts of His people here in the North, in southern Canada, in England, and in the United States. I was particularly happy that the little oratory chapel had been completed, making it a truly Christian hospital. On the wall of the vestibule hung a tablet stating that *The sick and suffering are welcomed here at all times in Jesus' name, without reference to race, colour or creed.*

I set off downriver to make my visits along the coast. I took passage on a motorboat owned and operated by one of our devoted Christian Eskimo, a man named Lester. It was a long trip and we had no time to spare if we were to be back at Aklavik when the governor-general arrived.

At each camp I held services but the week end spent at Maitland Point was a high-water mark. At Maitland Point there was no trading post or mission but only a very small Royal Canadian Mounted Police detachment with Lance Corporal C. Murphy in charge assisted by Constable G. T. Wareham. The corporal was an old friend. He was clean-cut, big-boned and yet spare, giving the impression of physical power, but his eyes attracted me most; they appeared cloudy and hid his thoughts. The constable was new to the country, good-looking, with a fresh open countenance.

Within a few hours of our arrival a private trader named Fred Matthews, traveling in a big freight canoe with powerful outboard motor and accompanied by other canoes bringing some three dozen Eskimo and fifty sledge dogs, drew in to the shore near the post. I had met Matthews several times on previous visits in the Western Arctic and had conceived for him a genuine respect. He had been living alone deep in the bush and away from the native trap lines. For companions he had a fine team of dogs of which he was justly proud and it was evident that the dogs loved their master. He was now on his way south to Edmonton to sell his fur in the market where the prices would be higher than in the North.

Here I also met a white trapper named Virville of whom I had heard but whom I had never known. As the trapping season was over he had come from the interior, hoping to get passage to Aklavik in order to dispose of his "take."

On Saturday morning I gathered the Eskimo together for a preparation service. Later that day I took the baptisms and marriages so that we might not be pressed for time during Sunday services. Before going to bed on Saturday I asked the

this was the first time in history that the flag of the Governor-General of Canada was flown from a building north of the Arctic Circle at the same time as a bishop's flag!

The visit of Lord Tweedsmuir will always live in my memory not because he was the Governor-General of Canada, but because he was a really great man. During the three days he spent with us at Aklavik he spoke freely on many matters. It was an unforgettable experience to sit and listen to his conversation, study his personality, note the delightful turn of a phrase, the surprising use of a word, and the penetrating judgment. Like most people, I had associated John Buchan with his romances but now he was revealed as much more than a novelist and historian. He was a noble man, true to the soul of things and because of his deep sympathy could put himself into the minds of his untold thousands of readers.

This brilliant Scot, the son of a Free Church minister, a lawyer, traveler, businessman, author, politician, orator, and the King's representative in Canada, was a personality greater far than even his many achievements might indicate. One evening when I ventured to express my humble admiration, he looked at me solemnly for a moment and then a flicker of a smile passed over his face as he said somewhat sadly, "Bishop, there is one thing I covet more than success and that you seem to possess—good health." He talked on a bit, revealing his thoughts. Then he shook me by the hand and said good night.

Miss Margaret Bourke-White, staff photographer of *Life*, and her friend Dr. Thomas Wood, of Oxford, England, had accompanied the governor-general on this trip.

On the morning of his departure from Aklavik, Lord Tweedsmuir asked me if it was true that they were traveling with me to Victoria Island. When I replied in the affirmative he said, "If she bothers you by clicking that camera when people are around, just call her Maggie and she will disappear!" Well! I never ventured to call her Maggie and in *Life* that autumn she had an article covering two and a half pages with many photographs entitled, "Strange Adventures of Archibald The Arctic!"

Four hours after the government party had departed I followed on a Canadian Airways plane with Arthur Ranken, pilot; Jack Dean, mechanic; and Dr. Wood and Miss Margaret Bourke-White as passengers. The weather was poor but we reached Fort Norman safely. There we found the governor-general and his party weather-bound and billeted with the Hudson's Bay Company who also kindly offered me hospitality.

I arose early in the morning only to find a stiff thirty-mile-an-hour wind driving great rolling clouds across the darkened sky and deluging the land with torrents of rain. After breakfast I visited the wireless station where the pilots and mechanics of the planes were staying. The weather reports from Cameron Bay were not encouraging. As I approached the H.B.C. house on my return, I heard my name called. It was the governor-general. He invited me to sit beside him on the verandah in a corner sheltered from the wind and rain. For the next hour I sat spellbound as he recounted the story of his life. His boyhood days in Fife; Glasgow University; his scholarships to Oxford; his amazing success as a writer so that even at college he earned more money than he required for his needs and was able to send welcome gifts to his parents then in the manse at Peebles. He said that Cosmo Lang, later Archbishop of Canterbury, had been his tutor and friend. He spoke of how just as he (Buchan) was called to the Bar in London he received Lord Milner's offer to go with him to South Africa; how he entered the publishing firm of Nelson and Company; married the finest girl in the world; became a Member of Parliament and was called unexpectedly to be the King's representative as Governor-General of Canada. He told me that owing to the variety of his experiences he felt he had been preordained for this work.

When his tale was finished, he asked me to tell him my story. When I hesitated he stated that he believed that if a man were sincere and diligent then God called him to his task, whatever that might be; that it should be accepted as such and that it was only mistaken or false modesty that blinded him to this fact. Then he added, "Your official signature 'Archibald The Arctic' is the most romantic signature in the world and just one point ahead of 'William of Argyle and the Isles.' "

At about four P.M. the storm had abated sufficiently to allow the planes to take off. The governor-general went to Eldorado Mines, and I to Cameron Bay.

Margaret Bourke-White and her friend were still with me. From Cameron Bay we went on to Coppermine where we were welcomed by our missionaries, the Rev. J. H. Webster and his wife, and then by all the white people and the Eskimo. There were quite a number of white people in the settlement, including the captain and crew of the H.B.C. schooner *Fort James* which had recently been crushed in the ice and lost. It was amusing to note the surprise on the faces of the inhabitants when they beheld a charming female with a vivacious smile and jaunty step, carrying a large press photographer's camera, approach them from the plane!

The next day we arose at four A.M. and took off at seven fifteen for Cambridge Bay. The first two hundred miles were covered in beautiful weather over ice-scattered seas, but after that we ran into dense fog and made a forced landing on an unknown island. There for ten hours we watched the fog roll by, wondering if and when it would lift. We were ill prepared to be marooned as we had left some of our equipment behind so that we might carry a little extra gasoline. On this occasion as on previous ones the outcome would be death from exposure and starvation if matters did not mend. The ten hours seemed interminable but at long last Art Ranken, in whom I had every confidence, decided that we might get through. So we took to the air. Near Cambridge Bay, we ran into a heavy rainstorm with a low ceiling so that Art Ranken was forced to bring the plane down very near the buildings as he searched for a landing place. As we skimmed over the two trading posts, the police barracks and the mission, we were surprised to see very few people about. There seemed to be no activity, no sign of life, no smoke from any chimney. This we could not understand. When we landed on the beach beside the mission we discovered that only two Eskimo families and the police interpreter were at the settlement. The white population had gone to the mainland on a small H.B.C. schooner. We had not enough gasoline to scout around the area to find out where they were. I was bitterly disappointed since the previous summer I had failed to reach Cambridge Bay. We found every place tightly locked except the police post where the interpreter was living. He had a warm fire burning in the kitchen stove and invited us to come there, which we were only too happy to do. Later in the evening I conducted a service with the Eskimo. To add to our troubles we very nearly had a catastrophe. During the refueling of the plane, some gasoline got onto Art Ranken's clothes. When he lit a cigarette after finishing work his clothes instantly burst into flames. With great presence of mind he ran into the sea and so no harm was done save a severe fright for us all.

The next day we returned to Coppermine, hoping to get on out on the succeeding day. Bad weather again detained us but eventually we reached Eldorado Mines and then Yellowknife. All five of us—that is, the two photographers, Art Ranken and his mechanic, and myself—went up from the plane to the best hotel in that thriving northern town where we were generously entertained by Victor Ingraham, the manager and part owner. When I asked Vic for my bill in the morning, he smiled and said, "Anytime you come here we will do our best to make you comfortable." There was a reason for his generosity.

In the late autumn of 1933 a high-powered motorboat was crossing Great Bear Lake with the last supplies from the south. Winter was at hand. Snow covered the ground, and ice was already forming on the lake. Suddenly an explosion was heard and the boat went up in flames. Victor Ingraham, who was in charge, tried to rescue two of the men who were cut off by the flames but without success. The men died. In his attempt he burned both his feet and both his hands. In this condition he and one other man managed to get ashore in a small rubber boat but in the intense cold his burned members were frozen. Dr. Thomas Bryne, at that time stationed at Cameron Bay, was able to give him some medical attention and then Ingraham was flown to All Saints Hospital, Aklavik. When he arrived there, little hope for his recovery was entertained by Dr. J. A. Urquhart and our nurses. Gangrene had set in and it looked as if in a few hours he would be dead.

However, Dr. Urquhart set to work. In all, Vic had fifteen operations but after five months in the hospital he was able to return south. Later he was equipped with artificial limbs and to see him moving around during our visit one would hardly believe that he had been so seriously maimed.

From Yellowknife we came down merely to refuel at Resolution, Fort Smith, McMurray, and finally reached Edmonton where, with only ten minutes to spare, I caught the C.N.R. transcontinental train going east and after two days and three nights reached Toronto. Since leaving home in June I had traveled four thousand, one hundred and forty-four miles by land; five thousand, two hundred and fifty miles by air; eight hundred and eighty miles by water; making a total of ten thousand, two hundred and seventy-four miles.

As I had come and gone from Aklavik all that summer of 1937 the need for a more commodious church impressed itself upon me. The population had increased with startling rapidity and it was evident that this once tiny settlement which in 1919 had been less than a dozen houses was about to become the center of the Western Arctic. We must erect a a new church that would meet the needs of the now large congregations.

In view of the tremendous expense involved in the construction of the new residential school and All Saints Hospital the question of finance loomed very large. On the other hand the people themselves requested that action should be taken. They asked that I see how much money could be raised in Aklavik itself, so the project was launched. The first gift was $100 from the Loucheaux Indian Women's Auxiliary. For them this was, of course, a very large sum of money. The second gift was a check for $25 from a private fur trader. Then it was announced that the collections at all services on a certain Sunday would be for the building fund and the plates were heaped to overflowing with muskrat skins. From then on gifts came tumbling in from Indians, Eskimo, and whites. So enthusiastic was the response that while still at Aklavik I decided to designate the new church as my cathedral and to spare no effort in making it as perfect as I could for the glory of God and the edification of His people.

Before I set sail for my labor in England I worked out with the architects Molesworth and Secord, Toronto, the necessary plans and specifications, and I made the Cathedral of the Arctic my chief appeal. Time and time again I have delivered my soul of its message simply because the care and supervision of a small part of the Lord's work had been entrusted to me. I have done so not knowing what specific result, if any, would follow. This was the case when I preached one Sunday morning during this winter of 1937–1938 in St. Philip's, Earl's Court, London. I told of the need at Aklavik and the sacrificial giving of the local people towards this object so near to their hearts. The next morning I received a letter from a lady who had been in the congregation, a Miss Violet Teague, who was on a visit to London from Melbourne, Australia. The writer explained that she was an artist by profession, a portrait painter, and that, having been moved by my sermon, she would like to paint an altarpiece for the new House of God in the land of ice and snow. She asked for an interview. Knowing nothing of her work I was a bit apprehensive but I soon saw that it was outstanding and that she herself was a sensitive, Christian woman. I accepted her offer. Then Miss Teague returned to Australia and I to Canada and the Arctic.

Two years later the completed "Epiphany in the Snows" was shown in Melbourne at a special exhibition opened by Archbishop Head. It attracted much attention and favorable comment. In due time it reached London where it was shown at Canada House. Here the exhibition was opened by the Hon. Vincent Massey (then Canadian High Commissioner). From London began its long journey to its final destination in the little Cathedral Church of All Saints at Aklavik, 120 miles beyond the Arctic Circle.

The picture conveys the message that Christ of God is for all people. The Madonna and Child are dressed in regal ermine obtainable in the North and both are wearing Eskimo boots. On the extreme right is a tall Nascopie-Cree Indian from the Ungava Peninsula bringing as his offering a live beaver symbolical of the beaver sanctuaries which are so beneficial to the people. Kneeling below him is a HBC man offering white Arctic fox pelts, the result of his labors as a trader. Behind stands a RCMP in northern garb who offers protection while two sledge dogs, one white and the other black, are harnessed ready for service. On the other side of the Madonna, an Eskimo dressed in caribou-skin parka, bearskin trousers and sealskin boots kneels in the snow offering the trophies of the hunt—two walrus tusks. Behind this man is an Eskimo woman from Baffin Land with a baby in her hood also bringing a gift. At the back instead of the traditional camels stand two reindeer, symbolical of the vast reindeer herds which are of such value to our people.

The press throughout the world has given this painting continuous praise, and even after all these years scarcely a season passes when we are not asked by some business or industrial firm for permission to reproduce it on their Christmas greetings. It was hung in place before the cathedral was consecrated by Archbishop Owen on St. Peter's Day, 1939.

The people of the Arctic have taken this picture to their hearts. I learned this poignant story on the Sunday following the consecration as I came around the corner of the cathedral unexpectedly and stopped to speak to some Indians who were

standing in earnest discussion. They were so serious that I
asked them what they were talking about. One replied, "We
were saying that we should be thankful to God and to the
woman who made that picture. We like it." I encouraged
them to say more so we sat down on the steps and I listened
with crowded emotions as they spoke.

It seems that some of the Indians had suffered a very critical
experience at the breakup in the spring and at one time were
in imminent danger of being drowned. After a terrible and
exhausting struggle they succeeded in reaching high ground
and were thus saved from the angry turbulent waters that
were pushing great broken masses of ice towards the sea.
When they realized their safety one of them suggested that
they give thanks for their rescue. This they did, using the
shortened form of Evening Prayer (note that as a matter of
course they had their prayer books with them). After the service they proceeded to light a fire and prepare a meal. While
they were sitting around the fire one man remarked that they
had had a close call and then went on to express his opinion
that he doubted if any Indian would ever get to Heaven.

When asked by the others to explain why, he said that he
had never seen a picture about Heaven with an Indian represented. There were only white people, "and," the Indian
added, "I think the white man will elbow us out in the Day
of Judgment."

"Now," concluded the man who had told me the story, "we
know that we were wrong for there is an Indian in this
picture."

I must mention one or two of the unusual gifts that make
the cathedral perfect of its kind. One set of hangings is the
work and gift of the Eskimo Women's Auxiliary of Pangnirtung in Baffin Land. The pattern, which is put together
with many small pieces of sealskin, is so beautifully executed
and the stitches so delicate and even, although sinew was used
for thread, that expert needlewomen in Montreal found it
hard to believe that it had been made by hand. When one
knows that this gift came from erstwhile pagan women who

had grown in grace to such an extent that they asked to make this sacrificial offering for "God's House faraway," who can doubt that "with Christ all things are possible."

The stained glass windows are second to none. Those in the transept are the work of Mr. Hugh Easton of England, who is perhaps best known for his distinguished Battle of Britain window in Westminster Abbey.

I have often been asked why I went to so much trouble to have the cathedral carefully designed by good architects and fitted with such artistic and interesting furnishings and why I felt it essential to have dignified services in view of the fact that it was well known that elsewhere I approved of having the simplest services held any place at all. My reply was that *always* the first matter of importance was to worship God and to help people realize that they were offering their prayers and praises to Him. But in Aklavik we are faced with a multi-racial problem. The native people are no longer simple no-mads but have advanced to a considerable degree in "civiliza-tion." Then there are many white people whose connection with any church is tenuous to say the least. The stately serv-ices, with a robed choir, such as we have in the cathedral, help these two groups of worshipers to realize that they are in the presence of the High and Holy One, the Maker of Heaven and Earth.

At this period when I went abroad for help, generosity met me at every turn and enabled me to care for my capital expenditures. The contrast between my present experiences in England and my early ones was often in my mind. Now I was invited to preach in Westminster Abbey and St. Paul's and to speak at packed meetings at the Albert Hall. As Bishop of the Arctic the doors of opportunity were flung wide open.

Through the courtesy of Dr. Iremonger who was then in charge of the religious department of the B.B.C. I was invited from time to time to speak over the air. Often my broad-casting brought interesting results. One Christmas Day mes-sage was heard on a ship in the Indian Ocean. Among the listeners was a businessman traveling home to Rhodesia. The contrast between the Arctic and the conditions that were familiar to him caught his fancy and he was kind enough to write me, enclosing a check for the work.

Now that television has become a commonplace and church services of all kinds can be seen at will, it may be of interest to record that I was the first bishop ever to be seen on the television screen. I would have been less than human not to have gotten a thrill out of this experience. I did not, however, enjoy the preliminary stages of having to be made up and I was distressed beyond measure when, before going into the studio, I saw my face in a mirror. And the lights and the moving cameras on trestles that came now near to me, now farther away, caused me mental confusion. I tried to look as if I had no fear in my heart. The result, however, was apparently satisfactory to the B.B.C. and certainly was to me in the contributions to the work that followed.

The people of the United States have been most liberal in their support of the Church's work in the Arctic. I traveled constantly and extensively there, doing the usual Sunday preaching and speaking at many schools. The bishops and clergy of the Episcopal Church were never-failing in their welcome. Once I spoke at the famous Explorers Club in New York—the only time in my life that I have had a multimillionaire on either side of me! I had also been present at the opening in England of the Scott Institute of Polar Research where I had been honored with an invitation not as a prelate but as an explorer.

Most of my work in the United States was, however, devoted to what are commonly called preaching missions though I preferred to call them renewal weeks because I usually took for my central theme the renewal of one's baptismal vows. I held these renewal weeks literally from Maine to Texas and during this time I often felt that my most useful work was in attempting to guide the troubled people who unburdened themselves to me in private interviews.

It is perhaps the general impression that the bulk of a parson's work is concerned with the vagaries of neurotic women. While there are undoubtedly some for whom the clerical collar has a magnetic attraction I have found throughout the many years of my ministry that it is mostly very normal people who seek either a solution to a problem, relief from a burden, or conviction in a doubt. I am convinced that there is scarcely a person of mature years who does not carry some form of cross and it is the parson's task to serve as the channel through which that individual may reach God.

How many times have I listened in the United States and in Canada, in the Old Country and in the Arctic, to the depressing stories of men's failures (they hesitate about admitting that they are sins), of men's doubts, imaginings, troubles and hatreds, their inability to believe in God. Everywhere men are the same and I always felt that these outpourings indicated on the part of the individual a desire for truth. I rejoice in the knowledge that some found their answer in God.

One of my happiest experiences in the United States was a week spent at the College of Preachers in Washington, D.C., where I deemed it a great privilege to be the first Canadian to direct a conference.

I told these young men that primarily it is the preacher's high and holy task to lead the thoughts of his people to the things that are uplifting. Preaching should seek to bring the Spirit of Christ, His Mind and His thoughts to the hearts of the listeners. Only as Christ is lifted up week by week in the pulpit can we constrain men to be loyal and obedient to the call of God to meet the needs of a stricken world. Christ's appeal is not primarily to the emotions or to the intellect but to the will, and when men find Christ, their passionate desire and purpose is to associate themselves with Him that through Him all men may be saved. The two great things for the preacher to remember are the power of Christ and the value of the human soul.

After compline the men would come to my room to talk over their problems until the small hours of the morning.

might be given the wisdom to meet their need. I remember one young man in particular with whom I wrestled over the problem of denominationalism. It was with the greatest difficulty that I was able to convince him that to be an Anglican or an Episcopalian did not give one a latchkey to a private and special gateway into the Kingdom of Heaven! And to all and sundry I quoted Benjamin Jowett, the Master of Balliol, who said, "You can do a great deal of good in this world if you don't want credit for it."

My main theme in these private talks was to show that Christ's death on Calvary was the inevitable result of His witness. He declared in His teaching and by His living that Love was of God because fundamentally God is Love. Through the sacrifice of Himself Jesus of Nazareth revealed the possibilities and the power of Love. I stressed that truth was eternal and unchanging and stood thus through the ages but that the interpretation of it must change with succeeding years. Some terms that embody a precious thought to one generation will be incomprehensible or repugnant to the next. The eternal truth stands that it was God Who gave out of love for erring and sinful humanity, and it was the Christ of God Who said, "And I, if I be lifted up, shall draw all men unto Me."

☆   19. Decision at Eskimo Point   ☆

THE SILENCE OF the Arctic is broken for a fleeting moment each year by the rattle of the anchor chain as the annual supply ship, having nosed her way through the scattered ice that still clutters up the harbors, drops anchor opposite the trading post and mission. But on our trip to the Northland in 1942, the vast silence was broken by the noises of war. The drone of airplanes and flying boats, the deep bass notes of the steam whistles of strange-looking vessels sounded in the lost fjords and harbors. The Eskimo stared in open wonder. And when these ships had discharged from their cargoes such things as bulldozers our people looked with amazement at the curious contraptions that the white man had brought.

It was a strange trip and yet a thrilling one—also the first on which my wife accompanied me. Heretofore the *Nascopie* had slipped out of the harbor at Montreal and worked her way north, fulfilling her commissions and returning to Montreal within a few days of her schedule. This year the only definite thing we knew at the beginning of the voyage was the hour of departure early in July. From then on the impact of the war was felt. Two and one-half days were spent anchored in the St. Lawrence off Quebec waiting for a convoy to assemble. The previous week three ships had been torpedoed by the Germans off the Gaspé coast. Instead of the usual bright lights the ship was blacked out each night and all were required to have their life belts with them day and night. It was an eerie feeling and while the passengers behaved sensibly, tension constantly manifested itself.

It was not until the convoy was well out to sea that the intercepting planes were seen no more and the escorting corvette came alongside with a message that gave Captain Smellie the freedom he so much desired. Now he could proceed north on his own responsibility.

This year, for the first time in history, the *Nascopie* was unable to make a port of call. Five years before, in 1937, the H.B.C. had established at Fort Ross at the entrance to the famous Northwest Passage. No vessel of the size and draught of the *Nascopie* had ever before navigated these uncharted waters and to do so successfully was indeed a proof of the great skill of Captain Smellie.

Each succeeding year this gallant little icebreaker got in to Fort Ross with the annual supplies but the attempt was always a source of anxiety to all concerned. In 1942 she could not make it. Had we been a week earlier all would have been well. But as it was, the ice had packed in Prince Regent Inlet and young ice was forming on any open water. The captain had to give up the struggle for fear that if he lingered we would be frozen in for the winter. Our hearts went out to Mr. and Mrs. Heslop and their apprentice clerk, for to them it meant bitter disappointment. There was no anxiety about their fuel or food since they had two years' supply, but they were deprived of their only chance of contact with their fellow men, of their luxuries, and of their mail. Eventually their letters were left at Pond Inlet in the hope that Canon Turner might be able to send them over by sledge and dog team in the spring.

The following year, in 1943, the *Nascopie* was again unable to reach Fort Ross. For three days the Heslops saw her smoke and then she disappeared. By this time their food was running low. As rapidly as possible arrangements were made for the rescue of the three white people. A Douglas C-47 of the

United States Army undertook the expedition which involved not only the parachuting of supplies but the first parachute jump to be made within the Arctic Circle. Captain (now Major) J. F. Stanwell-Fletcher dropped to mark out a landing strip. Three days later Mr. and Mrs. Heslop and their clerk were in civilization. Within a fortnight of this experience they had tea with us at our home in Toronto, Mrs. Heslop looking more like a fashion plate from *Vogue* than a heroine of the Arctic wilds! I told her that at the time of the first brave failure of the *Nascopie* in 1942 I was lying in my bunk with intestinal flu, delirious and running a temperature of 104°, thereby causing considerable alarm to my dear wife and to Dr. McKee who was the medical officer on the *Nascopie* at the time.

Mention has been made of Canon J. H. Turner who was stationed for many years at Pond Inlet and Arctic Bay and whose tragic death in 1947 was such a loss to the work. We had sweet fellowship with him for two days in 1942. His genuine devotion to his Master led him along heroic paths of love and duty. He was not afraid to face the rigors of life with the Eskimo and had little interest in wealth, for his needs were few. Indeed his soul was set on a great adventure and he feared neither man nor beast nor cold nor death. He knew right well that his was a lonely pilgrimage in the frozen realms of Arctic Canada.

Pond Inlet and Arctic Bay are so far north that for all but a few brief weeks each "summer" the cold is so intense and the snow and ice so abundant that it is impossible to differentiate between the land and sea. For many years Jack Turner was the only white man in this region. The worldly-wise might call his whole life folly but his heart bounded at the thought of the privilege that was his. He was the bearer of the message of love and salvation to those who sat in the terror and darkness of paganism. He was one of the few people I have known who would have gone to the stake cheerfully for his convictions. His mission might be difficult and in the first years the people unreceptive and uncouth but he never wavered from his belief that ultimate success was assured. All he asked was that he might be counted faithful unto the end.

It is not often that two brothers consecrate themselves to the same cause in the same field but Canon John Turner's brother, the Rev. Arthur Turner, was also for years a most faithful missionary at Pangnirtung. The Eskimo of Baffin Land owe much to these two men.

One of the greatest personal pleasures for me on this trip was to have my wife meet at Lake Harbour Sarah the widow of Pudlo whose death had brought me sorrow several years before. When we went to call on her in her tent which was crowded with her relatives she at once called me "the material of a son" and my wife "the material of a daughter."

As I watched Sarah's face, now old and wrinkled, I thought back to the early days when she had been bonnie and well-shaped, neat in her appearance and fond of pretty colors. In that long ago she had had a temper which she found difficult to control and a steely determination to have her own way. All this righted itself after her conversion and in her husband she found real companionship and sympathy. As I talked to her of Pudlo and of all that he had meant to me tears filled her eyes and mine and we were not ashamed.

How eager he had been to understand the mysteries of the Christian faith! The historical facts he soon knew and believed but he had wanted something more, for his analytical mind demanded it. Yet he knew in time that the love he held for his Lord transcended his understanding and his reason. He had grasped, too, that in the spiritual life God must pulsate into every nook and corner of the soul. Pudlo had a great longing to be a "complete Christian," as he was wont to call it. In the long and weary journeys we made together the superficial differences of race, language, and education faded away, and there emerged a man, a hero, a sincere friend and devoted saint of God.

The second evening at Lake Harbour another old friend came to see me, having traveled some hundred and fifty miles for this purpose. I sat down and spent an hour or so with him in the native room of the mission house and it was not until the interview was nearly over that he opened an old sugar bag that he had been holding in his hand. He shook it and out tumbled a foxskin, white and of beautiful quality. He shook again and out fell another and another until six perfect specimens lay on the floor beside me. "To help bring another teacher, In-nook-tah-kaub," he said.

And at Lake Harbour another extraordinary thing happened. When I had been in residence there first as a missionary a man named Nowdlak had for some months helped me around the mission house until I had sent him to Frobisher Bay as a licensed catechist because of his superior qualities and his living faith. Since that time I had kept in touch with him both directly and indirectly but I had not seen him again. Now he was traveling north with his family and I had the pleasure of renewing my acquaintance with him. To my amazement I discovered what I had never known before: he was the son of the Eskimo Shoudlo who had been brought to Scotland on a whaler some fifty years before and whose story my sister had told me on a Sunday evening. It was this incident of course when I was a little lad of nine that caused me first to say that I would be a missionary to the Eskimo. I cannot describe my feelings as I talked with the son of the man whom God had used to call me to my life's work. Strange indeed are the ways of Providence!

As always we found it awkward to arrange for services during the brief stops of the *Nascopie*. Two experiences in particular remain most vividly in my mind. At River Clyde, because there was no resident missionary, the services had to include marriages and baptisms as well as a sermon and a celebration of the Holy Communion so they were long, lasting well over two hours. It was past midnight when the Eskimo took me out to the ship in a canoe. The night was inky black with a sea running and sleet falling. After a bitterly cold, dangerous and strenuous struggle we reached the *Nascopie* side—and how welcome her bulk and lights looked as she loomed up in the darkness. Once there, however, we discovered that the companion ladder was too high out of the water for us to reach it. From the greater height of the launch we could have caught hold but not from the canoe. Not a soul was on deck and our shouting was to no avail against the noise of wave and wind. The Eskimo were tired, I was exhausted, and I knew that my wife safe in our cabin would be worrying. Then by the Grace of God, the steward Mr. Reid opened the door and stepped out onto the deck. The bobbing of our lantern caught his eye and in a flash he grasped our predicament. He ran for help but even when the ladder was lowered to our level we had great trouble with the canoe because of the angle at which the tide had turned in relation to the waves. The mate threw me a rope which we secured around my waist; on the upcrest of a wave one of the Eskimo helped to give me a hoist, I clutched the bottom step and on my hands and knees climbed the companion ladder which was glazed with ice. I shall never forget the anxious look on the faces of the little group who had come to my succor, nor the great kindness of Mr. Reid the steward in bringing me food and a steaming drink at that inconvenient hour.

At Resolution Island, an inaccessible pile of rocks rising from the sea, the tide is peculiarly savage, having a rise and fall of forty feet. I felt obliged to go ashore because there were two Eskimo families living there, caring for the men at the radio station. Two Eskimo families, six radiomen, that is all there are on the island year in, year out. The captain allowed us only a scant hour. He warned us that were we not at the rendezvous at a certain little cove on the minute he would not dare, with the terrible tide, to have the motorboat wait.

It was a stiff, steep scramble over wet rocks to the Eskimo dwellings. There we found five adults and six children. I had originally intended having a service but the parents were most anxious to have the children baptized so that was all there was time for. There was a great muddle about parentage as is so often the case. The names of three of the children—MacKenzie, Frankie and Pea Soup—told me the story, but what could I say? Who could expect these simple, natural Eskimo to resist the pressure put upon them or the lure of the bribes offered to them for "services rendered." My heart both burned and ached. The little maid at the radio house said that her Christian name was Elizabeth. When my wife told her that she, too, bore that name, this dark-skinned girl with a heart craving for affection pressed her face to that of my wife and from that moment until we stepped aboard the motorboat never let go of my wife's hand. For many years after this the Eskimo Elizabeth received an annual letter and a little Christmas present to gladden her drab life.

These Eskimo families on Resolution Island each possessed a radio and every day listened to a very worth-while broadcast in Eskimo from Greenland. By now this is a commonplace, but in 1942 it was new, startling, and progressive.

During my many journeys on the *Nascopie* I had made numerous friends. One of the most interesting people was Dr. I. M. Rabinowitch, familiarly known as Dr. "Rab." He was an international authority on metabolism and highly esteemed in Montreal for his work there. I soon discovered in him a friend as well as a great and lovable man. His whimsical mind and unexpected reactions were always stimulating.

He told me an interesting thing about the Eskimo. In answer to his questions I described how, when I first went to Baffin Land, the angakok who was also the doctor always bled his patients whatever the illness might be, just as the old leech doctors did in England centuries ago. To my surprise Dr. "Rab" claimed that they were perfectly right in doing so because, as the result of the experiments which he had carried out during the voyage, he had discovered that the Eskimo had generally an oversupply of blood due to the food they lived on, i.e., seal, walrus, white whale, and narwhal. He explained that too much blood in the body is just as bad as too little blood. I then for the first time understood why the Eskimo, both men and women but particularly men, often had terrible nosebleeds.

Of course no account of the *Nascopie* would be complete without a reference to Major McKeand. He traveled north annually as Secretary of the Northwest Territories and also as head of the government party which included the afore-mentioned "bug-hunters," the doctors, post office officials, and other representatives of the various governmental departments at Ottawa. The major's task was not a sinecure, but his abounding energy, his bluff kindly manner, and his keen sense of humor combined to make him well fitted for the task.

Another valued member of the *Nascopie's* annual company was Mr. J. W. Anderson, a quiet and canny Scot with a dry and keen wit, who was Fur Trade Commissioner of the Hudson's Bay Company. Through the years he dispatched his heavy responsibilities for the company with acumen and kindness. He has always been an honored friend.

And how shall I describe the captain, a redoubtable little man and as an Arctic navigator second to none. Time and time again when we had been in peril I have thanked God that Captain Thomas F. Smellie was in command. He had the reputation of being autocratic. But on the other hand his was the ultimate responsibility. He had to choose his path across the ice fields, to feel his way along uncharted coast, to sense the presence of an iceberg in the night.

Let me also put on record here the fact that I have always found the Hudson's Bay Company most cooperative in every connection. Occasionally an individual would fail to live up to the standard set by the company but that was the exception, not the rule. I have always looked upon my H.B.C. friends as emulative colleagues rather than as opponents, for I felt that we were both contributing to the welfare of the Eskimo. The H.B.C. is known in the North for its keen, hard, shrewd efficiency when it is a matter of trade, and for some of the personnel their soul's mistress was fur. But nearly always apart from trade the post managers and others are most helpful and generous. And year in, year out what appealed to me most in the Hudson's Bay Company men was their love for the land that give them little personally and their loyalty to the great company in whose service they displayed the noble austerities of courage and strength.

I have always taken a keen interest in the young men who come north for service in the trading companies, the Royal Canadian Mounted Police, and the other organizations. The majority were fine, healthy striplings anxious to do well. By the end of their term these youngsters had become *men;* steady and undeviating, or shoddy and inferior according to their inherent character. In the Arctic a man's traits become more pronounced than in the south and stand out more sharply for good or ill. In almost every case their time in the Arctic turned them into men of intense individuality.

One thing that has impressed me in connection with all these young men in the Arctic was the truth enunciated by Joubert that chastity is the mother of virtue. Time and time again the lust of the flesh called and, owing to the weakness inherent in human flesh, aggravated by the loneliness and isolation, one of these fine lads "got into trouble" with an Eskimo woman. In many cases he then became craven and sly. This situation has become much aggravated since the military and naval forces have entered the Arctic and has caused great anxiety to the Church. The simple native women need to be safeguarded; the young men need to be protected from themselves; and the chaotic complexity the half-breed must face is a source of pity and concern.

That there should be intercourse between white men and the Eskimo women is disturbing enough when the men are from among the rougher type, but when those who should be an example of the white man's standards fall a prey to their lowest passions it is humiliating.

There was an eminent traveler and explorer whose name is world-known who begat children wherever he went across the Arctic and took no responsibility for them although obviously they were his. At one place in the Western Arctic a man bears feature by feature the likeness of his progenitor and is called by his father's name. For many summers this man's poor mother piteously inquired of every newcomer if they had seen her husband; she said she knew he would come back for he had promised that he would.

Another, a writer whose works attract considerable attention, is considered by the Eskimo so lascivious that his name is literally spat from their mouths with revulsion and contempt. Surely the sins of men like these must sometimes lie heavy on their souls. One can regret but understand the moral lapse of a lad of nineteen but not the flagrant immorality of experienced men who repudiate in deed and word the Christian standards and who use the Eskimo women merely as a convenience for their desires. Is it any wonder that the blood of the missionary boils?

For the white dwellers in the Arctic it is in the nadir of winter darkness that the feeling of depression is most keenly felt and that men are apt to forget themselves. When a few men are cooped up in a small place with cramped quarters and no opportunity for getting away from each other the human frailties come to the surface. It is difficult then to keep a true sense of values. Little mannerisms irritate and infuriate in the most startling fashion and it requires more than a sense of humor to keep tempers from becoming envenomed. We all know that human personalities differ radically. In civilization congenital differences count for little but where men are forced into close personal contact each day in a lonely, isolated post those differences become the source of friction. Countless times as I recalled my own early experiences I had to admit, if I were to be honest with myself, that Bilby's dark moods and morbid fancies had driven me almost to the point of desperation. Nor was the irritation all one-sided, for later Bilby told me that my unconscious whistling of lilting Scottish airs induced similar thoughts in his mind.

Some men in the Arctic become incapacitated by sheer physical terror of the silence that surrounds them. Others become mentally unhinged and dangerous like David the

Eskimo or the mad trapper Johnson. Men do not generally suffer from the cold or exposure or lack of food but from boredom, and unless they take themselves in hand and cultivate steady habits of reading or have a hobby, they soon develop a nagging sense of frustration. This, in turn, causes mental, moral, and physical deterioration, and then tragedy may result.

But not all the effects of isolation are deleterious. It makes any intelligent man think and I have found time and time again that men who come north without any serious thoughts or religion or philosophy often become earnest seekers after truth. They study solid books on economics, sociology, and the like (I myself had a library of over 200 volumes at Lake Harbour). Many of the Scots have a deep-rooted love of metaphysics and enjoy discussing the problems together. They argue the relation between the rights of the individual and the power of the state to control the individual—or the value of purpose in human life. While few in the Arctic admit to being religious, many indicate that in working out their philosophy of life religon has its part. They ask very fundamental questions such as "Is there a God? If so what God? Has life any real meaning? Why evil? What happens at Death and after?" Many a time in private conversations as well as in sermons I asked them to declare how they took thought for their souls, for the soul is dyed the color of one's thoughts.

When it became clear that fundamentally the Christian does not simply accept certain dogmas and follow certain outward observances but seeks to know and to understand the Eternal Will they seemed to be greatly helped. Some accepted and demonstrated the fact that a man gains peace and fortitude only by yielding his will to the Eternal Will whom we call God. It is not without significance that the first two persons confirmed in All Saints Cathedral, Aklavik, were a Hudson's Bay factor and a corporal of the Royal Canadian Mounted Police. In the years that have passed, the latter officer has made a name for himself in the outside world and has received distinguished honors for the work he has done with that romantic police force. More recently an inspector of the R.C.M.P. was confirmed in All Saints Cathedral and at his own request was the last of the group, coming after all the native people for the laying on of hands.

As I have observed the many members of the R.C.M.P. whom it has been my privilege to know I have been inspired by their fine ideals, their courage, and their dogged attention to duty. Some of my ideas of the meaning of service have been changed because of their conformity and loyalty to the rules and regulations under which they were pledged. I could only pray that my will might be similarly obedient to the will of God.

Undoubtedly the greatest difficulty that has confronted men in the Arctic has been the absence of normal family life. We all of us crave domestic affection and the atmosphere of a happy home. It has been claimed that it is bad for a man to live always with women. I believe this to be axiomatic. But in the Arctic it has been demonstrated that it is equally bad for a man to live alone without the help and society of women. Indeed this has been one of the major problems for a century. Fortunately today even in the most remote settlements the amenities of civilization are being provided so that women are able to live there and to bring up their children in conditions that are not entirely primitive.

Most of the women I have met in the Arctic have had what the Scots call "innerliness" or a homely tenderness which means so much in that great, lone land. It lends tranquillity not only to their own homes and their own menfolk but to the single men and the casual weary traveler who may be privileged to enjoy their hospitality. To the Arctic women I pay tribute.

Despite all I have said of the temptations of loneliness, life in the Arctic teaches a man priceless things. One gets very close to other people and while very conscious of their weaknesses and idiosyncrasies, learns to appreciate their strong points and nobility and something of one's own faults as well. Above all one realizes very thoroughly that "no man liveth or dieth unto himself" and that each is dependent on the other. It is not possible to live happily without the fellowship of others and as one Scot put it, "Life is a heap sweeter if ye dae."

I should perhaps now take the opportunity to pay tribute for their steadfast devotion to all our missionaries whom I have not mentioned by name. They are remembered daily in my prayers and, had space permitted, their service in Christ's cause would have been recorded in these pages.

But all this digression has taken me a long way from traveling on the *Nascopie* and the vicissitudes of war. In 1942 when her own business was completed the little ship was sent to pick up a load of cryolite in Greenland. Through a succession of unfortunate incidents we were delayed in Greenland for six weeks and during this time were able to see something of the extraordinary activity of the United States forces. While there were inevitably some difficulties connected with their presence in large numbers they were, on the whole, welcomed and cordially received by the Danes. The majority of these boys were fine young men bearing their isolation with the greatest cheerfulness.

In point of fact this was not my first visit to Greenland but my third. Among other experiences I had stopped at Thule, which is the most northerly settlement in the world. Since then the whole settlement has been moved seventy miles to the north to make way for the huge American air base.

I had also had the privilege of preaching in the church at Godhaab. On this occasion Provost Bugge hoisted my personal flag to the top of the flagpole outside his house while the Danish flag flew from the pole near the church. I was given to understand that never before had a foreign bishop visited the Danish Church, nor had any bishop ever spoken to the people in their native tongue.

On all three visits to Greenland I was immensely impressed with the work done by the Danish Government among the Greenland Eskimo. While their problems were and are somewhat different from ours, the Danes have tackled them in an efficient, aggressive, and far-seeing fashion. The well-being of the native peoples now and in the future is considered as a whole and treated as a matter of prime importance. Moreover, to govern this colony to the best advantage of all, Denmark has considered it worth while to send out not inferior men as some governments do but officials of the highest caliber. There is nothing second-rate about the Danish personnel in Greenland.

Once we left Greenland, the voyage to Labrador took five days. There we slipped down a series of inland channels known as "the tickles" which saved us from passing through a submarine-infested area. As we neared the Straits of Belle Isle we were ordered to sleep in our clothes, which we did for three nights, holding the life belts we carried day and night. It was common knowledge that more than a dozen ships had gone down here since our departure in July. When we reached Port Alfred we had been on the *Nascopie* five months less two days. The events and emotions of this trip were not easily forgotten, and for a long time they cast a shadow on our life for others who had suffered more in these dark days.

For the first time now the thought of retirement began to simmer in my mind. The Arctic is a young man's country and the rigors that we had recently endured had made me aware that I was no longer young. As the ensuing pages will demonstrate, the following summers added to the physical strain. I realized that I must look to the future both for the work and for myself.

Fort George has always been a difficult place to reach and the trip which I now made there, accompanied by my wife, was no exception. It began by our receiving a wire from the H.B.C. which woke us from our sleep at two A.M. The message stated that the sailing date of the schooner from Moose Factory would be forty-eight hours earlier than previously scheduled. This change threw our plans into a turmoil and among other things necessitated our leaving Toronto on Dominion Day when the holiday travel is at its peak. There was no hope of obtaining proper accommodation and when we boarded the train to Cochrane amid the seething crowds at the Union Station all we had was one upper berth for the two of us as well as for Canon L. A. Dixon who was traveling with us! Canon Dixon as general secretary of our missionary society was to take part in the opening ceremonies of our new residential school. We were also accompanied by Dr. Arkell, a Toronto dentist, who was to work among the Indians that summer.

The next morning during the stop at Cochrane, Dr. Arkell very prudently thought to check on his luggage which with ours and Canon Dixon's had been sent in advance from Toronto the previous day. To his consternation he discovered that two cases were missing. He came running up the platform to tell us and to ask if ours were on the train. We all hurried back to the baggage car to investigate. We found ourselves all in the same plight! The dentist was without his instruments; the canon had his robes but no clothes; I had clothes but no robes while my wife had only the immediate necessities.

We had only minutes in which to work as our train was now due to leave. In fact we could not consult the stationmaster because he had already gone home. Some of the officials were most helpful, however, and suggested that if our luggage could be traced and found the railway might get it to us by speeder before the schooner sailed. Wires were dispatched in all directions and we continued our journey in unhappy suspense. At Moose Factory, our destination, a reply awaited us stating that our effects had been discovered at North Bay where in the confusion of Dominion Day travel they had been put off by mistake. We were advised that they were being sent on by speeder (a distance of 186 miles) and we were also told when to expect them. The time was twelve hours later than the *Fort Charles* appointed moment.

None of us could go north without our gear. Was the whole summer's schedule to be thwarted, the work neglected and the people disappointed? Skipper Neilson did his best and offered to wait until the turn of the next tide. His schedule was so heavy that he could not delay beyond that. It does not require imagination to understand the anxiety that filled the passing hours, nor the shout of relief that went up when the speeder "made it" with literally one hour to spare.

But more was in store for us that summer! The population of Fort George is mostly Cree Indian with a handful of Eskimo and my episcopal visitation had a twofold purpose—the opening of the new residential school and the confirmation of 93 Indians who had been prepared by the missionary-in-charge. Fort George is actually the oldest of our missions on Hudson Bay, having been established in 1852.

The dedication of the school was set for three o'clock the next day but as that was also a Sunday which necessitated many services I did not have an opportunity to inspect in advance the preparations made by the missionary-in-charge. A double classroom had been got ready for the occasion but when at the last minute I saw the numbers that had gathered to witness the event I hastily decided to hold the dedication outside. The opening of the school was a source of infinite satisfaction to the native people. They had earnestly longed that their children should have an education that had not been possible for them.

A special service had been translated into the Cree language so that all the people should understand. After the dedication I, as bishop, gave a short address and then called upon Canon Dixon to speak. He, the interpreter, and I were all standing on a small platform which had not been completed and which towards the rear had no flooring. At that part there were only the cross planks. I was most anxious that Canon Dixon should be seen and heard so, in my absorption forgetting the dangerous state of the platform, I stepped back and urged the canon and the interpreter to the fore.

The last thing that I heard was a cry of distress from my poor wife in the front row of the audience as she saw me fall. My robes to a certain extent saved me but the shock was enough to cause me to lose consciousness. As the men lifted me out and carried me over to my bed in the mission house,

I regained consciousness and was in great pain. With great presence of mind Canon Dixon continued his address and the service was closed as planned.

There was no doctor at Fort George but fortunately we had a nursing station in charge of Nurse Campbell, without whose knowledge and skill I should have fared badly indeed. She diagnosed the damage as cracked ribs and certain unpleasant internal injuries and reported by wire to Dr. Orford two hundred miles away. By return wire he gave instructions although, under the circumstances, there was little that could be done. Nevertheless I shall always be grateful for the wise care which I received. Nurse Campbell's time was almost fully taken up with attending a poor Indian who was dying so that she could not take care of me herself but she came over morning and evening to give a little relief to my wife who otherwise did twenty-four hour duty for a fortnight while I lay helpless.

Aside from the pain and a high fever our difficulties were increased by an acute shortage of food in the entire settlement. Owing to an oversight the food supplies had not been sent in to Fort George on the first trip of the schooner. Tinned sausage is not very alluring when one has a temperature of 103°. The skipper of *Fort Charles* kindly gave my wife a dozen eggs and a dozen oranges when he left, this being all he could spare, and the H.B.C. post manager, James Soper, most generously gave me his last two tins of chicken and all that he had left of clear soup.

In making our plans for this trip we had chartered a plane of the Austin Airways Ltd. to take us out to the Belcher Islands to visit the people there. When the plane arrived on the appointed day I was still confined to my bed. Fortunately there was other work in the vicinity that the pilot could do so he came and went, each time hoping to take us "out." On his third appearance he came to my wife with a report that the weather was changing and he feared that if we did not leave the next day we might be held up for another two or three weeks.

With my condition and the food shortage this was indeed a serious matter. On the other hand I felt that I was not free to go until I had confirmed the ninety-three Indians who had stayed in at the settlement and were expectantly waiting. With reluctance the pilot finally agreed to chance the weather's holding for thirty-six hours in order that I might fulfill my obligation. The next morning I was dressed and carried in a chair by the two Indian churchwardens from the mission house to the church. To shorten the ordeal of sitting upright I confirmed only the men and boys at that service. In the afternoon I was carried over again and confirmed the women and girls. Each time I was accompanied by Nurse Campbell, who tried to tell me that she was there *only* to play the little organ. My wife had to utilize the brief time that I was out of our room to pack our belongings because as soon as I returned Nurse Campbell sent me quickly to sleep.

At seven o'clock on Friday morning July 28, the men carried me from the mission house to the plane and twenty minutes later we took off. I pressed my dear wife's hand as we quietly gave thanks for God's many mercies and thought that within a matter of hours we would be at the Toronto Island airport and home. How little we knew! A strong south wind was blowing so we made slow progress but the pilot was in great hopes that once we reached the Height of Land the weather would improve. Instead it worsened and we had an extremely rough passage for we ran into blinding thunderstorms and torrential rain. Twice we saw below us the top of a tree burst into flames as the lightning struck. At one point we came down on an unknown lake to ride it out. It was a queer sensation to be bobbing about on the water, shut into the plane, to see the lightning flashing close by and to hear the pelting of the rain. This storm passed and we rose again but soon the visibility became so poor that we had to make another forced landing at Porcupine.

Here we were surprised to find several of the Austin Airways planes berthed on the lake and, fortunately for us, to discover that Mr. Austin himself was there. When this second storm abated he had us transferred to another plane, the men carrying me as gently as they could. One and one-half hours later we arrived at Sudbury, having been ten hours on the journey and still far from our destination. By now my state of exhaustion was alarming so despite the pilot's assurance that a couple of hours more would see us home, we sought accommodation for the night. When we awoke the next morning it was teeming rain. At the time this seemed a great disappointment but in reality it was a blessing because it gave us both twenty-four hours of much-needed rest. On the following day we came down at the Toronto Island airport, and it looked like the threshold of Paradise itself!

As I was convalescing I had much time in which to think and I came to know in my heart that the time to shift part of my burden was soon at hand. The decision to retire is difficult for any man. The knotty point of securing a successor in whom one has confidence is even more difficult. From now on that problem was ever in my mind, not so much as an immediate necessity as a matter requiring constant and prayerful consideration. I knew, of course, that the final decision was not mine because a bishop is elected, not appointed, but I hoped that my wishes in this important matter would be respected.

My mind cleared quite reassuringly along these lines when we went to Eskimo Point. Also the physical demands of that trip again demonstrated that my health and vigor were no longer equal to the strain of Arctic travel.

It is obvious that not every missionary, not even the most dedicated, has the qualities necessary for the work of a bishop. That office requires abilities both pastoral and administrative and the problems peculiar to the Arctic require much else. But at Eskimo Point I felt happy as I watched the energetic young missionary-in-charge with his direct blue eyes, his winning smile, and his gift of sympathetic understanding. I felt that he had the stamp of a man of God. It was clear that his compelling love for the native people was second only to his devotion to his Lord and Master. His untried but potential ability seemed to me capable of great development. My thoughts moved forward. Marsh was unacquainted with the Western Arctic; he had had no executive experience; I observed certain weaknesses but who among us is without weaknesses? I felt that given the opportunity all these things could be set right.

It was at this time that I marked in my mind Donald B. Marsh as my successor in office should God so will it.

INTERLUDE IV

*In order to give Mr. Marsh some experience in the Western
Arctic where conditions and problems were vastly different
from those he knew—particularly the complex multiracial
situation at Aklavik—I sent him down the Mackenzie and
appointed him Archdeacon of Aklavik. The slow wheels of
retirement were now set in motion.*

*For any of the clergy, bishops included, retirement almost
always means a change of residence, and so it was for us. For
some time we had been giving this matter superficial thought
but now we began to look around in earnest. We felt that for
our own sakes and that of our successors in office it would be
wise to leave Toronto. This would be a wrench for me as that
city had been home for nearly forty years, but the time had
come.*

*Our choice fell on Goderich, a charming county town on
the shores of Lake Huron. The lake was a vivid blue the
afternoon that we decided to buy the land. Gulls were wheel-
ing and drifting against the sky, the willows and the acacias
gently stirred, and the clear air off the water was invigorating.
Here we built high on the cliffs with the beauty of this inland
sea ever before our eyes. In this matter we were better guided
than we knew for while the house was yet in the process of
construction I was stricken with a severe coronary thrombosis.*

The blow fell on December 21, 1946, St. Thomas' Day and the anniversary of my consecration as a bishop in the church of God.

In the weeks and months that followed it became evident that I would not regain my health and that a life of semi-invalidism was the best that I could hope for. In this period of transition with retirement now quite definitely at hand I brought the Archdeacon of Aklavik out from the Western Arctic and established him in the diocesan office in Toronto. There his grasp of the problems inherent in the work and his acumen were a source of confidence and comfort to me. I decided now that as soon as I felt that his election was assured (unfortunately there were certain factions working to oppose it) I would send in my resignation. The letter was written and waiting.

To face resignation with equanimity; to admit that one can no longer carry on; to face the hard fact that younger minds and hands are more capable than one's own—this I take to be the final test of character. As I slowly won my inner battles it seemed to me that there were two factors to be considered in connection with all illness. In the first place it is not true that illness is "sent" by God. It occurs in the natural physical course of life for physical reasons. But equally it is a great mistake to assume that suffering is merely a necessary evil to be stoically endured. A careful study of the Saviour's life makes clear that if one's suffering is completely yielded to the will of the Eternal, good can follow. For one thing, pain dethrones vanity, selfishness, and pride. It also reveals the unfailing mercy of God and the wonderful sympathy of friends.

On the first of May 1947 I was able to be moved from Toronto to Goderich and into our new home. Despite the fact that for six years my activities have been drastically curtailed, I have enjoyed living. Now that I have retired I have discovered with satisfaction that there is no desire for distraction nor any sense of loneliness or frustration. Instead there is an inward sense of fulfillment. The task committed to me in 1927 has been entrusted to the man of my choice and I am glad that the responsibility is no longer mine. When I think of the life that I have lived, of the nervous exploitation and the subsequent exhaustion, I feel how fortunate I am to have such measure of health as is mine. I am happy in the quiet life that I can live. The tranquillity is healing.

At first I was reluctant to begin this book because I felt that every autobiography indicates a certain egotism on the part of the writer. But Sir Patrick Ashley-Cooper, former governor of the Hudson's Bay Company, convinced me that since my life work was, as he put it, "a page in the history of Canada," some account of it would inevitably be written. For that reason, he claimed, it was better that I myself write the true record.

Most of the book has been written sitting propped up with pillows. Each morning as I have felt able to work my wife has moved my bed up to the window where I can look out as I write. In summer the warm fragrance from the cedar hedge and the herbaceous border drifts in to give me pleasure. In winter the beauty of the snow has its own enchantment.

It is probably true that no one is a good critic of one's own career but I have tried to set out simply and with accuracy events and personalities as I saw them. I have described a small but solid core of facts and by relating actual daily happenings I have tried to preserve something of the color and the spirit of the early days. I have hoped that these pages will enable those who read them to understand the problems and pleasure, the struggles and the victories of life that belong to a generation ago.

20. Reflections

I HAVE REACHED the time of life when one is content to think
back across the years and to remember the joys and sorrows
of the past.

In youth the tendency is to pretend that there are no mists
of error or of self-deception but as the years roll on one has
no hesitation about admitting that there were strenuous internal battles before vital problems were faced and final decisions reached. Sometimes, alas, mistakes were made and these
cannot be erased even while one has learned much of value
from them. They are proofs of the frailty of human nature
and man's need for the guidance of the Spirit of God.

I know all too well that across the pages of my life there
have been failures and blots due to ignorance and disobedience. The wonderful thing is that in spite of the blots the
pages appear to have been not wholly in vain and for this
there is but one reason—the goodness and mercy of Him Who
in tenderest compassion forgives our sins and transgressions.

During the past forty years many have asked me how I
could love the Eskimo with all their dirty and degraded ways,
their primitive life and pagan customs. The answer is quite
simple. It is certainly not because I learned to "like" all
aspects of life in an Eskimo snow village in winter or tent
encampment in the summer. Much about life under such
conditions is repulsive to any civilized man. It is the fashion

now to say otherwise; to speak of the attractive and alluring simplicity of native life; of the harm done to the unspoiled native by the missionary and even by the trader. But those who make such statements are men who for their own reasons have adventured in the frozen north for brief months or for perhaps a year. Not just I with forty years' experience but any who have spent their working lifetime in the Arctic, men like Canon Turner, Canon Webster, and the others, are in a better position to know what it costs in self-abnegation to have endured over long periods the filth, the fear, and the famine that once ruled the Eskimo.

Nor are the transient strangers aware of the evolution of these people from their past to their present state. When I first knew them in the early decades of this century they were indeed children of nature—crude and cruel and cunning as well as simple and lovable. They were not a romantic people. To term them such is to do them the injustice of sentimentalizing their fine qualities.

I loved them because I soon discovered that they were real people, men and women and children just like the rest of mankind. They had warm, generous hearts and intelligent minds capable of responding to the "call Divine." As I lived with them away from the mission house either as a paying guest with a family in an igloo or in my own tent pitched among theirs I came to understand and to appreciate their fine characteristics—their courage, generosity and patience; their outstanding love for their children; and their utopian socialism as far as the sharing of food is concerned.

Above all I was conscious of the fact that they were living in the darkness of primitive pagan fear and therefore added to all else I loved them because of their need. I loved them because I had been called of God and commissioned by the Church to meet that need. When it gradually became clear that within each soul there was a deep hunger for the Light of Life and that by the teaching of the Gospel the longings of their hearts could be met and the black night of ignorance and superstition banished, it was the most natural thing in the world that I should love them. I soon recognized that the things which I so much disliked were largely due to the conditions under which they were forced to live in that black wilderness of rock and ice and snow.

Time and time again they went out of their way to help me, an ignorant foreigner, and so I changed from holding the typical superiority attitude of the white man towards the native and I came to see him truly as an equal. Whatever superior knowledge I possessed about some things, the Eskimo had superior knowledge about other things. I lacked many of their fine attributes and I became grateful for the privilege of knowing them, for all that I was learning from them and for all that they were doing for me. As Vinet puts it, "The property of gratitude and love is to identify the soul which feels them with the object which excited their feelings."

At first I was surprised and interested to find that the Eskimo who became my greatest friends were not necessarily those for whom I had done most but were those who had on some special occasion helped me in my time of need. It was as if with my having accepted *their* help they felt drawn towards me and wanted to maintain a special and personal association with me quite apart from that which existed between us as missionary and people. Of course when one stops to think one realizes that this principle is inherent in any friendship since it breaks down the barriers and places all on a common ground of feeling and action, mutual understanding, and reciprocity of service. These are bonds that attach us one to the other, establishing a true fellowship, and this fellowship has remained unbroken all these many years between my spiritual children and myself.

I have often felt that the Eskimo taught me much that I needed to learn, even regarding the inner meaning of some of the great truths which I had been sent to teach them. I received not a little inspiration from them. And some of my ideas had to be radically changed because of what I learned from trying to help them to understand what I thought I knew so well.

Perforce I lost the foolish idea that I had nothing to learn from them. It is fatally easy for the visitor from the south to assume that because of the material advance made by the white man he is therefore superior in every way to the Eskimo. This assumption hinders him from a proper appreciation of some of the fundamental qualities of their personality. In that wild land of ice and snow conditions are such that they demand from those who dwell there an alertness, a patience, a communal at-one-ness, unknown in civilization. The white man may be able to do all that the native does and with additional aids do it better, but if called upon to live the life the Eskimo is forced to live he would require experiences and some virtues not commonly found in newly arrived strangers nor, I may add, in those who write books reeking with inaccuracies after short visits with the Eskimo.

The fundamental purpose of the missionary is to link the spiritual and material man with God, and the missionary's task is twofold: first to be a witness to the Gospel of Jesus Christ and second to teach the people and through instruction to enlighten their minds so that their wills may be directed along the right way. The missionary is not an intermediary standing between the soul and his Maker but the messenger telling the Good News whereby the soul of man meets God through the mediation of the Saviour Christ. As John Morley puts it, "The spiritual light of Christianity has burned for centuries with pure flame kindled by the Sublime Mystic in the Galilean hills." It is to pass on this contagion that the missionary comes.

It was an inspiring study to watch the effect of the telling of the Gospel story on the minds of the Eskimo. At first it was simply a case of open wonder but step by step through the months and years the progressive realization of the consciousness of God in their minds became evident and was proved not only by their words but by their deeds and by their whole mental and spiritual outlook. It was as if amid these simple, humble people one of the approaches to Heaven was revealed.

It often appeared to me that some of these people had an

intuition for truth quite outside their knowledge. Perhaps it was due to a penetrative simplicity gained by the grim realities of the life they had to live. I saw the tussle going on between the forces that make for life and those that make for death and I saw the wistful search and desperate desire for things not seen and an instinctive belief that this life did not end with death.

It was no uncommon thing for them to be deeply moved during a service. At first I was puzzled because, while I prepared my addresses with care, I had no oratorical gifts likely to cause emotion. Gradually I realized that it was not my efforts that caused the disturbance but the marvelous truths of the Faith. To me the message was the "old, old story of Jesus and His love" but to the Eskimo it was new and it awakened within them fresh hope for it revealed to them the glory of God and brought the answer to their heart longings.

It surprised me to discover that the more intelligent apparently found little difficulty in understanding that in the Bible we have a record of the gradual manifestation of God to the children of men. To them some of the Old Testament stories that frequently disturb pious souls in civilization caused no perplexity whatsoever.

"Of course," they would say, "these men were even as we are and because they were ignorant God had to speak to them in that way." The thing that I kept stressing was that we had not come to give them *our* religion but *the religion of all men:* that God was their Father just as much as our Father; that Jesus did not speak English and live only in the south.

During my second term among them I had gained their affection and a working knowledge of the language. It was a constant source of interest and inspiration to watch the new truths filter into their minds. With a heart full of sympathy I noted how they triumphed over their fears and prejudices. Gradually the light dawned and in childlike faith they grasped the greatest of all truths that, unlike the capricious and malevolent spirits worshiped by their fathers, the great Spirit whom we call God is Love.

It was a constant marvel to me to see how the Spirit of God was at work in their minds and hearts. Coming out of the cavern of doubt they seemed at first to find it difficult to understand that religion is not some mysterious method, but a life to be lived in fellowship with the Eternal. It was not easy to win them from their old beliefs but once converted the majority manifested a capacity for self-discipline that was most impressive. And when they discarded the melancholy fear of future reincarnation as birds and beasts and fishes of the sea they discovered a holy peace. As children of God they radiated love so that their lives overflowed with happiness. What I saw taking place was much more than a revolt against paganism. It was the victory of the Spirit of God over flesh; of love over fear; of hope over the negation of fatalism; of peace over passion; of freedom over perpetual bondage.

The temperament of the Eskimo is not in the least contemplative. Essentially and quite naturally they are people of action and therefore belief in the magical clairvoyance of the conjurer had to be replaced by wholesome effort. When they became aware that each had a task to perform day by day in imitating the Christ and in sharing with others the new-found joy and peace they said, "Now we are happy inside."

It was the desire of my heart to interpret the great truths of the Gospel with pellucid clarity to these people and at times the continual repetition and explanation that seemed necessary caused me to question whether we were making any real progress. Suddenly one day it became clear to me that they *were* learning and *did* understand not only the vital issues but the details of the teaching. Like St. Augustine I could say, "They, as it were, in us speak what they hear and we, after a certain fashion, in them learn what we teach." As I listened to the murmur of their praying voices I was filled with a sense of awe. Here in this land of darkness and austerity was the warm, loving message of the Saviour of men. It had penetrated to the hidden recesses and inner sanctuary of life, bringing to them new hope and confidence for time and for Eternity. Life is full of mystery at all times but none so great or so inspiring as the power of the Gospel in the hearts of men. Faith which begins as an experiment ends as an experience.

Many of the angakoks and their followers were for obvious reasons unwilling to admit the cogency of our argument that the Gospel was the fulfillment of man's highest hopes. As I watched and studied these people I realized that some of them were brave and faithful to the inner light that they had. God does not leave any of His children without some fragment of the truth and although the light seemed dim to us the fact that they followed it at all was a guarantee of good things to come. In the years that followed I had every reason to believe that this was true. I also learned to comprehend the merits of some of the customs and taboos even though they were in conflict with my own viewpoint.

Unfortunately for us, the white men in the country at that time almost entirely favored keeping the natives in the pagan state. This was made abundantly clear by incidents such as that connected with the first converts at Blacklead Island related in Chapter 14. I feel required to record this so that the ruthlessness of their opposition be not minimized; that the patience and perseverance of the early missionaries be appreciated; and that the power of the Gospel of Jesus Christ to achieve results in the face of all the forces of ignorance and superstition and lust be acknowledged.

The problem of understanding the mode of Eskimo thought presented me with grave difficulties. That they accepted their mystical stories as true and that these had far-reaching implications influencing their life and conduct could not be doubted. But behind their myths there appeared to be a sincere attempt to interpret the problems of existence.

On the other hand close personal contact with them made it clear to me that in spite of their primitive simplicity their powers of reasoning were acute. It was both disturbing and puzzling. What I desired for them was that they should have freedom from their haunting fears of unseen, malevolent spirits and peace of mind and heart in the redeeming love of the Saviour. In a word, I longed to show them that the key to the enigma of life for them as for the rest of humanity was to see and to follow the polestar of Bethlehem. That this would be difficult I was well aware because, as Amiel said, "Life is a tissue of habits." Moreover the human heart improves but slowly. The invisible activities of the Spirit of God bring about startling changes but the greatest results are generally tardy in coming.

In dealing with human beings whether they be people of education and culture in civilization or children of nature in the Arctic we should recognize that there are two component and interdependent parts—the flesh and the spirit. It is because of this that we find both beauty and coarseness. It is the spirit that can control and quell the turbulent desires of youth and passion and ease the aching and fearful heart of old age.

I urged them to try to forget the poisonous shadows of the past. One night Simone and Keemalo his wife came in to visit me bringing a gift of seal liver. Simone was in a happy, talkative mood. He chatted away about some of his early experiences. I encouraged him and very soon he was telling me all sorts of queer stories that he had learned from his father. I listened with closest attention, not daring to speak lest I should interrupt his reverie.

Keemalo sat motionless too but suddenly she broke in and looking at me said, "Yes? That is so for I also remember those things. But why do you ask? You have told us to put away the old thoughts and now you ask Simone to speak of them."

It was with much difficulty and little success that I explained to her why it was important that I should understand their background. Just because it was steeped in ancient tradition and folklore it had to be given the greatest possible consideration and approached with humility as well as a questioning mind if I were to catch the glimmer of truth behind that which appeared to be of little value. It was soon made clear that their yearnings were identical with ours. To set them free from fear and despair and to lead them into spiritual freedom was the task committed to me. Only after many conversations with Keemalo in the succeeding days was I able to clear her mind as to the sincerity of my purpose, and then she as well as her husband gave me much valuable and detailed information.

Is the work worth while? Such a question does not enter into the missionary's consideration. He must go where God calls; and thank God there have always been men and women ready to obey the Divine command "Go tell," men and women desiring nothing beyond the knowledge that they were doing the will of the Most High.

Let me tell one story that carries conviction in its touching sincerity. Since archdeacon days part of my duty, as has already been stated, has been to see that the workers had adequate supplies. This naturally involved handling many invoices from the Far North and one year I was much surprised to receive a credit slip of $150 from the H.B.C. post manager at Baker Lake. This incident occurred just six years after we had established at Baker Lake and the reader will remember that I had had some misgivings as I looked at the sullen, wild, dirty pagans among whom we proposed to work. It seemed to me that nothing but a miracle could change these people. Yet they had been changed.

With great reluctance I had sent word that year to the missionary-in-charge asking him to minimize expenses as much as possible because I was having difficulty in raising funds. This request he passed on to the Eskimo, asking their co-operation. "In quietness and confidence shall be your strength." These people so recently pagan went down on their knees and prayed God to bless their hunting and then they sallied forth. They had good success and upon their return told the H.B.C. post manager that certain skins were for the work of the "teacher" in their midst. Hence the credit slip.

If after only six years of missionary endeavor the Spirit of God could so move these people that they knew how to pray and in their poverty to make sacrificial gifts surely there can be no doubt that it is worth while to tell them of the Eternal Love. If we fail them, Christ fails them, for He needs must work through us. If we fail them they must go down into the shadow without hope. Many, many times in my work among them I have been forced to recognize that they had more of the Spirit of Christ than many who profess and call themselves Christians.

It was wonderful to watch the spiritual development of these people whom I had learned to love and admire. The most truly satisfying experience of my life was to note their impulse to adore their new-found Saviour and to manifest that love by seeking to make their daily conduct agreeable to what they knew to be conformity to His will. Only a determined atheist could fail to see that there was something deep and powerful and essentially spiritual at work in the lives of these Eskimo.

To present a true picture of my life at this time I must admit that despite the increasing joy in my work I had some bouts of bitter loneliness. Being human, I experienced now and again a great longing to be with my friends and loved ones and to speak in my mother tongue. This was quite natural. But these occasions were relatively few because I had to apply all my powers of mind and body to the task committed to me. Indeed a strange thing happened and I found in the silence and loneliness a purifying power and element quite unexpected. The days were so full and the work so absorbing that there was neither time nor inclination for self-pity. Certainly most of the time I was so conscious of my many and great blessings that my heart was filled to overflowing with thanksgiving.

One of the things for which I am devoutly thankful is that while the isolation sometimes pressed hard upon me I never allowed myself to fall into the attitude of mind where I felt that I was exiled by my own doing. I was there because I had been called and chosen to share the life of these dear people and by mixing with them and suffering with them I was able to bring them something in the way of a spiritual gift and I received from them much that helped me to understand the meaning of St. John's words, "We know that we have passed from death unto life."

It is true that I was a pioneer and like all pioneers I was called upon to endure hardships. But it is equally true that I have been far lonelier when sight-seeing by myself in the great cities of Europe than when with the Eskimo in Baffin Land. The isolation of the Arctic determines the form that the trials of our life shall take but it does not determine what the issue shall be. The loneliness, the privations, the slowness in seeing results for years of patient labor, the doubts and struggles—these test the worth of the individual and reveal the essential quality of his soul.

In time of discouragement it is well for the missionary to remember that he is not really alone since he belongs to the Army of God. He and his bishop and all his fellow workers and those who hold him in daily remembrance at home are able to accomplish feats beyond the scope of any one individual. Sometimes his work may appear to be done in obscurity, or he is depressed by loneliness, disappointment, or defeat. There may be times when the spiritual realities and the joy and peace of humble worship are blurred. It is at such times that the soul is tested. But these periods are like clouds passing across the sky and shutting out the sunlight for a brief space. Have faith in God and you will "yet praise Him who is the health of thy countenance and thy God."

The important point in all Christian service is to see something of the Son of Man in all with whom we come into contact. The Master made this matter clear when He said, "Inasmuch as ye have done it unto the least of these, ye have done it unto Me." The wonderful thing is that one finds true joy and satisfaction in serving the least, whether it be sharing one's food and possessions or enlightening their minds and helping to meet their physical, mental, and spiritual needs. I learned to love the Eskimo because of what I discovered them to be and because of what I believed they could become by the mercy of God.

What the average white man coming to the Arctic does not understand is that there is no "race" problem. It is entirely a social problem. The white man has inherited many advantages because of the more favorable conditions in the south. He meets the Eskimo who have developed a culture suitable for their needs in that bleak and barren land, and the supposed superiority of the white man is not an anthropological question at all. When an Eskimo lives under conditions similar to those in the south there is little or no difference in intelligence and not the slightest repugnance in the closest physical propinquity.

Many years ago I brought out and placed in a well-known boarding school in Ontario two twelve-year-old Eskimo boys, Ben and Sam. They were handicapped in their studies by the lack of fluent English and required private tutoring to remedy this but the headmaster told me that their inherent intelligence and capacity to learn was in no way inferior to that of the other students. They quickly adapted themselves to their new environment, made friends with ease, and certainly displayed the most amazing scholastic progress. When at home during the holidays they were well-mannered and agreeable children, and during the long summer vacation were accepted as equals by a group of youngsters of their own age.

And a great many white men coming to the Arctic take the attitude of uninhibited individualism and advocate the right of self-fulfillment through the satisfaction of desire. When I queried them about the effect of their conduct on others they have simply shrugged their shoulders. These white men do not lack intellectual standing but they separate enlightenment and privilege from honesty and virtue and are entirely indifferent to the evil they work. They "couldn't care less" that their actions threaten the liberty and morality of those around them. It is the old story: Mephistopheles did not lack intelligence but goodness.

I have also had much searching of heart in connection with the free traders, i.e., men who have no stake in the country but who make a trip during the summer to buy fur from the native for cash. It has always seemed to me the epitome of meanness since they get the fur without having taken the risk inherent in the fur trade business. It is totally unfair to the regular trader.

With this general attitude prevailing through the years and dating back to the visits of the Scottish and American whalers is it any wonder that the Eskimo regarded the white men as having no religion at all? It was harder still to convince them of the moral character of the white man's religion in view of what they had seen and known. Moreover, men like a certain eminent explorer are not unwilling to use the full resources of their vocabulary, charm, invective, and ribaldry to discount the truth and the most elementary laws of morality held by Christians.

To present a fair picture, however, it must be stated that there were many white men who could recognize the open road to vice with all its seeming pleasures and yet exercise such will power that they were able to withstand the temptations. They are the real he-men of the North and can be found in almost every settlement. The attributes necessary for life in the Arctic are still the well-known qualities of vision, determination, and the capacity to endure discomfort without complaint. And to be forced to endure adverse conditions is a great test of character. When bravely faced it teaches discipline and develops fortitude and in the end brings blessing.

I have also discovered across the years that when dealing with the natives (or with those responsible for them) sincere good will is as important as good morals. Indeed it is sometimes all-important and the lack of it has often been most hampering and detrimental. It is easy for the visiting scientist or government official when on a brief cruise in the Arctic to get into a state of agitation over the deplorable condition of some of our Eskimo. It is still easier for them to place the blame on the resident white people whether missionary, trader, or government employee. These people, however kindly intentioned, seldom take the trouble to inquire about the past history of the native or to become acquainted with the degraded condition of his earlier state. Hence they are not aware of the development that has brought him from being but a little higher than the aborigines into his present state. It is also regrettable and harmful that the majority of such critics assume that those who are resident in the country for long periods of time and who wrestle with the problems daily at first hand are void of understanding, and unconscious of their obligations to one of the most lovable and worthy people in the world today.

An Eskimo's personality is not only precious but fragile. If one is to be really helpful to him one must understand something of his background and remember the conditions under which he lives. He will respond readily to sweet reasonableness but the moment the white man attempts anything stronger the native will develop complexes that will affect his whole outlook on life and spoil his proper development. The Eskimo will submit to tyrants when in special need but they have their own code of chivalry which is the result of their experiences through the centuries and the tyrant will not change these. They have dignity and are normally honest. Among themselves they are kind, tender, and trustworthy. But if the white man seeks to bully them as inferiors they soon develop deceit and dishonesty. The native knows well the cunning of the fox and wolf and wolverine and can be ruthless.

The day will come when the native be he Indian or Eskimo will become articulate. At present he is our brother but our younger brother. He is lovable, patient, and capable of the highest development but still a juvenile and not an adult.

As I watched the light dawn upon their darkened souls I felt as if I were in the presence of the Son of God Himself. Week by week, month by month, I could see these souls groping their way through the obscurity of their misconceptions towards an ever-clearer understanding of the meaning of the great Evangel. With deep interest and anxiety I watched the spiritual struggle that was taking place in the minds and hearts of these dear people. How true are the words of Savonarola, "Like a piece of iron between two magnets so does the human soul waver between divine and earthly things, between belief and feeling."

One of my greatest difficulties was to help them to understand that fundamentally there was no distinction between the ordinary and the spiritual. Christianity is a way of life that enters into everything and influences all our normal daily thoughts, words, and deeds. It gives both the motive and the power to do the will of God.

One day while sitting in the observation car of the transcontinental train and facing backwards watching the road over which we had come, it seemed to me that it was a valuable experience. It was a parable of life and looking back across my own life I realize that my strongest emotion is thankfulness. The way has often seemed long and lonely and has led through storm and stress, pain and disappointment as well as through joy and pleasure, success and comfort. Through it all God's mercy, love, and tender compassion can be traced.

The lessons learned have stood me in good stead and have survived the ravages of time. It is good for a man to be forced through varying circumstances to scale the heights and plumb the depths and so to catch a clear vision of the meaning of life. For life is something more than dust and ashes or even a terrestrial glory, for the Spiritual is of the Eternal. None of us can escape the vicissitudes which are the common lot of man. But in my own life I have proved beyond the peradventure of a doubt that we need have no fear regarding the future. If we have simple trust in God the Father of our Lord Jesus Christ and seek to put Him first in our daily life He will give us the courage to meet every situation as it arises. Pitfalls and difficulties will undoubtedly confront us but He gives clear guidance to those who seek. Pray and keep on praying. Prayer is often the occasion of serious disappointment but it is also the greatest source of hope in life.

Experience has taught me to believe that the disappointments and even the cruelties of life *make* character, whereas people who do not at times get rough treatment remain undisciplined and immature. The knocks of life are like the hammer blows upon the metal. Without them the metal remains soft and inferior, with them it is forged into tough, high-tensile steel with a fine temper and lasting quality. There is also a similarity in the development of character to the development of the ship or the airplane. The plane in the air and the ship in the water must be stripped of all obstructions. This is achieved by trial and error involving the labor of generations. Step by step the design is improved. So it is with character. Human personality is highly complicated and has to be divested of selfishness and self-will to achieve its highest form. This is a difficult and costly process requiring help from God.

Once launched into the sea of life we must breast the waves of joy and sorrow, of success and failure with stout hearts. We can best do this by looking not at them or at ourselves but to God in Whom we live and move and have our being. Life demands renunciation of self and obedience to the known will of God. This in turn gives strength for heroic action involving suffering and often austerity, but there is a concomitant joy. The reason for this is that the Christian life is based on love of God and of men. Someone called this life "the dream of a shadow" yet we must not forget that through life we can find Eternity and after the storm comes the calm. As a prisoner in the Tower of London carved on the walls of his cell, *Par passage pénible passons à port plaisant.*

There is and must be the contiguity and continuity of thought so that the human will becomes blended in the Divine Will. Neither primitive credulity nor modern utilitarianism will meet the need, not even the intense addiction to an intellectual passion. Noble men often seek to give themselves to what is called their best and link up this idea with the Greek tradition, speaking of it as common sense. To me common sense is most uncommon and is not to be confused with the idea of accepting what the majority at any one time or in any one group may think. Rather is it the result of careful thought and experience that causes the mind of man to become conscious that the "days which are seen are temporal and that the days which are not seen are Eternal" and that that intangible thing which we call Love is Eternal.

What is the good of all the trials and disappointments of life? Well, if we have a humble and a contrite heart they will develop within us patience and submission and we shall discover that "all things work together for good to them that love God." We shall be able to cry with Job, "Though He slay me yet will I trust Him." In looking back across the years I see the faults and failings, infirmities, and mistakes very clearly. They cannot be denied or deleted and they fill my soul with genuine regret. Yet when considered in retrospect they appear as clouds upon the distant skyline, lighted by the golden rays of the setting sun.

Life like the weather in this great Canada of ours is full of interest because it is ever-changing. Joy and sorrow, pain and pleasure, strength and weakness, virtue and shame, success and failure—these all have their place. During my threescore years and ten, whatever the cynic and doubter may say, I have found that God is good for His name is Love. In His mercy and with great gentleness He has led my soul step by step to the end of the road. Some may ask, "Does the Star of Faith that shone so brightly fifty years ago shine as brightly in the twilight of life?" The answer is "Yes."

I have deemed it proper to give details of my spiritual pilgrimage because I know from confidential talks with many men and women that the problems which confronted me and which in my young manhood all but wrecked my faith, confront others. My prayer is that my experience may make clearer the path for those who look for light.

For me my "conversion" in my twenties was a real awakening and I seemed to enter into a new sphere of life. I can still recall the thrill that came to me after that week of anxious thought. I was overwhelmed by the sense of the reality of God as the Creator and Saviour of man's soul—my soul. I walked with new strength and a certain hope for time and for eternity.

Ah yes, but I was only at the beginning of the road. I was so ignorant, so inexperienced in the things of the Spirit. Yet looking back across more than forty years, I know that the vision has never faded. Rather can it be said that through sorrow, sinning, success, defeat, and failure the background has become even more clear and the Christ of Calvary stands out not only as the symbol of the Love that is Eternal but as the express image in whom all things consist. Only the captive soul which has flung her rights away has all her powers free. To be willing to serve anywhere, at any time, in any capacity under the instant orders of the living God is the highest qualification for command.

I have never been either a scholar or a theologian but I do love people and hence the pastoral work that I have done has taught me something of the power of the Great Evangel to revolutionize human lives, giving inspiration and peace and power to help, which are the deepest needs of the ordinary man and woman. To me preaching was a tremendous privilege and I always felt with Saint Paul, "Woe is me if I preach not the Gospel."

My vision has been enlarged and I have gained a deeper understanding of the Gospel of Christ through personal contact with those from whom I differ profoundly about many things except that Jesus Christ is the supreme revelation of God and the Lover of the souls of men. At first my mental attitude was to judge people by comparing them with others whom I respected and admired but I gradually learned to accept them on their own merits no matter what their religious color might be. Things are not always black or white but may be dark grey, light grey, or mottled. It is possible to be both tolerant and charitable without either denying the faith or failing to rejoice with St. John that in Christ we have "beheld His glory, the glory as of the only begotten of the Father full of grace and truth." It would be of inestimable value for us all to put aside for a time our differences and problems and to face the task committed to us in the sim-

plicity that is in Christ Jesus our Lord. That has no reference to ritual in worship but to the recognition of the fact
that behind all the organization of the churches there must
ever be one vital issue: that we shall first be "like Jesus" in
our daily living and in our contacts one with the other. We
must ever try not to be obstinate in our opinions but with
honesty to ask the question, "What is our ultimate purpose?"
What we propose to do and desire to accomplish should
always be subordinate and subsidiary to the main issue.

Life is full of suffering and pain and disillusionment. Yet
all the same it is full of interest and pleasure. In the weaving
of the web of life we have to take our share of both joy and
sorrow but as we draw near to the end of the road it becomes
ever clearer that Love is the light which brings hope. It is
not difficult then to understand the meaning of Christ's
words, "I am the light of the world."

I have had my share of difficulties and discouragement, the
trials of failure and the reassurance of success; the discipline
of sorrow and the comfort of a supremely happy home where
loving companionship has soothed the wounds of labor and
restored the drooping spirit. On many occasions I have had
close brushes with death; at other times I have had a full
share of adulation and publicity. Thus it is the simple truth
to say that in these latter days I am blessed with happy
memories and full of gratitude for all God's mercies and I
say with the Psalmist of old, "I will sing praises unto my God
while I have my being."

I am all too conscious of the contrast between the actual
life I have led and the ideal set before me. I have become
increasingly aware of my unworthiness and lack of sufficiency
for the manifold duties and responsibilities. In moments of
discouragement I would picture the man who, wanting to
cross the river, sat down to wait until the water should have
all rolled by and so allow him to proceed on his journey. My
courage rose when I remembered the promise of old, "As thy
days thy strength shall be," which gave me the assurance that

the unworthy channel could be used of God to bring comfort
and healing to the hearts of those with whom I came into
contact.

Unfortunately there is only a certain quantum of power in
each of us. If it is spent as I had to spend it, it cannot be
spent in other ways. Moreover the excitement necessary to
good preaching and speaking and the constant traveling are
unfavorable to quiet reflection and put a heavy tax on the
physical and nervous forces of the body as well.

When my illness came I faced the hard fact that the signal
had been given, "Full Stop." I realized that as soon as matters could be satisfactorily arranged regarding the election of
my successor I would have to relinquish the work. It was
not an easy decision to reach as I was well aware that my
resignation meant the complete withdrawal from the work
for which I had given all I had. Every man, I expect, minds
to a greater or lesser degree losing a position of eminence if
he has held it for any length of time; we are happy in proportion as we believe our life and ourselves to be of value.
But I knew that in other ways this withdrawal would have
blessed compensation with a successor who would carry on
and extend the work so dear to my heart.

Resignation! What a word! Up to this point my whole
life's dream had been an eager endeavor to *do* things; to
conquer all obstacles in order to win the Arctic wilds for
Christ. In some ways the dream has been more than fulfilled
so that the apprenticeship of my life has not been in vain
and I am content. To withdraw all personal ambition and to
recognize that everything worth while is the gift of God; to
rejoice day by day in whatever falls from His ever-gracious
hand to this unworthy servant. Yes, in the renunciation which
is progressive there steals over the soul those great gifts of
peace and contentment which are from above. I have found
that by being forced to recognize my limitations I have become conscious of a deep freedom hitherto unknown. Although only in my sixties I have already found the circle of

old friends is growing narrower and I know that soon the dreams of life will fade away. That does not really matter for within the shadows I see the figure of the strong Son of God Who alone gives us that life which is Eternal.

My life has been a compound of organization, adventure, and evangelism—sometimes very thrilling, sometimes surprising, sometimes disappointing, but always revealing and rewarding.

An acquaintance of mine asked me recently what recompense I had received for all my years of labor. Perhaps some of my readers ask the same question.

I would reply that from the purely human point of view and in spite of all the difficulties, disappointments, poverty, and privations I can say quite honestly that I have enjoyed life. Having to face and to overcome opposition; the spice of danger when traveling by land, sea, and air; my several escapes from imminent death—these cannot be classed as pleasant experiences but from them I have learned many things of value and therefore they are not without their compensation. To be privileged to carry on and to extend the Church's work would be reward enough. But my exceeding great reward is the knowledge that I have obeyed the will of Him Whom I early learned to call my Lord and Master. Through His infinite mercy and loving condescension I have been able to bring help and succor to many souls in spiritual as well as physical need. Could mortal man ask for more?

I am often asked if I am disappointed not to be in the public eye now that my activities are curtailed. My answer is that I am very thankful to be freed from publicity. I am most thankful that I can hand over the lamp that lights the darkness of Arctic night to one who has had experience and has demonstrated his genuine love for the work and for the native people. It would have broken my heart to have seen it handed to some untutored stripling who might so easily stumble and let not only my life's labors but all that had gone before shiver into fragments. My mind and heart are at rest because I know that the Right Reverend D. B. Marsh, the second Bishop of the Arctic, will win new victories for Christ.

I have been surprised that the shock of giving up the Arctic work with the uprooting after all the years of labor and responsibility has not left me either lost or disconsolate. I do not feel that retirement is an anticlimax but rather a logical fulfillment of all my efforts. One of the lessons I have learned in recent days is to look upon life not only as an apprenticeship but as a progressive renunciation which prepares us for the life to come. It is not simply that as one grows older one's radius of action becomes narrower; one also learns to put away all personal desires. The wonderful thing is that as this happens we seem to gain freedom and a contentment and a satisfaction which are most precious.

When one gets to my age the stern realities have been faced. One does not live in an ivory tower, surrounded by perfumed sunlight, for one knows that one is now traveling on the shady side of the mountains. The shadows fall across the pathway and they have a purple tinge. The pocketbook is flatter than heretofore and we have to study economy too carefully to be extravagant. But we can still hear the music and laughter of life that echoes from love and affection and friendship and work accomplished and above all from the absence of fear because of the assurance that God is Love. And so with Lytton I cry:

Thou art strong and I am frail and I am man and Thou art God.
How I have striven Thou knowest. Forgive how I have failed
Who saw'st me strive.

LAUS DEO

Index

Adam Nowdlak, 256, 352

Aklavik, 281, 285, 287, 288, 289, 290, 291, 292, 296, 297, 298, 299, 307, 309, 310, 313, 314, 315, 316, 317, 322, 323, 326, 327, 328, 329, 332, 333, 334, 336, 340, 341, 342, 344, 358, 369, 370

Aleppo, 1, 2

All Saints Hospital, 285, 298, 307, 323, 334, 340

Amodjuak Bay, 89, 196, 220, 256, 257

Anarus, 2

Anderson, The Rt. Rev. J. G., 244, 263, 295

Anderson, J. W., 355

Anil-me-oob, 196, 197, 198, 230, 237, 257, 258, 259

Ar-a-ne, 150, 151

Arctic Bay, 350

Arctic Red River, 314, 316

Ar-na-king, 188, 211

Ashe Inlet, 50, 51

Ashley-Cooper, Sir Patrick, 371

Athabasca River, 282, 283, 301

Aulatsevik, 79, 81, 82, 83, 85, 87, 90, 115, 159, 216, 262

Austin Airways, 364, 365

Baillie Island, 296, 299

Baker Lake, 246, 247, 269, 270, 271, 272, 381

Bathurst Inlet, 130

Bay Chimo, 293, 295, 296, 299

Beaufort Sea, 310

Belcher Islands, 364

Bernard Harbour, 293, 294, 295, 297, 298

Bible Churchmen's Missionary Society, 276

Bilby, The Rev. W. J., 36, 37, 38, 40, 41, 45, 46, 50, 51, 52, 53, 54, 55, 56, 57, 58, 59, 61, 62, 64, 65, 66, 69, 70, 71, 72, 73, 74, 75, 76, 77, 79, 80, 81, 82, 83, 84, 85, 86, 87, 88, 92, 93, 94, 95, 101, 105, 110, 111, 112, 113, 114, 115, 116, 117, 119, 124, 125, 126, 128, 130, 132, 138, 139, 140, 159, 160, 161, 163, 167, 172, 174, 175, 184, 201, 203, 212, 272, 319, 357

Blacklead Island, 37, 50, 53, 89, 103, 104, 128, 140, 199, 200, 207, 224, 237, 256, 272, 379

Bloody Falls, 294, 307

Bompas, Rt. Rev. W. C., 281

Bourke-White, Margaret, 336, 337, 338

Bradford, Miss Dorothy, R. N., 299, 309
Britnell, Leigh, 312
Broughton, The Rev. Percy, 162, 163, 172, 173
Brown, John, Co., Ltd., 10, 11, 31
Buchan, John, Lord Tweedsmuir, 17, 331, 332, 334, 335, 336, 337, 338
Burleigh, 160, 161, 162

Cambridge Bay, 295, 296, 317, 328, 329, 338, 339
Cameron, Dr. M. V. C., 34, 193
Cameron Bay, 311, 329, 337, 338, 340
Campbell, Miss, R.N., 364, 365
Cantley, James, 171, 205
Cape Dorset, 89, 154, 156, 192, 193, 203, 207, 211, 213, 220, 225, 234, 237, 248, 249, 263
Cape Wolstenholme, 88, 234
Chartie, 187, 211, 213, 224
Chesterfield Inlet, 240, 245, 270
Churchill, 163, 182, 239, 320
Cody, The Rev. Canon H. J., 34, 322
College of Preachers, 346
Colonial and Continental Church Society, 276
Coppermine, 130, 145, 281, 295, 298, 311, 329, 338, 339
Cumberland Sound, 7, 103, 139, 212, 319
Cutty Sark, 2

David, The mad Eskimo, 250, 251, 252, 357
Davis Strait, 44, 119, 125, 139, 148, 199, 203
Dickens, Punch, 312

Distributor, 283, 284, 285, 287, 297, 298, 299, 301, 334
Dixon, The Rev. Canon L. A., 362, 363, 364

Easton, Hugh, 344
Eldorado, 315, 338, 339
"Epiphany in the Snows," 342
Erhardt, John Christian, 44, 46

Farrell, Con, 312
Feast of Sedna, 127, 129, 130, 131, 132, 190
Fort Charles, 362, 364
Fort Chimo, 241
Fort Fitzgerald, 283, 302
Fort George, 70, 241, 361, 363, 364
Fort McMurray, 282, 302, 311, 317, 329, 340
Fort McPherson, 281, 284, 286, 287, 313
Fort Norman, 285, 286, 300, 315, 329, 337
Fort Ross, 349
Foxe Channel, 67, 152, 196, 206, 207, 208, 213, 215, 217, 218, 220, 223, 250
Franklin Mountains, 286, 316
Frobisher Bay, 52, 136, 139, 140, 143, 145, 155, 158, 199, 205, 231, 307, 352
Fry, The Rev. W., 292
Fry, Mrs. W., 292

Geddes, The Rt. Rev. W. A., 287, 288, 290, 291, 292, 297
Gilbert, Walter, 316, 317, 318
Goderich, 369, 370
Grant, O. C. Forsyth, 139, 140, 146, 147, 148, 149, 150, 151
Great Bear Lake, 286, 311, 312, 315, 339

Great Britain, 1, 2, 6, 7, 8, 9, 10, 12, 13, 16, 17, 18, 24, 25, 28, 29, 31, 341, 342, 344

Great Slave Lake, 306, 311, 315

Great Whale River, 240, 241

Greenland, 38, 39, 43, 122, 138, 148, 164, 294, 300, 354, 360, 361

Greenshield, The Rev. E. W. T., 30, 37, 117, 139, 146, 200, 207, 224, 272, 319

Grenfell, Dr. Wilfred, 164

Grenfell Mission, 41, 170

Halley's Comet, 86, 216

Hamilton, Miss R., R.N., 323, 324

Hantzach, B. A., 207, 215

Harcourt, The Rev. C. C., 287, 288, 297

Harvey, Miss M., R.N., 324

Hathaway, The Rev. C. M., 295

Hawk's Head, 55, 114, 232, 248

Hay River, 284, 301, 315, 329

Hearne, Samuel, 182

Herschel Island, 287, 290, 291, 293, 298, 328

Heslop, 349, 350

Hockin, Miss Prudence, R.N., 321

Holmes, Rt. Rev. G., 29, 30, 31, 32, 33, 35, 37, 206, 287

Hudson's Bay Company, 61, 154, 156, 163, 169, 170, 172, 174, 177, 187, 193, 201, 203, 204, 205, 206, 224, 225, 237, 238, 239, 240, 245, 248, 259, 261, 263, 269, 270, 272, 274, 291, 292, 294, 297, 302, 307, 316, 317, 320, 322, 325, 326, 328, 330, 337, 338, 339, 342, 349, 355, 356, 358, 361, 364, 371, 381

Ing-mil-ayo, 102, 178, 205, 222, 231

Iremonger, Very Rev. F. A., 344

Ite, Ing-mil-ayo's wife, 102, 178, 205, 222, 231

Itinik, 183, 184, 185, 208, 210, 211, 213, 221, 250

James, The Rev. Canon W. J. R., 271, 272

James Bay, 70, 156, 170, 302

Johnny Penny, 119, 120, 121

Johnson, Albert, "The mad trapper," 313, 314, 358

Keary, Miss Gwendolyn, R.N., 322, 323

Keemalo, Simone's wife, 380, 381

Ke-ma-lo, 153, 154

Kemp, Inspector, R.C.M.P., 291, 293

Kilk-re-apik, 211, 212

Kimil, 215, 218

King-o-wat-se-ak, 113, 114

King's Cape, 178, 196, 199, 213

Kinguckjuak, 90, 92, 93, 96, 101, 102, 104, 107, 113, 114, 229, 230

Kitchen, Miss B., R.N., 323

LaBine, Gilbert, 286, 312

Lake Harbour, 51, 52, 59, 62, 75, 76, 78, 79, 81, 89, 90, 111, 112, 113, 127, 136, 139, 140, 146, 151, 156, 160, 161, 162, 163, 172, 173, 177, 183, 184, 187, 195, 197, 199, 203, 206, 207, 208, 211, 219, 220, 222, 223, 225, 229, 232, 236, 237, 238, 239, 248, 249, 250, 251, 257, 263, 269, 330, 351, 352, 358

Larch, 273

Liard River, 286, 300

Likert, Paul, 295

Lorna Doone, 36, 37, 38, 39, 40, 42, 45, 46, 47, 52, 54, 58, 59, 62, 64, 70, 107, 161, 169, 170, 211, 248

Lucas, Rt. Rev. J. R., 281

Lukesi Kidlapik, 139, 140, 141, 142, 143, 144, 145, 146, 150, 200, 204, 205, 207, 209, 237, 250

Luk-ta, 215, 216, 219

McCabe, Miss M., R.N., 285, 287, 288

MacDonald, The Rev. Robert, 281, 286

McKeand, Major D., 355

Mackenzie River, 157, 267, 282, 283, 284, 286, 297, 300, 306, 311, 312, 313, 314, 323, 369

McMullen, Archie, 312, 329

Maitland Point, 333

Ma-lik-tok, 105, 106, 198

Marsh, The Rt. Rev. D. B., Second Bishop of The Arctic, 367, 369, 394

Martin, The Rev. John, 288, 289

Mary Er-kak-tah-lik, 81, 183, 184, 185, 187, 209, 222

Matte, Kilk-re-apik's wife, 212

May, W. R. (Wop), 310, 311, 312, 313, 314, 315, 316

Moravians, 43, 44, 162, 172, 277

Morris, The Rev. John, 311

Murray, Captain Alexander, 60, 74, 75, 160, 161, 203, 295

Murray, W. G., 291

Naglikgeanilk, 213, 256, 259, 260, 261, 262

Nascopie, 169, 170, 202, 237, 240, 245, 246, 248, 250, 264, 270, 272, 295, 306, 322, 323, 348, 349, 350, 352, 354, 355, 360, 361

Neparktok, 188

Nicholson, The Rev. G., 321, 322, 324, 326

Noo-voo-le-a, 50, 51, 53, 90, 91, 97, 98, 99, 131, 161, 162, 163, 164, 172, 248

Northwest Mounted Police, 240, 298

Nottingham Island, 88, 273

Oakley-Reams, Inspector, R. C. M. P., 245, 246, 247

O'Meara, The Rev. Canon, 33, 34

Ottawa Island, 88

Ou-ang-wak, 246, 247, 248

Pangnirtung, 272, 321, 322, 343

Parsons, Ralph, 62, 163, 177, 205, 224, 234, 236, 238, 270, 295, 326, 328, 329, 330, 331

Peace River, 286

Peck, The Rev. E. J., 31, 36, 37, 38, 40, 41, 45, 46, 50, 51, 52, 53, 54, 62, 64, 68, 70, 71, 89, 103, 104, 128, 146, 160, 161, 162, 163, 164, 193, 206, 207, 244, 272, 319

Peck, Miss Margaret, 309, 310

Peel River, 281, 286, 313

Pelican, 163, 170, 171, 172, 175, 193, 201, 248, 250

Pelican Rapids, 283

Perry River, 130, 295, 296

Peter Too-loo-ak-juak, 272

Pit-soo-lak, the angakok, 74, 75, 120, 127, 128, 129, 131, 132, 134, 135, 136, 137, 138

Pit-soo-lak, Pudlo's daughter, 225, 226, 228, 229

Pond Inlet, 145, 272, 349, 350

Porsild, E. A., 300

Port Burwell, 272, 273

Port Harrison, 225

Port Hope, 244
Pudlo, 92, 93, 136, 137, 178, 179, 180, 183, 184, 187, 196, 197, 198, 199, 200, 205, 208, 209, 211, 213, 214, 215, 216, 219, 220, 222, 224, 225, 226, 227, 228, 229, 232, 233, 237, 248, 250, 251, 254, 255, 256, 269, 270, 272, 351

Rabinowitch, Dr. I. M., 354
Ranken, Art, 337, 338, 339
Rasmussen, Knud, 294
Resolution Island, 117, 301, 314, 340, 353, 354
Revillon Frères, 225, 239, 270
Richardson Island, 287, 327
Royal Canadian Mounted Police, 240, 245, 246, 247, 290, 291, 293, 297, 313, 314, 326, 333, 334, 342, 356, 358, 359

Saddleback Islands, 49, 52, 101, 109, 111, 115, 173, 204
St. John, N.B., 244, 265, 266, 306
St. Luke's Hospital, 322
Samuel Na-te-lah, 270, 271
Sarah, Pudlo's wife, 136, 137, 179, 351
Shingle Point, 290, 291, 297, 299, 310, 317, 326, 327
Silah, 215, 216, 217, 218, 219
Simon, James, 284, 285, 286
Simon, Sarah, 284, 285, 286
Simone, 380
Sittichinli, The Rev. Edward, 286
Slave River, 283
Smellie, Captain T. F., 299, 322, 349, 355
Smyth, The Rev. B. P., 269, 270, 271, 272

Society for Propagation of the Gospel, 275, 276
Sow-ne-ah-lo, 230, 231
Stanwell-Fletcher, J. F., 350
Stefansson, Vilhjalmur, 246, 292
Stella Maris, 162, 163, 164
Stewart, S. J. (Lofty), 171, 193, 220, 248, 249, 250, 261, 263
Stewart, The Rev. S. M., 241
Storkersen, S. T., 245, 246, 263
Strathcona, Lord, 172
Stringer, Rt. Rev. I., 281, 282, 292
Summers, Thomas, 326, 335

Teague, Miss Violet, 341
Terry, Miss, R.N., 288, 297
Thule, 360
Tuktoyaktuk, 328
Turner, The Rev. Arthur, 35
Turner, The Rev. Canon J. H., 145, 349, 350, 351, 374

Uluksak, 297, 298
Urquhart, Dr., 299, 324, 326, 340

Wallace, Mene, 38, 39, 164
Waterways, 282, 302, 314, 315
Webster, The Rev. Canon J. H., 145, 294, 295, 298, 338, 374
Whittaker, Archdeacon, 281, 287
Winnipeg, 306, 307, 318, 321
Wycliffe College, 32, 33, 35, 48, 167, 187, 224, 244, 276

Yarley, 65, 66, 67, 71, 72, 73, 74, 208, 209, 211, 213, 214, 215, 217, 220, 222, 224, 229, 230, 232, 233, 234, 237, 250, 258
Yellowknife, 339, 340
York Factory, 240